GAJAŚĀSTRAM
गजशास्त्रम्

Maharṣi Pālakāpya's

GAJAŚĀSTRAM

With the Sanskrit Commentary,
Bhāvasandarśinī of Anantakṛṣṇabhaṭṭāraka
with an English translation and 136 illustrations of various Elephants

Edited by

Dr. Siddharth Yeshwant Wakankar
Deputy Director, Oriental Institure,
M.S.U. Baroda

&

Vaidya Prof. V.B. Mhaiskar
Retd. Principal,
Govt. Ayurvedic College,
Baroda

BHARATIYA KALA PRAKASHAN
DELHI (INDIA)

First Published : 2006
Revised Edition : 2023

Published by C.P. Gautam *for*
BHARATIYA KALA PRAKASHAN
3480/1, Ground Floor, Narang Colony,
Tri Nagar, Delhi - 110035,
Contact No. : 011 71522860, 9811642997, 8595139625,
E-mail : info@bkpbooks.com; sales.bkpbooks@gmail.com
Website: www.bkpbooks.com

ISBN : 978-81-8090-016-7

Laser Type Setting
Creative Graphics

Printed by :
G.S. Offset Printers
Delhi

DEDICATED MOST HUMBLY

TO

H. H. The late

Shri Bhavanrao Shrinivasrao

alias

Balasaheb Pant Pratinidhi,

(24-10-1868 to 13-4-1951),

The Rajasaheb of Aundh

An Enlightened King and a Patron and Propagator of Indian Knowledge Systems, Fine Arts, Architecture and Literature.

CONTENTS

PREFACE

The Culture of a Nation survives on the active patronage received from the Enlightened Rulers/Kings and fortunately, our country produced many such Enlightened and Visionary Kings-who were not only scholars/ artists/patriots in themselves, but, also accorded very much impetus to scholars/experts from various fields,such as Poetry, Philosophy, Plastic Arts, Performing Arts etc. Some of the Kings or Rājās in the recent past have made excellent and everlasting contributions to their own small /big States or Kingdoms as regards the overall development in education, literacy,small-scale industies, fine arts etc. One such brilliant name is that of the late Shri Bhavanrao alias Balasaheb Shrinivasrao Pant Pratinidhi, B.A.-the Rājāsaheb of Aundh, a very small but progressive State near Satara in Mahara-shrea. He was born on the 24th October 1868 and breathed his last on 13th April, 1951. He ascended the Throne of Aundh in 1909 and till his death,he worked ceaselessly for the development of his small State, in respect of the small-scale industry, women' s education, fine arts, printing press, physical education, esp. *Sūryanamaskāra* (which has recently got recognized from foreign scholars also), architectute etc. He himself was a very good painter,a known connoisseur of arts, well-educated, with a bent of mind for reforms in his State. He not only believed in the *Sūryanamaskāras* as a physical exercise, but, also devoted his life and time for the propagation of that exercise-which is now being recognised everywhere as one of the best exercises for keeping our body fit and light. As a King, he patronised many experts from various fields and enriched his Court as well as his Library and Museum with the paintings of native as well as foreign painters of fame, specimens of plastic arts,rare and important books and manuscripts etc.At present, there are nearly 3000 manuscripts and transcripts of rare manuscripas in his rich and varied collection of antique pieces.The present work is based on one such very rare, important and unpublished manuscript. The *Gajaśāstra* by Pālakāpya. Folios: 393.Acc.No.1853.

This is a very wonderful Devanāgarī transcript got prepared by the Rājāsaheb of Aundh through the services of Pandit V. Vijayaraghavacharya, an Epigraphist and a sound Sanskrit scholar. This copy of the work was completed on 22nd November, 1926 AD. The work is rare in it that it contains a hitherto unknown and unrecorded Sanskrit commentary, written (composed) by one Anantakṛṣṇabhaṭṭāraka. Despite hectic efforts, we have not been able to locate the original manuscript, from which this transcript is prepared, neither any authentic information about this commentator from any source whatsoever. We sincerely request the readers/ scholars to kindly enable us to trace this original work. Our special request to our South Indian scholars to use their good offices and help us get the details about the original manuscript-which is most probably, in a Southern,esp. Telugu script. In the absence of any information about the original ms. we furnish herewith, the physical description of the Devanāgarī transcript.

The title page records: *Pālakāpyamaharṣipraṇītam Gaja-śāstram-Śrīmadanantabhaṭṭārakaviracita-bhāvasandarśinyākh-yayā vyākhyayā sametam.* Science of Elephants, containing 136 Illustrations of various Elephants and English Translation. 1926 A.D. The last page of this transcript records the details about the exact date when it was prepared and verified (22-11-1926). The size of the pages is: 30x21 cms, with 12-16 lines per page and 34-36 letters per line.

The English Translation by the Pandit is not a translation in the strict sense of the term, but, a summary or gist (or paraphrase) of what is given in the Text and the Commentary.

This commentary is being printed for the first time. It is our conjecture that the illustrations also must have been from the pen of the Pandit, who worked under the instructions or directions of the Rājāsaheb of Aundh, who himself was a very good painter.

There are in all 19 Chapters in this work and they contain information about:The origin of Pālakāpya; The curses to the Elephants; The forests in which Elephants are found; The different peculiarities of elephants belonging to various geographical areas; The description of the elephants since their birth, through the different stages in their life, the qualities of elephant's etc. etc. In short, it may be said without much exaggeration that this is a very important work or almost an Encyclopaedia on Elephants, because, everything about Elephants, except their diseases, and treatment is described here with graphic accompanying illustrations.

From our search for works on Elephant-lore, we found that there are mainly two titles/works, ascribed to Pālakāpya, viz. the *Hastyāyurveda*-published by the Anandashram Series, Pune and the *Gajaśāstra* (published from Tanjore as No. 76 and the present Devanāgarī transcript which is being published). (For details, pl. refer to the Bibliography).

The *Hastyāyurveda* as well as the *Gajaśāstram* of Pālakāpya Muni printed from Tanjore are only Texts, without any commentary in Sanskrit (unlike our present work). The Tanjore *Gajaśāstram*, however, is endowed with a Tamil Translation by Shri Mantramurti K.S. Subrahmanya Sastri and a Summary in English by Shrti S. Gopalan, the Hon. Secretary of the Saraswati Mahal Library, Tanjore. In addition to these useful aids, the Tanjore book furnishes some Extracts from other Sanskrit works and Coloured Illustrations in the form of Appendix. The Preface by Shri Gopalan clearly says that "This is a compilation from the classic on the subject by Pālakāpya Maharṣi with extracts from Vyāsa and Vaiśampāyana. The compilation was made during the days of the early Mahratta Kings. Each text is illustrated by coloured drawings.We have now included in this publication the text as compiled by order of the Mahratta Kings and added to it, by way of appedix, extracts from other texts on the maintenance, training and treatment of elephants when ill. A Tamil translation and a summary in English have been added. A select number of illustrations in colour from our Manuscript have been inserted." In this edition, at many places some authorities are specifically mentioned as *Vaiśampāyanīye granthe*, *Vaiyyāsike, Pālakpye* etc. and at times a general term like *Anyagranthe, Granthāntare* etc. is used to show the source of a particular passage. On page 18, it is said that the elephants were born from Praṇava (verse 20.). The total number of chapters of the Tanjore edition is only ten, while, our text contains 19 chapters. The comparison of these two texts will follow. T*he speciality of our Edition of Gajaśāstram is that*: It is endowed with a hitherto unknown and unpublished Sanskrit commentary, named, *Bhāvasandarśinī*, composed by Anantakṛṣṇabhaṭṭāraka, besides a very useful English translation/ paraphrase and wonderful black and white sketches or illustrations by the Scribe himself. Hence, we sincerely feel that this Publication with a Sanskrit Commentary, English translation and Illustrations would significantly add to our konwledge of the Elephants, as described in ancient Sanskrit Works and would be very much useful and informative to the readers/scholars/researchers etc. and it will be a welcome addition to books on the Lore on Elephants.

A comparison between the Tanjore Edition and our Present Publication.

The Tanjore Edition has in all ten chapters, while, our Text contains nineteen chapters. The *Pālakāpya-vacanas* from the Prayer to the end almost tally *verbatim*, but, some *Vyāsavaca-nas* are quoted as those of Pālakāpya.

The 9th chapter of the Tanjore Edition includes all the topics that are described from Chapter 10-19 in our Publication.

The 10th chapter of the Tanjore Edition deals with tectile and sonic signals to elephants, cutting of tusks, Elephant-games.

The matter under this head is a collection from various sources, including the *Hasti-āyurveda* and relates to the topics like: proper period for the capture of elephants, pregnancy in female elephants, *masti*, rearing of baby-elephants, features of healthy and sick elephants, treatment of various diseases, elephant-food, elephant-stables etc. etc.

Thus it may be very clear that the *Hastyāyuveda* Edition from Pune and the Tanjore Edition of the *Gajaśāstram* deal with the Ayurvedic aspects of the elephants, while, our Publication does not touch this particular aspect. It is just possible that though all these three treatises go under the name of Pālakāpya, the purposes of composing them were quite different. The earlier printed editions were written with the Āyurveda at its core, while, our Text deals with the general information about the elephant, its life-span and other matters, without giving importance to the Āyurveda aspect. Our book is meant for the general readers while the other two editions were more useful to the practitioners of *Hastyāyurveda* as a guide in their vocation/profession.

The comparison of the *Hastyāyurveda* and our *Gajaśāstra* is given elsewhere in this book (in the Introduction).

Though there are many Texts on *Gajaśāstra* going under or ascribed to Pālakāpya Muni, (like the *Hastyāyurveda*, *Gajaśāstram* of P. with extracts from other works and coloured illustrations, published from Tanjore in 1958 and the present one) we decided to take up the editing of this present Manuscript from Aundh-though the source of the original manuscript from which this transcript is prepared, is still unknown—on the following considerations:

(1) This is the only Devanāgarī transcript of the Text which is endowed with a Sanskrit Commentry, an English translation cum Paraphrase and the illustrations. Another Devanāgarī transcript of the original work (whose source also is unknown till this date), prepared on 17th August 1930 A.D. by the same Epigraphist

Pandit V. Vijayaraghavacarya, is also deposited in the rich collection of the Adyar Library, Channai, but, that is almost a *verbatim* copy of our transcript, but, unfortunately, without the English translation and illustrations/sketches. Hence, we decided not to take that into account.

(2) Sanskrit Texts on Scientific and technical subjects deserve to be published afresh, so that we get to know about the progress of these subjects/sciences in the olden days.

(3) Moreover, there may be some points of importance concealed in these unpublished treatises which are not available in the already known and printed works on Elephant-lore.

* * * *

ACKNOWLEDGEMENTS

First of all, we have to place on record our gratefulness to Dr. A.P. Jamkhedkar, the former Director of Archaeology and Museum, Govt. of Maharashtra, Mumbai, for kindly allowing us to visit the Aundh Museum and get the xerox-copy of the transcript; to Shri P.N. Potdar, the Curator of the Bhavani Citrasangrahalaya at Aundh, who helped us in getting the copy. We also sincerly thank the Librarian of the Adyar Library and Research Centre, Adyar, Chennai, for supplying a xerox-copy of the transcript of the *Gajaśāstra*. Our sincere thanks are also due to Prof. Dr. M.L. Wadekar, the Officiating Director of the Oriental Institute, Baroda, for his generous help. We are extremely thankful to the following members of our family for their kind and whole-hearted support, co-operation, encouragement and help in many matters connected with the smooth and speedy completion of this work. Sau. Vimalaben V. Mhaiskar and Sau. Sushama. S. Wakankar, Shri Bhaskar and Shri Rishikesh V. Mhaiskar (sons), Sau. Smita and Sau. Meena Mhaiskar (daughters-in-law) Sau. Nilima Gokhale (daughter of Prof. V.B. Mhaiskar) for their ready help on the computors and Miss Madhurima and Miss Tejaswini S. Wakankar for their over-all help.

We will be failing in our duty if we do not record our heartfelt thanks to these members of our family for their silent and valuable help.

Last but not the least, we are extremely thankful to our Publisher, Shri C.P. Gautam, of the Bharatiya Kala Prakashan, Delhi, for his patience and nice production of the book.

15 July 2005 **Editors**
Vadodara

INTRODUCTION

1. Elephants

It will be very pertinent to look at the line of thinking of the Āyurveda as regards the matter in the world. Caraka divides it into two groups, viz. *Cetana* (living or sentient), i.e. with senses and *Acetana* (non-living, insentient) i.e. without senses. (See: *Carakasaṁhitā*, S. S. 1/48). The other kind of division is *Sthāvara* (non-moving) and *Jaṅgama* (moving). The *Jaṅgama* is again divided into two groups: *Vanaspati*, *Vṛkṣa* (plants and trees) etc. form one part, the other part is *Prāṇi-varga* (animals). The *Prāṇi-varga* is again sub-divided into four groups:

(1) *Jarāyuja*: born from the womb, viviparous— Placental animals/mammals, like man, cow etc.

(2) *Aṇḍaja*: born from an egg, oviparous beings-birds, snakes etc.

(3) *Svedaja*: born of warm vapours/moisture/heat/sweat etc.—Lice, insects etc.

(4) *Udbhijja*: all animals born by breaking the soil-frogs etc. (see: *Caraka Sūtra* 3/16; and *Suśruta Sūtra* (1/29-30).

The elephant belongs to the *Jarāyuja* (placental) group.

It will be very interesting and informative too to see the actual position of the elephant in the animal kingdom.

In the process of getting orderly and correct information about the surroundings, the primitive man must have followed several ways and means. Naming an object and then knowing it by the same term is one of the most essential things. The names evolved out of keen observation of the surroundings, including life with its various forms. The things that were considered could be mentioned as follows: colour, size, shape, style of walking, using one or the other organ for the purposes of fighting, protection, various sounds made (indicative of different situations/emotions/feeling etc.), the way of building the nests, use of one or many sense-organs, mode of flight, cruelty or kindness towards other creatures, place of living such as on the land, inside a burrow or hole, alongside of water, in the water (fresh water or sea and oceans), capacity to swim in water, type of food consumed like, vegetables, flesh, eggs of other animals etc.; special appendages like wings, wings with feathers (like parrots, crows, swans, etc.), wings without feather (like a bat), presence or absence of teeth in the mouth, nature (like bold, timid) etc.

Now, let us turn to see how names would have been coined.

Kāṣṭha-kuṭṭa (Wood-pecker)—A bird that cuts out the wood to make a hole for its nest.

Ḍiṇḍimāṇavaka (Hornbill)—A bird that makes a high-pitched sound like a sort of drum (*ḍiṇḍima*).

We find many examples of classification based on the type of places, selected by the animals for their stay.

Guhāśaya—Those who live in caves (*guhā*), lion, tiger, wolf, bear, cheeta, wild cat etc.

Parṇamṛga—Those who live on the trees.

Madgu—a variety of snake.

Mūṣikā or **Vṛkṣamūṣikā**—a tree rat.

Vṛkṣaśāyikā—a Squirrel.

Avakuśa-golāṅgūla. Vānaraviśeṣaḥ—A kind of a monkey that-has a tail like a cow.

Bileśaya—Those animals that stay in burrows or holes—like Śvavit or a rodent having needle-like hair on the body; Śaśa-hare; Sarpa-snake or serpent; Nakula-mongoose or mungoose, Mūṣaka-rats etc. All these are the varieties of

Jāṅgalavarga, i.e. those beings that stay in desert, waste-land, forest etc. It means they are wild (and not necessarily tamed animals).

Anūpa-varga comprises of five types of animals, viz. Kūlacara (waders), Plava (swimmers), Kośastha (conches), Padin (having legs, foot) and Matsya (fishes). Of these, we will consider only the Kūlacarapaśus: Gaja (elephant), Mahiṣa (buffalo), Ruru (a types of deer that is usually found in the Cedideśa), Varāha (wild boar), Khaḍga Gaṇḍaka (a rhino) etc. The elephant belongs to the Kūlacara-class, that is, those animals who prefer to stay by the side of water-reservoirs like, lakes, river, streams etc.

It will be very informative to know if there existed any kind of a classification of insects, animals, birds, or fish etc.

Honey is one of the most popular things that has been used and prescribed by the Vaidyas since very ancient times. There are many kinds of honeys, named after the flowers from which the bees collect it. The commonly known names are Haraḍe-honey, Neem-honey, lotus-honey etc. All these are the varieties pertaining to the flowers from which the honey is taken and hence, this type is known as the *Pauṣpika-madhu*. Another aspect of the substance Honey is the honey collected by different types of bees having different qualities. Caraka supplies the names of four types of honey-bees, Pauttika viz. Bhramara, Makṣikā (big bee), Kṣaudra (small bee) and Paitika (large bee). The words can easily be translated as: honey collected by the Bhramara type of bee; ordinary honey-bee; small-sized bee and the one collected by the Puttika type of bees which are large-sized. Suśruta, on the other hand, gives eight types of honey-bees, but, in the end, all these eight types could be converted into four. Ḍalhaṇa, the commentator, supplies certain characteristics of the following bees: Puttika-bee is large and has the *piṅgala-varṇa*, i.e. reddish brown, yellowish, brown or tawny colour; Bhramara is the well-known bee; Kṣaudra-bee has also *piṅgalavarṇa*,but is of a smaller size, while, Makṣikā-bee is large-sized, with again the *piṅgalavarṇa*. The other four types of bees given by Suśruta are: The Chatta-bee, yellowish and called 'bug' by the locals. This is to be found in the Haimavata and Malava-vanas. Arghya-bee-yellow-coloured, with a very hard sting (*tīkṣṇadaṁśa*). These look like the six-legged ants and are found in the Malva region. They are known to collect honey from the Madhukapuṣpa (flower), also known as Śvetaka. Uddālaka-bee: this appears to be an insect collecting honey and living in ant-hills. Dal-bee is brownish in colour and small-sized that collects the honey (in the beehive) within the hollow of a tree. (See: *Suśrutasaṁhitā, Sūtrasthāna*, 45/113, with the commentary of Ḍalhaṇa).

Moreover, Suśruta also gives the names of the six varieties of cats, known as Mārjāras, which are: Grāmya (living in villages); Vanya (living in forest); Toyajāta (living, lit. born in water); Pakṣimārjāra (bird-cat)-(Pākhamāñjara); Vijjaka-cats living on trees, also known as Ijaṭa (or Udamārjāra) and Sugandhavṛṣaṇamārjāra-Musk cat, also known as Pūtighāsa (Musk-cat) (see: Suśruta, *Sūtra*. 4.41/36 and 46/76 with the commentary of Ḍalhaṇa).

Suśruta gives three varieties of Hariṇa or deer, viz. Eṇahariṇa—of black variety (Blackbuck); Raktahariṇa-red-coloured and Ciṅkārahariṇa-neither black nor red Kuraṅga. (See: S. S. 46/57, with Ḍalhaṇa's commentary).Three varieties of Tittira are also described. They are: Kṛṣṇatittira—black, having a mixture of coloured spots on the wings; Kapiñjalatittira; Gauratittira—with a mixture of whitish and reddish coloured tinges.

It is very surprising that Suśruta has not classified the Elephants as a class (*varga*), neither does he give any names or *lakṣaṇas*-characteristics-of different types of elephants.

The most important Sanskrit work for the classification of the plant world and animal- world is the *Tattvārthādhigamasūtra* by a great Jain scholar, Umāsvāti, who flourished in the first century A.D. The speciality of his classification is that the number of senses possessed by an organism is taken into account and subsequently, an animal is placed in an ascending order, according to the number of senses, with which it is endowed. The details are supplied below:

(1) Animals which posses two senses, viz. Touch and Taste.:

- (a) Apādika – Worms without appendages, Legs.
- (b) Nūpuraka – Ring like, with pendants-amelia.
- (c) Gaṇḍūpada – knotti-legged animals-arthropada, including crustacea.
- (d) Śaṅkha (conch), Śukti (pearl oyster) and Śaṁbūka (spiral shell) etc.
- (e) Jalauka-leeches.

(2) Animals possessing three senses, viz. Touch, Taste and Smell.

- (a) Pipīlikā – ants.
- (b) Rohiṇikā – red ants.
- (c) Upācikā-Kunthu, Tuburaka – bugs and flees (any of an order of wingless, very agile, blood-sucking insects).
- (d) Trapusabīja and Kārpāsāsthika – cotton-seed lice.
- (e) Śatapadī and Utpātaka—Centiped and Spring tail.
- (f) Tṛṇapatrāla—Plant lice and
- (g) Kāṣṭhahārka—wood-destroyers, termites or white ants.

(3) Animals with four senses, viz. Touch, Taste, Smell and Sight.

- (a) Bhramara, Varāṭa and Sāraṅga – bees, wasps and hornests.
- (b) Makṣikā, Puttikā, Daṁśa and Maṣaka—dipterous flies, gnats, mosquitoes.
- (c) Vṛścika and Nandyāvarta – Scorpions and spiders.
- (d) Kīṭa-Pataṅga – flying and non-flying insects.

(4) Animals/Humans (Men and *Tiryakyonis*), with five well-developed and active senses.

(a) Matsya – fishes.

(b) Uraga – limbless reptiles, snakes.

(c) Bhujaṅga – limbed reptiles and amphibians.

(d) Pakṣī – Birds.

(e) Catuṣpāda – Quadrupeds, mammals.

This group is again sub-divided into the oviparous.

(a) Aṇḍaja-Sarpa (snake), Godhā (monitor lizard), Kṛkalāsa (chameleon or chamaeleon and garden lizard), Nakra (crocodiles), Śiśimāra (dolphins and porpoises), Graha-godhikā (wall lizard), Matsya (fishes), Kūrma (tortoises) and Lomapakṣa – birds with the feathered wings.

(b) Jarāyuja-Placental animals. Here, the word *jarāyu* is limited to mean those animals that have non-deciduate placenta, e.g. man, cow, buffalo, goat and sheep, horse, camel, deer, yak (Camara), hog, gavaya (mithuna), lion, tiger, bear, panther, dog, cat, etc.

(c) Potaja-Mammals with deciduate placenta-which is thrown off after birth, such as Sallaka (porcupine), Hastī (elephant), Śvavit and Lopaka (hedge-hog and other insectivorous), Śasa and Śāyikā (hares and squirrels), Nakula (mongoose), Mūṣika (rats and mice) and Carmapakṣapakṣī (birds with leathery wings), i.e. bats and Valgulī (flying fox), Pakṣivirala (microcheiroptera) and Jaluka (desperately blood-sucking bat or vampire). (See: *Ch.* 2, *Sūtra*-22, 23 and 24, along with the commentary).

In brief, elephants are *Jarāyuja* animals and belong to that group which posseses all the five well-developed senses and it falls under the sub-class termed as *Potaja*.

It is a *Kūlacara,* i.e. an animal that stays by the side of water-places like, lakes, rivers, streams etc. According to the *Deśabheda*, it is to be found in all the three types of *Deśas*, viz. Anūpa, Jāṅgala and Sādhāraṇa, as already described, in keeping with the Āyurvedic texts.

2. Gajaśāstram by Pālakāpya Maharṣi

Gajaśāstra by Maharṣi Pālakāpya is one of the famous and classical works by Pālakāpya. The *Hastyāyurveda* is the other often-quoted work by him. There is a difference between these two works. The *Gajaśāstra* mainly deals with the following different aspects about the Elephants:

The creation and origin of the creature: The mythological stories about it. Its mythological form, grandeur and special powers etc. The curses and the solutions thereto, along with the advent—coming of Maharṣi Pālakāpya. (Chs.1-3).

The major and minor Elephant-forests and the features of the elephants from those forests (Ch.4); the age-wise growth of the elephant from the first month of its birth till the age-limit of 120 years (Ch.5). The account of fifty seven ancient countries clubbed under ten groups. (Ch.6).

Different methods of capturing the elephants (Ch. 7).

Different types of elephants and their features (Ch. 8).

Different creeds (mental attitudes) of elephants (Ch. 9).

The colour, brightness, body-odour, patience, physical strength, mental growth of the elephant (Ch.10-14).

The gait and walk of the elephants (Ch.15).

The various circles and figures on the body of the elephants and their significance (Ch.16).

Congenital bodily defects (Ch. 17).

Measurements in three dimensions of the elephants and the various types or kinds of elephants according to the same as well as units of Measurements (Ch.18).

Seats and their types used for rides on the elephants (Ch.19).

Thus, in short, the work deals with almost all the important factors/points related to the elephants as seen in the forests as well as in captivity. The work puts more stress on the healthy aspects of the elephants as also the natural ones and less stress is laid on the diseases of the elephants (which actually forms the Āyurvedic aspect which is not at all discussed herein).

More emphasis is laid on the purchase value as well as acceptability for maintaining the elephants/taming them. In a way, it may be said that the principal subject-matter of this treatise is "a healthy and acceptable elephant, which is worth training and retaining as a sign of symbol of pomp, glory and power and a not an elephant which is a patient—a suffering creature".

3. Comparison between the two works by Pālakāpya, viz. *Gajaśāstra* and *Hastyāyurveda*.

The *Gajaśāstra* refers to the *Dhātus* and *Doṣas* etc. as and when necessary. No separate description of the *Śarīraracanā* (Anatomy) or *Śarīrakriyā* (Physiology) is given in the *Gajaśāstra*. In all,not more than fifty technical terms are used (See, App, III.). In *Hastyāyurveda*, there are separate chapters about the *Śasīra* and *Śarīrakriyā*. In the *Śalyasthāna*, we find separate *Adhyāyas* on *Garbha-saṁbhava* (Ch.8), *Garbhāvakrānti* (Ch. 9), *Doṣa-dhātu-māna* (Ch. 6), *Danta-nakha-śirā* etc. (Ch. 8), *Śarīravinaya* (Ch. 9), Śīrāvyūha (Ch.16), *Marmapramāṇa* (Ch. 20), *Pradeśajñāna* (Ch. 29). The *Pradeśajñāna-adhyāya* describes fifteen areas of the body of an elephant, with several sub-divisions of each one of them, as under:

Pradeśa (Area)	*Pradeśa-bhāgas* (Sub-parts)
(1) Trunk	28
(2) Mouth (Internal)	30
(3) Teeth	10
(4) Face	33
(5) Netra	23

(6) Head	24
(7) Ears	30
(8) Neck	23
(9) Chest	7
(10) Heart	10
(11) Legs (fore)	96
(12) Body (*Kāyamadhya*)	40
(13) Legs (hind)	74
(14) Penis	11
(15) Lāṅgūla (Tail)	7
Total	**446**

Similarities and Differences

Similarities between the two works:

Mythological story is the same.

The author of both the treatises is the same.

Mānaparibhāṣā-technical terms are the same for measurements.

Types of Elephants are similar in terms and numbers.

The questions and answers between King Romapāda and the Maharṣi Pālakāpya are similar.

Differences: The *Gajaśāstra* describes the *Gajavanas* in detail, but, no such description is found in the *Hastyāyurveda*.

The GS. gives details about the *Deśas* or countries and features of the elephants living therein. The HA. doesn't give these.

The GS. has a unique chapter on the *Kālīyagaja* (i.e. the (physical) age-wise growth of the elephants. No such description is found in the HA.

The HA. is divided into four main sections, termed as:

Mahārogasthana (On major ailments), *Kṣudrarogasthāna* (Minor ailments), *Śalyasthāna* (Ailments which could be surgically treated or the causes of grief or pain for the elephants) and *Uttarasthāna* (Detailed treatment of some other important diseases and topics). It includes chapters on anatomy, physiology, different habits like mating-habits etc., seasonal changes, creation of stables and food, sterility and madness (frenzy due to rut or ichor) of the elephants.

The symptoms or signs of the diseases and their treatments/ indications of the imminent death of elephants etc. are also described in the text.

The GS. has a totally different layout. The diseases, their signs and treatments are not at all discussed in it.

The HA. is comparable to the *Caraka-saṁhitā* in many ways. Like the CS., HA is written in the form of questions and answers between King Romapāda and Pālakāpya. In the GS., a similar pattern of questions and answers is followed in the first three chapters and from the fourth chapter, the King Romapāda does not seem to be asking questions any more and Maharṣi Pālakāpya directly starts giving information on some specific topics.

In the HA., the information given comes from Pālakāpya while in the GS. the opinions of Vyāsa are given along with those of Pālakāpya (in the original text as well as in the commentary-*Mūlam* and *Ṭīkā*).

To be more specific, there is no special reference to the opinion of Vyāsa (or Vaiśaṁpāyana) in the first three chapters of the GS, but, in the subsequent chapters, Vyāsa is almost invariably quoted in the *Mūlam* in the words: *Vyāsaprokte gajaśāstre*: In the HA.,Vyāsa or *Vyāsaprokta gajaśāstra* is not at all referred to by Pālakāpya. It is, however, very evident that the verses attributed to Vyāsa do not form the original part of the GS. and seem to be the later additions by some one else.

It could be gauged from the difference in the wordings of

the languages, metres used etc. that Pālakāpya basically composed his treatise in the Anuṣṭup metre, while, the verses ascribed to Vyāsa show a variety of metres. The gs has a little-known commentary *Ṭīkā* named *Bhāvasandarśinī* which is composed by one unknown/untraced scholar, viz. Anantakṛṇa-bhaṭṭāraka. It is very difficult to say anything about this scholar in the absence of any kind of authentic biographical informa-tion, neither is the original manuscript of this commentary available. We have just one Devanāgarī transcript (possibly from an original Telugu manuscript which seems to have been irretrievaby lost-as we could not get any kind of information about its existence even from the Southern Indian Libraries/ Research Institutes-) which was got prepared in 1926 A.D. by the Rājāsaheb of Aundh, Balasaheb Pant Pratinidhi. This King was very much enlightened and got many such rare works transcribed through the commissioned services of a Telugu Pandit, V. Vijayaraghavacarya-who was an accomplished Epigraphist from the South and enriched his Library in Aundh, which is nearly fifty kms. from Satara in Maharashtra. This GS., by the way, is still unpublished. The HA. by Pālakāpya is published as No. 26 in the famous *Ānandāśrama Sanskrit Granthāvalī* from Pune in Śālivāhan Śaka 1816 (1894 A.D.) and does not contain any commentary. It does contain the text in *Padya* as well as *Gadya*. A cursory glance at the contents of this treatise will leave no doubt in the minds of the readers that this work pertains to 'The diseases of the elephants and their treatment'. One fails to find this subject-matter dealt with in the GS-which is being printed now, along with the rare and still unpublished commentary and illustrations and English transla-tion-cum-paraphrase by the Copyist, viz. Pandit V. Vijayaragha-vacarya, an Epigraphist and Sanskrit Scholar.

The elephants are scientificially termed after their most important and conspicuous feature, viz. the trunk, otherwise known as Proboscis. The term Proboscidea is given to that type of mammals that possesses a Proboscis, a long and flexible snout. Only two varieties exist, viz. Indian and African. These are only survivors of about 7-8 varieties that were known to exist in the past. They are:

The Elephas or the Asian Elephant and
The Loxodonta or the African Elephant.

The elephant is an awe-inspiring yet attractive animal. Its size and shape, gait and strength are the main features of attraction for the old and the young, rich and the poor, educated as well as uneducated, men in authority or without it. Its general looks and non-harming yet fearful sight is not common with any other creature that walks on the surface of the earth. The strange part of it is that though it is fearful, still, people like to wait and see it from a close yet safe distance. In the case of a tamed elephant, one dares to go forward and offer a bunch of grass or fruit and then watch it eating it. The elephant is an enjoyable sight on land and especially in water when it is playing. Till recently, elephants used to be a common sight in towns and cities, especially, in the capitals of the Princely States. The status of a King was measured by the number of elephants he was able to possess, as wealth and prosperity as well as prowess and strength were a pointer to the affluence of the owner. The gift of an elephant with an *Ambārī* (seat) was a sign of a very special honour given in recognition of bravery, honesty and dedication. All the other graces were a follow-up of this.

This mighty creature formed a very important part of the Four-fold Army (*Caturaṅgasenā*) of a king. It was a very ferocious force to reckon with in a battle or a war. The number and quality of training were very decisive in the battle-fields till the days just prior to the invention and use of guns and other early explosives (which frightened them). A warrior mounted on an elephant was supposed to be more than a match for a horseman, a foot-soldier (*Padāti*) etc. The same is the case in the Game of Chess also, wherein the elephant was one of the very powerful pieces and it was to be protected from all sides, due to its paramount place because of its wide ranging movement on the chess-board.

The very sight of this powerful and faithful animal,

renowned for its courage and training and leading a formidable army in the medieaval times, was sufficient to create a psychological impact, turning into the defeat of the opposition and an army deficient in or devoid of elephant-force used to be at the receiving end. In course of time, however, the limitation of the elephant-force was exposed by the opponents who were endowed with superior weaponry, fire-arms in particular, firing from a distance. Gradually, the elephant lost its position in the army, though, they were put to other uses, like, recreational purposes, as a valuable mode of transport, pompous processions, religious processions and other ceremonies like coronation, for joy-riding, for crossing jungles, water-barriers and lastly, in the circuses in modern times.

The elephants, however, did not completely disappear from the scene. The Princely States like Baroda, Mysore etc. kept elephants in various strengths, depending on the capacity. The erstwhile State of Baroda, now, Vadodara, was very well-known for its Elephant-stable, which was popularly known as *Hāthī-khānā* or *Pīlakhānā* and *Gajaśālā* in Sanskrit. There were more than one hundred elephants at the Baroda *Hāthīkhānā* in 1875 A.D. The then rulers, viz. H. H. Maharaja Malharrao Gaekwad etc. used the elephants for the entertainment on weekly events like *Hāthī-ṭakkar* (elephant duel fight), *Sāṭhamārī*, Ḍāgadāri etc. The animals in that *Gajaśalā* were very strong and they carried heavy seats (*Aṁbārīs*) of gold or silver, for which ordinary elephants were not of much use. The details about the Baroda *Hāthīkhānā* are given elsewhere in this book.

Āyurveda and Elephants

Āyurveda is the knowledge (*Veda*) of life (*Āyuṣ*). It is applicable to all types of living-beings or the *Jīvasṛṣṭi*, consisting of the humans, animals, plants and all the living world is the subject-matter for Āyurveda. The *Aśva-āyurveda*, *Gaja* or *Hasti-āyurveda*, *Vṛkṣa-āyurveda* are the separate treatises that pertain to the discussion about the health as well as the diseases and the remedies thereof in the case of the animal-world and the plant-world respectively. The basic or fundamental Theory of *Vāta*, *Pitta*, *Kapha-doṣas* is applicable like the consideration of the *rasādi* seven *dhātus* and the *malas* like *mūtra* and *purīṣa* (urine and feacus). The concept of *Bala* is also nicely narrated in the *Hasti-āyurveda*. It states that the elephants born and brought up in the jungles, more freely, play happily in the water and mud. By playing more and more, the *Ojas* or *Dhātuprasāda* is produced, resulting in the good health, which in turn gives good strength and the *Bala* (strength) or *Ojas* (*Prāṇa*) keeps away all the diseases (*rogas*). The *Hasti-āyurveda* specifically says :

पांसुकर्दमतोयैश्च ततः क्रीडन्ति हर्षिताः।
धातुप्रसादं शीघ्रं हि क्रीडतां जायतेऽधिकम्।।
धातुप्रसादादारोग्यमारोग्याद्बलमेव च।
बलाच्च सर्वरोगाणां निवृत्तिः स्यादतःपरम्।।

(*Hatyāyurveda Mahāroga* Chapt. 1 *Sūtra* 211-12)

The books on Āyurveda frequently refer to the *Hasti-āyurveda* of Pālakāpya. In the chapter on *Jvara* in the *Nidāna-sthāna* of the *Aṣṭāṅgahṛdaya*, the author says that *Jvara* (fever) affects everything, like, the humans, birds, animals, plants, fishes, different finished corns (*dhānyas*), but, the terminology is different in different cases.

The terms for *Jvara* in animals, plants, corns, earth etc. are as under:

Elephants—*Pākala*
Horses—*Abhitāpa*
Dogs—*Alarka*
Dhānya—*Cūrṇaka*
Bhūmi (Land, Earth)—Ūṣara
Jala (Water)—*Nīlikā* and

Jalaja (fishes etc.)—*Indramada* Man—*Jvara*.
Oṣadhi (Plants)—*Jyoti*

(REF: *Aṣṭāṅgasaṅgraha*, *Nidānasthāna*, Ch.I, *Sūtra*-4)

Pālakāpya in his *Gajaśāstra* gives the following list :

Sr. No.	Things affected by *Jvara*	Term used
1.	*Nara* (Human)	*Jvara*
2.	*Haya* (Horse)	*Abhitāpa*
3.	*Khara* (Donkey)	*Khoraka*
4.	*Go* (Cow)	*Īśvara*
5.	*Uṣṭra* (Camel)	*Alasa*
6.	*Vyāla* (Tiger)	*Akṣika*
7.	*Aja*(Goat)	*Pralālpaka*
8.	Sarisṛpa (Serpent)	*Kaśniṣa*
9.	*Mahiṣa* (Buffalo)	*Haridraka*
10.	*Mṛga* (Antelope)	*Mṛgaroga*
11.	*Pakṣī* (Birds)	*Avatāpa*
12.	*Śvā* (Dog)	*Alarka*
13.	*Matsya* (Fishes)	*Indramada*
14.	*Gulma* (Cluster of trees)	*Gucchaka*
15.	*Oṣadhi* and *Vanaspati*	*Jyotiṣka*
16.	*Mālya* (Flowers)	*Parvaka*
17.	*Nalinī* (Lotus)	*Ṛṣabhaka*
18.	*Dhānya* (Food-grains)	*Cūrṇaka*
19.	*Kodrava*(Sanwamillet)	*Lalha*
20.	*Śāka*(Vegetables)	*Madhūka*
21.	*Bhūmi* (Earth)	*Ūṣara*
22.	*Āp* (Water)	*Nīlika*
23.	*Gaja* (Elephants)	*Pākala*

The word *Pākala* means that which brings about the *pāka* or results in the destruction of the *Dhātus*. Different varieties of *Pākala* are described in the *Hasti-āyurveda* of Pālakāpya.

Caraka includes the *hastinī-mūtra* (urine of a female-elephant) in the eight types of *mūtras* (urine) used in the therapy. He also gives its qualities and indications for use (*C. Sūtra*. I/102).

Caraka and Suśruta describe the qualities of the elephant's milk. Caraka's commentator observes that though the characteristics of the elephant's milk are given, its use in the treatment is not seen in the later chapters. (*Caraka.Sūtra*. 27/217-224.Cakrapāṇi). Suśruta had also given the properties of elephant's curds in *Suśruta Sūtra*.45-74.

Another noteworthy reference to the elephants in the Āyurvedic texts is again from Caraka in connection with the *Basticikitsā* (the therapy through enemas) in different animals. *Bastipūṭakas* or the Urinary-bladders of different animals are used in different cases. The length of the *Bastinetra* (nozzle) to be used in different animals, the substances to be used for the preparation of the *Basti* (*kvāthratail*) etc. and their quantity are discussed under this topic. In the case of the elephants, they are as under:

1) Choice of *bastipūtaka*—goat or sheep-bladder.

2) Length of the *basti-netra* (Nozzle-tube)—one *aratnī* or the length of the fore-arm, approximately 18 inches.

3) Quantity of *kvātha* (decoction) for *Nirūha-basti* (Evacuative enema) should be 1/8th of the *Nirūha*, i.e. 128 *tolās*.

4) Kurchi-seeds (Indrayava), costus liquoris (Kustakuliñjana), long pepper-sweet-flag (Pippali), (Vacā), Dill seeds (Śatapuṣpa), Emetic nut (Madanaphala), Extract of Barberry (Rasāñjana), Gur (Jaggery), Rock-salt (Saindhava) and decardices (Daśamūla) are useful in the prepartion of all kinds of veterinary enemas. Holy-fig (Aśvattha), Banyan tree (Vaṭa), Aśvakarṇasāla, catachu (Khadira), purging cassia (Āragvadha) and Palmyra Palm (Tāla) are especially useful in the enemas to be given to the elephants. (See:*Caraka, Siddhisthāna*-11 verses 20-24).

4. GAJAŚĀLĀ OR HĀTHĪKHĀNĀ (PĪLAKHĀNĀ) AT VADODARA

Maintaining elephants has been a sign of affluence and it was a practice with almost all the Royal Families to maintain *Gajas*-which was considered to be the measure of their prowess as well as prosperity. The Kings of Baroda (modern Vadodara) were also not lagging behind in this respect. The Baroda Mahārājās had an extensive area which was known as the *Hāthīkhānā*, which has now been turned into a whole-sale market-place. In this small chapter, an attempt is made to acquaint the readers with the *Hāthīkhānā* at Baroda-a pride in those days.

The Gajaśālā or Stable for Elephants: These *Gajaśālās* were very spacious structures-clean and well-ventilated. Every elephant was provided with a 20'x 20' well-paved space, with 15 feet open space separating two such areas. The flooring with a gentle slope was provided with a channel at the end for the easy flow of the urine and excreta, passed by these animals. The excreta were removed at least twice a day, since, it is very injurious for the feet of the elephants to trample on it or to crush it under their feet. It also becomes the breeding ground for flies, mosquitoes and other insects, which may trouble the animals. The stables were high-roofed, measuring more than 16 feet.

There used to be as many as 125 elephants in this *Hāthīkhānā* at Vadodara in the early eighties of the 19th century (1875AD). Some of the famous and favourite elephants were named as: Sundara-gaja, Śambhuprasāda, Fateh-gaja. The names of the female-elephants were Rūpamālā, Caṁpā, Gaṅgāpyārī etc.

The urine of an elephant in '*Masti*' (intoxicated or in frenzied state of mind) has a very bad and strong odour which is almost unbearable. Hence, these animals are to be kept away from others, neither it is good nor advisable to keep them in the open. Therefore, they should be placed in a sheltered space.

The *Hāthīkhānā* had been a very vast area near the old Nazarbaug Palace, adjoining the modern Mandvi Gate. The ever-growing city area now surrounds both the *Hāthīkhānā* as well as the Palace. Consequently, the *Hāthīkhānā* is now converted into a whole-sale food-grain market, as the number of the elephants is dwindling. A look at those original structures with high roofs, mighty walls and broad passages will give you an idea of the grandeur of those days.

The *Hāthīkhānā* was not only a stable, but, it also was required to house everything that the elephants need, such as: water-tanks, fodder, *Aṁbāris* of various types, chains, ropes, workshops for the iron-smith, carpenter etc. for the maintenance and repairs, special ornaments and decorative articles for the elephants for ceremonial purposes, living-rooms for the staff on duty, *Mahautas*, helpers etc.

An elephant's main requirements are:ample water, fodder, food-grains and vast areas for daily walks. They need water for playing, bathing as well as drinking.

हस्तीनामुदकं प्राणास्तद्गतिस्तत्परायणाः।
तस्मात्सलिलमेतेषां कामतोऽनुप्रसाधयेत्।।

(Ref. *Hastyāyurveda, Mahārogasthāna*, 1.2.5)

The daily average requirement of drinking water for an elephant is 196 lbs at a time for a large-sized elephant, while, medium and small-sized animals require about 150 lbs and 100 lbs respectively at a time. They normally drink water twice a day or in summer, even thrice a day. Elephants are choosy about the water in that they accept very clear and preferably odourless water. Some elephants drink water before taking food, some take after the food. There are many ways in which they show their satisfaction, like, spilling out small amount of water at the end, by making strange sounds by themselves or with the help of their chains. Some prefer drinking directly from a tap, rather than from a storage tank. It so happens that sometimes, the elephants open the taps and quench their thirst.

Water is as good as life for elephants. Watching elephants drink water is a sight of rare pleasure. They show special liking for a particular animal accompanying them on such drinking sprees. The sight of an elephant being bathed is also pleasant, with so many persons at work washing different parts simultaneously for nearly two hours. It is always advisable to bathe the elephants before they are taken out for riding, hunting or even in ceremonial processions. It is the wont (habit) of the elephants to put dust on their body, immediately after a bath, if they are not properly taken care of. At times, the elephants are given a hot-water bath, for which, nearly 15 to 20 large buckets of water are needed.

It is observed that the tamed elephants crave for a dip in the lake or bathe in running water of a stream or a river. At times the urge is so intense that the animal escapes from the clutches of its master, despite the chains and rushes to the water-reservoirs. On such occasions, it is very difficult to control, capture and bring it back to the pavilion if not allowed to take the bath to its heart's content. We hear a lot about such instances of elephants breaking off to indulge in such a water-sport.

FEEDING ELEPHANTS

Elephants were classified into three different categories, on the basis of the size, digestive power and the type of work to be done (i.e. taken from) by the elephants.

Food substance (in lbs)	1st type	2nd type	3rd type
Wheat flour	50 lbs	40 lbs	32 lbs
Ghee	3	1½	3¼
Jaggery (gur)	3	1½	¾
Salt	½	½	½
Dry fodder	320	320	240

The condiments in the following measure were given for all the three categories.

Substance (Name)	Amount in *tolas.*
Turmeric	5
Black pepper	5
Garlic	5
Kutki	5
Fenugreek	½

This measure is for the animals used mainly for much lighter work in days when they were not supposed to participate in wars and battles. In earlier days, there were seven categories of these animals and corresponding seven types of food to be given to them.

Normally it is taken for granted that these animals, i.e. elephants, are strictly vegetarian—grass-eater. In captivity, however, they are fed on mutton soups, blood, eggs, animal fats etc. Many of the medicinal preparations contain these substances in large amounts. Apart from diseases, these substances were given to them for some specific uses such as duel fights, for engaging them in games like *Sāṭhamārī*, *Ḍāgadārī* etc. They were also given alcoholic drinks, like, Surā, Vāruṇi, Āsavas, Ariṣṭas and sour-fermentations like *Kañji*. In the *Gajaśāstra,* we find references to the mention of some of the elephants from the Upavanagajas, living in the North-western Himalayan forests, indulging in eating blood and flesh, as also some sort of natural alcohol *(Madyam)*.

Since the elephants like green fresh grass, a special pasture was maintained at Dumad (दुमाड), six miles away from the city. This was used for the free movement of the elephants during September to January every year. Another favourite food of the elephants is the sugar-cane, which was also given to them during the season. It was also ensured that there is a kind of a variety in the daily diet of the elephants and a thought was also given to the amount of food which should ideally be equal to the weight the elephants are required to carry. Pālakāpya makes a point when he says that

Ajasram hastino bhakṣyam—*Hastyāyurveda Mahāro-gasthāna* अजस्त्रं हस्तिनो भक्ष्यम्। Chap 2-74-75

According to the *Hasti-āyurveda,* the quantity of the food to be given to an elephant has to be decided on the basis of its bodily measurements. They are measured in all the three dimensions, length, height and circumference. This is very significant because these measurements collectively give a very good and clear idea of the total mass to be nourished. There are three categories, viz. *Uttama*, *Madhyama* and *Kaniṣṭha* and they are to be fed accordingly and the quantity of food required is also prescribed. (See: *Hastyāyurveda*, *Uttarasthāna,* chap. 3/22 and *Hastyāyurveda Mahārogasthāna.* chap. 3/61 to 67.

MEASUREMENTS OF GAJAŚĀLĀ ACCORDING TO HASTYĀYURVEDA

The HA. specifically gives the measurements of *Gajaśālā* for all the three types of elephants, as under:

Type		Breadth	Length	Height
Uttama	*Artanīs*	24	48	26
	Feet	36	72	39
Madhyama	*Aratnīs*	22	44	20
	Feet	33	66	30
Adhama	*Aratnīs*	20	40	16
	Feet	30	60	24

FACING-EAST OR NORTH

Prāgjīva (प्राग्जीव) Fore-ground-half the breadth in each case.

Several instructions are given regarding the floor, its slope, channels for the easy flow of excreta, walls as well as fixed and movable shutters. The *Hastiśālās* are to be disinfected by fumigation to get rid of the flies and the mosquitoes. In summer, they were ventilated by removing the movable shelter portions and other such sections which could be easily adjusted. In winter, fire-places were arranged in suitable portions of the *Gajaśālā* for keeping the animals warm. It was made a point to keep the sick or ailing elephants away from the healthy ones to avoid being affected by the diseases (*Rogasaṁparka*). (See: *HA*. *Āyuruttarasthāna* ch.6)

It is a well-known fact that the elephants like putting dust and mud on their bodies. It is interesting to note that the *Hasti-āyurveda* has devoted a special chapter, termed as "*Pāṁsudāna*" (giving a dust-bath). Pālakāpya says that the *Pāṁsudāna* is very refreshing for the elephants and they do relish it. It also provides strength, it increases *rasa-dhātu* and wards off lice and insects. (*Hastyā Uttarasthān*. Ch.30)

It is interesting to note that the *Hāthīkhānā* at Baroda has maintained a record of the heights of certain elephants as under:

Śrīprasāda measured	10'-7" (1909)	Rūpamālā-8'-8"
Bājabahāddara "	10'-4" (1910)	Caṁpā-8'-6"
Śambhuprasāda "	10'-0" (1910)	Gaṅgāpyārī-8'-4"
Sundaragaja "	9'-10" (1910)	(1910)

(Pl.See *Hastivijñāna* by Shri M.M. Joshi)

There are many methods of measuring the elephants. One method is to measure the circumference of the fore-leg of the animal and then multiply it by two which gives the height of the elephant. Yet another method is to measure the distance between the tip of the lower lip to the ground, while the animal is standing naturally and then multiply it by two which also gives the height of the elephant. But, both these methods do not give the exact idea of the figure or the height of the elephant. They, however, are very useful for getting a somewhat correct idea of the height of the elephant when one has to guess the size of the animal from its foot-prints in the forest.

PRAKARAṆA-1.

Who Was Pālakāpya

In the first chapter (*Prakaraṇa*) of the *Gajaśāstra,* the mythological story-traditionally known-is narrated as under:

As per the promise given by Brahmā to the elephants, Pālakāpya was born to a Yakṣiṇī-who had assumed the form of a very beautiful female elephant-of a pious sage, named Sāmagāyana. Pālakāpya was endowed with the knowledge of that part of Āyurveda, pertaining to the Elephants. Soon after the delivery, the mother carried her sons having a human form-in her trunk and delivered it to Sāmagāyana Maharṣi in his hermitage, who brought him up. The etymology of the word Pālakāpya is given as follows :

Pālanāt gajayūthasya kāpyagotrodbhavo yathā/
Pālakāpya it śrīmān nāmadheyam cakāra saḥ//.

The mythological element in the story apart, certain facts must be taken into consideration. A human off-spring born to an elephant certainly sounds strange. There are, however, many examples, where an orphaned human off-spring is reared, protected and brought up by the birds and animals. Here it may be brought to the notice that Śakuntalā—the human baby of Menakā and Viśvāmitra, abandoned in the forest-was protected and reared by the birds. We also know of the instances wherein human child is protected and reared by a pack of wolves. Pālakāpya is perhaps one such rare example. Another reason for this is: The female elephant gave birth to a human child after ten months.

The elephants have a gestation period of 21 to 24 months. (See: *Mṛgapakṣiśāstra* of Haṁsadeva, *Śreṇī*.6; verses 255-56.

The original wording in the Text is : *Samaye tam asūta sā/* The commentator explains it as : *Daśame māsi sūryāga-nitejasam mānuṣarūpam hastyāyurvedapāragam munikumā-ram svāsyatalenaiva suṣuve.*

In fact, it is just possible that the orphaned human child must have been located by one of the female elephants from the herd staying near the hermitage, picked up by her trunk, held near to her mouth and then that clever female-elephant 'delivered' that child at the door or gate of the hermitage. "*Svāsyatalāt suṣuve*" can very well be interpreted in this way. The matriarchal system in the elephant-herds, the kindness shown by the elephants towards human babies and children only adds to this type of interpretation. Generally, the elephants don't hurt the young ones of any species and carefully pass along without hurting them.

Asked by the King Romapāda as to how he knows all the details of the elephants, the great sage Pālakāpya answers him in the following simple way : See : *Gajaśāstra*, Ch.1, verses :

हस्तिन्याः वक्त्रसम्भूत...........जानास्येषां हिताहिते।।

Prayer by Maharṣi Dhārmika

In addition to these usual prayers, we also come across yet another prayer by one Sage, named Dhārmika. It appears that he flourished after the King Romapāda in the region of the Naimi-ṣāraṇya. The Sanskrit *Ṭīkā* (commentary) specifically mentions the following:

(1) Dhārmika was a student (*śiṣya*) of Pālakāpya.

(2) He lived and preached in the Naimiṣāraṇya.

(3) He addressed a congregation (*pariṣad*) of the Sages (*Ṛṣis*) and narrated to those assembled there the subject-matter relating to the Elephant Lore, by enumerating the Tradition of the authors on *Gajaśāstras* like Lord *Śaṅkara*, Lord Viṣṇu,

Lord Indra and Lord Brahmadeva, stressing the point that this Tradition is continued in later periods also.

Surprisingly, hereafter, there is no reference to Dhārmika Maharṣi in the Text (*Mūlam*) and the Commentary (*Ṭīkā*) either.

PRAKARAṆA-2.

THE CREATION OF THE DIGGAJAS

The chapter gives the famous mythological story of the creation of the original eight Divine Elephants, brought into being by Brahmā (the Creator) at the request of the seven sages (staying in the seven *lokas* or worlds). Thus, a new *Jāti* of creatures, viz. the elephants, came into existence.

The Divine Elephants had their own peculiarities like: They were endowed with wings for flying. They had four tusks. Each and every elephant with his wife ruled over the eight Directions or *Diks*, hence, they were known as *Dig-gajas*. They were very beautiful, strong and capable of going anywhere on land, in water or air. This made them powerful and very proud, as no other creature could match their might. As a result, they created havoc wherever they went and thus were very dreaded creatures.

Each pair of the elephants (*Dig-gajas*) gave birth to sons (in all 30 sons and one daughter). They in turn produced several off-springs. Thus, their progeny went on multiplying and thus covered all the land on the earth. Their supreme might turned them into troublesome creatures, bringing about destruction wherever they went. When they went near the hermitages of the Sages and started destroying those secure and peaceful areas, the angry Sages cursed them and curbed their might in different ways.

The *Dig-gajas* had four tusks and wings like the Mastodons and Four Tuskers. Millions of years ago, there lived an animal much like the elephant which was called Mastodone-which is now extinct. These elephant-like animals were termed as Four Tusker Mastodones. They were stronger than the modern day elephants. The earlier species had tusks in both the jaws.

Gradually, some of the later species lost their lower tusks naturally and others developed great flat lower tusks. They were called 'Shovel Tuskers'. It is very surprising that no species having wings-corresponding to the ones described in the Sanskrit literature-has been found amongst the ancient groups of elephants.

PRAKARAṆA-3.

CURSES BEFALLING THE DIG-GAJAS AND SOLUTIONS THEREFOR

We are told in this chapter how the *Dig-gajas* lost their four tusks and the wings and the span of life due to the curse pronounced on them by the Sage Dīrghatamas, as a result of their destructive deeds. Hence they became mere carriers or the vehicles of the royalty and the nobles and remained as the underlings of the humans. They also lost their enormous might and became unaware of their physical strength. The elephants insulted the wife of the Fire God (Agnideva) and as a result were cursed by the God that they will have voracious appetite. Subsequently, they went to Brahmā to get a solution, but, Brahmā knew the facts and cursed them in yet another way, viz. the elephants would throw mud and dust on their own body to get rid of the burning sensation.

The elephants consume about 150 kgs. of food every day. Unlike other quadrupeds like cows, the elephants have a 'single stomach'. They do not ruminate like cows or buffaloes and the food taken in is virtually ground between the huge molars (weighing about 4 kgs or more each) and then swallowed. The Gods riding on the back of the elephants at the time of the wars or battles against the Asuras found that their seats (on the back of the elephants) became slippery with the profuse perspiration of the elephants, hence, they requested Brahmadeva to find a solution to this problem. Brahmā in turn cursed the elephants and deprived them of their perspiration or sweating. In the fifth chapter of the *Gajaśāstra*, it is said that an elephant calf of two years of age constantly sweats from the skin portion near the nails. In chapter twelve also, the odour of the sweat (*Sveda-gandha*) is mentioned.

It is a fact that the elephants do not have sweat-glands and in the absence of sweating, keeping the body cool becomes very difficult. It becomes almost an uncontrollable urge to keep the body wet by taking recourse to water, putting muddy-water or even dust and grass to have a cooling effect. The elephants drink a huge amount of water, nearly 150-200 litres per day.

Brahmā also thought that the heavy and huge testicles hanging between the hind legs of the male elephants must be a hurdle in their normal speed, hence, He made them disappear from view by placing them mingled with other structures (bodily) in the portion of the tail in between the hind legs. It is also a fact that the testicles are hidden. It is considered as a physiological norm when the *Gajaśāstra* says that the '*Sa-muṣka gajas*' or the males whose testicles-are visible are considered to be abnormal. It is said that the testicles do descend and are visible when the male elephant is in rut (*must* or *masti*). In fact, the testicles are high up in the pelvis. Pālakāpya in his *Hastyāyurveda* has given a detailed account of injuries to the testicles, the causes thereof, features and the treatment recommended.

MAMMOTHS : The Mammoth is a pre-historic animal. Closely related to the present-day elephants, they were huge, lumbering beasts. Some of the Mammoths measured 4-5 metres in height at the shoulder. They had trunks and tusks too. Many times, some have been found to be having 4-5 metres long tusks curved upwards. They were wooly animals and lived in the icy lands of Asia, Europe and America. They belonged to the Elephantidae-the family of elephants and they are comparable to the Arala and the Atyarala varieties of elephants, described in the 18th ch. of this *Gajāśāstra*.

This noble creature seems to be very much endangered and all the nations have banned the capturing and killing of elephants. Licensed killing, however, is still in practice, in view of the uncontrollable and destructive nature of this animal; but, that is rare. In the ancient times, the mythological Divine Types were not an exception to this; even in those days, the elephants were punished for their destructive nature/attitude/ acts. That is the reason why they were cursed by the Sage whose hermitage was destroyed by the elephants and consequently, lost their wings and two tusks. Another *Ṛṣi* cursed them that they shall be controlled and dominated by the humans. The King Romapāda was the first to use them for war, hunting and entertainment. He, however, did not have any idea about how to control them and treat them in their illness and Maharṣi Pālakāpya obliged him by narrating this *Gajaśāstra*.

The importance of the elephants in wars and battles came to an end, with the gradual advent of long-range fire-arms. Despite this, the capture of elephants went on for their use in the field of entertainment, i.e. circus-shows, elephant-fights, hunting and games like *Ḍāgadārī* and *Sāṭhamārī*. Inspite of the legal ban, the killing continues for the precious tusks they are endowed with. This is a very hard and lasting material, known as Ivory-which is used for making the handles of the swords, daggers, walking sticks, decorative objects such as idols, inlaying material for ornamental dishes, trays, boxes, table-tops, chess-pieces and making seals, especially, in Japan.

We close this chapter with a very interesting observation:

All the literary material from ancient times abounds in the details regarding the tusks, their beauty, the way they are to be cut, fixing them with (in) the rings of noble metals like the gold, silver and last but not the least, their protective power for the animal itself-who is endowed with these priceless tusks. The animals were mainly captured and trained for their use in war, hunting, carrying loads and various other tasks like religious and social processions. The interesting fact that we come across while perusing the ancient literature is: nowhere it is mentioned that the elephants were to be captured or killed for the purposes of extracting their tusks and the valuable ivory. On the contrary, the great authors have insistently advised the people to protect the aged and disabled/ailing male and female elephants. Another possible reason for not killing the elephants in olden days, esp. for ivory, is that many elephants used to be killed in the wars/battles etc. and consequently, abundant amount of ivory must have been available in those days, without much efforts at purposely killing the elephants. This must have been the reason that killing of elephants for ivory must have been unheard of in those days. Gradually, the use of elephants in wars became obsolete and ivory became scarce. This prompted the people to kill the animal expressly to obtain ivory. On the basis of this fact, we may say that 'possessing tusks' seems to be their last curse in modern times. This perhaps has proved to be one of the most important causes endangering this species today. Fortunately, there are some animal-lovers who are making frantic efforts to preserve such noble species-enabling the modern day-man to have a look at this giant and extremely useful and friendly animal.

PRAKARAṆA 4.

ELEPHANT FORESTS

The present chapter supplies information about the different habitats of the elephants or the *Gajavanas* as they are called, that were there in existence in and around India in those days. These sixteen Forests surround many countries, as is clearly mentioned in the Text as follows:

तत्रास्मिन् चतुर्थे प्रकरणे गजानामुत्पत्तिस्थानानि षोडशवनानि शास्त्रनिर्दिष्टानि। एषु षोडशवनेषु बहवो देशाः अन्तर्गताः इति भावः।।

This points to the proportion of the forest and the countries in the ancient period. The elephants found in these forests are known as Kaliyuga-gajas. The author has just named only sixteen main areas from where elephants of one's choice could be available. These sixteen forests are divided into two groups, viz. Eight Main Forests from the Prācya-gajavana to the Pañcanada-gajavana and the Eight Sub-territories located in the Himalayas, beginning from the Kirāta-viṣaya (country) and ending with Īśāna-upavana. The details of these are given below:

(1) The *Prācyagajavana* is 200 *yojanas* in extent, i.e. spread over about 8000 to 10000 sq. miles. The main Upavanas are given with their well-marked boundaries as well as well-defined sketches in the original manuscript. The sketches give a fairly good idea of the geographical locations of these forests. A gross idea of the area covered by these forests is given for the following four forests.

(2) **Kaliṅgagajavana**:spread over an extensive area of 100 *yojanas*, i.e. approximately, 4000 to 5000 sq. miles. It is also known as the Dakṣiṇāpathavana or the Daṇḍakāraṇya. Its Sanskrit description is furnished here in the original for better understanding.

सह्यपर्वतस्योत्तरस्यां दिशि..........कलिङ्गवनमित्युच्यते।।

(3) **Saurāṣṭragajavana-**Its expanse is 50 *yojanas*, i.e. approximately 2000 to 2500 sq.miles. We may profitably refer to some interesting information given in the Gujarati Book, "*Vanya-jīvana*", published by Prakashana and Sampark Vibhaga, Gandhinagar, January, 2001 : The total areas of the Sanctuaries and National Parks in Gujarat are 16442.71 sq. kms.and 479.67 sq. kms. respectively and these are the housing grounds for animals like the lions, cheetahs, tigers, blackbucks, various kinds of nilgais, hyena, cinkara, bees, birds (both local and migratory), monkeys, deer etc. as well as marine life. It may be noted that wild elephants are no more to be found in Gujarat. From amongst the areas of both the National Parks and National Sanctuaries, Saurāṣṭra has the following share: N. Ps: 455.68 sq. kms; N. San.: 4738.48 sq. kms. None of these areas harbours wild elephants.

(4) **Pañcanadagajavana**-Its expanse was more than 200 *yojanas*, i.e. 8000-10000 sq.miles approximately.

The main Gajavanas mentioned in this chapter are: Prācya; Cedikarūṣaka; Daśārṇa; Āṅgareya; Kaliṅga; Aparānta; Saurāṣṭra and Pañcanada.

The geographical locations. i.e. mountains, rivers, cities and the then existing countries mentioned in connection with these forest are:

(1) **Prācya-gajavana (Eastern) :** They are bounded by the Ganga Yamuna rivers in the north and west, by Prayag (Allahabad) city in the south east & Brahmaputra river on the east. This forest was spread over 200 *yojanas*, i.e. an area of about 8000 to 10000 sq. miles. The elephants from this forest freely roam and are naturally spread over the following geographical areas and countries: They are: (a) Along the banks of the rivers Sarayu, Yamuna, Ganga and Gomati; (b) Mālavadeśabhūmi-Malva/Malwa; (c) In the mountains of the Aṅgadeśa and nearby places; (d) In the different parts of the Magadhadeśa; (e) In some parts of the Puṇḍradeśa; (f) In parts of Kashmir; (g) In parts of the Kosaladeśa; (h) In parts of the Pāñcāladeśa; (i) In parts of the Kaliṅgadeśa; (j) Along the banks of the river Gomati. These elephants are generally not seen in other parts.

(2) **Cedikarūṣaka-gajavana :** Tripurathala in the north, Daśārṇadeśa on the east and the Mekhalā river on the west.

(3) **Daśārṇa-gajavana :** To the east of the Vetravati river (Betwa), to the south of the Śrīparvata, to the west of the Daśārṇadeśa and to the north of Balaparvata.

(4) **Aṅgreyaka-gajavana :** To the south of the Reva (Narmada) river, to the east of the Vidiśā country, to the north of the Pāriyātra-hills and to the west of the Brahmavati river.

(5) **Kaliṅga gajavana :** To the south of the Vindhya Mountain, to the west of the Bay of Bengal (*Maho-*

dadhi), to the north of the Sahyaparvata (i.e. Western Ghats in Maharashtra). This *vana* was spread over 100 *yojanas*, i.e. 4000 to 5000 sq. mls. Kalingavana is the modern Orissa forest.

(6) **Aparānta-gajavana :** To the north-east of the Reva river, to the south-east of the Krishnagiri mountain, to the west of the Paścimasamudra (Arabian Sea), to the north-west of the Astamayagiri.

(7) **Saurāṣṭra-gajavana :** To the south of the Avanti-country and the Reva river, to the east of the Dwarka town, with an expanse of 50 *yojanas*, i.e. 2000-4000 sq. mls.

(8) **Pañcanada-gajavana :**

The following five points are quite helpful in identifying the qualities of the Elephants found in the eight forests in our Nation. The *Gist* of the cry, of colour, of size and bodily measurements, of nature and conduct and of strength.

In the case of the eight *Upavanas* or sub-forests, the case seems to be different. From the descriptions, it is clear that these *upavanas* are different parts of the great Himalayan ranges, extending in its full length from its eastern-most part to the north-west frontier province. The commentator puts it in the following words:

अधुना शास्त्रकारस्तावत् हिमवत......
......स्थाननिर्देशपूर्वकं तत्र जातानाम्–इत्यादि।

It means that these elephants were found in all the directions surrounding the Himalayas and at places very near to the Himalayas-which were considered to be the *Adhama-vanas* or inferior forests.

One thought may naturally come to our mind that our Text should have referred to some Himalayan states, located in the north of India, such as Sikkim, Bhutan and Nepal. It is surprising that their names do not occur either in the original Sanskrit Text or in its Sanskrit commentary. The principal *Vanas* and their locations make it clear that they are also located to the south of the Himalayas. Taking the central position and then working on all the eight main directions within the length and breadth of the Himalayas, we find the following picture.: Eastern forest- Kirātadeśa; south-eastern forest—Līla mountain; southern forest-Viśāladvīpa; south-western forest-Barbaraka-deśa; western forest; north-western forests; northern forests and north-eastern forests.

Viśāladvīpa : To the south of the Himalayas is a territory named as the Viśāladvīpa (large country surrounded on all sides by water). It is very difficult to say anything exact about this particular region because the Upavanas are situated in all the eight directions of the Great Himalaya, and no such land portion covered on all the sides by water is to be found in this particular geographic area.

Northern forests of Himalaya : The commentator says that there are numerous very wide forests in this region, but no reference is made to Nepal, Bhutan, Sikkim and Tibet. The names of Nepal and Bhutan appear in the sixth chapter in connection with the *Deśa-bheda-gajas* etc. Some modern books assert that the elephant-tracks are found at a height of 12000 ft. in Sikkim, while, in Burma, the elephants wander all around in all the seasons upto the height of 10000 ft. (See:BNHS *Book of Indian Animals*).

The *Gajaśāstra* furnishes some information/guidelines regarding the elephants that are considered to be Very good (*Uttama*), Medium (*Madhyama*) and Inferior (*Adhama*) by giving thought to certain aspects.

Name of the Vana	Quality of elephant
1) Prācya, Kaliṅga, Aparānta	Extremely good
2) Cedikarūṣaka, Daśārṇa, Āṅgareya	Medium
3) Saurāṣṭra, Pañcanada	Inferior.

A word about the Principal Forests and the five-fold examination employed for the gradation of the elephants will not be out of place. We furnish that information in a tabular form in order to have an idea at a glance.

Sr.No.	Vana	Nature of Cry	Colour	Size/Measure	Nature/Conduct	Strength/Price
1.	Prācya	Pleasant	Whitish black	Stout stomach, broad cheeks, long trunk	Look etc. calm, swift, active, intelligent, easy to control	Very powerful in war, hunting Price: very high
2.	Cedikarūṣaka	—	*Kapila* (tawny)	Little short in size	Beautiful, not so easy to control	Proportionately strong P : very high
3.	Daśārṇa	—	*Piṅgala* (brown)	Very tall	Very good natured	Verv strong; P: very high
4.	Āṅgareyaka	—	Very dark	Very tall	Beautiful, smooth, very beautiful eyes	Strong; P:very high
5.	Kaliṅga	—	Black	Medium size	Stout, Pleasurable, slow in movement	Strong;
6.	Aparānta	—	Jet Black	Tall, very smooth	Beautiful, very bold in war and hunting	Very strong, P: high
7.	Saurāṣṭra	—	Jet Black	Narrow head and face, small nails	Dull	Inferior, short-lived P:
8.	Pañcanada	—	Very dark	Physically very strong, huge body	Not easy to control, some bad qualities	Very stong P:

The gist of the cry is of special importance. An elephant's cry is similar to the cry/barking of other wild beasts of the surrounding forests, specially, in regard to the intensity and the shrill, like the cry of a lion, tiger, hyena of that forest (See, ch. 4). Some Upavana-gajas have a very killing instinct towards other animals, like the cows, deer as well as towards human beings and they do have liking for wine and flesh too.

PRAKARAṆA 5.

KĀLĪYA-GAJALAKṢAṆAM-FEATURES OF THE AGEWISE GROWTH OF THE ELEPHANTS.

Before we actually turn to the proper treatment of this topic in the *Gajaśāstra* chapter fifth, it will be better to touch upon certain points regarding the mating season, gestation period, birth of the calf and its initial two/three days, which were recorded by Haṁsadeva in his *Mṛgapakṣiśāstra*.

Our *Gajaśāstra* specifically mentions that the males and females attain adulthood by the 7th or the 8th year. According to the modern studies, after attaining this age, a male may try to unite with a female of his choice and age, but, is not much successful in doing so, on account of the dominance of the other stronger and elder males. The *Gajaśāstra* says that male elephants, belonging to the second decade age group (11 to 20 years), are capable of causing pregnancy. For some males, this may be possible at such an early age, but, for the others, it could be as late as thirty years (according to the modern view), depending upon the number of senior and stronger males in a herd. The females generally become pregnant by the age of ten to twelve years. According to Haṁsadeva, they mate on land or in water. The mating season generally is Vasanta or Prāvṛṭ (spring or early rainy season). The gestation period is from twenty-one to twenty-four months. Pālakāpya surprisingly says in his *Hastyāyurveda* that an elephant cow gives birth to a calf at the end of the 10th , 11th or 12th month (See:*H.Ayu. S.S.* 8/110).

On giving birth to a calf, the female generally does not eat or drink for 2/3 days. She devotes her time in breast-feeding the new-born. She is extremely alert in protecting her calf., as the calf is completely dependent on the mother in the first year of its life. It frequently drinks breast milk and follows the mother very closely. (See:*Mṛgapakṣiśāstra*, *śreṇī* 6, ślokas). The *Gaja-śāstra*, however, does not give these details. According to the workers at the breeding centre for the elephants at Chitvan (in Nepal), the weight of a new-born elephant calf is 80 lbs.

Pālakālpya compares elephant (*gaja*) with man (*puruṣa*), especially, as regards a human child and an elephant calf. Both in the *Gajaśāstra* and in the *Hasti-āyurveda*, the elephants are described as having *sāttvika, rājasika* and *tāmasika prakṛti. Sātmya-jāti-prakṛti* etc. are also described in detail (*H.Ay.S.S.* 6). The terminology regarding the *Śarīra* and *Śarīrakriyā* (body and bodily actions) is almost similar. Suśruta has said that the *puruṣa* is the main or all important thing and all else is secondary to the *puruṣa* (S.S. 1.).

This is stated in the following words by Pālakāpya in his *Hastyāyurveda*.

तेषामेव भूतानां पुरुषः श्रेष्ठः पशूनां गजः।

"From amongst the *bhūtas* (living beings), the man is superior and from amongst the beasts, the elephant". (HA. *Śalyasthāna*-3 pA02)

Similar idea is expressed by Haṁsadeva in his *Mṛgapak-ṣiśāstra*, S.6/339:

"The elephant is the top-ranking *rajoguṇātmaka* amongst all the animals". About the mind, the *Hastyāyurveda* says that it doubts and desires :

संशयोत्पादनमभिप्रार्थनात्मकं मनः।

(*H.Ā.S.S.*7, p. 404)

The 8th *adhyāya,* named the *Garbhāvakrāntiḥ*, in the 3rd chapter, viz. *Śalyasthāna*, verse :402 cd and 403 ab, p. 435, of the *Hastyāyurveda*, abounding in similarities between a man and an elephant, specifically says that: "The *doṣas*, *dūṣyas* and *indriyas* in the humans and the elephants are similar. The diseases in both these species have similar features".

दन्तिनां मानुषस्तुष्यो दोषो दूष्येन्द्रियाणि च।
व्याधयश्च भवन्त्येषां प्रायशस्तुल्यलक्षणाः॥

Now, we turn to the actual contents of this chapter: *Kālīyagajalakṣaṇam*—the chronological (Age-wise) growth of the elephants.

This is a unique chapter of the *Gajaśāstra*, as no other book or text gives such a detailed information about the development of an elephant from the first month of its life to about 120 years of its age. The sketches are wonderful and give a fairly clear and good idea. This is applicable to all the elephants that are found in all the 16 *Gajavanas*, irrespective of whether they are males. females or belonging to different types like Bhadra, Manda, Mṛga and Saṅkīrṇa. The growth in the first year, from the birth to the 12th month, is described in great details and is well commented upon by the learned scholar, viz. Anantakṛṣṇabhaṭṭa. Similar is the case with the period from the 2nd year upto the 10th year. The life span from the age of the eleventh year upto the utmost age of 120 years is divided in eleven stages of ten years each. Stage-wise bodily changes, increase in body and strength, growth of tusks, food types and quantity thereof, sleep and wakefulness, sexual behaviour and changes, appearance of different coloured spots and the colour of the skin, the peculiar behaviour of the youthful male and its attitude towards the herd, the females and their attitude towards the equals and elder males in the herd, their liking for water and mud etc. etc.-all these aspects and things are very clearly given in great details. It will be a pleasure to read all these things from the original Sanskrit Text, with the help of the excellent and explanatory commentary in Sanskrit and the English translation, so capably done by Pt Vijayaraghavacharya, the scholar from Tirupati, who has not only drawn the sketches but also has prepared in 1936 A.D. the Devanāgarī transcript of this manuscript for the Rājāsaheb of Aundh.

Roughly speaking, the life of an elephant can be divided into two major parts: from birth to the end of the 5th stage, i.e. up to 50 years. These are the years when the elephants seem to gradually attain to the top of bodily growth and strength.

From the birth to 12 months (1st year)

In the first month after its birth, the baby-elephant is very weak and does not even know how to suck breast milk and is totally dependent on the mother. One may think that the baby-elephant sucks milk with the help of the trunk, but, it is not so. It curls up the trunk on its head and then reaches the breast-nipple and then sucks by the mouth. Very frequent feeding is required in the earlier months. An important mile-stone, viz. getting away from the herd for a short distance and quickly coming back, is attained by the 3rd month. The term used for this is '*yūthaniṣkrama*'. Along with this, the baby manages to muster courage to face the other elephants in the herd, slowly finds some interest in the surroundings, tries to eat tender grass, leaves of trees, pluck them with its own trunk, gradually becomes interested in water play, goes on getting stout and its sleeping hours shorten, gets very angry if something is not to its liking. By the 7th month, its walk is not so shaky and starts walking with speed in the 8th month, still, prefers to be near the mother, eats a lot and sleeps more as compared to earlier two months. By the end of the 12th month, the face assumes a beautiful black colour and the body becomes plump, the look is quite attractive. Hereafter the skin starts getting thick. It becomes very strong and occasionally drinks milk and eats a lot. In the 3rd year of their life, they grow so strong that they are able to uproot small and medium-sized trees. The tusks grow a little out of the jaw, almost protruding.

In the 2nd year elephant, the skin portion near the nails is seen to be wet with sweat.

By the 4th year, their teeth become strong and this is the age when they should be captured and training started.

Pālakāpya opines that this is the proper time for the teaching and training of the elephants, as, in the fourth year itself, the elephant acquires the capacity to know and remember the passage on its way for going to and returning from the training and work-place etc. By the end of the fifth year, the tusks come out fully. The appearance of spots on various parts of the body is a continuous process in all these years. Hair-tufts also keep on showing/growing and the elephant understands various commands and meaning of the sounds made by the Mahouts and promptly carries out the orders. An all round progress takes place in the next two years. In the 8th and 9th year, the elephants become sexually active and the erection of penis is often seen, goading them to go near the females of their age for enjoyment. By the 10th year, they attain full bodily growth and thus become fit for employing in the wars.

In the second and the third decades (11-30 years), they attain the capacity to father a baby-elephant. (*Garbhaprado bhavet//*). They have the strength to break open the strong walls of the fortress (*Durgabhedī*). It tends to make them enter into a fight with other elephants and uproot trees.

In the fourth decade (31-40 years), they are very strong and are always in a mood to have sexual enjoyment, that too with a passion. The '*masta* or *dāna* or *mada* (rut, ichor)' generally appears in this period and when they become angry, they may even injure their keeper or the Mahout.

In the fifth decade (41-50 years), though they are stronger, they become calm, endure pain and physical exertion of a very severe nature.

From 50 to 60 years of their age, the elephants start losing their strength gradually. The decline is evident in the form of the weakness of the organs of locomotion and of sense (*Hīyamānedriyagrāma*), body-tissues also show regression (*Tanudhātucayaḥ*), the base of the tusks gets open, digestion suffers (*Alpāgnipitte*) and *Vāyu* (gastric problems) dominates (*Bahu-mātariśva*), the gait becomes uncertain, i.e. faltering

(*Kiñcit skhalitagatiḥ*) and they do not remain fit for war or other laborious works/tasks, as they keep on losing strength. They prefer to be alone, away from the herd, sleep becomes irregular, are not able to eat hard stuff and go to the areas where soft food like grass and water is available. They become lean and thin, due to the loss of fat, lying down and getting up also becomes difficult, pass urine and stools with difficulty and the voice becomes very weak.

Although the life span of the elephants is said to be of 120 years, many elephants perish before that age-limit. It is really very rare that one is able to see and identify an elephant in the 11th or 12th stage of life (i. e. 100-110 and 110-120 years).

Despite the fact that he has put down so many minute details in the various stages of the life span of the elephants, the great Sage Pālakāpya openly accepts the limitations of the knowledge of the humans about the elephants in the following verse :

Āyurmānam vayojñānam garbhiṇījñānameva ca/
Munayo'pi ca muhyanti kim punaḥ māṁsacakṣuṣaḥ//

Pālakāpya gives specific names of the elephants for the different age-groups from the very birth upto 120 years.

Age	**Term used by Pālakāpya**	**Term used by Vyāsa**
Upto one month	—	Viklava
2nd month	Haṁsa	Mandaka
3rd month	—	Yūthaniṣkrama
4th month	—	—
5th month	—	—
6th month	—	—
7th month	—	—
8th month	—	—
9th month	—	—

Age	Term used by Pālakāpya	Term used by Vyāsa
10th month	—	—
11th month	—	—
12th month	—	—
2nd year	Cūcuka	Cūcuka
3rd year	—	—
4th year	Barbara	—
5th year	Kalabha	Kalabha
6th year	Vikārika	Vikārika
7th year	—	Sisa
8th year	—	—
9th year	Prabhava	Prabhava
10th year	—	Vikka
11th-20 years	—	Kalabha
21st-30 years	—	Javana
31st-40 years	—	Kalyāṇa
41st-50 years	—	Yūtha
51st-60 years	—	—
61st-70 years	—	Vikarṇaka
71st-80 years	—	Viravi
81st-90 years	—	Purāṇa
91st-100 years	—	Sthavira
101st-110 years	—	Pūrvaka
111th-120 years	—	—

Pālakāpya in his *Gajaśāstra* divides the life span of the elephants in three groups as under :

No.	Age-group	Grade
1.	1-14 years	Medium : Considered best for all teaching/training
2.	14-32 years	Best: Prime youth fit for war, hunting and traction
3.	32-70 years.	Inferior : Age not fit for war, hunting etc.

It may be noted that the English translation gives a different grading, possibly, due to the progress/advance in knowledge of the modern scholar/translator.

This *Prakaraṇa* abounds in several details regarding the age-groups of the elephants and this sort of information is very much difficult to find even in the modern books on elephants. While' we go through this chapter, we always feel that we are watching it live in the wild-life telecast on the Discovery channel.

It may be noted that the description herein is mostly regarding the male-elephants. Even then, while commenting on the elephants in their second decade of life, the commentator says :

एतावता प्रबन्धेन सर्वेषामपि करिणां च मासक्रमवर्षक्रमवयस्सु स्वरूप-गुणादिकं प्रतिपादितम्।

Haṁsadeva in his *Mṛgapakṣiśāstra*, *śreṇī*-6, verses-330-335, notes clearly certain peculiarities special to the females thus: Even though the female elephants have the same appearance and movements like the male elephants, they differ in the following aspects: They do not have tusks; are calm, shy and smaller in size; possess abundant intelligence and are very strong; are beautiful; are not at all cruel; their skin is soft and walk (gait) is pleasant; eat less and bear 3-4 off-springs in their life time; extremely love their young ones and are kind towards all living creatures. Their (both of males and females) prime youth is up to the age of forty years and thereafter they are unfit for any hard work, hence, both should be cared for and looked after properly by the owners, Kings as well as Rulers.

It will not be out of place to supply some more information about the female elephants here only which will be a pointer to the character of a Mother in any species. We have seen that the adult males tend to slowly move away from the herd by about the age of 5-7 years. The females, however, do not leave the herd, but, very much stay in the herd along with their mother and other elder females. The eldest of the females dominates and guides the herd. The herd slowly gets dependent on such a female leader for its daily and seasonal activities, like: search for food and water, resting and safe breeding places, for long travels and migrations in difficult times of famines, shortage of food and water etc.; gradually, the other females of the herd coming of age assume these skills of leadership. In the case of a dangerous situation, the calves are kept safely in the herd. A female who has just delivered a child, is usually helped and protected by the seniors in the herd. The leading female (Matriarch) or the ruling mother is the carrier of knowledge, because the elephants have a strong matriarchal society. It is very rare that a female joins another group. Generally, the males keep themselves at a distance from the herd and they may move in a loose group, in two or three or at times as loners. They may occasionally go to other herds nearby, but, this is a rare thing, because the males in the other group usually chase them away. The adult males have a phase in their life, termed as '*Masti*', when large amount of strong-smelling, thick fluid flows from the temple-glands, situated between the eye and the ear. It is a dark and oily substance which stains the face of the elephant and occurs about once a year for 3 to 4 months. During this period, the elephant becomes short-tempered and uncontrollable and may not even heed to the instructions of the Mahout and his helpers. At times, the flow is so abundant that the animal in that state is termed as '*Dāna-varṣī*' (Showering *dāna*). In addition to this, the '*mada* or *dāna*' fluid may come out from the feet, ears and *kaṭa* (temple). It is nicely described in the Text in the following words:

कर्णे कटान्ते वेष्टे च पिङ्गूषे मस्तकेऽपि च।
दानवर्षी च सततं वारणस्तु मदान्वितः।।
पादयोश्चापि कटयोः कर्णयोरपि दानवान्।

The modern workers say that the phenomenon of '*Masti*' is difficult to be fully understood. The *Hastyāyurveda* has given various causes for the occurrence of the '*mada*', like the season and other causative factors, like colour-variations in certain cases. They are as under: The '*masta*' which is caused by the *Vātadoṣa* has the colour of barley-water (*Yavodaka*), the season being Prāvṛṭ-early rainy season.

The *mast* which is due to *Pittadoṣa* is yellow-coloured and the season of its appearance is Śarad-autmn.

The *mast* due to *Kaphadoṣa* is like water mixed with grain-flour, i.e. white-coloured and occurs in Hemanta-early winter.

The *mast* caused by all the three *doṣas* (*Sānnipātika*) has varied colours and the season depends upon the predominance of the *doṣa* concerned. The *mast* caused by the vitiation of *Rakta* is red or yellow in colour due to *pitta*—the season when it occurs is Nidāgha/Grīṣma-summer season.

Abhijñānābhidhāna-mast appears on a full moon day (*Paurṇamāsyām*)—A male born to a female who in turn is born of a male which had been in *masti* at the time of the union is called *Abhijñānābhidhāna*.

Harṣa—Harṣa or overjoy or elation, as a result of the surroundings or circumstances conducive to sexual arousal, such as Spring season, blooming flora, intoxicated peacocks and other birds like the cuckoo, swan, Sārasa etc., an atmosphere full of aroma and fragrance and the presence of the favourable cows (she-elephants) around set in the *Mast*-flow.

Pāriṇāmika is the *Must*-flow appearing in an aged elephant, which is lean and thin; though the flow is scanty, it is very troublesome.

Naisargika-Sometimes, the flow occurs as a result of an insult (*nirbhartsanā*), at the sight of killing (*Vadha*), as a result of being tied down to a place for a very long time (*Bandha*) etc. The must occurring in such circumstances is termed as *Naisargika*.

Santāpaja—This type of *must* is caused as a result of excessive heat (*Santāpa*), over work, over exertion, carrying heavy loads, uprooting huge trees etc. Excessive heat generated through such activities results in the breaking out of the *must*-flow, which has a foul smell and is followed by vomitting.

Puṣṭya—Many times, the elephants are fed on very rich food having much nourishing value, which ultimately results in the flow of the *Must* or *Dāna*. This type is traditionally known as *Paitika Mada*.

Vyādhija—The *must* occurring as a result of some *vyādhi* or diseases like *Śiroroga*, *Mūtraroga* or as a result of a variety of *Jwaras* like *Śuddha-pākala* etc. is known as the *vyādhija*-rut.

Upadhānaja

Śauryaja-It is just possible that on the battle-field, excited or roused by the circumstances and the likelihood of the victory of its master, the elephant-with its special (or sixth) sense, may start having the *mada*/dāna-flow and may turn into *masti*. The courageous acts are the provocative factor for the flow of *mada*.

In all, there are fourteen types of *Madas*/*Musts*. The first five are *doṣaja* and the remaining are connected with special causative factors. Pālakāpya in his *Hastyāyurveda*, *Kṣudrarogasthāna*, ch.61, termed as *Prabhinnādhyāya*, pp. 305-310, includes *Mada* or *Must* as a *roga* (minor disease) of the elephants and gives signs, symptoms as well as a detailed treatment of every type. The readers will definitely benefit by reading the original, published in 1894 A.D. from Pune, as No. 26 of the famous Ānandāśrama-Sanskrit-Granthāvalī.

It will be proper to supply the details about the general characteristics of the elephants.

The elephant is the largest animal living on the land, second in tallness only to the giraffe. Elephants are the only animals that have a nose in the form of the long trunk, which also helps them in pulling the leaves and twigs from the branches of the trees and for sucking water, which then is *squared* in the mouth. They have a very keen sense of smell and they often use their trunk to test the air and sense danger, if any. They have ears larger than any other animal and their tusks are the largest teeth. They have a short and muscular neck and enormous head, flanked by triangular ears. The trunk extends from the upper jaw, while, the tusks grow from each side of the jaw, at the base of the trunk. The body is supported by the massive legs and the tail is very small in relation to the body.

THE TRUNK : The trunk is formed by the elongated upper lip and the nose. It consists of a strong mass of flesh, its length in adults being 1.5 metres and weight is about 140 kgs. It is useful in many ways for breathing, eating, drinking water, smelling, pulling/pushing objects, guiding their young-ones and making a trumpet like sound or cry. Young elephants use it in friendly fight, but, in the real fight, the trunk is protected by the elephant by curling it under the chin. The trunk is also used for sprinkling dust waster/mud etc. on its body. While going through deep waters, the body may get submerged and only a small portion of the trunk is above the water level and the elephant breathes through it. The sense of smell of the elephants is so keen that they can smell from as long a distance as three kms. The strong trunk can easily lift weight upto 275 kgs. And heavy logs of wood can effortlessly be pulled/pushed/ carried from one place to another. The trunk being a very vital organ, it is always protected by the animal especially during a fight.

TUSKS AND TEETH : The tusks are long curved upper teeth (incisors) and are made of ivory. About 2/3rd of the portion extends out from the upper jaw. The tusks are used for digging soil for taking water and roots of trees and also in fight. The baby elephants grow small tusks known as 'milk-tusks', which fall out by the age of two years. Thereafter, the permanent tusks grow and they keep on growing throughout their life. The molars are just behind the tusks and measure upto 30 cms. and weigh upto 4 kgs. In an adult elephant, the teeth virtually grind the food, leaves, twigs, branches, grass, sugar-cane, barks of trees, roots and anything that comes their way. The elephants do not ruminate like the cows and the buffaloes.

SENSES : The trunk provides a keen sense of smell, on which the elephants depend more than on any other sense. The wild elephants dislike or hate the smell of a man and the term used for that in the *Gajaśāstra* is '*nara-gandha-asahiṣṇu*' (intolerant of human odour/smell). They can smell a human being from as long as 1.5 kms and their huge ears can pick up a very faint sound from a distance of 3.5 kms. Their ears stand stretched out when they intend to listen to a sound. It is a pity that despite such strong senses, the elephant's eye-sight is very poor (See:chapter 14-*Gajanetra-varṇa-lakṣaṇam*).

DAILY FOOD REQUIREMENTS : An adult elephant in captivity needs about 800 pounds (363kgs) of fodder per day, while, wild elephants may eat between 800-900 pounds (408 kgs) per day. Following are some of the things that the elephants prefer: green grass, sugarcane, tender leaves or branches of Karṇikāra (*Cassia fistula*), Khadira (*Acacia catechu*), Śālmalī plantain trees and banana leaves/branches/ twigs, Babbula (*Acasia Arabica*) as well as leaves of all the thorny trees, their branches as well as twigs. The elephants may enter a paddy field and devour it as they do in a sugarcane field. They also like bamboo leaves and tender shoots. Different roots, tubers and fruits also form a part of their favourite food. They also relish palm-leaves, coconut leaves and coconuts too, the *Tapioka* root, sweet potatoes and many other roots, while in captivity, they eat millet, wheat, moong and a variety of other corns and drink about 200 pounds of water per day.

The third *adhyāya*, named *Annapānavidhi-adhyāya*,

verses 67-72, of the *Uttarasthānam* of the *Hastyāyurveda* by Pālakāpya (p. 563), gives a fund of information about the qualities of the Yavasa-grass, as under : The grass, especially, green, is a very important food-item for the elephants, both wild and in captivity. The grass 'quenches the thirst, is satisfying, nourishes the mind, strengthens the *Grahaṇī* (place of Agni-*jāṭharāgni*), helps in equalizing the imbalance of *Vāta, Pitta* and *Kapha* (humours) *Doṣas,* as also the *Doṣas* of *Rakta* (blood). It eliminates the vitiated *doṣas*. The grass imbibes life and thereby nourishes the organs of sense. It also does away with exhaustion, tiresomeness, stupor, restlessness and excessive sleep in the elephants. Thirst (*Tṛṣṇā*) is produced by the water (*Jala*), which has the Soma predominant and a thing created by Soma is nourishing. Moreover, the elephants themselves have originated from the Soma and that is why the Soma-predominant grass is having all these good effects on the elephants'.

LIFE-SPAN OF AN ELEPHANT : The fifth *Prakaraṇa* states in the following verse the features of the elephant in its 12th decade.

समाहितः स्थिरमनाः सुदीर्घाङ्गुलिपुष्करः।
सविंशतिवर्षशतं समं जीवति वारणः।।

The opinion of Vyāsa, however, is that there is no sure method to assess the accurate age at this later stage of the life. He comes up with a very general remark as under:

आयुर्ज्ञानं वयोमानं गर्भिणीज्ञानमेव च।
मुनयोऽपि च मुह्यन्ति किं पुनः मांसचक्षुषः।।

Even the Sages (most learned and wise) are not able to give an exact assessment about the stage of life at a given point of time, the age-limit and about pregnancy (in case of creatures well-known to them), then what to speak of or expect from ordinary people like us. The commentary gives yet another explanation.

In practice, however, the elephant generally lives upto the

end of the 10th decade, i.e. 100 years. In case of very few elephants, it is seen that they live upto 11th -12th decade of their life, but, it is very rare that elephants attain the age of 120 years. In any case, it is very difficult to exactly assess the age of an elephant, especially, at the late stage, it is a very difficult task, involving very fine intelligence coupled with experience. Hamsadeva in his *Mṛgapakṣiśātra*, Śreṇī 6, vs. 336, states that the life of elephants is upto 100 years. (*Śatam varṣāṇi kariṇām paramāyuritīritam*/). Nīlakaṇṭha in his *Mātaṅgalīlā* says that life of an elephant in general is upto 80 years. Mr. G.P. Sanderson in his book, "*Thirteen years among the Wild Beasts of India*" (published from London in 1879 AD) says that he has seen a she-elephant, named Bhīmarati (in the Mysore Maharaja's stable) who was looking quite young at the age of 74 years and must have lived upto nearly 150years, his argument being based on the fact that elephants who are not in captivity and enjoying their natural habitat, definitely live longer than the ones in captivity and subjected to hardships/torture etc. (See:p.103 of the Marathi book, "*HASTIVIJÑĀNA*" written by Shri Mahadev Mukund Joshi, an ex-staff-member at the Baroda *Hāthīkhānā*. It was published from Baroda in 1910 AD).

Pālakāpya in the 6th chapter, named, *Dvādaśopakramādhyāyaḥ*, of the third *Śalyasthāna* of his *Hastyāyurveda* (p. 392)-which is similar to the writings in many respects of Caraka, has discussed the topic of *Āyuḥparīkṣā* of the elephants. He gives 31 different ideal features of an elephant's body and says that when all of these are present, then the elephant enjoys the full length of life. They are as under :

(1) Firm body joints —Āsannasandhibandhanaḥ.

(2) Skin covered with shining hair —Romaśāyatacchaviḥ

(3) Having long hair —Dīrgharomaśaḥ

(4) Knowledgeable —Mahāviduḥ

(5) Well developed scrotum —Paripūrṇāṇḍakośaḥ

(6) Having large bumps on the head —Mahākumbhaḥ

(7) Having large ears —Mahāśravaṇaḥ

(8) Having soft, long and curled hair —Mṛdudīrghakuñcitasnigdhakeśaḥ

(9) Having double type of hair —Yugmajaikaromāḥ

(10) Having a broad and larger face —Pṛthvāyatamukhaḥ

(11) Having a large neck —Mahāgrīvaḥ

(12) Having a uniform archlike backbone —Dhanuṣpariṇatavaṁśaḥ

(13) Having well protruding tusks —Suniṣkrāntaviṣāṇaḥ

(14) Having a trunk with a long tip —Dīrghāṅgulikaraḥ

(15) Having broad shoulders —Vyūḍhoraskaḥ

(16) Having soft, long bodily hair —Mṛdudīrghavālaḥ

(17) Having a stout hind portion —Avaruddhajaghanāparaḥ

(18) Having smooth and round legs —Ṛjuvṛttagātraḥ

(19) Having well-developed and well-distributed network of vessels, nerves, veins, arteries etc. —Suvibhaktaśirāḥ

(20) Having the upper portion of the trunk studded with fine and well-distributed spots —Sūkṣmabindubhir-vibhaktāvagrahaḥ

(21) Having the head with well-knit joints and bodily structure —Vyūhavidvanta-ramastakaḥ

(22) Having a long trunk or channels of nourishiment in the body —Mahāsrotāḥ

(23) Having a good body smell/odour —Sugandhiḥ

(24) Having very beautiful eyes —Sucārunetraḥ

(25) Having a good sound (voice) —Susvanaḥ

(26) Having a large penis —Mahāmeḍhraḥ

(27) Having well-built muscles —Sūpacitāṁsaḥ

(28) Always making sounds with the ears —Nityamāsphoṭanādikarṇaḥ

(29)	Having unctuous, crystal-like and half-moon-shaped and well developed twenty nails.	—Snigdhasphaṭikārdhacandrapari-pūrṇaviṁśatinakhaḥ
(30)	Having an elegant walk or gait.	—Sugatiḥ
(31)	Having a prominent raised fore-portion of the body	—Purastādudagraḥ

These are generally the features of an elephant that enjoys a full length of life, but, very few elephants have been seen to have these features. It is also observed that if an elephant possesses any three features (*lakṣaṇas*), it may attain the 3rd or 4th decade of life (upto 30-40 years); those that possess five features, may attain the 5th to 8th decade; those having seven features may reach the 9th or 10th decade and those having any eight features may live upto 11th or 12th decade.

This description is altogether different from what we find in the *Gajaśāstra* of Pālakāpya.

The life span of an African elephant is supposed by the modern scholars to be upto 50 to 60 years only.

The ethics of medical science says emphatically that a doctor or a *vaidya* should be very compassionate towards all living beings as with his own self (*Ātmavat satatam paśyet api kīṭapipīlikam.* Aṣṭāṅga 2/23) and he should not even think of even injuring/hurting or insulting even the smallest of living beings. This traditional view is the substratum of the modern awakening or awareness of the activists of the movement of kindness or non-cruelty to animals and now they have been trying to make it a crime. They rightly think that tamed or domesticated animals should be strictly protected from this kind of abuse and advocate the necessity of creating various rules and regulations for stopping this abuse to animals. Surprisingly, this compassion was existent in India throughout the centuries, even without the written laws and regulations and it was a moral binding. The credit for this humane approach may be given to Pālakāpya. Subsequently, a view came into existence that there should be some age-limit for taking work from the elephants, something like the 'Age for Retirement' for the animal, especially in captivity, because they are put to a variety of uses like: carrying heavy loads/pulling-pushing them, entertaining through the circus etc. in two or three shifts, participating as fore-bearers in the processions-royal/religious etc. going on for long hours and involving a walk of over 30 to 40 miles in 12 to 15 hours, obliging them to stand constantly without food or water for hours together at ceremonial locations etc. Besides these light-natured things, they were also put to formal tasks like pulling gun-carriages, participating actively in the wars/fights, engaging for breaking open the strong and sturdy walls of forts or very strong fortified gates of forts, taking heavy arms and other materials across the mountain ranges, crossing rivers with loads/ warriors/noblemen and their entourage on the backs etc. etc. Considering these points with some concern, it is definitely necessary to give them some humane treatment and look after their welfare too. One thing must be stressed here that the point of their strength and the tasks given to them in accordance with their capacity were never lost sight of by the earlier writers. We come across statements highlighting this fact.

cf. (अष्टांगहृदय सूत्र 2/23)

The present work has statements like the following :

An elephant at the age of 50 is fit for tasks like carrying loads and participating in wars. At the age of 60, it starts losing physical strength and power (i.e. intensity) of the sense-organs, its gait becomes uncertain, that is, faltering. It the 7th decade, an elephant looses its charm, flesh and colour complexion and at times excessive exertion makes it breathless. In the 8th decade, it becomes tired of war effort, its look is no more charming, physical strength and courage starts declining and all the while seems tired, intelligence decreases and the eye-sight weakens. In the 9th decade, the elephant shirks away from heavy tasks like carrying loads, breaking open fortresses, despite leing beaten and forced to do these. They also suffer from dental disorders like loosening or falling of teeth. In the 10th decade, the elephant is not in a position to bear the weight of its Mahout (Rider) also; likewise, other types of loading are also disliked by it and at this stage, it is rightly termed as '*sthavira*'—an old elephant.

Broadly speaking, the following divisions are given: From 10-32 years-Fit for superior tasks like fighting/participation in wars/fights etc.

From 33 to 70 years, they are good for inferior tasks like load-carrying. From 70 to 100 years and onwards, the elephants are good for none of these tasks and hence, should be allowed to be at peace with themselves.

There is yet another classification given in this chapter. The elephants from 10 to 14 years of age are good for all sorts of training; those between 14 and 40 are good for traction and load-carrying while those above 70 years are not fit for any work whatsoever.

Haṁsadeva in the *Mṛgapakṣiśātra*, *śreṇī* 6, verse 339, says that the elephants live for one hundred years and they are fit for all sorts of work upto 40years of their age and thereafter they are to be specially cared for their welfare and not for employing in any kind of tasks-small or big, light or heavy.

Pālakāpya in his *Gajaśāstra* says that the limit for retirement of an elephant should be 70 years, considering its life span to be of 120 years, while, Haṁsadeva opines that they should retire at 41+. According to the modern activists of elephant welfare movement, the animal should be put to use only upto 65 years of its age.

Pālakāpya in the *Hastyāyurveda*, *Mahārogasthāna* chapter 3, verses 10-14, enumerates the following causes for the death of the elephants: *Parvatāt patanam*—falling from a mountain; *Paṅka*-getting trapped in very deep mud or quagmire/marsh; *Viṣa*-poison; *Vallī*-getting trapped in strong and thick creepers; *Jarā*-old-age; *Anala*-wild-fire; *Kūpa*-falling into a deep well; *Pratigaja-graha*-fighting with opponent elephant; *Vidyut*-struck by the lightening; *Bhujaṅga*-biting by a poisonous snake; Vyāla-killed by a tiger or lion; *Bālye māturvivarjanam*-separation from the mother in childhood, i.e. orphaning by the mother, due to her death or such other reasons.

Pālakāpya emphatically says that in the case of the elephants staying in the forest, the imbalance of the three *doṣas* is not the cause of their death, but, the above-mentioned causes are the only causes for their death and not any diseases as such. By the way, it may be noted here that the diseases and their treatment etc. given in the *Hastyāyurveda* is in connection with the elephants in captivity only.

PRAKARAṆA 6.

ELEPHANTS FROM DIFFERENT COUNTRIES / AREAS

The 4th chapter *(Prakaraṇa)* of this work described the principal and subordinate forests wherein elephants are found, but, the description therein pertains to the wild (untamed/ undomesticated) elephants. The 5th chapter gave us a good idea about the physical growth of the elephants in the following age-groups: 1 to 12 months; 1 to 10 years; 11 to 20 years upto the 120 years of their life-span, counted in decades. That has dealt with elephants-wild as well as in captivity. The present chapter no. 6, gives us the details of the elephants belonging to different areas or *Deśas* or the countries or the ancient geographical habitats. The particulars suggest that in those days also the elephants were captured, trained and employed for different purposes and sold as well as purchased. It is really a very difficult task to identify each and every place/location with the present-day *Deśas* or countries due to a variety of reasons/ difficulties such as : many names of those times are now out of use or have undergone many changes and some are even non-existent. The scholar who supplied the English translation/ paraphrase has tried his best to mention and co-relate many of them, to the best of his capacity. Here, we venture to say that in olden days, there was a large population of the elephants and they must have been roaming on the streets and their sight was not a rare thing like it is today. Here, we are concerned with the geographical sections, described in the work, where the elephants must have lived and walked through, as their natural habitats. Some of those areas are as under:

Kamboja— Hindukush mountain and near to Tibet. Latapura- West of the Narmada river, including the forests of Bharuch, Baroda State and Ahmedabad.

Sindhu— Upper Indus, including the forests in Sind (Sindh), Kapurtala, Patiala and Suketa Rajya.

Vanayuja or **Parasika**— Persian forests (i.e. forests from the Persian-territory) Anga-Forests in modern Bhagalpur (in Bihar and Orissa) areas.

V(B) angala— Eastern Bengal, including Tripura and Cooch Behar Forests.

Nepalaka— All forests from Nepal.

Avanti— North of the Narmada river-forests including Dhar, Mahuwa, Alwar, Bharatpur, Bikaner, Bundi and Jaipur, Jodhpur, Kishangarh, Udaipur and Pratapgarh forests.

Vidarbha— Modern Berar, including Bidar forests.

Yāvanta— Kabul forests.

Saurastra— Raivataka of Junagarh (Girnar), Rajkot, Dharampur, Navanagar (Jamnagar).

Kasmira— All forests of Kashmir.

Matsya Virata— Western forest of the Dholpur State, including the forests of Jaipur State (Kingdom).

Trigarta— Ludhiana forests.

Malava— Bundelkhand forest, including the forests of Bhopal, Devas, Gwalior, Indore, Rewa and other nearby States.

Aśmāntaka— All forests of the Travancore State.

Sauvira— Forests in and near Thaneshvar.

Balhika— Forests in the eastern Punjab.

Tihari— Modern Tehri Garhwal forest including northern forest of Delhi.

Matsya— Western Rajaputana forests.

Bhota— All forests from Bhutan.

Karnataka— All forests of the Mysore State (Karnatak).

Andhra— All forests between Krishna and Godavari rivers.

Malayala— All forests of the Western ghats (Southern).

Vikunta— All the forests from the South and North Canara districts.

Pandya— Madura forests and the ones in the adjoining areas.

Pāścātya— Forests in the Mangalore district.

Tuluva— Forests near Goa.

Kong (k)· aṇa—Western forest of Hyderabad in the Deccan.

Gauda— Forests in Benares and western forests in Bengal.

Keralanita-
Visaya (Desa)—Cochin and adjacents from Kerala.

Sahyagiri— Western Ghats (in Maharashtra).

Maharastra— Forests in the Maharashtra State.

Gurjarastra—Forests of Gujarat.

Kalinga— Orissa forests including those of Rajnandi, Cuttack, Puri.

Kurudesa— Kurukshetra, Delhi and adjacent forests.

It is very difficult to identify the following *Deśas*: Pulinda, Samanda, Huna, Vatsa, Barbara, Dasarna (is it modern

Mandasor in M.P.), Giravana, Bhuka, Marala, Hataka, Tailagiri, Ahiralagiri, Nilavala, Karnakamakhya, Surasena and Kukura etc.

The author has discussed ten groups-each comprising of a number of *Deśas* or countries and they are discussed. The learned translater, Pt. V. Vijayaraghavacarya of Madras, has given details of many of these old countries, but, he was also not successful in identifying some other places. We, therefore, sincerely request the scholars and interested for help.

The following Chart gives us a rough idea of the known and unknown (i.e. identified and not identified) countries from each group.

Sr. No.	Group	Total no. of Deśas	Identified	Unidentified
1	Kambojādi	5	5	0
2	Pulindādi	7	4	3
3	Saurāṣṭrādi	6	5	1
4	Matsya-barbarādi	5	4	1
5	Sauvīrādi	3	2	1
6	Girvanadi	4	1	3
7	Matsyādi	9	9	0
8	Karṇātādi	9	9	0
9	Keralānta	1	1	0
10	Tailagiryādi	10	4	6
	Total	**54**	**37**	**17**

The Ayurvedic texts, however, enumerate three different *Deśas* according to the physical geographical locations and the classification is based on the rainfall and vegetation, flatlands and hilly and mountainous ranges, as given under:

(1) ***Jāṅgala Deśa*** : It is a dry, arid zone, wherein are found scanty vegetation, thorny bushes, small trees, ample wind, poor rainfall etc.

(2) ***Anūpa Deśa*** : Heavy rains, thick vegetation, water-logged marshy lands and plenty of wild life.

(3) ***Sādhāraṇa Deśa*** : A mixture of these two types.

The *Gajaśāstra* refers to the Jāṅgala and the Anūpa types of areas and their effects on the elephants. The original Sanskrit text reads like the following and the commentary makes the point clear as regards the type of elephants that are available in that country.

कुरुदेश्याः शौरसेनाः...........।
महाजवबलाः शूराः...........॥
ते च जाङ्गलजाः शूराः...........।
आनूपजाः पित्तदेहाः...........॥

The elephants from the *Jāṅgala Deśa*-which is devoid of water (*jalahīna*) and having hard (*kaṭhina*) type of forests-have great speed, strength and they are all the time in an angry mood and have rows of long white hair on their body and head.

The elephants belonging to the *Anūpa Deśa*-where there is excessive water-are not very strong, possess a small body or stature, have a little fat (*medas*) and fall into the *pitta* type of body.

All these minor details are supplied so that their utility for war, laborious works/tasks, learning capacity and ultimately their selection for capturing and their costs could be determined. For these purposes, following things are taken into account: physical features of the elephants, their colour, hair, height, shape of the head, trunk-its colour and length, size-small, medium, big, shape, colour of the tusks, body odour (good or bad), defects in the body (*vicitra-tanu*), length, colour and other details about their penis, body parts and their proportion, colour of the eyes, leanness or fattiness of the body etc.

With regard to their mental attitude, they are classified as per the dominance of this or that humour, like, *Sattva*, *Rajas* and *Tamas*.

Sr. No.	*Guṇa*	***Deśa* or Group of *Deśa* of the forest**
1.	*Sattva*	Keralānta-gaja, Pulindādi, Sahyagiri-sānubhāga, Tailagiri etc.
2.	*Rajas*	Kambojādi, Gīrvāṇādi.
3.	*Tamas*	Saurāṣṭrādi, Matsyādi.
4.	*Kaphadoṣa*	Dominance is noted in Pulindādi and the Sauvīrādi groups.

The different *Kulas* or Families of elephants are also named after these countes, like the following: Gurjarādikulaja-gaja; Keralakulajagaja; Avantīkulajagaja; Nepālakulajagaja; Lāṭa-kulajagaja; Anūpakulajagaja; Pārasīkakulajagaja; Cchuncchu-mallakulajagaja; Aśmakāntakulajagaja, Cauryakulajagaja etc. The elephants are again graded as under: Best variety-32 *kulas*; Medium variety-10 *kulas*; Inferior variety-16 *kulas*; Mixed variety-40 *kulas*—thus, in all there are 98 *kulas* of the elephants mentioned in our Text.

In the case of the other quadrupeds also kept in captivity as pets or for other purposes, the same type of classification is seen, e.g. the horses are named from the places wherefrom they hail, like Arabian, Kathiyāwadi, Bhimathadi (hailing from along the banks of the river Bhīmā in Maharashtra); cows and bulls belonging to the Khillāri-class in Maharashtra; Gir lions, Bengal tigers, buffaloes from Jafrabad etc. etc.

It may be noted that rearing and training of these elephants is a very special subject, which has not been covered in this work.

Looking to the descriptions in chapters 4 and 6, it is quite evident that elephants were found in abundance throughout the length and breadth of the then known Bharatakhaṇḍa-from the northern stretches of the great Himalayas to the southern tip of this vast country, viz. Kanyakumari, from Dwaraka in the west to the Kirātadeśa in the east. There were very vast and spanning forests known as *Gajavanas*, out of which eight were principal and other eight were *upavanas* or sub-forests. The smallest of them-the Saurāṣṭra-gajavana-had an expanse of 50 *yojanas*, i.e. 4000 to 5000 square miles and the largest one having an expanse of more than 200 *yojanas*, i.e. an area of more than 8000 to 10000 sq. miles.

From the way of describing found in the *Gajaśāstra,* we often feel that in those days one could always come across an elephant, walking or grazing nearby. Though unbelievable now, it is not at all surprising. Even if we consider the conditions that prevailed nearly 100 years back when we could read different stories and incidents involving elephants walking on the roads/railway tracks etc. blocking the road-traffic and inconveniencing the public. The elephant menace was so great -dreadful-that the British travellers and European officers and their families were warned to be on their guard and be very cautious because in those days one could come across a lion, a tiger, an elephant, a cobra snake etc. at any place which was a little bit remote to main towns/cities and in the interior from the village. This situation is often reported in the autobio graphies, travel accounts and such other literature of the foreigners.

Though basically the elephants love water and mud, they have a good capacity to accommodate in a variety of geographical surroundings like mountains, forests etc. and could scale heights upto 10000 ft-12000 ft. in the snowy regions also.

The Book of Indian Animals, a 1997 publication of the Bombay Natural History Society, furnishes a fund of information about this.

PRAKARAṆA-7.

METHODS OF CAPTURING THE ELEPHANTS

Elephants were used on a very large scale in India for the purposes of wars since times immemorial, as they formed a very important and winning part of the Indian four-fold army (*Caturaṅgasenā*). For putting them to this significant use, it was absolutely necessary to catch them and then train them for these purposes. Their use in hunting, as an attacking force and for ceremonial parades, on religious and social occasions as well as for joy-riding and entertainment (in the circus etc.) has been very secondary aspect of their character. Mythologically, King Romapāda is supposed to be the first person to catch the elephants, for which five special methods were in practice, as under:

(1) *Vāri-bandha*-Using a deep trench full of water surrounding a vast area (one *krośa* by one *krośa*) of land.

(2) *Vaśā-bandha*-Capturing them by employing a tamed female elephant.

(3) *Anugata-bandha*-A male in love and passion coming close to a female (trained) elephant and getting captured.

(4) Āpāta-bandha-Capturing them in shallow pits and

(5) Avapāta-bandha-Capturing them in deep pits.

The last two *bandhas* were considered to be inferior because in these, the animals sustained injuries which many times crippled them or were fatal at times.

These methods are popularly known as '*Kheḍḍā*,' which are now banned by law in our country. It may be noted that the last '*Kheḍḍā*' was officially arranged during the last phase of the second term of Presidentship of the late H.E. Dr. Rajendra Prasad.

Haṁsadeva in his *Mṛgapakṣiśātra*, 6th *śreṇī*, verses 336-337 has suggested yet another variety. Another way suggested by him is the *Jalabandhādiyoga*' (without giving any details. Such calves as are abandoned by a female elephant or are orphaned due to Jungle Fire or any other reason, which are starved, hungry, thirsty and consequently have gone weak, can be offered water, food and addressed in kind words and then captured. This is possible in the case of only those calves that are very young (i.e. in their 1st, 2nd or 3rd year of age). Capturing the elephants is a very elaborate process and various methods as mentioned above are employed. After capturing, their training in methodical ways starts which is a bit easy if the elephants are caught very young, say, from the 2nd, 3rd, 4th year of their age and should be completed by the age of the 9th year, when the elephant is termed as in its '*Bālyavayaḥ*-younger age'.

The training procedure is as under :

(1) *Ālānabandha*—Tying the captured elephant to the pillar which is meant for it and ensuring that it stays there.

(2) *Svadatta-āhāra-swīkāre eva abhilāṣā-bandhanam*—Compelling the elephant to accept only such food as is offered by the owners' or trainers' hands.

(3) *Kopanīcīkaraṇam*—Bringing down the level of anger or wrath of the elephant and teaching it self-restraint.

(4) *Śramasahanam*—Training the elephants as to how to cope with strain and exertion brought about by the bearing of weight, traction and such other laborious tasks.

(5) *Nirdiṣṭamārge eva gamanāgamanam*—Following the fixed track/route only for going and coming

(6) *Puruṣādi-pratyantarādin prati tarjanādiviratiḥ*—Training them not to be aggressive towards human beings or other creatures in the surrounding areas.

(7) *Yantṛ-vaco'nukaraṇam*—Obeying the orders (words) of the trainer or the *Mahout*-who controls them.

(8) *Yuddhādi-sāhasakāryeṣu-abhīrutvam*—Developing fearlessness in participation in war and other such adventurous acts.

All these-though looking very simple-were to be completed by the end of the 10th year of age. These tasks must have been very difficult to be achieved, as they were time-consuming, painstaking and involving great skill on the part of the trainers and were extremely hard for the calves and young ones of elephants to grasp. It is really very difficult to imagine or visualize the various tools and methods employed by the then trainers and teachers. This also suggests that there must have been a very methodical and scientifically advanced branch or lore which unfortunately is lost to us now.

There are many qualities with which the elephants are endowed, the most important being their Intelligence.

Elephants have a large brain and they are capable to learn and remember very fast, with their retentive memory. In the forest, they are required to know about their surroundings-friendly or otherwise-presence of food and water, vegetation, high and low level, smooth and rough ground, their own herd and its members, their family and family groups, the area of the forest of such herds and groups, communication skills, expressing different emotions/feelings like fear, anger, pain, alarm, closeness, love, affection etc. etc. This is apparently stored on a large scale by the leading female or the ruling Mother. She is the main carrier of the knowledge and passes it on to the next eldest female in the herd, who eventually, becomes the next Matriarch. Such knowledge generally relates to the migration routes, places of food and water, the ways to find water in conditions of drought and such other vital information necessary for their survival.

In captivity, the elephants can learn a variety of things, like the skills and tasks as well as tricks. The teaching methods generally consist of beating and goading by sharp instruments, by breaking their own sweet will and making them follow the commands. Some trainers do follow some gentle methods with good results, but, that is very rare. A well-trained elephant can follow nearly upto 40 commands.

All elephants are not equally good or bad in this respect. Following are some of the expressions used to describe their qualities.

(1) Saurastra-vanagaja-*Mūḍhacetas*-ignorant.

(2) Uttaropavanagaja-Northern Forest Elephant is also ignorant.

(3) In the 4th year of its life, the elephant is—"*Yātāyātasya Vettā*", knows and remembers the routes of coming and going.

(4) In the 5th year, it is capable of making out different sounds of drums etc. (*Śabdādīn vetti*) and obeys orders of the *Mahout* or the teachers/controllers-*Yantṛvaśo bhavet*.

(5) In the 3rd decade of life, he fights well-*Raṇadṛḍho bhavati*.

The *Mṛgapakṣiśāstra* is more specific when it observes:

Dantavālagaja has a very sound memory; Gaja and Dvirada know very well the mind of the *Mahout*; Manda-gaja remembers whatever is taught-*Śikṣaṇe smaraṇopetaḥ*; Mṛga-gaja is of unsound intellect and forgetful—*Buddhibhramśayuktaḥ*; Saṅkīrṇa-gaja follows the order of the rider—*Yantṛcittānuvartin*; besides, it is also very expert in all the skills-*Sarvakarmasu dakṣaḥ*; Mataṅgaja is intelligent, forgiving and of kind attitude— *Buddhimantaḥ, Kṣamāyuktāḥ*; Padmin is capable of learning fast/easily-*Svalpaśikṣāparāyaṇa*; while, Stamberama can easily be trained-*Sukhaśikṣākṣamaḥ*.

The love and craze of the elephants for waters is very well known. Pālakāpya sums up that in the following verse:

हस्तिनामुदकं प्राणाः तद्गतिस्तत्परायणाः।
तस्मात्सलिलमेवेषां कामतो न निवर्तयेत्।।

Elephants love water because it is as good as their own self; it is like their life-breaths. Hence, they like and prefer, in fact, relish to swim and frequently bathe in waters of lakes and rivers. They are very good at swimming and can pass through powerful water-currents without much efforts, even though submerged fully into water with only their trunk kept above the water level. Elephants also enjoy rolling in the mud. Its excessive urge to be in water is so intense that even in captivity, whenever it gets a chance to enter into a lake or a river, it is found to be very difficult to pull it out of the water, because on their own, they are very reluctant to come out of water and they will just neglect any order or threat, whence, we have got a phrase, viz. *gajani-mīlitam*.

The *Gajaśāstra* of Pālakāpya mainly deals with the following aspects of the life of elephants-wild as well as captured type of animals. Account of the first capture of the elephants by King Romapāda on the banks of the river Śaṁpā. Birth of the divine elephants. Curses given to the elephant. *Gajavanani-rūpaṇa*-Description of the forests where elephants stay or are found. Age-wise growth of the elephants throughout their life. Elephants in different countries. Methods of capturing them. Types and creeds of elephants. Colour, brightness and mental attitudes, their gait, circles on the body, figures formed by the coloured dots and their significance, bodily defects, measures of their body and the details regarding the seats of the riders etc. Though he does not exactly deal with the diseases and their treatments, the great Sage does refer to the *Tridoṣas* and the *Triguṇas*, viz. *Vāta, Pitta* and *Kaphan* and *Sattva, Rajas* and *Tamas* (bodily and mental). In the first chapter itself, he has given the secret of the sound health of the wild-elephants in the following words:

पांसुकर्दमतोयाद्यैः..........।
धातुप्रसादं क्षिप्रं तु..........।।
धातुप्रसादादारोग्य..........।
बलाच्च सर्वरोगाणां..........।।

The sequence goes as under :

The elephants freely enjoy playing in the dust, mud and water upto their hearts' content.

The rigorous play and exertion quickly results in the full growth of body tissues (*Dhātuprasāda*)—which leads to good health, which in turn, culminates into strength (or *Prāṇa* and *Ojas* as it is termed in Āyurveda).

Bala (*Ojas*) can prevent the advent of all the diseases (*Rogas*). Pālakāpya further says that this natural course of life gets basically changed or altered in captivity.

वधबन्धपरिक्लेशैः यदा क्लाम्यन्ति नित्यशः।
न ते पुष्यन्ति मातङ्गाः दुःखशोकसमन्विताः।।

So, to give at least a partial relief to them, a King or a captor should see to it that the elephants get ample water to play and to keep themselves cool (and thus, away from the mental stress) and feed them properly and sumptuously, so that the *Bala (Ojas)* is kept up or maintained. It is our bounden duty to keep them happy and cheerful, so that their health-maintaining power is not lost. One important point made by him is that the elephants should be kept in captivity till such time that one is capable to look after them properly and to feed them to their hearts' satisfaction. बन्धनीयास्तावदेवैते यावच्छक्यास्तु पोषितुम्। Otherwise, they will turn out to be 'White Elephants' - a term which is more proper now-a-days than in those days.

PRAKARAṆA-8.

TYPES OF ELEPHANTS

This chapter deals with the types of Elephants and their features. There are four principal types (*Jāti*) of the elephants in the following chronological order:

Yuga	Gajajati	Quality
Kṛta	Bhadra	Superior
Tretā	Manda	Medium
Dvāpāra	Mṛga	Inferior
Kali (Saṅkīrṇa)	Mixed	Mixed

From the point of view of height and largeness of the body, it seems that the Bhadragajas were the largest and most powerful and high-quality animals amongst them. The Manda and Mṛga types followed them in quality. There are eighteen types of the

Saṅkīrṇa variety, depending on the nature of mixture (cross-breed) resulting from the *Anuloma* and *Pratiloma* mating between the animals. This subject has been discussed in great details by the commentator, with very good diagrams showing the distinct features of the types in the vertical and transverse dimensions of their own at the given age. It will be better if the experts in the subject undertake a detailed study of this aspect. The Mṛga-jati *gajas* at times go along with other quadrupeds such as cows, sheep etc. It is a normal practice of the elephants to maintain their own herds.

PRAKARAṆA-9.

THE CREED OF ELEPHANTS.

Description of the *Aṁśa* or creed of certain elephants.?

It is a well-known belief that the elephants endowed with specific good physical characters as well as psychological characteristics brought victory in war, enormous wealth, fame, long life and happiness to their owners. Therefore, they were meticulously examined, carefully and critically evaluated and then selected and employed for various kinds of purposes. Some guidelines were followed while selecting the elephants. These, after selection, were in turn compared to certain very high-quality super-human beings, such as Brahmā, Indra, Kubera, Varuṇa, Candra, Agni and Viṣṇu (the Creator, Chief of Gods, God of Wealth, God of Rain, the Moon, the God of Fire and Lord Viṣṇu respectively).

The features examined were mainly connected with the following:

(1) Different spots on the body, face, trunk and their size, shape, colour, various figures formed by them (like the Conch, Moon, Wheel etc.).

(2) General complexion and the colour of the skin.

(3) Colour of its hair, lips, trunk, tusks, tongue.

(4) Consistency of the '*Mada*' or rut or ichor and its flow.

(5) Folds on the body, neck, throat etc.

(6) Size of the body as a whole, size of the head, of legs, of trunk, of ears and penis.

(7) Psychological aspects like calmness, happiness, anger or short-temperedness etc.

Taking into account all these minute details, the elephants were employed on various occasions like war, coronation, ceremonial parades, *Yajñas* and other religious ceremonies and processions, occasions of pomp, show and glory etc. All these things are very nicely given in the Text, explained in the Commentary and the English translation, throwing very good light on this subject.

PRAKARAṆA-10.

THE COLOUR OF THE ELEPHANTS (*VARṆAGAJALAKṢANAKATHANAM*)

This chapter deals with the various colours and their shades which are possessed by the elephants. Many colours like green, red, black, blackish-red, yellow, white etc. are mentioned. These colours or their shades are to be seen on the skin, hair, nails etc. The inter-mingling of colours (*Antar-varṇa*) is also mentioned. The commentator, however, very correctly remarks that the various colours of the elephants like red, white, green, yellow etc. are not to be seen in the present Kaliyuga and the elephants generally seen in the Kaliyuga are black-coloured only. Jet-black colour, black having a bluish tinge are considered to be of good omen. White-coloured elephants are much discussed, but, are not seen anywhere. Whatever is considered as 'white or whiteness' is the presence of the light-coloured spots on the trunk and the face portion of an elephant. The sketches of the elephants in this chapter or for that matter throughout the manuscript which are shown as red, black etc. are not coloured like that, but, are only in black and white colour. In fact, there are simply outline sketches without colours throughout the text of the *Gajaśāstra*. There is ample description of the skin and the hair of an elephant in chapters 4, 5 and 6. Let us see, what the present-day workers in the field say about this aspect.

The skin is gray and wrinkled and hangs in folds and measures about three centimeters in thickness. The weight of the skin can be upto 900 kgs. The elephants are technically termed as '*Pachyderms*', i.e. thick-skinned animals or quadrupeds. The skin of this huge animal is surprisingly very tender, and insects including flies and mosquitoes can bite into the skin. The elephant has no sweat -glands, hence, the excess heat is lessened by flapping its enormous ears or by spraying water on itself with its trunk. They also keep themselves cool by resting in the mud. The mud dries on the skin and shields them from the sun as well as the flies.

At the time of the birth, the elephants are covered with a sparse brown, black or reddish or brown hair, which gradually wear off as the elephants grow old. Sometimes, small tufts can be seen around the ear, eyes, mouth and a bunch of them at the end of the tail.

PRAKARAṆA-11.

COMPLEXION OF THE ELEPHANTS

***Cchāyā-nirūpaṇam*—Description of the brightness of the skin of the elephant.**

Cchāyā or the brightness of the elephant's skin is discussed in this chapter. The *cchāyās* are related to the predominance of the Five Primary Elements (*Pañca-mahā-bhūtas*), viz. Pṛthivī (Earth), Salila (Water), Agni (Fire), Vāyu (Air) and Ākāśa (Space, Ether). The *cchāyā* is the hue or colour shade describing the complexion.

It is practically impossible to find a member of the elephant family without dust, grass or mud on its body. A fortunate person may happen to witness an elephant emerging out of the clear water of the river with its original colour. In the captive elephant, however, one can see the original colour of the skin of the elephant for a very short time, because, the elephants like (or are wont) to put dust and grass on themselves as soon as they get a chance. It is very difficult to keep them away from this habit of putting dust and mud on their bodies, especially, when they are cleansed and painted for ceremonial purposes.

PRAKARAṆA-12.

SMELL (ODOUR) OF THE BODY OF THE ELEPHANTS.

This chapter supplies us the details about the smell or odour emanating from the body of the elephants, which is basically of two types, viz. good and bad. They are to be examined in respect of the urine, faeces, sweat, the fluid that trickles from the trunk and that of the *Mada*-fluid (ruttish-flow). The various kinds of smells (good or bed) are compared with the smells of different flowers, ghee, rice, fibres of lotus, khus and with mutton, crow, tortoise and fish respectively. Owing to the curse pronounced on them, the elephants do not sweat or perspire outwardly. (See: *Svedo na syandatām bahiḥ* Ch. III).

According to modern knowledge or observation, elephants do not have sweat glands. As a result of this, they put a lot of water, mud and dust on their bodies for keeping themselves cool. Pālakāpya, while giving the features of a two-year old elephant in the fifth chapter, says: These calves constantly sweat from the skin portions near their nails—*Sadā svinnanakhāṅkurāḥ2/*. This fact is corroborated by the workers at the elephant-breeding centre at Chitvan in Nepal. This requires to be verified.

The commentary on the fifth chapter says that at this age, the elephants always give out *sveda* (perspiration/sweat) at the level of the nails. Does it mean or suggest that the sweat -glands are present on some parts of the body of an elephant? The examination of sweat for identifying good or bad smell, therefore, sounds a little bit out of place here.

In the *Gajaśāstra*, many different types of elephants are

stated to have good or bad smell (Pl. see chapter, 4 and 6). The elephants of Saurastra and Gurjaradeśa smell like onions (*kandarpagandhāh.* Ch.6.)

The *Mṛgapkṣiśāstra* of Haṁsadeva notes the following varieties as good-smelling-(1) Dantavāla-*Sugandhideśa*; (2) Bhadragaja-*Śubhagandha-śarīra*; (3) Padmin-*Puṣpagandhi* and (4) Stamberama-*Śubhagandha*. Only one variety, viz. Mṛga-gaja is mentioned as *Durgandha*-foul-smelling.

PRAKARAṆA 13.

STRENGTH AND PATIENCE OF THE ELEPHANTS.

The chapter gives details about the examination of the strength and patience of the elephants. Elephant, as is well-known, is the largest of all the creatures walking on the surface of the earth. In tallness, it is next only to the giraffe. The size, height or beauty are inferior to the strength, which, in its turn, is only second to the patience. While selecting elephants, one must keep in mind the Strength (*bala*) and patience (*sattva*) of the animal. The *bala* is tested by measuring the capacity of the elephant to easily carry a given weight to a given distance, without being exhausted, as mentioned under:

Sr. No.	Load	Distance covered without exhaustion	Category
1.	18000 *palams* of gold, copper or silver (i.e. 839.8 kgs.)	10 *yojanas* or 40-50 miles	Strongest
2.	14000 *palams* etc.	7 *yojanas* or 28- 35 miles	Medium
3.	100 *palams*.........	5 *yojanas* or 20- 25 miles	Ordinary
4.	1000 *palams*	Exhausted at a Distance of 5 *yojanas*, or 20-25 miles	Inferior

The commentator very nicely describes the four categories like Strongest, Middle-class, Third-class ordinary and Inferior one.

The measures of *Pala* and *Yojanas* are stated approximately as under : One *Pala* is equal to four *Tolā*. One *tolā* comes to nearly 11.664 grams-One *Yojana* is approximately four to five miles.

Sattva-parīkṣā: *Sattva* is the mental state or psyche. The mental strength of an elephant is measured by its capacity to tolerate or put up with pain or suffering. The *Gajaśāstra* gives a novel method for this kind of assessment and the English translator has given it in detail. The elephants which are able to bear pain and jolts while bringing down the strong pillars, are worth employing in wars, fighting duels and other elephant-games such as *Ḍāgadārī*.

PRAKARAṆA 14.

MENTAL SET-UP OF THE ELEPHANTS.

Mind has been the most important organ of all the living beings, hence, Indian writers have stressed the soundness of mind as the most significant feature of a living entity. This has been the way of thinking since at least the Vedic times. The Āyurveda has used the word *Sattva* for Mind and says that it has three properties, known as the *Guṇas-Sattva, Rajas* and *Tamas*. Individuals are dominated by either one or the other of these properties which are seen in different proportions. This predominance is seen from the very birth which results from the dominance of anyone of these in the parents. The qualities of the individuals are decided on the proportion of the *guṇas*. When the *Sattva-guṇ* is predominant, the individual is calm, quiet, peaceful, happy, intelligent and balanced minded. When the *Rajo-guṇa* is dominant, the individual becomes angry, restless, very active, short-tempered etc. The dominance of the *Tamo-guṇa* results in inertia, idleness, lethargy, ignorance, poor understanding and more of sleep. Like the human beings, the animals (elephants) also have their psyche (mind-*manas*) dominated by these three *guṇas* and they exhibit similar behavioural patterns. The Sanskrit commentary and the English translation make a very good and interesting reading in this regard. The Āyurveda has compared the *Manobhāvas* (mental attitudes) in altogether a different context. The mental set-up is compared with different super-human as well as inferior (low-grade) creatures.

The Pure (*Śuddha*) *Sattvaguṇa* results into the following seven varieties: *Brāhma-sattva; Ārṣa-sattva* (*Ārṣa*-like a ṛṣi-a sage); *Indra-sattva* (like that of God Indra); *Yama-sattva* (like that of the God of Death); *Kaubera-sattva* (like that of the God of Wealth/Riches); *Varuṇa-sattva* (like the God of Rain) and *Gandharva-sattva* (like the Gods of Music).

The dominance of *Rajoguṇa* is seen in the following six varieties: They are known as *Rājasa-sattvas*. *Āsura-sattva* (like an *Asura* i.e. non-divine giant); *Rākṣasa-sattva*-like a *rākṣasa* (giant); *Paiśāca-sattva*-like that of evil spirits; *Sarpa-sattva* like snakes/serpents; *Preta-sattva* like a corpse; *Śakunta-sattva*-like birds;

The dominance of the *Tamo-guṇa* results in the following three types: *Pāśava-sattva*-like beasts; *Matsya-sattva*-like fish and *Vānaspatya-sattva*-like the vegetable kingdom-trees etc. (Ref: *Carakasaṁhitā*, *Śārīra-sthāna, Adhyāya:* 4/33-39, Nirnay Sagar Press, Mumbai).

A similar type of classification is seen in the *Gajaśāstra* of Pālakāpya, which is as under: *Deva-sattva*-Mind like the gods; *Mānuṣa-sattva*-mind like human beings. In this, there are sub-types like:*Brāhmaṇa-sattva*-like a Brahmin; *Kṣatriya-sattva*-like a warrior; *Vaiśya-sattva*-like a trader and *Śūdra-sattva*-like a servant.

Gandharva-sattva-like a musician; *Piśāca-sattva*-like an evil spirit; *Sarpa-sattva*-like a serpent and *Rākṣasa-sattva*-like that of a giant.

The knowledge of this mental make-up is very useful while assigning different jobs to the elephants, in keeping with their mental set-up or behavioural attitude, a list of which is supplied at the end of this chapter.

The *Deva-sattva* elephants are fit for the Kings and the Emperors to ride at the time of their coronation. The *Kṣatriya-sattva* should be posted at the main gates of the Palace in order to show off the pomp and the grandeur of the Rulers. The *Vaiśya-sattva* are fit for carrying loads while the *Piśāca-sattva* and the *Rākṣasa-sattva* elephants should be employed for the destruction of the enemy-armies.

Haṁsadeva in his *Mṛgapakṣiśāstra* (6th *śreṇi*) says: The Bhadra-gaja should be used at the time of the *Paṭṭābhiṣeka*-Coronation Ceremony of the Kings. The Manda-gaja is *Dṛḍha-bhāravāhī*-able to carry very heavy loads and is also expert in war and hunting. The Saṅkīrṇa-gaja is very attentive in all the tasks allotted to it. The Padmin-gaja is fit to be used for riding by the *Mantri* (Minister), *Senā* (Army-men) and *Yuvarāja* (the Prince). They are also fit to be employed in hunting. The Ibha-gaja should be employed by the Kings as the leading elephant of an army, almost like a shield for other elephants (*ḍhāla-gaja*) and also be used for protecting the tents or the army camps.

One important point to be noted here is that the Sanskrit commentary of Pt. Anantakṛṣṇabhaṭṭāraka is available up to this portion only and the remaining topics are not covered in the commentary that is available at preset. Consequently, the English translation by Pt. V. Vijayaraghavacarya also abruptly ends here and we are denied the benefit of both these-the commentary and the English translation-in truly understanding the Text and its nuances. It is just possible that there is any other manuscript of this portion available somewhere, but, we were not successful in procuring that portion despite our sincere efforts for the last three four years. Scholars are earnestly requested to kindly lend their hand of support/co-operation in this matter and oblige and enable us to bring the complete text to light.

***Gajanetravarṇanam*—Description of the eyes of the Elephants.**

The original text gives only a few details about the eyes of elephants, emphasing the fact that those elephants having such type of eyes bring victory in war to their owner. The qualities are like the following: eyes having the colour like honey, colour and appearance like a ball of ghee, like that of a semi-precious stone called gomedaka, eyes as bright as the sun or fire or fiery red. The eyes are very small as compared to the huge body of the elephant, hence, at one place, it is said that they resemble the eyes of the sparrow (*Kalaviṅkanetra*) (See: *Prakaraṇa* 8, Bhadra-gaja); they are also said to be like the eyes of a lion (*haryakṣa*-Ch. 8-Mṛgagaja); elephants are called *sthūlākṣa*-big-eyed (Ch. 8-mṛgagaja). The examination of the eyes is very important while grading the Miśra-jāti-gajas (Chs. 8 and 9). As we have already noted, the elephants have a very poor eyesight and they cannot see objects farther than 50-60 feet. The movement of the neck is also limited, hence, in order to see an object at its back, an elephant has to turn around. This drawback is sufficiently compensated by the intensity of their senses of touch and smell. The sense of touch is very acute at the tip of its trunk and it can recognise the size, shape, roughness, smoothness, heat and cold etc. with the help of the tip of the trunk.

***Gajasvaralakṣaṇam* Description of the voice of the elephants.**

The *Gajaśāstra* says that the following types of sounds made by the elephants are considered to be of good omen. They are like: that of a conch, a thunder (of the cloud), a swan, a drum (*dundubhi*), roar of a tiger or a lion or like a bull; that of a parrot, a cow, a wild bear and like monkey are supposed to be of bad omens.

The elephants make a variety of sounds, which serve as a means of communication. While in a herd, they make sounds in the form of screams, roars, bellows, groans etc. and a baby elephant, when frightened, makes a loud hoarse rumble and its mother makes a low humming rumble to comfort the child. The cry of the elephant is termed as '*Bṛṁhita*' (*Bṛhita*), otherwise known as *Riṅkāra* (*Ṛīṅkāra*). It is observed that the elephants make only three types of sounds, viz. *Bṛṁhita,* the place of its origin being the palate (*tālu*); *Garjita* from throat (*kaṇṭha*) and *Fenāyita* coming from the base (root of the tongue. (Cf. Ch.14). There is yet another version or theory about the sounds and their places of origin, as given under:

Bṛṁhita comes from palate (*tālu*) or *gaṇḍa* or *śirā* (head), *kaṇṭha* (throat), *jihvā* (tongue), *hasta* (trunk), *udara* (abdomen-belly) and *śruti* (ears). *Garjita* and Śaṅkhasama from *Gala* (*Kaṇṭha*)-throat and *Meghanādasama* (thunder of the clouds) from heart (*hṛdaya*). *Hamsadhvani*-like that of a swan or *Dundubhi* (a sort of a drum) from *jihvā* and *karṇa* (tongue & ears). *Utkrośa* from *Gaṇḍa*.

Roar like a tiger or a lion or a bull from head (*hastiśiras*). It is also noted that there are certain special elephants and the sounds made by them are considered to be of good omen. They are: *Mṛdaṅgarava*-sound like a special drum (a musical instrument) made by the trunk-*Hastena*; *Dundubhisvara*-drum like in a war-made by ears-*Karṇa*; *Darduradhvani*-a crushing sound made by mouth-*mukha*.

PRAKARAṆA-15.

WALKING STYLE OF THE ELEPHANTS.

Pālakāpya in his *Gajaśāstra* gives many minor details about the different aspects connected with elephants, as well as their traits.

An elephant calf is able to stand within an hour of its birth. It gradually starts walking, running nearby its mother. Though it plays about, its walking and running etc. is not stable. In the 7th month, the walk becomes stable (*Padaistu na virodhaḥ syāt* (*saptame māse*) (Ch.5.); On this original version, the commentator says that the elephant in its 7th month assumes a stable walk, as in its earlier months, it is unstable. In the 8th month, it assumes speed (*Aṣṭame capalo gantā*). The milestones in the development of its walk can be put as under:

Age of the Elephant	Walk and other related things
(1) First month	Stands only
(2) Second month	Begins to play in the mud
(3) Third month	Walks away from the herd for a short distance
(4) Fourth/fifth month	Runs, movements are fast
(5) Sixth month	Runs, movements are fast and walk is not stable
(6) Seventh month	Walk becomes stable
(7) Eighth month	Walks with speed, runs
(8) Third year	The leg and foot-joints become strong and leaves clear foot-marks on the path it traverses
(9) Fourth year	Knows about the track it goes
(10) Seventh/eighth year	Walks very swiftly
(11) Second decade	Walks very fast like an arrow
(12) Third/fourth/fifth decades	Becomes strong in every aspect like strength etc.
No direct words are used to describe walk, run etc.	
(13) Sixth decade	Decline in speed and other aspects
(14) Seventh/eighth decade	Becomes breathless on walking fast or on exertion
(15) Ninth decade	Does walk with the herd, but, prefers to live in a cave aloof
(16) Tenth decade	Walks very slowly and avoids to go uphill
(17) Eleventh/twelfth decade	Prefers to stand at a place and stays put wherever it goes

The *Mṛgapakṣiśāstra* of Haṁsadeva (6th *śreṇi*) supplies information about the *gaja* and *gajagati* in the following way:

Type of Gaja	Gati or Walk
(1) Dvirada	*Mandasañcāraka*-slow walking
(2) Gaja	*Śaravadvegagāmī*-walks fast like arrow
(3) Bhadra	Usually goes slowly, but, assumes great speed when angry
(4) Manda	Walks slowly
(5) Mataṅgaja	*Mahāvega*-very fast walking; *santatam vegagāmi*-continuous fast walking; *Śaravadvegagāmī*-goes/ walks fast like an arrow
(6) Ibha	Often walks very fast, frequently runs and when irritated it runs fast and is uncontrollable-*Nitarām vegagāmī*-extremely fast walking
(7) Dantavāla	Extremely speedy
(8) Hastinī (Female elephant)	*Manojñagamanopetā*-endowed with a graceful walk

The legs and the feet

The legs of the elephants are very strong and sturdy and support the massive body like the pillars support the edifice. The feet are almost round and heavily padded with fat which acts as a cushion; expands under its heavy weight and contracts while lifting the legs, thus helping it walk through deep mud also. The elephants make very little sound of their steps while walking or running fast enabling them to appear suddenly on a track or path or road as if from no-where and take other animals and men by surprise. The normal speed of an average elephant is 8 to 10 kms/hour, while the speed could be upto 16 kms/ hour when walking in a family group for long distances. A frightened or angry or otherwise charged elephant can attain a speed of more than 40kms/ hour for a short distance. The walking or running is of a shuffling type and the elephants cannot jump because of their enormous weight and the structure of the feet.

The migration of elephants is also a topic of special study, but, our Text does not treat of it.

A few words about the English translation given in the original work:

The walk of the elephant or its gait should be like that of a wrestler, lion, parrot, tiger cub or like a bull. It should be provided a stable seat, the stepping should be equal and its body well-balanced while walking. Such a walk is considered a good omen. Even while fast-walking, it should be balanced and light-footed and should not disturb the rider. The same features in the case of a horse are also considered to be of good omen, despite its mood being good or otherwise. An elephant walking like a wolf (*kṛkalāsa*), donkey (*khara*) mongoose/mungoose (*nakula*) is of a bad omen.

The chapter ends with two opinions of Pālakāpya and Vyāsa which are as under:

Unevenness in the back, irregular seat-place, inability to walk with speed, having a swing of the seat while walking or having a faulty walking style are considered by the experts in *Gajaśāstra* to be the bad qualities of an elephant.

According to the opinion of Vyāsa that elephant brings victory to its owner who keeps an eye and moves with speed with an intention to crush or destroy the objects like an anthill, a pillar, a bush, a tree or a plant, with its mouth raised high, making a loud sound and moving its flanks and body and at the same time winding its left or right tusk with its trunk.

PRAKARAṆA 16.

CIRCLES AND MARKS ON THE BODIES OF ELEPHANTS.

Almost all the living beings have some birth-marks on some part of their bodies-which are supposed to be good or bad as far as their fortune is concerned. Such marks are to be seen on both the sides. They are like: circles and figures like a conch, earthen pot, fish, mirror or looking-glass, bull, lamp, decorative hangings (*toraṇas*), sacrificial fire-place (i.e. *yajñakuṇḍa)*, arrow, Cāmara (chowrie), elephant, umbrella, in the form of small red spots or large folds created by the group of such folds. The clock-wise formation of these circles on the right side and the anti clock-wise on the left side is supposed to be of good omen—bringing fortune; while, the other ones are considered to be bad omen—bringing misfortune. Similarly, it is also believed that appearance of the circles on the following parts is not good: Anywhere else on the parts other than the ones mentioned earlier; on the cheeks and temples, throat, heart, jaw, chin, penis, flanks, hips, nails, scrotum (when it is hanging down at the time of rut) and thighs. An elephant having a skin disease is also considered to be unfit for use.

Such references to these features are to be amply found in the books from the orient, while, no comparable modern literature on this aspect of the elephants is available. The Devanāgarī transcript of our work (manuscript) does have a few pictures/sketches/drawings, giving an idea of the nature of such circles and figures.

In the end, the author furnishes some vital information about the desirable good parts nullifying the bad effects of such circles on the other parts, as follows :

Desirable parts	Nullifying bad effects
Aṅgulas	Trunk
Trunk	Tusks
Tusks	Mouth
Mouth	Eyes
Eyes	Mouth
Nails	Hips
Apara	*Vāla*
Vāla	*Keśa*-hair

Nirdoṣa-koṣa (faultless scrotum)	All the body
Toes	All the body. Outside/inside
Mukha	Teeth

This aspect seems to have been neglected by modern scholars, majority of whom do not believe in the ancient Indian science of palmistry or *Sāmudrika* and do not feel it to be of much importance, despite the fact that this was one of the many tests for the selection of elephants and subsequent purchase by the Royals/Rulers/Wealthy persons, exhibiting their affluence.

PRAKARAṆA 17.
MAIN BODILY DEFECTS (CONGENITAL)

The author deals with the topic of the main defects in the body of the elephants, which approximately number nearly forty as under: having three tusks, extra body part or devoid of one or two parts of the body or limbs, extra leg, enlarged abdomen like that of a pregnant female, dumbness, deafness, absence of hair on scrotum, trunk, ear, umbilicus, nose, fingers, having a hunch-back, lustreless skin, hair entering the trunk, ugly hair, crooked penis, belonging to a wretched type of class, having uneven growth of hair etc. These are considered bad for use by the wise, but, no corresponding views of the modern scholars are to be had in this regard.

From amongst the several defects listed by our author, the one termed as '*Samuṣkagaja*' is very important. It is a well-known fact that in the case of the male elephants, the scrotum (*Muṣka*, testicles and the bag/sack containing the testicles) is not visibly hanging out as is seen in the case of other quadruped animals like the bull, horse, buffalo, goat, dogs etc. Most of the time the *Muṣka* or the Scrotum remains concealed and only at the time of the rut the scrotal-sack can be seen. This anatomical peculiarly has been ascribed to a curse given to the elephants by Lord Brahmā—the Creator-on the complaint of the Gods that "the large testicles with the scrotal sack (*samuṣka*) become a hurdle for the elephants engaged in carrying heavy loads, arms and other things in the war". Brahmā, realizing this genuine and practical difficulty of the Gods, said, "Let all the male elephants have their scrotum placed (hidden) in the space known as '*Trigākhyapadasandhitale*' (space between the upper portion of the hind legs) where they (i.e. hind legs) support the body and thus be out of the vision or sight". Actually, the testes are high up in the pelvis. It is very interesting to note that such peculiarities of the body and their causes are said to be the result of the curse of the Creator. Actually, the bodily development and defects therein is a part of the anatomical genesis. On this background, is the word Brahmā equivalent to the things connected with growth?. The congenital defects are a result of the developmental shortcoming, peculiar deformity-due to creation/creator (*Brahmā*).

An interesting fact about some of the male elephants is that they have very short tusks, not much longer than in the females. They are termed as *Mukaṇās*-tuskless males. Though they are large in build and have extra-ordinarily well developed trunks, the elephant-cows (females) usually don't allow them to approach and keep away from them.

PRAKARAṆA 18.

MEASUREMENT OF ELEPHANTS.

In this chapter, the measurements of different bodily limbs of the elephants are given. The *Hastyāyurveda*, *Uttarasthānam*, *Adhyāya* 3, verses 3-7, supply some details about this aspect, which are as under:

Measurements of a New-born elephant-calf (*Jātamātra-dantin*) in the case of the Superior class of this animal are:

	Height	Length	Circumference
Aratnīs	1¾	2¼	2½
Feet	3"	3'-3"	3'-9"

The yearly growth in all the three dimension in *aṅgulas* is :

Aṅgulis	4.5	5.4	6
Inches	3"	3½"	4½"

All these are true in the case of a perfectly normal animal.

Sr. No.	Type Hands	*Āyāma* Length Feet	*Āyāma* Length Hands	*Utcchrāya* Height Feet	*Utcchrāya* Height	*Nāha* Circum-ference Feet	*Nāha* Cir.	*Quality*
1.	Bhadra	9	13.5	7	10.5	10		*Uttama*-Best
2.	Manda	9	12	6	9	9	13.5	*Madhyama*-Medium
3.	Mṛga	7	10.5	5	7.5	8	12	*Kaniṣṭha*-Inferior
4.	Saṅkīrṇa	4	Uncertain	Uncertain	Uncertain	Uncertain	Uncertain	Of no use
5.	Arala (P. & Vyāsa)	10	15	8	12	11	16.5	,, ,, ,, (Ref: *Hastyā. Mahārogasthāna.* Ch.2, vs. 58-59)
6.	Atyarala	11	16.5	9	13.5	12	18	(The same as above)

Measurement: 1 *Hasta*=18 inches or 1.5 foot

7. Vāmana : Those elephants are termed to be Vāmana (Dwarf) which are one Hand (i.e. 1.5 ft.) less in all the three dimensions from the first three varieties.

8. Kubja (Hunch-backed) : An elephant which is smaller than the Vāmana in all the measures is termed as *kubja*. Both these are useless.

Of these eight varieties given in the *Gajaśāstra*, Arala and Atyarala (no.s 5 and 6) could be comparable to the Mammoths of the ancient ages. These Mammoths (large extinct elephants) were very huge lumbering creatures which were very tall measuring nearly 4 to 5 meters.

The *Hastyāyurveda* gives a very elaborate way of measuring the height of an elephant. In this method, the height has to be measured at the level of the shoulder only by using strong wooden staffs (*daṇḍas*)-one for vertical placement and the other horizontal, taking the help of a strong rope. The *Uttama* measured 7 *Aratnīs*, *i.e.* 10.5 ft.; the *Madhyama*-6 *Aratnīs*, i.e. 9.5. ft. while the *Adhama* measured 5 *Aratnīs*, *i.e.* 7.5 ft.

The length was measured from the *Kumbha* (the frontal globe on the forehead of the elephant) to the *Pecaka* (the root of the elephant's tail). The Best, Medium and the Inferior-lengthwise measured 9, 8 and 7 *Aratnīs*, *i.e.* 13.5, 12 and 10.5 ft. respectively.

The *Pariṇāha* (circumference, expanse etc.) was to be measured at the *Kakṣa-bhāga* and 10, 9 and 8 *Aratnīs* (i.e. 15 ft, 13.5ft. and 12ft.) were the measures of the Best, Medium and Inferior types respectively. An interested person may look into the *Uttarasthāna*, *Adhyāya* 7, *Annapānavidhi* of the *Hastyāyurveda* for these details, which are given in a table like this :

Sr. No.	Type	*Āyāma* Length *Hasta*	*Āyāma* Length Ft.	*Utcchrāya* Height *Hasta*	Utc. Ht. Ft.	*Nāha* Circumference	*Nāha*
1.	Uttama	8	12	6	9	9	13.5
2.	Madhyama	7	10.5	5	7.5	8	12
3.	Adhama	6	9	4	6	7	10.5

The height of a quadruped in modern times is measured from the ground (forefeet) to its shoulders, while, in ancient times, the highest point on the curved back of the elephants was taken into consideration, by standing on one side and putting a rope over the highest point on the back and measuring the elephant for its height. That was a crude but correct & practical method. The shoulders are at a low level than the highest point of the arched back, hence, a measure at the shoulders fails to give a correct idea about the 'true functional height' of the animal. This is clear when we take into account the purposes for which these creatures were used in the past, like, in wars, battles, hunting etc. On all these occasions, the functional height, i.e. the highest point on the curved back, is certainly advantageous to its rider.

In the case of an elephant, the average height of an adult male is 9ft. (2.7 metres), while, the female member is nearly one foot (30 cms) lower. (Ref. p. 224, *The Book of Indian Animals*, Bombay Natural History Society Publication, 1997).

In the *Hāthīkhānā* of Baroda, the elephants were made to stand against a thick, strong wooden vertical plank, having carved figures denoting the measurement of feet. An easily moving transverse wooden scale adjusted at the level of the animal's shoulder, gave the measure of the height. (Ref: p.45, Chapter 5 of *Hastivijñāna*-a Marathi book, written by Shri Mahadev Mukund Joshi-a staffer at the *Hathikhana* of Baroda, 1910). This seems to be only a modification of the method used in the *Hastyāyurveda*, described earlier.

The *Mṛgapakṣiśātra* of Haṁsadeva has given 13 *Jātibhedas* or Types of the Elephants, including the principal four varieties, viz. Bhadra, Manda, Mṛga and Saṅkīrṇa, Śuddha. It could be given in a tabular form as under:

JĀTI (TYPE)	SPECIAL FEATURES
1) Dantin	*Pṛthudanta* (Broad tusks)
2) Dantavāla	*Kumbhadvayayukta*-having two frontal bumps on the forehead and *Tuṅgakāya*-very tall.
3) Hastin	*Mandasañcāra*-slow walker
4) Dvirada	*Svacchadantadvayayukta*-having very clean two white tusks.-prolonged breathing
5) Gaja	*Bṛhatkāya*-huge-bodied and *Kiñcitkṛṣṇarada*-the tusks are slightly black.

6) Bhadragaja	*Bhṛśam tuṅgakāya*-very tall; *sthūlamātra* very large bellied.
7) Mandagaja	*Nātituṅga*-not very tall; *sthūlakāyodara-śuṇḍa*-having broad body, belly and trunk
8) Mṛgagaja	*Kṛśadeha*-having lean and thin body; *kṛśaśuṇḍa*-thin trunk; *kṛśadanta*-thin tusks; *vikṛtāvayavopeta*-having defective bodily limbs
9) Saṅkīrṇagaja	*Saṅkīrṇaguṇa*-having mixed features (from 6, 7 & 8 years). They are easily tamed
10) Mataṅgaja	*Mahāvega*-very speedy; *mahākāya*-huge-bodied; *śuṇḍācālanaśīla*-habituated to swinging their trunk; *santata-vegagāmī*-having consistently fast speed.
11) Padmin	*Durguṇavivarjita*-devoid of all bad features; *kṣuttṛtsaha*-tolerating hunger and thirst; *saṅgīta-śravaṇarata*-engaged in listening to music; *ghaṇṭādukūlapaṭṭeṣu dattacitta*-having a bent of mind (*liking*) to put on bells, silk cloth spreads and such other decorative objects on their bodies (comparable to the *Kṣatriya-jāti-gaja).*
12) Ibha	*Parjanyanināda*-having a sound like a thunder-cloud; *satatakopa-yukta*-always full of anger; *nātituṅga-nātinīca-medium* sized (not very tall not very dwarf); *garvasamanvita*-very proud; Karkaśas-parśadeha-having very rough bodies.
13) Stamberama	*Hrasvatanu*-having short body; *vayaḥ-krameṇa bhinnaguṇavanta*-having changing features according to the change in

age; *samāvayavasamyuta*-possessing proportionate body parts; *nātisthūla-nātikṛśa*-not too bulky not too thin; *sarva-prāṇihite rata*-kind to all creatures;

Haṁsadeva does not give any body-measurements of the animal in *hasta*, *aratnī* units. He has just used the words like: *hrasva* (short), *dīrgha* (long), *tuṅga* (tall), mahākāya (huge bodied), laghukāya (light bodied), *nātisthūla nātikṛśa* (neither too obese nor too thin) etc. etc.

Of the many kinds of elephants that existed in the past, only two kinds exist now, viz. Asian and African Elephants, scientifically termed as: Genera: Elephas-Asian/Indian and Laxodonta-African Elephants.

It will be very interesting to have a look at the main differences between the Asian/Indian and the African Elephants.

	African Elephants	**Asian/Indian Elephants**
1)	There is a dip in the back.	The back is arched.
2)	A loose fold of skin joins the hind legs and the sides of the body.	No such skin fold is present.
3)	Hind legs have three *toes*.	Hind legs have four *folds*.
4)	Forelegs have 4 or 5 toes.	Forelegs have five toes.
5)	Two nobs of flesh are there on the trunk.	Only one nob of flesh on the tip of the trunk.
6)	Forehead forms a smooth curve	Forehead has two bumps on it.
7)	Ears cover the shoulders.	Ears do not cover the shoulders.

One more speciality of this Text is that from chapter 1 to 17, there are very beautiful sketches of the elephants, showing various details. The tip of the trunk in all these sketches has two nobs. The sketches are that of an Indian elephant and every one of these sketches has an evenly curved (Convex) back and the ears do not cover the shoulders. The two nobs on the tip of the trunk is a speciality of an African elephant and not of an Indian/Asian elephant. Hence, this aspect of the sketches is rather puzzling or confusing. As the luck would have it, we do not have any clue whatsoever about the artist who drew these sketches nor of the period when they were incorporated therein. *It is just possible that the Rajasaheb of Aundh in whose rich collection only this manuscript with so many sketches is preserved-must have commissioned the services of some very good artist for drawing these sketches OR he-himself being a very good painter-must have drawn these OR the transcriber, viz. Pt. Vijayaraghavacharya must have tried his hand at these-to give a fairly good idea of the elephants as they might have looked in the past-possibly*, he based his imagination on the descriptions of the elephants found throughout the Sanskrit literary works-of which he was a very sound scholar. Any way, it is only our conjecture in the present state of our knowledge (or otherwise). One thing must be accepted that the Rajasaheb of Aundh was a connoisseur and an enlightened King/Ruler and a patron of artists or experts in different arts, as well as a person interested in acquiring knowledge of different branches of learning, for the noble purpose of the furtherance of and patronage to knowledge.

Pālakāpya has described different units of measurements that were in vogue in those days. We give below some of them.

It starts with the almost invisible measure of a *Paramāṇu*-the minutest particle as the primary unit of measure.

1)	*Paramāṇu*	=	Primary unit-Invisible (very minute not to be easily seen)
2)	Eight *paramāṇus*	=	One *trasareṇu*
3)	Eight *trasareṇus*	=	One *rathareṇu*.
4)	Eight *rathareṇus*	=	One *vallāgra*.
5)	Eight *vallāgras*	=	One *likṣā*.
6)	Eight *likṣās*	=	One *yūkā*.

7)	Eight *yūkās*	=	One *yava*
8)	Eight *yavas*	=	One *aṅgula*
9)	Ninety-six *Aṅgulas*	=	One *pada*
10)	One *vitasti*	=	12 *aṅgulas*
11)	Two *vitastis*	=	One *aratnī* (hand)
12)	Four *vitastis*	=	One *Kiṣku*
13)	Two *Kiṣkus*	=	One *dhanu*
14)	1000 *Dhanus*	=	One *gola*
15)	Two *golas*	=	One *krośa*
16)	Two *krośas*	=	One *gavyūti*
17)	Two *gavyūtis*	=	One *yojana*
18)	8000 *Dhanus*	=	One *yojana*

In the case of the elephants, we are concerned with the following units: *Hasta*/*Kara*(Hand)/*Aratnī*-were used for the measurements of the body of the elephant. (1 hand = 1.5ft.). *Yojana* was used for measuring the forest area and perhaps the speed of the elephants per 'a time unit' (an hour). One *yojana*=4 to 5 miles. The speed of the elephant, however, is not given in this unit in our *Gajaśāstra*.

PRAKARAṆA 19.

ĀSANALAKṢAṆAKATHANAM.

This chapter describes the proper *Āsana* or a seat to be arranged on the back of an elephant. The seat should be *Sama* (even, equipoised) *Samalagna* (well-tied) and *Dṛḍha* (firm). It should be *Jānu-sama* (knee-high) and be placed in the front portion (*Purastāt*), just behind the *Mahout* (driver) who sits on the shoulder-portion. The purpose of an *āsana* is to goad the elephant (*gajasya preraṇam*). There are three types of *Gajas,* viz. Bhadra, Manda and Mṛgagajas, and three types of *āsanas* too, viz. *Utkṛṣṭa* (the best), *Madhyama* (medium) and *Avakṛṣṭa* (Inferior). The best type of *āsana* is recommended for occasions of war and such other important events. The original text does not say anything about the other two types of *āsana*. The *Madhyama*-type of *āsana* should be used looking to the nature of the occasions, such as religious processions, ceremonial parades, marriage and such other events. For occasions such as hunting, *Avakṛṣṭa* type of *āsana* is to be used.

Here ends the treatment of the *Āsana* in the original Text. We, however, give below certain details as gleaned from a Marathi book, named, *Hastivijñāna* (chapter 8, pp. 85-88) written by Shri M.M. Joshi, who was the In-charge of the *Hāthīkhānā* at Baroda.

The *Āsanas* are also called *Aṁbārī* or *Hauda*. The *Aṁbarīs* are made of gold, silver, copper, brass and iron material and are heavily decorated with pearls, jewels, precious stones, silk and other rich-costly clothings and laced with ribbons of colourful material. Golden chains and pearl strings are also fitted with beautiful and richly made huge umbrellas. The choice, of course, depends upon the purpose for which it is going to be used as well as the status of the rider. The mounts are very heavy structures, equally strong and sturdy. Calm, quiet and seasoned elephants are selected for the purpose, which are, of course, well-trained for such occasions.

PAINTING AN ELEPHANT: Elephants are painted with pictures and beautiful scenes, on the front portion of the face, on the trunk from its base to its tip, on the ears and on the sides also if no backseat is mounted. The painters who are skilled workers use red, blue, green, yellow and many other colours and their shades and this painting procedure goes on for one and a half to two hours, during which time, the animal is denied to have its natural movements and is reprimanded by the *Mahouts* for whatever movements it does. Hence, the elephants are not at all happy about this painting process which is time-consuming and almost so to say torturing to them-since, they are deprived of their natural movements. They are helpless in this kind of captivity which is painful. At times, the elephant gets angry and puts a lot of dust on itself, thus, bringing severe punishment on itself. After the painting is finished, they mount on the special seat on its back. Very beautiful and artistic seats of gold, silver, wood, steel, copper, brass etc. are mounted on the back. They are very heavy, but, are pieces of art, as they are decorated with precious and semi-precious stones.

MOUNTING ON THE SEAT OR *AMBĀRĪ/HAUDA*:

First of all, a soft mattress of one inch thickness is put on the back, with a view to making it sure that the heavy metal seat does not come in direct contact with the skin of the animal and injure it. This mattress is known as *Namadā* and is made of cotton which is very soft. On it is placed a mattress of rags of six to eight inch thickness with small holes for air-ventilation. Then the seat or the *Aṁbārī,* as it is popularly known, is securely tied on the back. The whole thing goes on into a fine sequence of minute details, known traditionally, by the *Mahouts* only. One missed detail results into several re-arrangements, consuming precious time. The *Aṁbārī,* the mattress, the ropes of various sizes, hanging of different materials of metals, wood and other articles etc. are very heavy. The head, trunk, and ears of the elephants also are decorated with studded gems, gold, precious stones and are decked with the pictures of the sun, moon, stars etc.-giving a grand appearance to the animal.

॥श्रीः॥

॥श्रीगणाधिपतये नमः॥

श्रीपालकाप्यमहर्षिप्रणीतं

गजशास्त्रम्

श्रीमदनन्तकृष्णभट्टारकविरचितभावसन्दर्शिन्याख्यया व्याख्यया समेतम्॥

तत्रादौ मंगलाचरण्

मूलम्

ओंकारात्मकशालायां नादस्तंभे महत्तरे।
निबध्य ध्यानपाशेन कलये कलभाननम्॥

भावसन्दर्शिनीव्याख्या प्रारभ्यते

तत्र व्याख्यातुः मंगलाचरणम्

अजमव्यक्तमीशानमनन्तं जगतां पतिम्।
नमामि सूरिभिर्ध्येयं नमतामिष्टदायिनम्॥

गुरोः प्रसदनान्मन्दोऽप्यहं शक्तः प्रसन्नधीः।
गजशास्त्रार्थसन्दर्भं व्याकरोमि क्वचित्क्वचित्॥

वारणैरेव भूपानां जयलक्ष्म्यादिमंगलम्।
इत्याकलय्य वृद्धोऽपि कृष्णभट्टः कुतूहलात्॥

पालकाप्यकृतस्यास्य गजशास्त्रस्य चोत्तमाम्।
भावसन्दर्शिनीं व्याख्यां करोति विदुषां मुदे॥

व्याख्या—इह किल **भगवानाचार्यः पालकाप्यो महर्षिः** परमदयालुः सर्वेषामपि महीपालानां विविधानि मंगलान्यापादयितुमनाः सुमेरोर्दक्षिणभागस्थिते भारतवर्षाख्येऽस्मिन् पुण्यभूमितले गजशास्त्राख्यमिममुत्तमं कल्पं प्रचारयितुमु-

द्युक्तः सन् तत्रादौ विशिष्टेष्टदेवताभजनात्मकमंगलं ग्रन्थमुखे निबध्नाति–ओंकारात्मकशालायामिति। अयं तु मंगलश्लोकगुंफः पुराणशैल्या स्पष्टार्थक एव। तथापि संक्षेपेणास्यार्थाविष्करणं क्रियते। यथा–भूपालादिभिर्धन्यैः पूरुषैः यथा वा मदाविलकटमदावला गजशालामध्यं नीताः पाशशृंखलादिना निबद्धा-स्तदभीष्टसाधका भवन्ति। तेनैव क्रमेण ओंकारात्मकशालामध्यतलभासुरबीजा-क्षराख्यस्तंभे कुंजराननं कमपि देवं सन्ततध्यानाख्यपाशेनाबध्य मामकीनाभिमत-सिद्धये तदंगसौष्ठवचेष्टागुणादिकं कलये भक्त्यतिशयेन स्तौमीति **वाक्यार्थक्रमः**। एवंशैल्या निर्विघ्नपरिसमाप्तये **गजशास्त्रस्यास्य** ग्रन्थमुखे गजाननभजनात्मक-मंगलश्लोकनिबन्धनेऽपि शालापाशबन्धनाद्युत्तममंजुलपदग्रथनेनास्य **शास्त्र-कारस्य पालकाप्यमहर्षे**रन्यादृशीं कविताचातुरीं कथमहं वृद्धः **(व्याख्याता)** स्तोतुं शक्नुयामित्यस्माकमेतावानुद्यमः प्रकृतकार्यसौकर्यापादनाय संक्षेपेणार्थवि-वृतिमाकलयति तोषाय सतामिति।।

Abridged translation of the text and commentary of Gaja-śāstra or Science of Elephants

Author's Introduction

Psalm of Gaṇeśa

I entreat to the Elephant-faced god Gaṇeśa, with the ropes of concentration in the stable of broad sky (Omkāra) tied to the pillars of sounds and even pray to Him to accomplish my attempt without any hindrance.

मूलम्

शुक्लां ब्रह्मविचारसारपरमामाद्यां जगद्व्यापिनीं
वीणापुस्तकधारिणीमभयदां जाड्यान्धकारापहाम्।
हस्ते स्फाटिकमालिकां विदधतीं पद्मासनस्थां स्थिरां
वन्दे तां परमेश्वरीं भगवतीं बुद्धिप्रदां शारदाम्।।

व्याख्या–सर्वस्यापि शास्त्रस्य वाङ्मूलकत्वात् तां वागीश्वरीं प्रणमति–शुक्लामिति। परमानन्दपीठाख्यकमलविशेषे निषण्णां स्वकीयकरकमलैः वीणाक्षमालापुस्तकादीन् धारयंतीं स्वपादांबुजं प्रणमतां मतिजाड्यं तत्क्षणादेव निरस्यन्तीं मरालशरीरकान्तिसोदरश्वेतामतिशयभासुरांगीं सरस्वतीं नमामीति शिष्यशिक्षायै **शास्त्रकारोक्तिः**। एवमेतादृशशास्त्रप्रवचनादये निरर्गलधिषणा-

पाटवाद्यनेकविधश्रेय:प्राप्यर्थं सर्वैरपि ग्रन्थमुखादौ शारदाया भजनं कलनीयमित्याशय: **शास्त्रकारस्य पालकाप्यमहर्षे**रादरणीय एव। किं चायं श्लोक: पूर्ववत् पुराणशैल्या स्पष्टार्थक्रम:। तस्मादस्माभिरस्य विस्तारार्थकथनं न कलितमिति मंगलाय।।

Psalm of Saraswatī—

I pray to the Goddess of Learning (Saraswatī) white in complexion, sitting on the lotus, offering wisdom, ever concentrating her mind towards the Creator Brahmā, surrounding all the universe, having sitar, books, beeds (*Japamālā)* and *abhaya* in her four hands with a cheerful face to remove the devotee's dullness.

मूलम्

हरित्करीन्द्रैरभिषिक्तदेहां
हस्तारविन्दादृतफुल्लपद्माम्।
पद्मां भजे मंगलमाल्यभूषां
पद्मासनस्थामखिलार्थसिद्ध्यै।।

व्याख्या—अथ निखिलजगन्मातरं मुकुन्दवल्लभां प्रफुल्लपद्मासन-पीठनिषण्णां करकमलकलितकोकनदां मंगलाभरणदिव्यमालादिमनोहरमूर्तिं पार्श्वयो: दिग्गजपुष्करधृतकनककलशगलितविमलगंगासलिलधाराभिषिक्तां श्रियं देवीमप्यत्र ग्रन्थमुखे **शास्त्रकार: प्रणमतीति विवेक:**। एवं स्वकीयापांग-तरंगवैभवेन सर्वेषामपि भक्तानां अनश्वरैश्वर्याद्यनेकमंगलदायिन्या रमाया: पादारविन्दभजने कृते सति अभीष्टसिद्धिरहमहमिहाकलितेति मति:।।

Psalm of Lakṣmī—

I humbly pray to the Goddess of Lakṣmī sitting on the lotus, with the best ornaments on her body and with two divine elephants on her either sides, pouring sacred water on her head.

मूलम्

प्रणम्य साम्बमीशानं विष्णुं नाकाधिपं विधिम्।
पालकाप्यादिकमुनीन् गजशास्त्रमहं ब्रुवे।।

व्याख्या-एवमुक्तप्रकारेण इष्टदेवतानमस्काराद्याकलनानन्तरं **शास्त्रकारो भगवान् पालकाप्यमहर्षिः** तदिदं **गजशास्त्रं** नातिसंक्षेपविस्तारं प्रणीय **अंगदेशाधिपस्य रोमपादभूपालस्या**स्थानसभायां सकललोकहिताय कथयामासेति **सन्दर्भः**। अयं किल विषयस्तूत्तरत्र द्वितीयप्रकरणारंभे स्पष्टं प्रतिपादयिष्यते। तस्मादेतादृशगजशास्त्रप्रणेतुः **पालकाप्यमहर्षेः** शिष्येण **धार्मिकमहर्षिणा** नैमिशारण्यवासिभ्यस्तदिदं **गजशास्त्रं** समयान्तरे पठितमिति च **पूर्वकथाप्रसंगः।** अतो नैमिशारण्यवासिभ्यो महर्षिभ्यः पठनसमये तेन किल **धार्मिकमहर्षिणा** प्रणम्य साम्बमीशानमित्ययं श्लोकः मंगलाचरणधोरण्या निर्गुंभित इति **व्यवस्था** चोह्या। किं चात्र मंगलश्लोके प्रतिपादिताः कैलाशशिखरनिलयः परमेश्वरः वैकुण्ठलोकधामा रमापतिः स्वर्गलोकाधिपो वासवः जगत्सृष्टिकर्ता पद्मासनश्चैते सर्वेऽपि कल्पान्तरकालेषु **गजशास्त्रप्रणेतार** आसन्। अतस्तेषां सर्वेषामप्याशयमनुसृत्यैव **पालकाप्यो महर्षि**स्तदिदं **गजशास्त्र**मुत्तमं रचयामास। तदेव यथाश्रुतं नैमिशवने मुनिपरिषदि तेन **धार्मिकेण** पठितम्। तस्मात्परंपरया आचार्यगोष्ठीमासेदुषां तेषामुमेशरमेशवासवपद्मासनानां पादारविन्दभजनमपि **स्वाचार्यस्य पालकाप्यमहर्षे**रन्येषां **व्यासादीनां** नमनमपि मंगलायैवेत्यालोच्यैव तेन **धार्मिकमहर्षिणा** प्रणम्य सांबमीशानमित्ययं श्लोकस्तु स्वकीयमंगलाचरणशैल्या निर्गुंभित इति **सन्दर्भक्रमार्थपरिपाटी** च सूक्ष्मतो **ज्ञेया**।।

Dhārmika's prayer—

I (sage Dhārmika, the pupil of author) worship my guru, the sage Pālakāpya and his four gurus, Brahmā, Śiva, Viṣṇu and Indra, who had written the science of Elephants in detail in different ancient generations (*Kalpa*).

1st chapter: Birth of Sage Pālakāpya.

There was a famous kingdom of Aṅga, situated on the south of the river Ganges and north of the Vindhya mountains with its capital Champāpuri. King Romapāda was ruling over that country Aṅga with great pomp like Indra. On one occasion many sages, Gautama, Agniveśya, Śaunaka, Jārgya, Gābāli, Parāśara, Yājñavalkya etc. visited his court or Darbar, when he welcomed them with great joy and gave them *Arghya*, *Pādya* and respected seats. He then requested them to shower their blessings on him in his attempt of capture of all the elephants spoiling his whole country and to which they gave permission heartily.

The Mahārājā Romapāda gave imperial order to his courtiers to search and capture all the elephants in the thick jungles and forests. Accordingly, the expert hunters took noose and requirements for hunting and set out to find the elephants in the Himalayan and other forests. In the course of their hunting, they spied in a hermitage a great sage with long knotted hair with astonishment in the midst of elephants, talking to them with signs and symbols, giving them food etc., playing with them at all times except in the midday to perform his religious rites in his hermitage. These hunters thought that it was impossible to capture the elephants as they were protected by the sage doing penance and so they returned home with fear and sorrow to narrate this story to their ruler.

The Mahārājā Romapāda then started himself to the woods on horse-back with his retinues and these expert hunters to capture the elephants, when he was able to capture all of them very easily with chain and ropes at midday, for, the sage was away from them to his hermitage to perform his religious rites as usual as they were once cursed to be so. After capturing them he brought them with him at the sage's dwelling on the banks of the Champā river belonging to them and expressed to them thus—I have captured these elephants only by your good grace and now I request you to teach me and the *Mahauts* how to protect and control them both at happy and angry times, give food and talk to them, as I am quite ignorant of doing so. The sages gladly complied with his request and asked him to go to his capital. Then they tied them (elephants) with chains and ropes in rows on the banks of the Champā river and gave instructions to the *Mahauts* how to control them easily. This was the first instance of controlling the elephants.

अथ प्रथमं प्रकरणम्

पालकाप्योत्पत्तिक्रमकथनं

मूलम्

धार्मिक उवाच–

अंगानामधिपः श्रेष्ठः श्रीमानिन्द्रसमद्युतिः।
येनेयं पृथिवी सर्वा सशैलवनकानना॥

चतुःसागरपर्यन्ता भुक्तासीन्मित्रतेजसा।
दानेन चन्द्रसदृशो दीप्तिमान् दिव्यतेजसा॥

स रोमपादनृपतिश्चक्रवर्ती महायशाः।
रोमेति नाम पद्मस्य रेखाकारस्य विश्रुतम्॥

तद्रोमयुक्तपादत्वात् रोमपाद इति श्रुतः।
आसने स्वोचिते दिव्ये रत्नवैडूर्यभूषिते॥

उपविष्टो महीपालो राजा राजीवलोचनः।
गंगाया दक्षिणे तीरे ब्रह्मर्षिगणसेविते॥

अंगदेशे स्वनगरे रम्ये चास्थानमण्डमे।

व्याख्या–एतावता प्रबन्धेन इष्टदेवतानमस्कारात्मकमंगलाचरणानन्तरं श्रीमतां महीपालानामनितरलभ्यराज्यलक्ष्मीसौख्यनिदानभूतस्य **गजशास्त्रस्यास्य** प्रवक्ता यः **पालकाप्यो महर्षिः** प्रसिद्धः तस्योत्पत्तिप्रकारप्रतिपादनात्मक-**मिदमाद्यं प्रकरणं** वक्तुमादौ तस्य ऋषेरवतारक्रमश्रवणोत्सुकस्य **रोमपादमहीपाल**स्य पूर्वरंगप्रसक्तिं विस्तरेणाह अंगानामधिप इत्यादिना। अंगानामधिप इत्यारब्धमिदं प्रथमं प्रकरणं तावत् तस्य किल **महर्षेः पालकाप्यस्य शिष्येण** पूर्वोक्तेन तेन **धार्मिकमहर्षिणा** पठितमिति सन्तो गजशास्त्रावतारक्रमवेत्तारः। तस्मादस्मिन् शास्त्रे द्वितीयप्रकरणस्यादौ भगवन्

वारणोत्पत्तिमित्यादिकमेव भगवता तेन **महर्षिणा पालकाप्येन** निगदितमिति सन्दर्भक्रमव्यवस्था। किं च-अंगानामधिप इत्यादिकं सर्वमपि पुराणशैल्या स्पष्टार्थकमेव। तथापि तत्र तत्रास्मिन् शास्त्रे संकेतार्थक्रमादिकमेव संग्रहेण स्पष्टीकर्तुमस्माकमयमुद्यमः शेषे वयसीत्यवगन्तव्यम्। तत्र विन्ध्यस्योत्तरभागे **आर्यावर्ताख्यपुण्यभूमिस्तु** देवादीनामप्यत्यन्तश्रेयोवृद्धिकारिणीति घण्टापथ एव। अतस्तस्यां पुण्यभूम्यां प्रसृताया गंगाया दक्षिणतीरतले लसमान **अंगाख्य** उत्तमदेशः **याज्ञवल्क्यगौतमपराशरादिभि**र्मुनीन्द्रैः श्लाघितपूर्व एव। एवं प्रसिद्धिमतस्तस्यांगदेशस्याधिपती **रोमपाद**नामा **महीपाल**स्तावत् चक्रवर्ति-पट्टभाक् यथापूर्वं वर्णाश्रमपरिपालनादिकमाकलयन् सन् विरराजेति **वाक्यार्थक्रमः**।।

मूलम्

अकस्मादागतान् तांस्तु मुनीन्द्रान् भसितव्रतान्।
गौतमं चाग्निवेश्यं च राजपुत्रं च शौनकम्।।

काशिपुत्रं नरं काप्यं रैभ्यं चैव बृहस्पतिम्।
गंगायनं च गार्ग्यं च जाबालिं च पराशरम्।।

याज्ञवल्क्यं हिरण्याक्षं भृगुमंगिरसं तथा।
दृष्ट्वैव परमं प्रीतो राजा विस्मयमागतः।।

सहसोत्थाय तान् नत्वा तोषयामास भक्तितः।
अर्घ्येणासनदानेन पाद्येन च परन्तपः।।

स्तूयमानैश्च तैः श्रेष्ठैः स्वागतं व्याहरत्तदा।
पृच्छद्भ्यः कुशलं तेभ्यो जगाद परया मुदा।।

व्याख्या–एवंप्रकारेण तस्यां**गदेशस्या**लंकारमणौ शंपानगरे शंपापगातरंग-वातांकुराधूनितबाह्योपवनमण्डिते स्वकीयप्रासादास्थानमण्डपे सिंहासनारूढे सति तस्मिन् **रोमपादमहीपाले** कदाचित् **गौतमाग्निवेश्यराजपुत्रशौनक**प्रभृतयो महर्षयो लोकहिताय तत्राजग्मुः। तथागतान् तान् दूरतोऽवलोक्य स महीपालमणिः सकौतुकः प्रत्युत्थायाभिगम्य अर्घ्यपाद्यमधुपर्कादिसमर्पणेन तदन्वासनपरि-कल्पनेन च नितरां तोषझरीं नीत्वा तेषां स्वागतमप्यवादीदिति **वाक्यार्थः**।।

मूलम्

ततश्च वदतां श्रेष्ठः सामात्यः सपुरोहितः।
नयकारान् गुणश्रेष्ठ अभिवाद्येदमब्रवीत्।।
अहं जिघृक्षुर्द्विरदानिति ते तु महर्षयः।
अनुग्रह्य तथेत्याहुर्नयधर्मविशारदाः।।
अथ राजा वचः श्रुत्वा विधिना गजचारिणः।
वीरांस्तान् प्रेषयामास सकामान् हितकारिणः।।
अन्वेष्टव्यास्तथा नागा गतपृष्ठाश्च सर्वतः।।

व्याख्या–एवं स्वागतकथनानन्तरं तस्मिन् किल सदसि तेषां मुनीन्द्राणां चिराय परस्परं सल्लपनकथाप्रसंगे स तु **रोमपादमहीपालः** सांजलिपुटं तेषां पुरतः स्थित्वा भो भो महर्षयः युष्माकमनुग्रहमवलंब्यैवाहमिदानीमेतद्देशक्षोभ-कारिणां करिणां ग्रहणबन्धनाय उद्यमं करिष्यामीत्याचचक्षे। एवमस्य महीपालस्य मुखारविन्दगलितां शुभां वाणीमाकलय्य ते सर्वे महर्षयः पुलकितांगा भो राजन् तथा ते मंगलं भूयादित्येकवाक्यमूचिरे। अतः सोऽयं महीपालः धर्मशास्त्रवैद्यशास्त्रसंगीतशास्त्रशिल्पशास्त्राद्यनेकशास्त्रप्रणेतृणां परावरत्रिदां निग्रहानुग्रहशक्तिभासुराणां तेषां मुनीन्द्राणामनुज्ञां शिरस्याकलय्य स्ववशवर्तिनः शूरानुपायज्ञान् बहूनाहूय नानादेशक्षोभकारिणो मदावलान् तान् सर्वानपि अस्मद्वशवर्तिनः कारयितुमचिरादेव यूयं गत्वारण्यतलं तत्र सर्वतो दिक्षु गिरिगह्वरेष्वटवीबिलेषु उपवनमध्यभागेषु निखिलेष्वपि कुंजेषु संघशो लीना व्यापृताश्च ते गजघटा मृग्या निःशेषगुप्तितलमिति आज्ञापयामास।।

मूलम्

अन्वेष्टितुं तथारब्धा मुदा परमया सह।
अपश्यन्नाश्रमपदं नानाद्रुमलतायुतम्।।
शैलराजाश्रितं पुण्यं लौहित्यं सागरं परम्।
यक्षगन्धर्वनिलयं सिद्धचारणसेवितम्।।
शैलराजस्य पार्श्वस्थं वनराजिविराजितम्।
अप्सरोभिः समाकीर्णं मृगव्यालादिसेवितम्।
तमाश्रमं प्रविष्टास्ते तस्य यूथस्य यतः पदम्।।

अपश्यन् ते मुनिं तत्र निवसन्तं तदाश्रमे।
मदोत्कटैश्च मातंगैरुपेतं हि मनोहरैः॥

चारुगाभिर्वशाभिश्च हिताभिः प्रियदर्शनैः।
तेजसा नियमैर्युक्तं कृशदेहं कृपान्वितम्॥

धृतिक्षमाभ्यां युक्तं च तपःसामपरायणम्।
शरण्यं सर्वभूतानां जरावल्कलधारिणम्॥

युक्तं धर्मेण हर्षेण क्रीडन्तं सह वारणैः।
कलभैर्धेनुकाभिश्च भ्रमरोद्गीतशाखिषु।
नानापुष्पसमृद्धेषु हंसचक्रवकैः सह॥

कमलोत्पलरम्येषु गाहमानं सरस्सु च।

व्याख्या—एवं तेन **रोमपादचक्रवर्तिना** प्रचोदितास्ते वीरा गजग्रहण-कौतुकतंगितमानसः तेषु देशेष्वरण्यमध्यस्थलानि हिमवतः सानुभागाटवीतलानि आलौहित्यमापारावारतटं वनराजिमध्यतलानि यक्षगन्धर्वसिद्धचारणाप्सरोभिरा-सेवितान्यतिमनोहराणि दिव्यस्थानान्याश्रमपदानि च प्रविष्टा अपि तादृशगज-संघास्तेषां वीराणां नयनपथं नैव प्रापुः। अतस्ते वीराः सर्वे श्रान्ताः किं कुर्म इति यावद्विषादाकुलितास्तावदेवाचिरेण तेषां पुरतः कस्यचिन्महर्षेरा-श्रमस्थानमविरासीत्। तदनु ते सर्वेऽपि वीरास्तस्य किलाश्रमपदस्य नातिदूरस्थले बह्वीभिर्वशाभी रमन्तं नरेन्द्रनिर्दिष्टं गजयूथमद्राक्षुः। अथ तस्मिन्नेव गजमण्डले कैश्चिन्मतंगजैः साकमिंगितबृंहितादिना सल्लपन्तं जटावल्कलधारिणं वाचंयमं तपोनिष्ठं कमपि मुनिवरमवलोकयामासुः। किं चैवंप्रकारेण घटिकाकाले व्यतीते सति तस्यैवाश्रमपदस्य पार्श्वान्तरवर्तिनि कमलसरसि वारणैरन्यैश्च साकं स्वयमपि मज्जनोन्मज्जनपरं तमेव मुनिवरमाकलयांचक्रिर इति **वाक्यार्थक्रमः**॥

मूलम्

उत्पन्नेयं मतिस्तेषामनेनैतद्धि रक्षितम्।
अनेन मुनिना यूथमत्र याम यथासुखम्॥

अथ मध्याह्नकाले तु सोऽगमन्मुनिराश्रमम्।
सायाह्नकाले तु मुनिर्यूथमध्यं पुनर्गतः॥

व्याख्या–एवमुक्तप्रकारेण गजवृन्दैस्तैः साकं सल्लपननिमज्जनोन्मज्जन–खेलनादिकमाकलयन्तमतिमानुषचरितं तं मुनिवरमवलोक्य ते तु वीराः सभय–कौतुकाः क्षणमालोच्याहो बताश्चर्यचर्याः अनेनैव हि मुनिना गजमण्डल–मिदं संरक्ष्यते। तत्र तत्र किल चाल्यते। क्वचिन्नियम्यत इति च परस्परं ब्रुवाणाः सन्तः सर्वथा नास्माकं शक्तिरेतस्य गजयूथस्य मुनिरक्षितस्य संग्रहण इति निश्चित्य किं कर्तव्यमजानन्तः स्वनायकस्य **रोमपादमहीपालस्य** पदकमल–दिदृक्षया तेनैव मार्गेण प्रतिवृत्ताः **शंपानगर**मवापुः। एवं तेषु वीरेषु स्वस्थानगतेषु सत्सु तैश्च वारणैः क्रीडनासक्तः स मुनिर्मध्याह्नसमये स्वाश्रमतलमवाप्य स्वकीयव्रतनियमपरोऽभूत्। पुनरपि सायंसमये संप्राप्ते तादृशगजमण्डल–संरक्षणायाचिरात्स तु मुनिवरस्तस्य गजवृन्दस्य मध्यतलमाविवेशेति **कथासन्दर्भः**।।

मूलम्

तस्मै नरा बहिर्भावं तथागम्यं न्यवेदयन्।
मूर्ध्नि कृत्वांजलिं भीता महीमास्थाय जानुभिः।।
दर्शनीयानि वीर्याणि नादवन्ति महंति च।
बहून्यदृष्टपूर्वाणि सत्त्वानि भुवि कानिचित्।।
सर्वसस्यविनाशं च तानि कुर्वन्ति नित्यशः।
तेषां देशहितार्थाय प्रतियत्नो विधीयताम्।।

व्याख्या–तस्मै नरा इति। एवं तस्य **रोमपादमहीपालस्य** आस्थान–सभांगणमागतास्ते वीराः सर्वेऽपि सांजलिबन्धं प्रणम्य भो नाथ भूलोकभागधेय चक्रवर्तिन्। भवदाज्ञानुसारेणैव चिरायारण्यतलं प्रविष्टैरस्माभिः कस्यचिन्महर्षे–राश्रमपदे भवन्निर्दिष्टानि तानि गजमण्डलानि निखिलसुरासुरयक्षगन्धर्व–किन्नरोरगादिभिरपि दुर्निरोध्यबलपराक्रमचेष्टानि नयनानन्दकारीणि देशक्षोभनि–दानानि दृष्टान्येव। तानि सर्वाणि तेनैकेन महर्षिणैव सन्ततं संरक्ष्यन्ते। तत्र तत्र प्रचाल्यन्ते। शिक्षाविधिमप्यानीयन्ते। तत्र हेतुस्तस्य तपःप्रभावो ननु। न विद्मः। तस्मात् तेषां ग्रहणे बन्धने च वयमसमर्था भवत्पादपद्ममूलं प्राप्ताः। भवानेव तद्ग्रहणे समर्थो नान्य इति च विज्ञापयामासुः।।

मूलम्

ततस्तेषां वचः श्रुत्वा ग्रहाय कृतनिश्चयः।
प्रस्थितो हृदि तं कृत्वा यः कालस्तैर्निवेदितः।।

गृहीत्वा वागुरादींश्च स्वपुरान्निरगात्तदा।
अचिरात्समनुप्राप्तस्तं देशं यत्र ते गजाः।।

स तान् शापवशं प्राप्तान् गजान् जग्राह पार्थिवः।
तस्मिन् काले तदायाते यूथं बद्धं नृपेण तत्।।

शंपातरंगिणीतीरे प्रतिपूज्याभिवाद्य च।
अथाब्रवीदंगराजः प्रहृष्टमनसा मुनीन्।।

विधिना शास्त्रदृष्टेन यूथमेतन्नियम्यताम्।
प्रत्यब्रुवन्नंगराजं सर्वे ते नयकोविदाः।।

स्वकार्यमेतदस्माकं शेषं कार्यं विचिन्त्यताम्।
शंपाप्रवेशः क्रियतां राजन् स्वस्थमना भव।।

ते राजनि प्रयाते तु यूथं स्तंभेष्वबन्धयन्।।

व्याख्या—तत इति। एवंप्रकारेण तेषां वीराणां वचो निशम्य झटिति विकसितशेमुषीविलासोऽय**मंगराजः** तादृशगजमण्डलबन्धनानयनार्थं कृतनिश्चयः सन् तैश्च वीरैरन्यैर्मृगयातत्त्वज्ञैश्च परिवृतः सन् दृढपाशशृंखलावागुरादींश्च गृहीत्वा अचिरेणैव कालेन तत्प्रदर्शितवर्त्मना महर्षेस्तस्याश्रमस्थानमागत्य क्वचित्कोणे स्थितिमवाप्य यस्मिन् किल समये तान् गजान् दूरतो विसृज्य स मुनिवरः स्वकीयाश्रमस्थितो भवेत् तमेव समयं समुचितमन्विष्यन्नवर्तत। एतस्मिन्नन्तरे स मुनिवरः प्रातःकाले यथाक्रमं गजयूथस्यान्तिकमवाप्य तेषां वांछानुगुणं तैः साकं सल्लपनखेलनादिकं कृत्वा मध्यंदिने संप्राप्ते यावत् स्वावासस्थलमुटजांगणमवाप तावत् सत्त्वरं स **महीपाल रोमपादनामा** तुरगारूढो निभृतमनुचरैः साकं वारणानां तेषामन्तिकतलमवाप्य स्वकरप्रसारित-वागुरापाशशृंखलादिना सर्वेषामपि वारणानां पादशुण्डादिस्थलेषु बन्धनमकार्षीत्। तथा च आसृष्टिकालं मानुषवशमप्राप्तानां तेषां गजानां बन्धनमेवमचिरादनायासेन समजनीति यत्तत्र हेतुस्तु नरेन्द्राणां वाहनत्वं गमिष्यथ इति तादृशगजान् प्रति मुनिशापप्रसार एवेति **व्यवस्था ज्ञेया**। अयं किल **विषयस्तूत्तरत्र स्पष्टं प्रतिपादयिष्यते**। तस्मादेवं तस्य **रोमपादमहीपालस्य** दर्शनमात्रेणैव मुनिशापफलानुभवाय सज्जीकृतास्ते सर्वे वन्यवारणाः विगलितगर्वमदाटो-

पाद्यनेकदुर्गुणाः शुद्धसत्त्वमापन्नास्तत्करगता अभवन्। अत एवमनायासेन बद्धान् तान् सर्वान् वारणानप्याकर्षन् सोऽयं महीपालः **शंपानद्यास्तट**भुवि कलिताश्रमान् **शौनकादीन् मुनीन्द्रा**नुपसृत्य यथाक्रमं प्रणम्य भो भो महर्षयः पूर्वोक्तरीत्या भवतामनुग्रहादेव मया बद्धा इमे वारणाः स्थलमिद-मानीताः। तथापि बहुकालस्थितये शिष्यशिक्षायै चैतेषां गमनागमनचालनप्रचारण-सांत्वनपरिरक्षणादिविधिः भवद्भिरेव उपदेष्टव्य इति प्रार्थयामास। एवमुक्तवति सांजलिपुटे महीपाले त्रिकालज्ञास्ते सर्वे महर्षयः भो राजन् करिणामेषां रक्षणादिविषये चिन्तां त्यज। तत्सर्वं वयमेव साधयिष्यामः। भवान् किल स्वस्थमानसो भूत्वा स्वास्थानसिंहासनारूढः सन् प्रजापालनधुरं वहतु। स्वस्ति ते भूयादित्यनुगृह्य प्रेषयामासुः। ततस्तस्मिन् महीपाले स्वस्थानस्थिते सति ते तु महर्षयो निखिललोकक्षेमाय सस्याद्यभिवृद्ध्यै च तान् सर्वान् वन्यवारणान् आलानस्तंभेष्वनेकेष्वबन्धयन्निति **कथाप्रसंगः**।।

मूलम्

अथ शिश्रूषणं कृत्वा स निष्क्रम्याश्रमान्मुनिः।
तं देशमभिसंप्राप्त आसीद्यत्र स्थितं च तत्।।

तस्मिन्नपश्यत् तद्यूथं मनसा व्याकुलेन च।
प्रारब्धोऽन्वेषणं कर्तुं पुरासीद्यत्र तत्सुखम्।।

येषु येष्वावगाहन्त तेषु तेषु सरस्सु च।
नापश्यत्तेषु सर्वेषु शंपामभ्यागमत्ततः।।

पदेन मुनिशार्दूलः शोचन् स्नेहेन हस्तिनाम्।
तपोनियमसंपन्नाः स्थितास्ते वनमध्यगाः।।

ददृशुर्युगपच्चैव तस्मिंस्तु गजमण्डले।
ततो बद्धांस्तु तान् दृष्ट्वा वारणान् मुनिसत्तमः।।

आसीत्पर्यश्रुनेत्रश्च वैक्लव्यं च जगाम सः।
एकरात्रोषितास्तत्र सूत्रकारा महामुनेः।।

शोकस्य कारणं किंवा पप्रच्छुर्विनयान्विताः।
केनानुकंपसे नागान् केनैषां लुंपसे व्रणान्।।

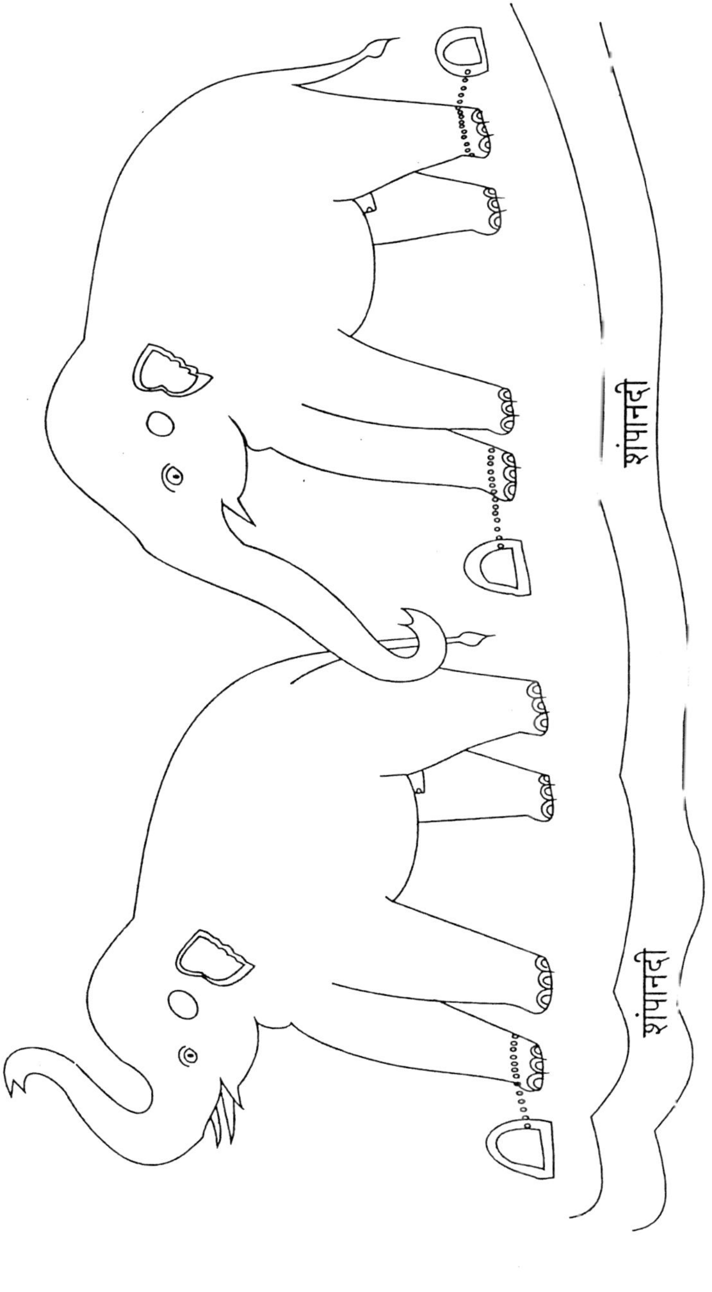

Fig. 1 शंपानदीतीरे रोमपादमहीपालेन प्रथमतो बद्धाः गजाः

Fig. 2 शंपानदीतीरे रोमपादमहीपालेन प्रथमतो बद्धः गजः:–

ऋषिभिः पृच्छ्यमानोऽपि न किंचित्प्रत्युवाच सः।
अनभिव्याहृतास्तेन जग्मुस्ते विस्मयं तदा॥

व्याख्या—अथेति। तत्र तु गजमण्डलमण्डिते स्वाश्रमस्थले स्वपित्रोर्बन्धूनामतिथिवर्गाणां च अर्घ्यपाद्यासनमधुपर्कश्यामाकनीवारादिभोजनप्रदानानन्तरं विहितनिजनियमविधिः स तु महर्षिः पूर्ववत् तदेव स्थलमवाप्य मधुरेण रवेण स्वस्नेहपात्रान् गजान् तानाहूतवान्। तदा न कोऽपि मदावलः प्रत्याजगाम। किमिदमिति क्षणं विचार्य व्याकुलितमानसः स मुनीश्वरः पर्यन्तारण्यकुंजसरसीप्रमुखेषु विविधेषु स्थलेष्वदृश्यान् गजान् तानन्विष्यन् सर्वत्राप्यनुपलब्धतदीयवृत्तान्तो नितरां दुःखितस्ततः कृच्छ्रेण तेषां गजानां पदपंक्तिसरणिमवलोक्य तेनैव मार्गेण **शंपानगर**समीपमुपेत्य तत्र नदीतीरे वृन्दशो निबद्धान् स्वेनैव संवर्धितान् तानेव गजान् पश्यन् सन् अहो किमर्थमियं दयनीया दशा वारणानामेतेषामापादितेति तेषु स्नेहवशेनाश्रुपूर्णवदनो वैक्लव्यमवाप। एवं प्रकारेण तथा बद्धान् गजान् प्रति अनुशोचन्तं तं मुनिवरं निरीक्ष्य तत्रत्याः पूर्वोक्ताः सर्वे महर्षयस्तदन्तिकमुपेत्य—भो भगवन् महर्षे! किमर्थमेतान् प्रति भवाननुशोचति। किमर्थमेषां बन्धनव्रणवेदनामपनोतुमुद्युक्तोऽसीत्यब्रुवन्। एवं **शंपानदी**तटतलनिवासिभिर्मुनीन्द्रैः पृष्टोऽपि स मुनिवरः किंचिदपि प्रतिवचनं नैवादात्। अतस्ते विस्मिता अभवन्निति **वाक्यार्थक्रमः**। शेषं स्पष्टम्॥

मूलम्

तेभ्यो निशम्यांगपतिर्महर्षिमभिगम्य तम्।
अर्घ्येणासनदानेन पाद्येन च महामुनिम्।
प्रणिपातेन चाभ्यर्च्य पृष्ट्वा व्याधिषु कौशलम्॥
सान्वयं परिपप्रच्छ नियमेन कृतांजलिः।
भगवन् श्रोतुमिच्छामि जन्म नाम तव स्वयम्॥
जन्मप्रभृतिरूपं च दयादृष्टिं च हस्तिषु।
इति तं परिपप्रच्छ भूमिपालः कृतांजलिः॥
मुनिना भाषितस्तेन खेदाद्वारणबन्धनात्।
ततो ब्राह्मणमाराध्य पृष्टवान् पार्थिवस्तदा॥
अथासौ धर्मविस्तारं शशंसात्मन आत्मवान्।

व्याख्या–तेभ्य इति। एवं प्रकारेण **शंपानदी**तटं प्रति कस्यचिन्महर्षेरागमनं तदनु तं प्रति तत्रत्यानामुपसर्पणकुशलप्रश्नादिकथनं तान् महर्षीन् प्रति तस्य मुनेः प्रतिवचनाप्रदानं च तेषां महर्षिणामाश्चर्यभाषणेन विदित्वा स किल **रोमपादभूपालः** सहसोत्थाय सचिवपुरोहितपरिवारपरिवृतः सन् **शंपापगा**तीरमागत्य तत्र स्थितं तं मुनिवरमभिसृत्य तत्पादयोः प्रणम्य अर्घ्यासनदानादिना प्रतिपूज्य भगवन् महर्षे किमर्थमेवं भवता गजेषु दयादृष्टिराद्रियते। तस्माद्भवतो विचित्रचरितस्य जन्मवृत्तान्तादिकं सर्वमप्यहं श्रोतुमभिलषामि। कृपया तदेतत्सर्वं मे वक्तुमर्हसीति प्रार्थितवान्। तदन्वंगीकृतभूपालप्रार्थनः सोऽयं मुनीश्वरस्त्रिकालज्ञः स्वकीयजननक्रमवृत्तादिकं यथाक्रमं वक्तुमारब्धवानिति **पंक्त्यर्थः**।।

मूलम्

मुनिरुवाच–

पुरा हि वारणा राजन् कामगाः कामरूपिणः।
विचेरुर्मानवे लोके देवलोके च पार्थिव।।

अथ तीरे हिमवतो महान् न्यग्रोधपादपः।
द्वियोजनशतं राजन्नुच्छ्रयायामविस्तरः।।

ऋषिर्दीर्घतपा नाम तस्याधः सपरिग्रहः।
न्यग्रोधं च कदाचित्ते समाजग्मुरनेकपाः।।

निषेदुस्तस्य शाखायां सहसैव तथा गजाः।
अतिभारेण तेषां च सा शाखा शतयोजना।

विदारयन्ती तं देशं निपपात महीतले।
ते चापि वारणाः सर्वे शाखामन्यां समाश्रिताः।।

ततः क्रोधसमाविष्टस्तान् गजान् मुनिरब्रवीत्।
बलदर्पोज्झिता नागा मम शापपरिग्रहात्।।

विमुक्ताः कामचारेण भविष्यथ न संशयः।
नराणां वाहनत्वं च तस्मात्प्राप्स्यथ वारणाः।।

अथान्तरिक्षान्महती राजन् वाणी विनिर्गता।
यैर्हता दानवा दैत्यास्तान् मुक्त्वा शपथं कुरु॥
वाणीं श्रुत्वा हितामेनामेवमस्त्विति सोऽब्रवीत्॥

व्याख्या—अथ स मुनिवरस्तस्मै **रोमपादमहीपालाय** स्वाविर्भावक्रनादिकं वक्तुमादौ कृतयुगारंभसमये गजानां शापप्राप्त्यादिकं पूर्वरंगशैल्या विशदयति पुरा हीत्यादिना। पुरा किल कृतयुगारंभसमये ब्रह्मणा सृष्टाः सर्वेऽपि मतंगजाः दिग्गजा इव स्वेच्छागृहीतविविधरूपा रसातलभूतलनाकादिषु सर्वेष्वपि देशेषु संचरणशीला अभवन्। एतादृशवैभवशालिषु तेषु गजेषु केचिन्मतंगजाः पुरा कदाचित् हिमवतः सानुभागस्थितस्यात्युन्नतस्य न्यग्रोधपादपस्य शाखायां महत्यां यदृच्छयागत्य निषेदुः। तथा निषण्णानां तेषामतिभारं वोढुमक्षमा सा वृक्षशाखा तत्क्षणादेव भग्ना सती तस्य वृक्षस्याधःस्थले निजधर्मपत्न्या सहितस्य द्वितीयाश्रमे धर्मसुखमनुभवितुः **दीर्घतपोनामकस्य महर्षेरा**श्रमं तदन्तिकस्थलं च क्षोभयन्ती भूमौ पपात। अथ तस्याः शाखायाः पतनं निरीक्ष्य दर्पान्वितास्ते मतंजगाः शाखान्तरमास्थाय तत्रैव मुदा सुखं स्थिताः। तदनु तस्य वृक्षस्याधःस्थले स्थितः स तु **दीर्घतपोनामा महर्षि**रेवमकाले शाखायास्तस्याः पतनहेतुं स्वाश्रमस्थलक्षोभादिकं च विदित्वा नितरां क्रोधाक्रान्तः सन् भो वारणा यतो यूयमत्यन्तबलगर्वसमेता निरपराधस्य ममाश्रमक्षोभं कृतवन्तस्तस्मादित आरभ्य युष्माकं तादृशबलगर्वयोर्नाशो भविष्यति। एवं तत्र तत्र कामचारशक्तिश्च नश्यतु। इत्थं यूयं युष्मद्वंशजनिताश्च सर्वे गजाः स्वतंत्रत्वं विहाय राज्ञां वाहनत्वं च प्राप्स्यथेति शशाप। तस्मिन्नवसरे गगनमध्यतलात् काचित् वाणी निःसृता। यथा–भो भगवन् **दीर्घतपोनाम महर्षे** सर्वलोकहिताय भवता शापमेवं प्रापितानामेतेषां दुष्टानां गजानां एतद्वंश्यानां गजानां च कामचारशक्तिहानिः महाबलगर्वहानिः महीपालादीनां पराधीनत्वं च भवतु। एतत् युक्तमेव। परन्तु स्वर्गलोकस्थितानां विबुधवैरिनिषूदनपराणां केषांचिदेव वारणानां कामचारशक्त्यादिकं यथापूर्वमस्त्विति भवाननुगृह्णातु। एवमिन्द्रादेशादागताहं त्वामभ्यर्थय इत्यदृश्या काचित् गन्धर्वी वाणीमेवमवाकिरत्। अथैवं प्रकारेण तया हि गन्धर्व्या प्रेरितां वाणीं स्वर्गलोकहितकारिणीं शुभां मत्वा स किल मुनीन्द्रस्तथा-स्त्वित्यब्रवीत्।

मूलम्

अथ ते वारणाः श्रुत्वा शापमात्मापराधजम्।
परं दैन्यमुपागम्य ब्रह्माणमुपतस्थिरे॥

अथ तान् पूर्वमेवाह ब्रह्मलोके पितामहः।
माकार्ष्ट वारणाः शोकं न हि शक्यं तदन्यथा॥

कर्तुं यत्तेन मुनिना वचनं समुदाहृतम्।
एतद्वाक्यं ततः श्रुत्वा प्रत्यूचुस्ते दिशांगजाः॥

अस्माकमन्वयानां तु गजानां वनवासिनाम्।
रोगाः प्रादुर्भविष्यन्ति विषमात्यशनादिभिः॥

दिग्गजानां वचः श्रुत्वा प्रत्युवाच पितामहः।
उत्पत्स्यतेऽचिरान्नागा गजबन्धुर्महामुनिः॥

आयुर्वेदस्य वेत्ता वै मत्कृतस्य भविष्यति।
तेषां तु रोगानुत्पन्नानौषधैर्वारयिष्यति॥

एवमुक्त्वा तु दिङ्नागान् विससर्ज यथादिशम्।
ततस्ते प्रययुः स्थानं स्वं स्वमैरावतादयः॥

दिग्वारणान्वयास्ते तु लोकं मानुषमागताः।
विचरन्तो महीं कृत्स्नां सशैलवनकाननाम्॥

शतशो यूथसंख्याभिः प्रवृद्धाश्च सहस्त्रशः॥

व्याख्या—इत्थमनेन **दीर्घतपसा मुनिना** प्रेरितशापस्य दुष्फलं विदित्वा भग्नमानसास्ते वारणाः सर्वे संघीभूय ऐरावतादीन् दिग्गजांश्च पुरस्कृत्य **विधातुः** सन्निधिमवाप्य प्रणम्य स्वकीयापराधेन संजातशापं प्रति परमां शुचं **ब्रह्मणे** प्रदर्श्य का वा गतिरस्माकमित आरभ्येत्यब्रुवन्। इत्थं दिग्गज-प्रमुखानां वारणानां विषादवचनं श्रुत्वा स तु **कमलासनः** भो गजोत्तमाः तादृशमुनिवचनमन्यथाकर्तुं को वात्र प्रभवति। विधिवशादापतितस्य शापस्यानुभूतिं प्रति शोको न युक्तः। तदपि मुनिभाषितं लोकहितायैव विदितम्। तथापि युष्माकं वैभवगौरवादिकं तु सर्वथा न हीयेत। एतदलं किलेत्यवादीत्। अथ

पुनस्ते वारणा अस्मद्वंश्यानां यदि कदाचित् रोगोद्रेकः स्यात्तदा भवता को वा उपायो विचिन्तित इत्यूचुः। तदाकर्ण्य **विधिरेवं** व्याजहार–भो भो दिग्गजमुखा वारणाः स्वल्पेनैव कालेन भूलोके **गजबन्धु**र्नामा कश्चिन्**मुनि**रुद्भविष्यति। स एव मुनिः पूर्वं प्रतिकल्पं मया ग्रथितस्य **गजायुर्वेदस्य** वेत्ता प्रचारयिता च भविष्यति। किं च समुचितौषधप्रदानादिना सर्वान् गजरोगान् दूरतो निरस्य सर्वेषामपि गजानां श्रेयःपरंपरामापादयिष्य- तीत्यनुग्रह्य तिरोदधे। अतस्त **ऐरावतप्रभृतयो दिङ्नागा ब्रह्मणा** प्रोक्तामेतां शुभवाणीमाकर्ण्य किंचिन्मुदितमानसाः स्वं स्वं स्थानमवाप्य यथासुखं विचेरुः। तेषां दिग्गजानां पुत्रपौत्रादिकुले संजाता वारणास्तु भूलोकमिममागत्य हिमवद्विन्ध्यादिगिरीन्द्रतटगुहारण्यतलादिषु स्थितिमासाद्य स्वपत्नीषु करिणीषु कालक्रमेण शतसहस्रसंख्यकानुत्तमान् पुत्रानुत्पादयामासुरिति **वाक्यार्थः**। तस्मादेवमुक्तप्रकारेण ऋषिशापवशादेव ते तु वारणा **रोमपादभूपाल**वशंगताः **शंपानदी**तीरे प्रथमं बद्धा अभूवन्निति **भावः**।

मूलम्

राजन् हिमवतः पार्श्वे महर्षिः सामगायनः।
सागरं प्रतिलौहित्यं तपस्तीव्रमतप्यत॥
तस्याश्रमपदाभ्याशे आजगाम यदृच्छया।
सवृन्दजालः सुमहान् गजयूथपयूथपः॥
तं स्वप्ने दर्शयामास यक्षिणी कामरूपिणी।
उत्थाय स्वासनात्तूर्णं मुनिर्मूत्रं चकार सः॥
विसृष्टमूत्रे नियमं यातेऽस्मिन् ऋषिसत्तमे।
देवकारणसंयुक्तं तस्य तद्रेतसान्वितम्॥
अपिबद्धस्तिनीमूत्रं ततो गर्भमधत्त सा।
तस्य तद्वचनं श्रुत्वा राजा वचनमब्रवीत्॥
कथं करेणुस्तच्छुक्लं पीत्वा गर्भमधत्त सा।

मुनिरुवाच–

वसूनां कन्यका राजन् नाम्ना गुणवती किल॥
तदाश्रमे मतंगस्य कदाचित्प्रविवेश सा।

धर्मविघ्नकरीं मत्वा शक्रेण प्रहितां स्वयम्॥
ततः शशाप संक्रुद्धः तापसस्तु स कन्यकाम्।
अरण्ये विचरस्येका यस्मान्मानुषवर्जिते॥

तस्मादरण्यनिचये करेणुस्त्वं भविष्यसि।
माभूदरण्यवासेऽपि विनाशः स्वस्य चेतसः॥

ततः शापवशात् त्रस्ता ह्यपतत्पादयोर्मुनेः।
कौतूहलात्प्रविष्टाऽहं रमणीयं तवाश्रमम्॥

प्रसादं कुर्वनागस्याः शापान्तेन ममानघ।
गुणवत्या वचः श्रुत्वा मतंगो मुनिरब्रवीत्।
उपस्पृश्य ततो ध्यात्वा ज्ञात्वा विगतकल्मषाम्॥

नापराधोऽस्ति ते भद्रे धात्रा पूर्वकृतो विधिः।
भविष्यति च ते पुत्रः सामगायनसंभवः॥

दीर्घकालतपोवीर्यान्मौनमास्थाय सुव्रतः।
चरिष्यति गजैः सार्धं शीर्णपर्णांबुभोजनः॥

स्वयंभूः प्राक् ददौ यस्मै गजायुर्वेदमुत्तमम्।
पालकाप्य इति ख्यातो मुनिर्वारणबान्धवः॥

संप्रसूयाथ संवर्ध्य त्वं तु मूर्त्या पुनः स्वया।
विसृज्य हस्तिनीभावं विशापा दिवमाप्स्यति(सि)॥

व्याख्या–एवं प्रकारेण वारणानां प्रथमशापप्राप्त्यादिक्रममुपपाद्याधुना स तु मुनिवरः स्वाविर्भावक्रमं कथयति–राजन् हिमवत इत्यादिना षोडश-श्लोकगुंभेन। पुरा किल **सामगायननामनि मुनीश्वरे** हिमालयस्य दक्षिणभृगुतटे चिरायातितीव्रतपश्चर्यां परिसमाप्य कालं कंचित् विश्रान्तिमनुभवति सति जातुचित् तस्याश्रमस्यान्तिके करिणीभिरनेकाभिः परिवृतः कोऽपि गजयूथाधिपः सपरिवार यदृच्छया किलाजगाम। तत्रान्तरे विधिबलप्रेरिता कामरूपिणी काचन यक्षिणी गगनमार्गेण तत्रागत्य नितरां मनोहरांग्याः स्वस्याः स्वरूपं तस्य मुनेर्मनस्तटाके प्रतिफलितं कारयामास। तथा विश्रान्तिभाजो निमीलित-

चक्षुषस्तस्य **सामगायनमहर्षे**र्मानसे यावत् यक्षिण्याः स्वरूपमतिफलनं संजातम् तावदेव झटिति क्षुभितेन्द्रियवर्गः सन् स तु मुनीन्द्रः स्वाश्रमात्सहसा बहिर्निर्गत्य नातिदूरस्थले गलितस्वरेतसा संयुक्तमूत्रोत्सर्जनं चकार। तदनु स मुनिवरः पादौ प्रक्षाल्याचम्य यथाक्रमं स्वाश्रममवाप्य नियमाकलयन्नवर्तत। एवमस्मिन् विसृष्टमूत्रे मुनौ स्वाश्रमं प्रविष्टे सति तत्र गजवृन्दैः साकमागता-स्वनेकासु करिणीषु मनोहरांगी काचित् वशा तत्स्थलमवाप्य महर्षेस्तस्य शुक्लेन संयुक्तं मूत्रजलं तत् स्वशुण्डादण्डेन सादरमादायापिबत्। तदानीमेव सा करिणी अन्तर्वत्नी च बभूवेत्युक्तवति तस्मिन् मुनिवरे तस्य मुनेः शुक्लसंमिश्रं मूत्रं पीत्वा कथं सा धेनुका गर्भवत्यासीत्। अत्याश्चर्यवृत्तान्तः किलायम्। तत्र निदानं किन्नु वा। तच्च सर्वं वदस्वेति **रोमपादमहीपति**-रपृच्छत्। तच्च युक्तं मत्वा स तु मुनिवरस्तत्पूर्ववृत्तं च कथयितुमुपक्रमते। वसूनां कन्यका राजन्नित्यादिना। पुरा किल गुणवती नाम्नी निखिलगुणाढया वसुकन्या काचित् **मतंगमुनेरा**श्रमतलमाविवेश। स तु मतंगः शक्रप्रेषितां स्वतपोविघ्नकारिणीमप्सरसं तां मत्वा भो बाले मानुषसंचाररहितेऽस्मिन्नरण्ये त्वमेकाकिनी निर्भया यतः किलैवं विहारवती तस्मात् त्वमचिरादेव काचित् करिणी भव। किं च तादृशकरिणीदशायामपि तव मनसि पूर्वजन्मज्ञानाद्यावि-र्भावो भूयादिति शशाप। एवमकाण्डे शापपतनमाकलय्य सा वसुकन्य भो-भगवन् महर्षे नितरां रमणीयं त्वदीयाश्रममहं केनापि कौतूहलेनैव प्रविष्टास्मि। न तु तपोविघाताय। अतो भवता निरपराधायां मयि कथमेवं शापः प्रसारितः। शापविमोचनप्रदानादिना वाद्य मे प्रसीदतु भवानिति तत्पादयोः प्रणम्य प्रार्थयामास। अथैवं क्रन्दन्त्यास्तस्या वसुकन्याया दीनवचनमाकर्ण्य स तु **मुनिर्मतंगः** ससंभ्रममुपस्पृश्य स्वज्ञानचक्षुषा तां निरपराधां विदित्वा पश्चात्तापयुक्तः सन् भो बाले त्वदुक्तप्रकारेण त्वं निरपराधैव। तथापि दैववशादेव शाप एवमापादितः। मद्वचनं तावन्नान्यथा भवेदेव। तथापि कालान्तरे त्वदुदरे **सामगायनाख्यमहर्षे**रिन्द्रियसंपर्कवशात् कोऽपि धन्यो मुनिपुत्रो भविष्यति। स तु महातपोवीर्यात् गजबन्धुर्भूत्वा पूर्वं ब्रह्मणा ग्रथितस्य **गजायुर्वेदस्य** प्रवक्ता च भविष्यति। तस्मात्तादृशसमये त्वद्गर्भे प्रादुर्भूतं **पालकाप्यनामानं मुनिपुत्रं** त्वं त्वदीयास्यतलात् प्रसूय तं च पुत्रं वर्धयित्वा ततः शापावधिं प्राप्य प्रणम्य तादृशकरिणीशरीरं विसृज्य स्वकीयया

दिव्यया मूर्त्या संयुक्ता सती यथापूर्वं स्वर्लोकस्थिता सुखभाक्भवितुमर्हसीत्यनुगृहीतवान् स **मुनिर्मतंग** इति **पूर्वकथाक्रमः**।।

मूलम्

अथ विज्ञाय तेजस्वी आत्मनस्तमतिक्रमम्।
आत्मनस्तेजसा तस्य भव एव मनो दधे।।

मनसानुगृहीतस्तु गर्भस्तेन महात्मना।
अवर्धत ततो माता समये तमसूत सा।।

हस्त्यायुर्वेदपारज्ञं दीप्यमानं स्वतेजसा।
जातं मानुषरूपं तु दृष्ट्वा जातभयं तदा।।

कृत्वा विरावं तद्यूथं विदुद्राव समन्ततः।
सा तु गर्भस्य मूलज्ञा करेणुः सुतमात्मजम्।।

आदायाश्रममागत्य प्रायच्छत् ब्राह्मणाय तम्।
प्रतिगृह्य तु तं प्रीतो महर्षिः सुतमात्मजम्।।

जातकर्मादिसंस्कारान् चकारास्मै यथाक्रमम्।
संस्कारे तु कृते तस्य वागुवाचाशरीरिणी।।

कल्पे कल्पे गजानेष ह्यमितौजा महायशाः।
पालयिष्यति धर्मात्मा रोगार्तान् भृशदुःखितान्।।

पालनात् गजयूथस्य काप्यगोत्रोद्भवो यतः।
पालकाप्य इति श्रीमान् नामधेयं चकार सः।।

पिता साधूंश्च संमान्य सन्तर्प्यर्षिगणांस्तदा।
आश्रमादविदूराच्च धेनुका विचचार सा।

वर्धमानस्तु पुत्रस्तामन्वगच्छत्स धेनुकाम्।
तं मां विद्धि महाराज प्रसूतं सामगायनात्।।

हस्तिन्या वक्त्रसंभूतं विवृद्धं च सह द्विपैः।
जानामि भक्ष्यं भोज्यं च तथैवेंगितबृंहितम्।।

ते यथा च विचेष्टन्ते प्रकुप्यन्ति च येन तत्।
नागाः कुर्वन्त्यरण्येषु तत्सर्वं विदितं मम॥

एवं मामभिजानीहि गजाः सर्वे प्रियात्प्रियाः।
भक्ष्यं वा क्रीडनीयं वा तदुपाहर एव वा॥

आश्रमेऽस्मिन् महाराज महद्यूथमिदं त्वया।
दशवर्षसहस्राणि दशवर्षशतानि च॥

त्रीणि पंचैव वर्षाणि मया चीर्णं सह द्विपैः।
बहुकालोषिततत्वाच्च जानाम्येषां हिताहिते॥

पांसुकर्दमतोयाद्यैः तृप्ताः क्रीडन्ति हर्षिताः।
धातुप्रसादः क्षिप्रं तु क्रीडनाज्जायतेऽधिकम्॥

धातुप्रसादादारोग्यमारोग्यात् बलमेव च।
बलाच्च सर्वरोगाणां निवृत्तिः स्यादतः परम्॥

हस्तिनामुदकं प्राणास्तद्गतिस्तत्परायणम्।
तस्मात्सलिलमेवैषां कामतो न निवर्तयेत्॥

आयोजनशतं स्थानं विचरन्तोऽपि कुंजराः।
सत्यमेव न सीदन्ति सलिलेनैव केवलम्॥

यथा न परिशुष्यन्ति कर्दमोदकशीकरैः।
भवन्ति सुखबोध्याश्च येन हृष्टेन हेतुना॥

बन्धनीयास्तावदेते यावत् शक्यास्तु पोषितुम्।
वधबन्धपरिक्लेशैर्यदा क्लाम्यन्ति नित्यशः॥

न ते पुष्यन्ति मातंगा दुःखशोकसमन्विताः।
कुलं राज्ञां दहन्त्येव मानिता निदहन्त्यरीन्।
तस्मात्प्रयत्नः कर्तव्यः सुमहान् गजरक्षणे॥

तस्मादपीतभुक्तेषु वारणेषु सदा नृप॥

स्वयं न भोजनं कुर्यात् यदीच्छेत् श्रेय आत्मनः।
नवग्रहे च मातंगे क्षीणे वृद्धे तथातुरे॥
यत्नतो रक्षणं कार्यं स्वयं चैवान्ववेक्षणम्॥

इति पालकाप्यमहर्षिप्रणीते गजशास्त्रे पालकाप्योत्पत्तिकथनं नाम प्रथमं प्रकरणम्॥

व्याख्या—अथ विज्ञायेति। पूर्वोक्तप्रकारेणाकाले तस्या यक्षिण्या दर्शनेन संजातं स्वमनःकालुष्यं **तष्यत्द्द्वारा** झटिति स्वरेतसो विसर्जनं करिणीकृततत्पान क्रमादिकं सर्वमपि विदित्वा स तु **सामगायनमहर्षिः** क्षणमनुशोचन् पुनरप्या-दृतदृढनियमविधिः सन् मुहूर्तद्वयकालं तथा स्थित्वा समाप्तनियमो लोचने निमील्य निरीक्ष्य स्वाश्रमस्य नातिदूरस्थले तिष्ठन्त्यास्तस्याः करिण्या उदरगतः स्वरेतःप्रसारः सर्वलोकहिताय दिव्यतेजोविशिष्टः कश्चिन्मुनिकुमारो भूयादिति यावन्मनसानुग्रहं चकार तावदेव सा हस्तिनी गर्भिणी भूता तत्प्रभावेनैव प्रत्यहं संरक्षितगर्भसत्त्वा सती दशमे मासि सूर्याग्नितुल्यतेजसं मानुषरूपं हस्त्यायुर्वेदपारगं मुनिकुमारं स्वास्यतलेनैव सुषुवे। तेन प्रकारेण हस्तिन्या उदरतलान्मानुषरूपं जनितं मुनिकुमारं विल**क्षत**नुं ज्ञात्वा तत्सहचराः सर्वेऽपि मातंगाः संजातभयसंभ्रमाः रींकारं कुर्वन्तः समन्ततो दिशो दश विदुद्रुवुः। सा तु करिणी पूर्वोक्त**मतंगमुने**रनुग्रहमहिम्ना विदितस्वपूर्वजन्मवृत्तान्ता स्वोदरे तस्य **सामगायनाख्यमहर्षेः** रेतःप्रवेशक्रमं तत्प्रभावेनैव स्वस्या गर्भवृद्ध्यादिकं च ज्ञात्वा निर्भया सती तथा स्वास्यतलात् बहिरुपेतं मुनिकुमारं नितरामादरेण संगृह्य मुदा तस्य महर्षेरन्तिकमनयत्। सोऽपि महर्षिस्त्रिकालज्ञस्तथा तस्या वदनतलात् संजातं स्वात्मजं ससंभ्रममादायालिंग्य देवपितृब्राह्मणादीन् नांदीक्रियादिव्रताचरणेन संमान्य तस्य कुमारस्य जातकर्मादिकं सर्वमपि यथाक्रममकरोत्। तस्मिन्नवसरे काचिदाकाशवाणी शुश्रुवे। यथा–भो भगवन् **सामगायनमहर्षे**! विधेराज्ञाबलेन करिण्यामेतस्यां मानुषरूपो जातोऽयं भवत्कुमारो धर्मात्मा प्रतिकल्पं लोकत्रयस्थितानां मदावलानां सर्वेषामपि पालयिता। काप्यगोत्रोद्भवश्च अतोऽस्य **पालकाप्य** इतीदं नाम युक्तं जगन्मंगलायेति। मुदा तदाकर्ण्य सोऽपि **मुनीश्वरः सामगायन**स्तं सुतं **पालकाप्य**नामानं कलयित्वाऽन्वग्रहीत्। एतादृशं तं मुनिकुमारं सादरमादाय सा करिणी

तस्याश्रमस्यादूरस्थले कंचित्कालं पोषयामास। स च मुनिबालकस्तामेव धेनुकां मातरं मुदान्वितोऽन्वगच्छन्नवर्धत। भो राजन् तथा वर्धितः स मुनि-कुमारोऽहमेव एवं मम जननं तावत्तस्या हस्तिन्या वदनतलादाकलितम्। तत्सहचरयूथैः साकमेव मे बाल्यक्रीडादिकमभूत्। तस्मादहं सर्वेषामपि गजानां भक्ष्यभोज्यादिद्रव्यस्वरूपं तदिंगितबृंहितचेष्टादिकं तत्प्रकोपसान्त्वन-क्रमादिकं सर्वमप्यहं जानाम्येव। एवंरीत्या स्वतपोनियमविधिमप्यंगीकृत्य तैर्गजयूथैः साकं संचरतो मे कोट्यधिकदेववर्षकालो व्यतीत एव। तस्मादेवं चिरपरिचयाद्विविधवनस्थानां विविधजातीनां सर्वेषां गजानां लक्षणादिकं सर्वमप्यहं जानामीत्युक्तवानिति **पूर्वेणान्वयः**। एवं प्रकारेण **पालकाप्यमहर्षि**स्तस्मै **रोमपादभूपालाय** स्वाविर्भावक्रममुक्त्वा संग्रहेण तस्मै गजरक्षणविधिमुप-दिशति पांसुकर्दमतोयाद्यैरित्यादिना। भो राजन् भूलोकेऽस्मिन् निवासभाजः सर्वेऽपि वारणाः पांसुकर्दमसलिलादिभिः शीतलद्रव्यैर्नित्यं क्रीडन्ति। अत एव तेषां धातुप्रसादो भवति। तद्द्वारा तेषामारोग्यमुपजायते। आरोग्यात् बलवृद्धिः। बलवृद्ध्या प्रायशो रोगनिवृत्तिश्च भवति तस्मात् स्वच्छमुदकं महीरुहः छायादिकं च गजानां मुख्यप्राणाः। अतिभारवहनादिना योजनशतदूरमार्ग-गमनागमनादिना च गजानां श्रमलवोऽपि न भवति। परन्तु सलिलाप्राप्त्यादि-नैवेति क्रमः। विमलजलमृदृतृणेक्षुकाण्डकदलीदण्डादिप्रदानेन प्रत्यहं संमानिता वारणाः स्वनायकानां विशेषतो महीपालानां जयारोग्यैश्वर्याद्यनेकसुखलक्ष्मी-र्वर्धयन्ति। एवं स्वनायकस्य रिपुबलानि कालक्रमेण क्षीणदशां नयन्ति। तस्मादुत्तमकुलजा मातंगा **नवं** गृहीतमातंगा भारवहनादिना क्लान्ता मातंगा वृद्धा गजाश्च नितरां यत्नतो रक्षणीयाः। तेषां भुक्तिप्रदानानन्तरमेवं भुंजीत। एवं कलनमेव नितरां मंगलाय भवतीति संग्रहेण **रोमपादमहीपालाय** गजपरिपालनक्रममुपदिष्टवान् **पालकाप्यो महर्षि**रिति **धार्मिकमहर्षे-र्वाक्यार्थक्रमो ज्ञेयः**।

इति श्रीमदनन्तकृष्णभट्टारकविरचितायां भावदर्शिन्याख्यायां गजशास्त्रव्याख्यायां प्रथमं प्रकरणम्॥

After completing his religious rites, the Sage came to the spot and began to call them but none came to him. Seeing that all of them were away simultanously, and feeling sorry for this absence, he started to find them out where they went. He managed to find out their feet-steps and followed them which led him to the banks of Shampā river where his elephants were tightly fastened with chains and ropes in rows. After seeing them like that, he felt sorry and shed tears. Those sages, seeing this new Sage feeling sorry and shedding tears asked him why he was so; to which he paid no heed. At that time the *Mahārājā Romapāda* came to that place and happened to see the new sage shedding tears for the sake of elephants. He then worshipped him with *Arghya-pādya* and then requested him to state what relationship he had with them and who he was as it was impossible for the human beings to control the wild elephants like that. Then the new sage began to narrate his life and relationship with them.

In ancient days, all the elephants were flying in the air with wings freely whenever they desired. On one occasion they parched on the branches of a big banyan tree in a valley of the Himalayas, which fell down into pieces owing to their huge heaviness on the hermitage of a great sage doing penance from a long time. The sage after seeing his hermitage being spoiled thoroughly, grew indignant and cursed them that they in future must not be over proud, indifferent and independent and must be controlled by the human beings.

Hearing the cruel curse of the sage, the king of elephants went to the Brahmā and represented their curse by a sage and requested him to mitigate their distress from the attack of sickness. Then Brahmā replied :—Oh elephants! don't be discouraged. Any how you must undergo the curse given by the sage. Shortly there will be another great sage, by name *Pālakāpya* born in the womb of elephants only, who will look after you all with great care and affection and you and your inheritants will be ridden of any sickness. After hearing the consoling words, they went to their abodes with great joy. Then their inheritants began to multiply in thousands on the face of the earth. Then the sage, *Pālakāpya*, after describing their first curse, began to describe his own birth thus.

Oh! King *Romapāda*! once there was a great sage by name *Sāmagāyana* in the Himalayan frontiers. As he was taking rest after completing his penance and religious rites, some herds of elephants came to that place when he fell in love with a very beautiful female elephant owing to the will of *Brahmā*.

No sooner had he fallen in love with her than he came out of his hermitage and passed semen alongwith urine, which she devoured and became pregnant. Having heard this, the *Mahārājā Romapāda* with astonishment questioned the sage as how could a female elephant devour a man's semen and become pregnant. The sage replied—Oh King! a daughter of one of the eight Vasus by name Guṇawatī went to Mataṅga's hermitage (*āśrama*) when she was very young, as the hermitage was very charming and beautiful. At that time, the sage Mataṅga with closed eyes was doing penance in a secluded place. After completing his penance, he saw her standing before him and cursed her in anger to be a female elephant that Devendra might have sent her (divine maid) to spoil his penance. In receiving the curse, she entreated the sage that she was only a young daughter of one of the eight Vasus (Divine beings) and she came to his hermitage as a pastime but not as he thought.

Then that sage understood who that girl was and why she came there by the power of his Yoga and consoled her that the curse given to her could not be retracted as it was the word of Brahmā. Again he added that she would be with bright senses though she was an elephant. Then she asked him when and how her curse could be ridden off. To which he replied that another great sage *Sāmagāyana* would pass his semen which she should devour. After doing so, a great sage *Pālakāpya* would be born to her through her mouth and with his birth her curse would be relieved, abandoning her elephant body and a girl of that Vasu once again. The sage *Sāmagāyana* repented much for his hasty action, and saw the elephant devouring the semen. He then blessed that a sage-like son should be born to her. He was then protecting that elephant for 10 months till her delivery in his *āśrama* only. The female elephant gave birth from her mouth to a beautiful sage-like son and then went away after handing over the child to the sage by her trunk. He brought me up for some time and called me by the name of *Pālakāpya*.

That son was none else except myself. Therefore I remained with the elephants thousands of years and I know their nature, conduct etc. much better than any one else. They must be well fed and given good water to drink and good shelter. As long as they are pleased, there will be no danger and fear to the kings and they will increase the prosperity and long life of their masters.

द्वितीयं प्रकरणम्

दिग्गजोत्पत्तिकथनम्

रोमपादमहीपतिरुवाच–

भगवन् वारणोत्पत्तिं बोद्धुमिच्छामि तत्त्वतः।
इत्यंगपतिना पृष्टः स महात्मा बहुश्रुतः॥
राजपुत्रनरेन्द्राय व्याचचक्षे यथागतम्।

पालकाप्य उवाच–

ससर्जादौ जलं ब्रह्मा तत्र वीर्यमपासृजत्।
हैमं तदण्डमभवत् तत्र भूतानि जज्ञिरे॥

ततो मृत्पिण्डमादाय यद्भास्वत्तेजसान्वितम्।
तन्मार्ताण्डाख्यपुत्रार्थमदित्यै प्रददौ प्रभुः॥

तद्गर्भं धारयामास सादितिर्लोकसंमता।
धृत्वा वर्षसहस्रं तत् समयेऽर्कमसूत सा॥

तस्मिन् प्रसूते सप्ताश्वे विभांति स्म दिशो दश।
तद्भित्त्वाण्डं महातेजाः भास्करः प्रययौ दिवम्॥

यदपश्यन् द्विधाभूतं सप्त ते परमर्षयः।
विस्मितास्ते तदादाय दीप्तं जग्मुर्महर्षयः॥

ब्रह्मणो भवनं भास्वत् परमं प्राप्य विस्मिताः।
पावकादित्यसंकाशैः महर्षिभिरकल्मषैः॥

सतताभ्यागतैः पुण्यं ब्रह्मघोषाभिनन्दितम्।
तत्रासीनं महात्मानं ज्वलन्तमिव पावकम्॥

प्रभवं सर्वभूतानां ददृशुस्तं महर्षयः।
तेऽभिगम्य त्रिलोकेशमभिवाद्य प्रणम्य च॥
तदण्डं दर्शयामासुर्वचनं चेदमब्रुवन्।
हस्तीह भगवन् यातः संयोक्तव्यश्च तेजसा॥
भूतानां जनने व्यक्तं स समर्थो भवेदिति।

व्याख्या—अथ **शास्त्रकारो महर्षिः पालकाप्यः** गजोत्पत्तिकथनं नाम **द्वितीयं प्रकरण**मिदमारब्धवान्। तत्रैव पूर्वकथाप्रसंगः। यथा पूर्वप्रकरण-प्रतिपादितरीत्या तस्मै **रोमपादमहीपालाय** स्वकीयजननक्रमं स्वस्य गजवृंदेषु दयादृष्टिप्राप्तिक्रमादि चोक्त्वा तस्मिन् **पालकाप्यमुनिवरे** विरमति सति भो भगवन् महर्षे पूर्वं सृष्टिकाले कथमेतेषां दिग्गजादीनां सर्वमदावलानां सृष्टिरभूत्। कया वा विधया। तत्सर्वमपि श्रोतुमभिलषामि। कृपया वदस्वेति पुनरपि प्रार्थयते तस्मै नरेन्द्राय गजोत्पत्तिक्रमं सविस्तरं वक्तुमुपचक्रमे **ससर्जादा**वित्यादिना। पूर्वमादियुगारंभे सर्वप्राणिसृष्टिकर्मणि प्रवृत्तश्चतुरान-नस्तावदादौ स्वच्छसलिलं सृष्ट्वा तेन स्ववीर्यमयोजयत्। तत्प्रभावतस्तत्सलिलं हैममण्डमभूत्। तदनु कालक्रमेण तस्य विधेः संकल्पवशेन तस्मात् सुवर्णाण्डा-देव देवगन्धर्वयक्षकिन्नरोरगमानुषपश्वादया जननमवापुः। एतद्विस्तारक्रमस्तु-**विष्णुपुराणा**दौ ज्ञेयः। एवं प्रथमतो विरचितसृष्टिक्रमः कमलासनः अन्यस्मिन् समये मृत्पिण्डं गृहीत्वा तत्र स्वतेजोविशेषसंयुक्तं-कारयित्वा देवमातरमदितिं स्वान्तिकमानीय भो देवजननि! निखिललोकहिताय एतस्मान्मृत्पिण्डात् किमपि ज्योतिरुद्भविष्यति। तदर्थं त्वमेतत् नियमयुता संरक्षेत्युक्त्वा तदण्डं तस्यै प्रायच्छत्। सापि सकुतुका तदण्डमादरेण कराभ्यां परिगृह्य तद्रक्षणजाग-रूकासीत्। एवं देववर्षसहस्रकाले गते सति शुभसमये तदण्डं भित्त्वा तन्मध्यतलात् सहस्ररश्मिः बहिरुपेत्य सर्वजीवहेतुर्भूत्वा दिवमवाप्य विधेराज्ञावशेनैव चन्द्रादिग्रहैः समेतः गगनसंचरणशीलो बभूव। एवं मृत्पिण्ड-मध्यतलात् नितरां तेजस्विनः सूर्यस्याविर्भावमाकलयन्तः तत्र सत्यलोके स्थिताः परमर्षयः विस्मिताः सन्तः तदण्डं परिगृह्य ब्रह्मर्षिभिर्भासुरां ब्रह्मणः सभां प्रविश्य यथाक्रमं प्रणम्य भो भगवन् कमलासन! विधातः! एतस्मादण्डात्

सर्वतेजोनिधिः सूर्यः जनिमवाप्य सप्ताश्वनेयमेकचक्रं रथमाकलय्य दिवि भासते। तस्मात् प्राणिजननशक्तिभासुरादस्मादण्डात् हस्तिसृष्टिमपि भवान् करोतु लोकहितायेति प्रार्थयामासुरिति **वाक्यार्थक्रमो ज्ञेयः**।।

Chapter-II

BIRTH OF ELEPHANTS

After hearing the birth of sage *Pālakāpya*, the king *Romapāda* asked him how the divine elephants were born. The sage *Pālakāpya* said—The creator Brahmā created water first and spelled some sacred divine powers in it, which became a powerful golden egg, out of that, Devas, Gandharvas, men etc. were born. At another time he took the earth and made it two (skulls) (*kapālas*) and gave them to Diti, mother of Devas. She kept them with her for thousand years repeating the *mantras* (spells) every now and then, out of which skulls, the god of light Sūrya was born. This the seven sages watched and requested Brahmā to create Elephant first out of those skulls. Accordingly, he created Irāvata-diggaja with his wife Abhramu from his right hand skull repeating the seven *Sāmaveda* hymns to the entire satisfaction of the seven Ṛiṣis.

अथ–ऐरावताख्यदिग्गजोत्पत्तिः

ततः कपाले भगवान् पाणिभ्यां प्रतिगृह्य च।
ऋषीणां तच्छुभं वाक्यं अर्थयुक्तमपूरयत्।।

अथ दक्षिणहस्तस्थात् कपालादसृजन्मृगम्।
अभिगायन्नचिन्त्यात्मा सप्तभिः सामभिर्विधिः।
जविनं बलिनं शूरं रौप्यपर्वतसन्निभम्।।

युक्तं सर्वैः प्रमाणैश्च द्युतिमन्तमनेकपम्।
मृदुना परिपूर्णेन सुवृत्तेनायतेन च।।

करेणैकेन चोपेतमाहाराघ्राणकर्मणा।
चतुर्भिरायतैस्तीक्ष्णैर्युक्तं दन्तैर्मधुप्रभैः।।

पृथुकर्णं चतुष्पादं दीर्घमाभूमिवालधिम्।
श्रीमन्तं नामधेयेन ख्यातमैरावतं नृप।।

इरावतीपुत्रभावादैरावत इति स्मृतः।

ऐरावण इति पाठे तु निरुक्तिः-

रवेण महता गायन् ससर्ज भुवि यन्मुदा।।
जन्म तस्य करेणैव तस्मादैरावणः स्मृतः।
अयमैरावतः सर्वगजश्रेष्ठः शुभावहः।।

तथा चोक्तम्-

यस्मात्सप्तभिरेकस्तु संभूतः सामभिर्गजः।
सविशिष्टतमस्तस्मात् प्रथमस्तु मतंगजः।।

कल्पान्तरे सामप्रणवादैरावतादीनामुत्पत्तिरपि श्रूयते-

सूर्यस्याण्डकपालमादिमुनिभिः सन्दर्शितं तैजसं,
पाणिभ्यां प्रतिगृह्य सप्रणववाक् सव्ये कपालं करे।
धृत्वा गायति सप्तधा कमलजे सामानि तेभ्योऽभवन्
मत्ताः सप्त मतंगजाः प्रणवतश्चान्येऽष्टधा संमतः।।

अभ्रमूत्पत्तिर्यथा-

तादृग्लक्षणसंपन्नां चतुर्दन्तविवर्जिताम्।
हस्तिनीं सव्यहस्तस्थात् कपालादसृजत्प्रभुः।।

नाम्ना च या भ्रमुः ख्याता तस्य भार्या बभूव सा।
कायेन कर्षतीवाभ्राण्यभ्रमुस्तेन गीयते।।

लक्षणव्यंजनोपेतः सोऽभ्रम्वा सह भार्यया।
वनानि विचरन् क्रीडन् रम्याणि सुरभीणि च।
आत्मानुरूपानेतस्यां जवनेन बलेन च।।

तेजसा चापि संपन्नान् पुत्रांश्च जनयिष्यसि।
सर्वान् लोकांश्च गच्छ त्वं कामरूपी भविष्यसि।।

इति स ब्रह्मणादिष्टो विचचार यथासुखम्।

व्याख्या—तत इति। एवं सप्तर्षिप्रार्थनामंगीकृत्य स तु कमलासनः स्वकराभ्यां तदण्डमादाय तच्च स्वकरकमलधृतकपालान्तःस्थलं नीत्वा क्षणकालं मौनमंगीकृत्य ध्यात्वा मनोहराणि सप्तसामानि गायन् सन् कपालादस्मात् कोऽपि मनोहररूपो हस्ती भवत्विति संकल्पमकरोत्। तथा विधिना तेन संकल्पे कृते सति तत्क्षणादेव तदीयदक्षिणकरस्थितकपालात् कोऽपि मतंगजो बहिरागतः। स किल वारणः कीदृश इति चेत् तदंग-स्वरूपलक्षणादिकं संग्रहेण विशदयति **शास्त्रकारः**—जविनमित्यादिना। स तु मतंगजः सर्वगजापेक्षया नितरां वेगवान्। गगनतलादिगननोचितमनोहर-पक्षयुगलसमेतः। नितरां बलशाली। सर्वेष्वप्यवयवेषु रौप्यखण्डवन्मनोहर-श्वेतवर्णयुतः। उत्तरत्र वक्ष्यमाणभद्राख्यगजोत्तमप्रमाणसहितः। नितरामायत-मृदुशुण्डादण्डोपेतः। मुखभागे मधुवर्णभासुरपृथुदन्तचतुष्कसहितः। पृथुकर्ण-युगलोपेतः। चतुर्भिः पादैरुपेतः। दीर्घवालधिश्चेति। अत एवं लक्षणोपेतं कपालादुत्थितं तं गजरत्नमाकलय्य कमलासनः परमानन्दभरितः सन् भो मृग त्वमेव सर्वगजेषूत्तमः। ऐरावत इति नाम वोढुमर्हसीत्युक्त्वा प्रीत्यतिशयात् स्वकरतलेन तदंगान्यामृज्य आशीर्वचनान्युदीरयत्। अत्र **ऐरावत इति पाठस्यार्थक्रमो** यथा—इरावती सरस्वती। तस्याः पुत्रत्वेन तद्व्यवहारो युज्यत इति। **ऐरावण इति पाठे** तु **शास्त्रकार** एव निष्पत्तिमाकलयति—रवेणेति। अस्य **विशदार्थस्तु**—पूर्वोक्तरीत्या यस्मात्स विधाता उच्चैः स्वरेण सप्तसामगीतिं गायन् सन् गजमिममसृजत्; तेनैव कारणेन ऐरावणनामभाक् स बभूवेति **केषांचित् पूर्वतनमहर्षीणामा**शयमपि व्यक्तीकृतवानिति **तत्क्रमः**। किं चास्यैव गजस्य श्रेष्ठत्वे हेतुस्तु—यस्मादित्यस्मिन् श्लोके प्रतिपादितः। यथा—सप्तसामशक्तिवशादेव अयमेको गजो निर्मितः। तस्मादस्यैव विशिष्टतमत्वं युज्यत इति। किं चात्र गजसृष्टिक्रमे **अन्येषां केषांचिन्मुनीनां मतान्तरम**प्याह **शास्त्रकारः** सूर्यस्येति। पूर्वं गजसृष्टिसमये विधाता तावदादिमुनिभिर्निर्दिष्टं सूर्यजनकमण्डमादाय स्वपाणिभ्यां धृत्वा सानन्दं प्रणवोच्चारणपूर्वकं सप्त-सामगीतिं यावदाकलयामास; तावत् तेभ्यः सामस्वरूपेभ्यः सप्तमतंगजाः प्रणवस्वरूपा**दय**मैरावतश्चाविरासीदिति। एवं प्रकारेण सर्वगजश्रेष्ठस्यास्य ऐरावतस्य सृष्टिं विरचय्य रचयित्वा तस्य पत्नीमभ्रमुनामधेयां तत्सदृशलक्षण-

Fig.3 : ऐरावत-दिग्गज
Airāvata-diggaja, a divine elephant.

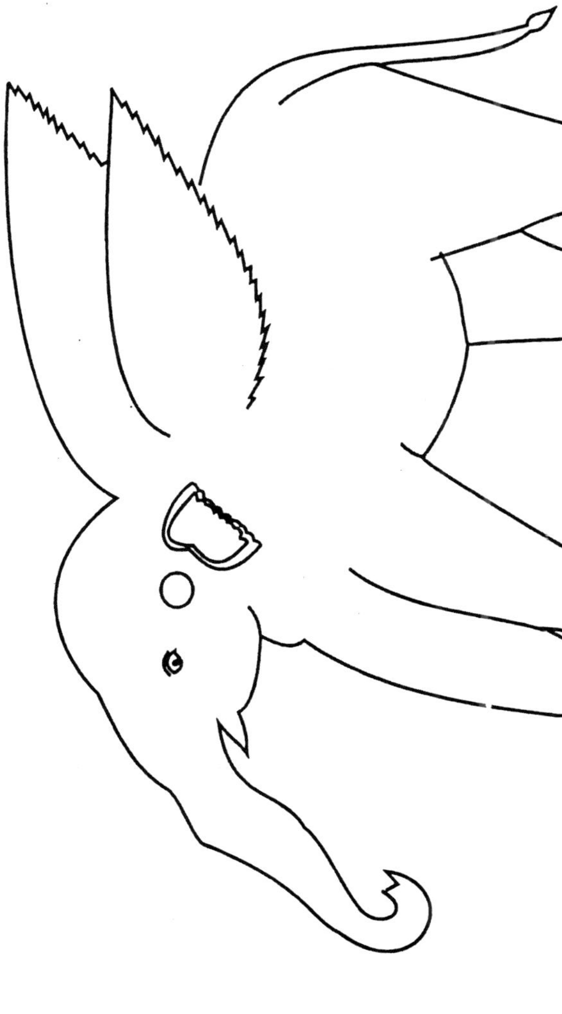

Fig.4. : अभ्रमु–Abhramu, a female-elephant, wife of Irāvata-diggaja.

गुणादिनोपेतां तादृशचतुर्दन्तहीनां हस्तिनीमसृजत्किल एवमादिगजदंपती सृष्ट्वा मुदिताशयः कमलासनः भो गजराज ऐरावत। सकलसद्गुणोपेतस्त्वं कामरूपी सन् सर्वलोकसंचारशीलो भूत्वा अनया अभ्रम्वाख्यया भार्यया सह रमणीयप्रदेशेषु विहरन् सन् त्वत्सदृशसौशील्यादिसद्गुणमण्डितान् पुत्रान् सृजन् मोदस्वेत्यनुगृह्य प्रेषयामासेति **वाक्यार्थक्रमो ज्ञेयः**।।

Nature and conduct of Airāvata-diggaja

Irāvata-diggaja is white throughout his body like silver and he has four big tusks, two wings and a long tail. He is very tall, strong, powerful and most beautiful.

अथ-पुण्डरीकाख्यदिग्गजोत्पत्तिः॥ (2)

मुनयः-

अथ विश्वसृजं देवमिदमूचुर्महर्षयः।
दृष्टिकान्तमिदं सत्त्वं सृष्टं भगवता महत्॥
यथैष हि तथैवान्यान् सृजस्व भगवन्निति।
ततस्तेषां वचः श्रुत्वा भविष्यत्सप्रयोजनम्॥
अनुपश्यन् पुनः सृष्टान् ससर्जान्यान् मृगोत्तमान्।
साम्ना रथन्तरेणाथ पत्न्या कपिलया सह॥
पुण्डरीकवनप्रख्यं पुण्डरीकं मृगोत्तमम्।

पुण्डरीकशब्दनिरुक्तिः-

श्वेतांभोरुहवर्णत्वात् पुण्डरीक इति स्मृतः।

व्याख्या—अथेति। एवमभ्रम्वाख्यया हस्तिन्या सहितस्य ऐरावतस्य सर्वगजश्रेष्ठस्य सौन्दर्यसौशील्यादिकं विलोक्य परमानन्दकन्दलितान्तः-करणास्ते आदिमहर्षयः अन्यस्मिन् समये पुनरपि ब्रह्मणः सविधं गत्वा यथाक्रमं प्रणम्याभिवाद्य भो भगवन् विधातः नयनानन्दकरोऽयमैरावतो भवता निर्मितः किल; एवमेव भवानन्यांश्च कांश्चित् गजोत्तमान् लोकहिताय सृजत्विति प्रार्थयामासुः। सोऽपि विधाता तां च प्रार्थनां साधु मत्वा पूर्ववत् विविधसामगाथापठनेन तस्मात्कपालादेवान्यान् सप्तमदावलानसृजदिति **वाक्यार्थः**। तत्रैवं तेषां सृष्टिक्रमो ज्ञेयः। यथा रथन्तराख्यसाम्नः पठनेन कपिलाख्यया भार्यया सहितं श्वेतवर्णभासुरमैरावततुल्यस्वरूपादिकं पुण्डरीकाख्यं गजमथो ससर्जेति।

After some time Brahmā created another elephant, Puṇḍarīka-diggaja, with his wife Kapilā, white in colour like lotus, almost equal to Irāvata, repeating the Rathantara-

Fig. 5. : पुण्डरीक-दिग्गज Puṇḍarīka-diggaja, a divine elephant.

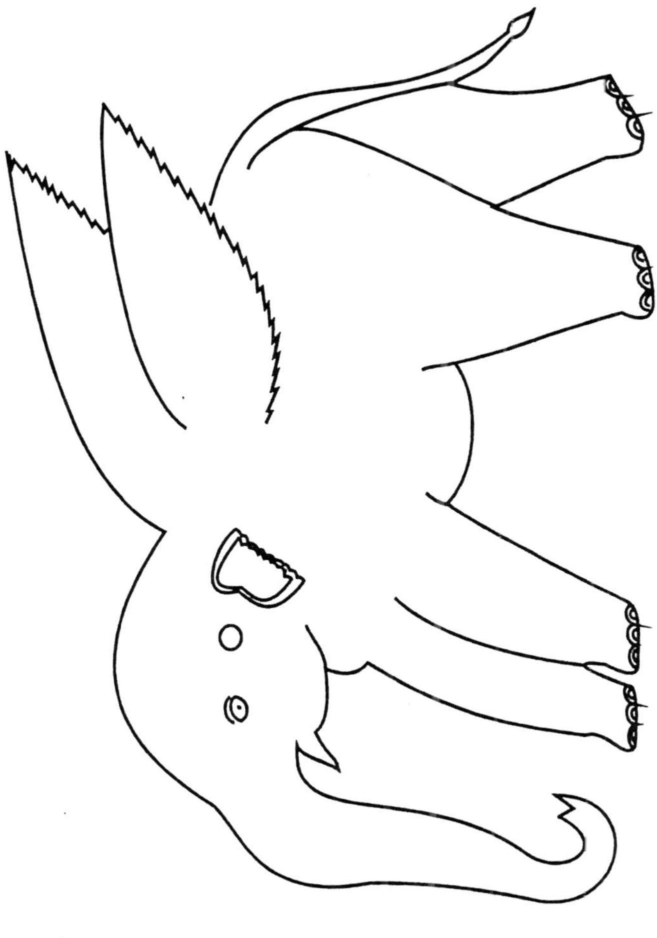

Fig.-6. : कपिला–Kapilā, a female elephant, wife of Puṇḍarīka-diggaja.

sāmaveda-hymns, at the request of the seven sages, the councillors of Brahmā.

अथ पुण्पदन्ताख्यदिग्गजोत्पत्तिः (3)

ततोऽसृजत् बृहत्साम्ना ताम्रकर्ण्या समं प्रभुः।
दन्तैश्च पुष्पवर्णाभैः पुष्पदन्तं महामृगम्॥

पुष्पदन्तपदनिरुक्तिः-

षट्पुष्पवर्णदन्तोऽयं पुष्पदन्त इति स्मृतः।

पुष्पाणि तान्याह–

चंपकारुणराजीवमल्लिकाकेतकांबुजम्।
बन्धूकप्रसवश्चेति षट्पुष्पाणि प्रचक्षते॥

व्याख्या–तत इति। एवं पुण्डरीकाख्यं गजं सृष्ट्वाऽनन्तरं स विधाता बृहत्साम्नः पठनेन पूर्ववत् तस्मात्कपालात् ताम्रकर्णाख्यया हस्तिन्या समेतं रक्तांबुजवत् किंचिद्रक्तवर्णभासुरशरीरं विकसितमल्लीकुसुमवत् श्वेत-वर्णैर्मनोहरैश्चतुर्भिरायर्दन्तैश्चोपेतं पुण्डरीकगजतुल्यस्वरूपं पुष्पदन्ताख्यं गजश्रेष्ठं च क्रमान्निर्मितवानिति **वाक्यार्थक्रमः**॥

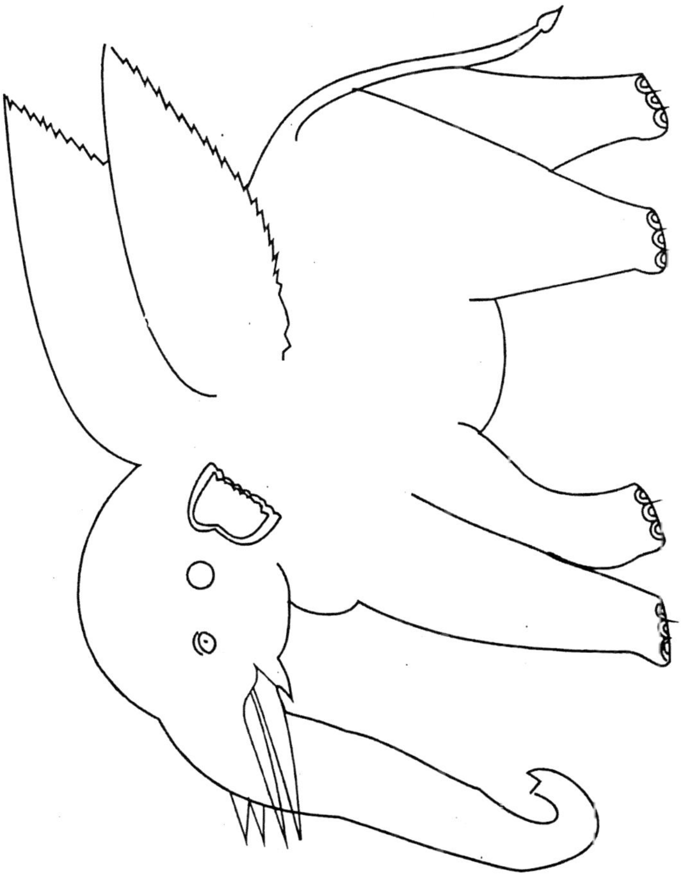

Fig.-7. : पुष्पदन्त-दिग्गज Puṣpadanta-diggaja, a divine elephant.

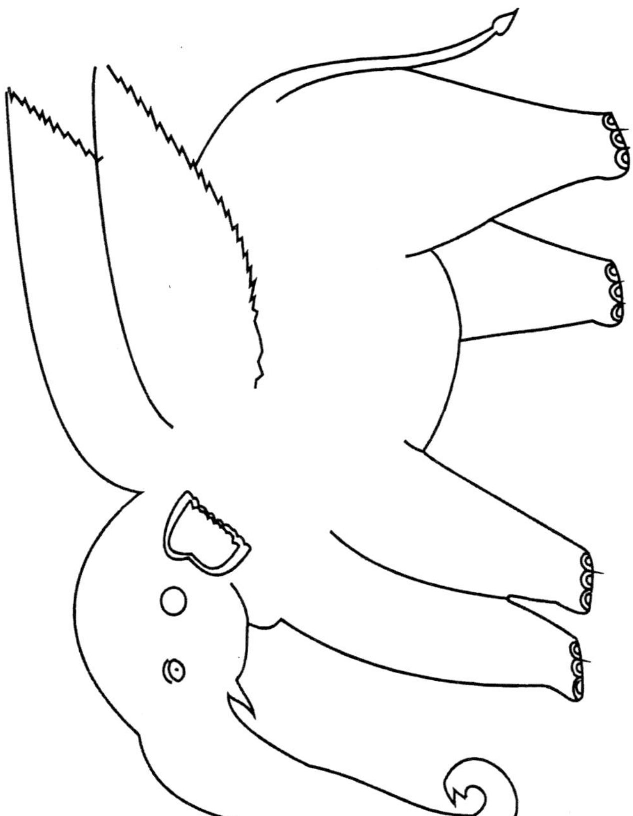

Fig.-8. : ताम्रकर्णी, Tāmrakarṇī, a female-elephant, wife of Puṣpadanta diggaja.

Again Brahmā created another elephant, Puṣpadanta-diggaja, with his wife Tāmrakarṇī, white in colour as jasmine flowers, repeating the Bṛhat-sāmaveda-hymn.

अथ वामनाख्यदिग्गजोत्पत्तिक्रमः (4)

श्यामं श्यामघनप्रख्यं वशयांगनया सह।
वामनं वामदेव्येन साम्ना नागं च निर्ममे।।

वामनशब्दनिरुक्तिः-

वामनो वामनैर्दन्तैः मातंगः परिकीर्तितः।

व्याख्या—श्याममिति। एवं पुष्पदन्ताख्यं गजोत्तमं सृष्ट्वाऽनन्तरं स किल पद्मासनः यथाक्रमं वामदेव्याख्यस्य साम्नः पठनेन पूर्ववत् तस्मात् कपालादेव अंगनाख्यया हस्तिन्या समेतं सजलमेघवत् नीलवर्णछुरितांगं वामनाख्यं दिग्गजमप्यसृजत्। किंच-एवं प्रकारेण निर्मितोऽयं वारणः पूर्वोक्तैरावतपुण्डरीकपुष्पदन्ताख्यानां गजश्रेष्ठानां प्रमाणापेक्षया किंचिद्वामनस्तथैव वामनदन्तचतुष्कभासुरश्चाविरभूदिति क्रमः। तथापि पूर्वोक्तपुण्डरीकादितुल्यसौशील्यपराक्रमादियुत एवेति व्यवस्था चोह्या।।

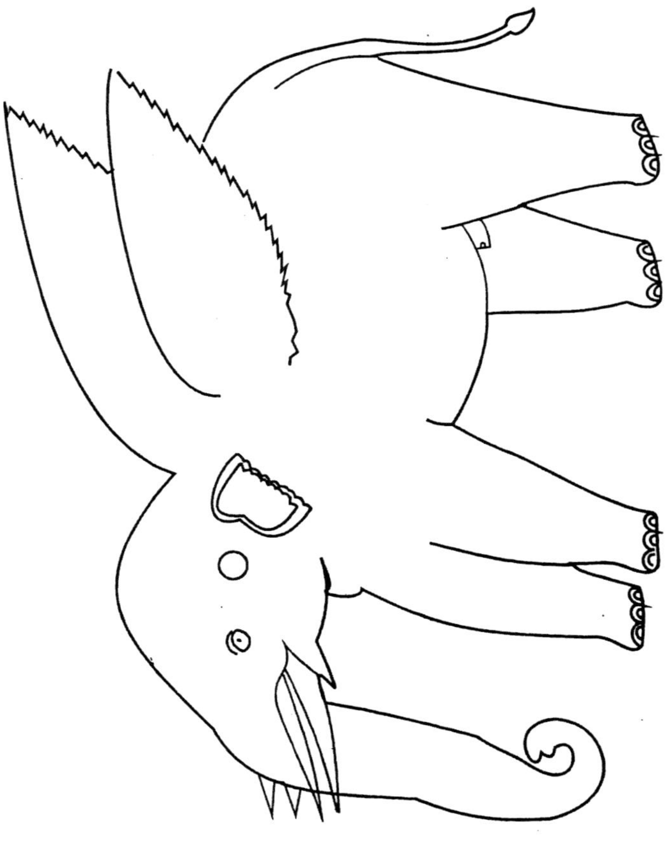

Fig. 9. : वामन दिग्गज—Vāmana-diggaja, a divine elephant.

Fig. 10. : अंगना-Aṅganā, a female elephant, wife of Vāmana-diggaja

Then Brahmā created another elephant, Vāmana-diggaja, with his wife Aṅganā, blue in colour like clouds, shorter than the previous ones, repeating Vāmadevya-sāmaveda-hymn.

अथ सुप्रतीकाख्यदिग्गजोत्पत्तिक्रमः (5)

सुप्रतीकं महावीर्यं सहानुपमया प्रभुः।
वैरूपेणैव साम्ना च नागं नाम्ना विनिर्ममे।।

सुप्रतीकशब्दनिरुक्तिः-

सुन्दरावयवा यस्य सुप्रतीकः प्रकीर्तितः।

व्याख्या–सुप्रतीकमिति। एवं वामनाख्यं दिशागजं सृष्ट्वाऽनन्तरं स किल विधाता वैरूपाख्यस्य साम्नः यथाक्रमं पठनेन पूर्ववत् तस्मात् कपालमध्यतलादेव अनुपमाख्यया नितरां मनोहरांग्या हस्तिन्या समेतं राकाचन्द्रमरीचिनिचयप्रसारवत् श्वेतवर्णछुरितांगं सुप्रतीकाख्यं गजोत्तममप्य-सृजत्। एवं निर्मितस्यास्य गजश्रेष्ठस्य मुखशुण्डाद्याः सर्वेऽप्यवयवाः पूर्वनिर्मितगजसौन्दर्यापेक्षया सौन्दर्याधिक्यभासुराः। अतोऽस्य सुप्रतीकव्यवहारत्वं युक्तमिति **परमर्षयः प्राचीनाः**।

Afterwards, Brahmā created another elephant, Supratīka-diggaja with his wife Anupamā, white in colour like moon-light, repeating Vairūpa Sāmaveda-hymn. This pair is the most beautiful of all the others.

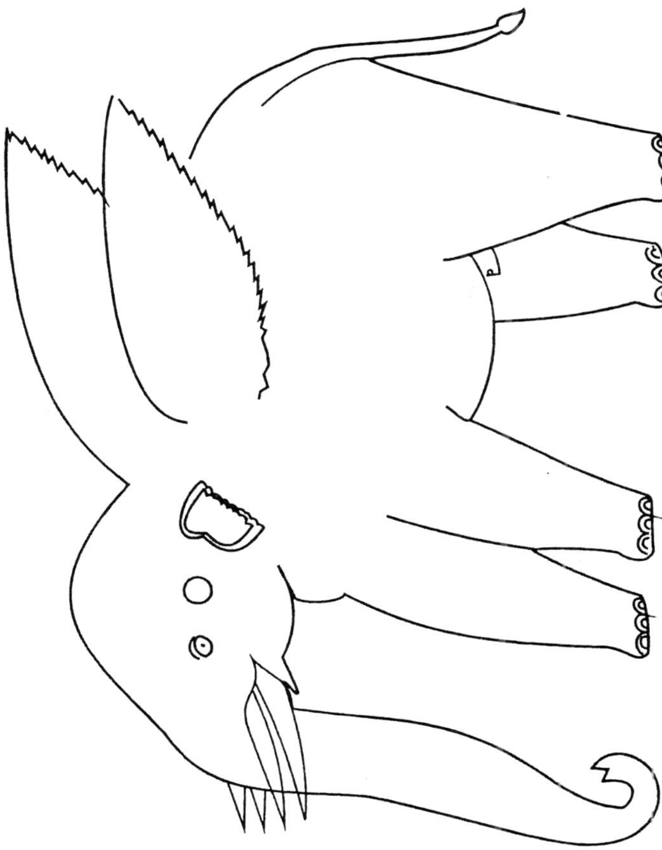

Fig. 11. : सुप्रतीक–दिग्गज—Supratīka-diggaja

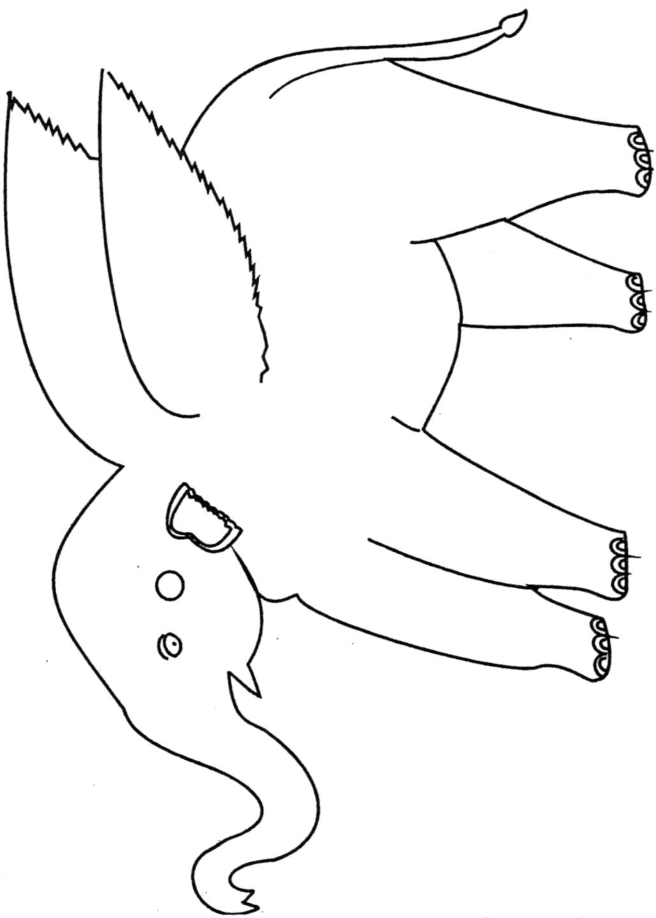

Fig.12. : अनुपमा–Anupamā, a female elephant, wife of Supratīka-diggaja.

अथ-अंजनाख्यदिग्गजोत्पत्तिः (6)

साम्ना च परमानेन गजमंजनसन्निभम्।
वशयांजनवत्यासावंजनं नाम निर्ममे॥

अंजनशब्दनिरुक्तिः-

अंजनाद्रिसवर्णोऽयं सोंऽजनः परिकीर्तितः।

व्याख्या—साम्ना चेति। एवमुक्तप्रकारेण सुप्रतीकाख्यं गजोत्तमं सृष्ट्वाऽनन्तरं स तु विधाता यथाक्रमं पवमानाख्यसाम्नः पठनेन पूर्ववत् तस्मात्कपालादेव अंजनवत्याख्यया करिण्या संयुक्तमंजनगिरिकान्तिपुंजवत् निबिडकृष्ण-कांतिझरीछुरितसर्वावयवं अंजनाख्यं दिशागजमपि निर्मितवान्। एवं निर्मितोऽयं गजश्च पूर्वोक्तगजतुल्यपराक्रमसौशील्याद्यन्वित एवेति क्रमः॥

Again Brahmā created another elephant, Añjana-diggaja, with his wife Vaśā, jet black in colour, repeating Pavamāna-sāmaveda-hymn.

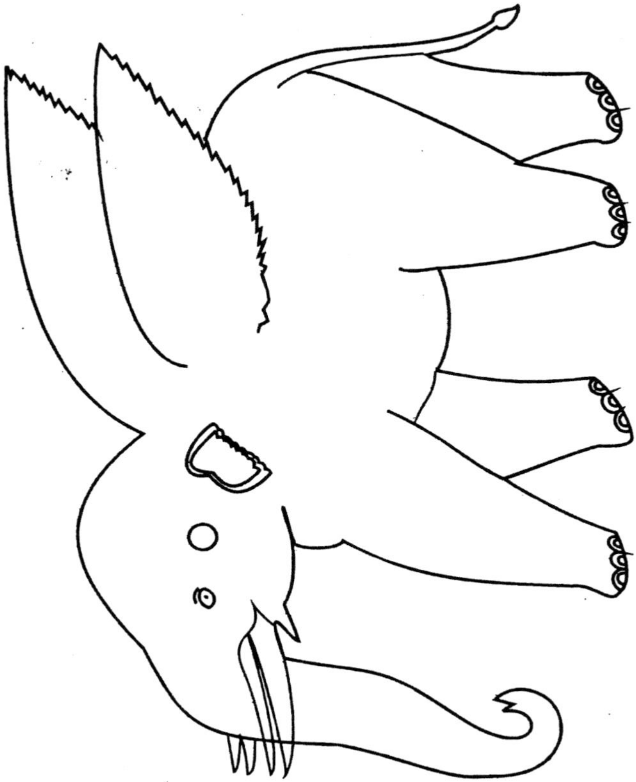

Fig. 13. : अंजनदिग्गज–Añjana-diggaja, a divine-elephant.

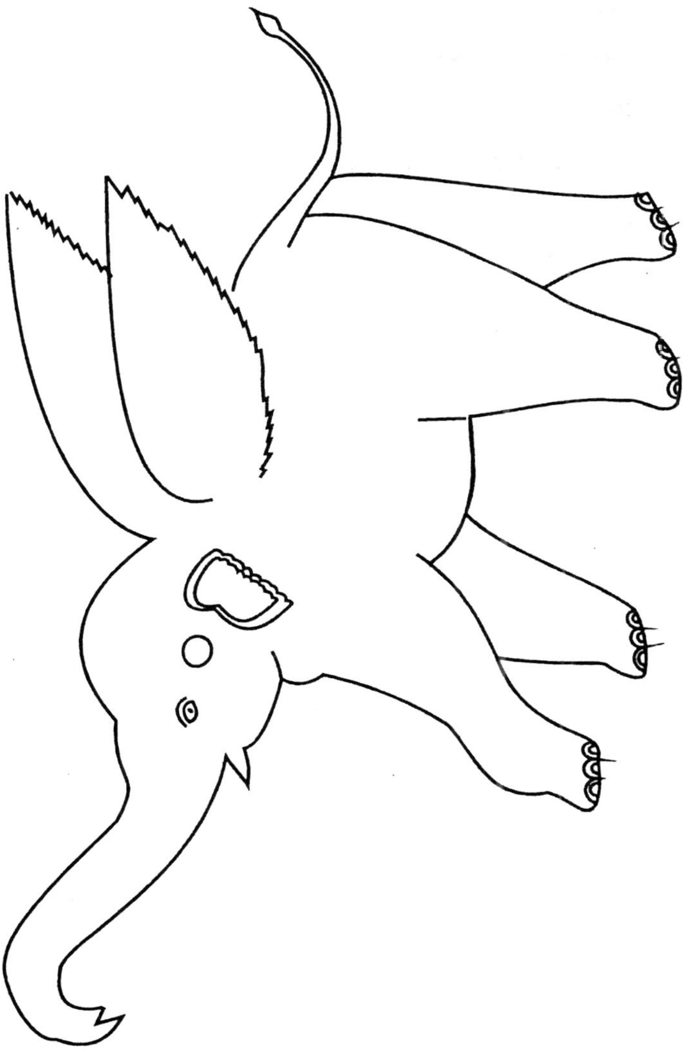

Fig. 14. : वशा–Vaśā, female elephant, wife of Añjana-diggaja.

अथ-सार्वभौमाख्यदिग्गजोत्पत्तिः (7)

वैराजेनैव पद्माभं पद्मिनं पद्मसंभवः।
असृजत् सार्वभौमं च शुभ्रदन्तां च दंतिनीम्॥

सार्वभौमशब्दनिरुक्तिः-

सर्वस्मादधिको भूम्ना सार्वभौम इति स्मृतः।

व्याख्या–वैराजेनैवेति। एवमंजनाख्यं वारणोत्तमं सृष्ट्वाऽनन्तरं स तु पद्मासनः पूर्ववत् यथाक्रमं वैराजाख्यमुत्तमं साम गायन् सन् तस्मात् कपालादेव शरत्कालविकसितकमलोदरकान्तिपूरवत् किंचिच्छ्वेतरक्तवर्णझरीकवचित-सर्वावयवं मनोहरातिदीर्घशुण्डादण्डं शुभ्रदन्त्याख्यया वशया संयुक्तं सार्व-भौमाख्यं गजोत्तममप्यसृजत्। एवं प्रकारेण सृष्टोऽयं वारणः पूर्वनिर्दिष्टैरावतादि-वारणापेक्षया बलपराक्रमसौशील्यसौन्दर्यादिषु किंचिदाधिक्यशाली। अतोऽस्यैव सार्वभौमव्यवहारो युक्त इति॥

Then Brahmā created another elephant, Sārva-bhauma-diggaja with his wife Śubhradantī, white in colour like lotus, repeating Vairāja-sāmaveda hymn.

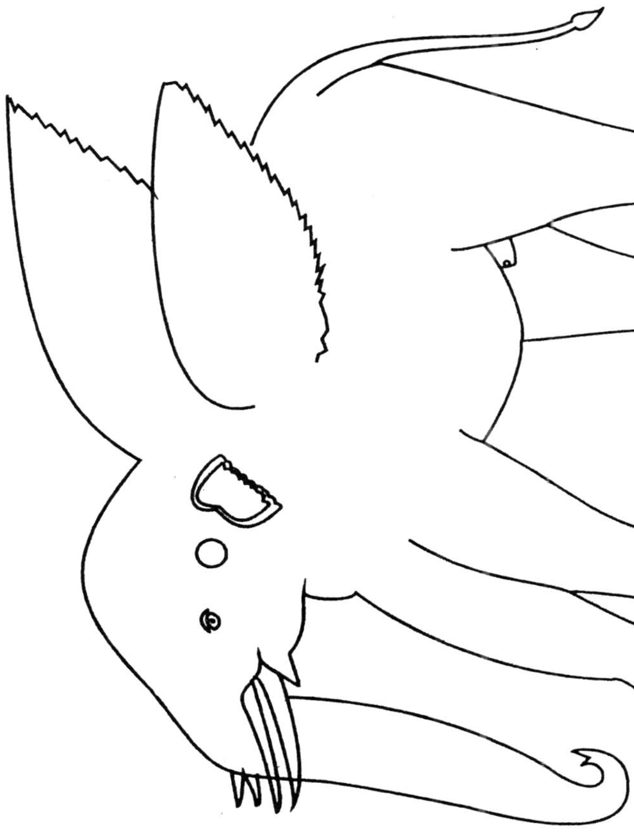

Fig. 15. : सार्वभौम–दिग्गज–Sārvabhauma-diggaja, a divine elephant.

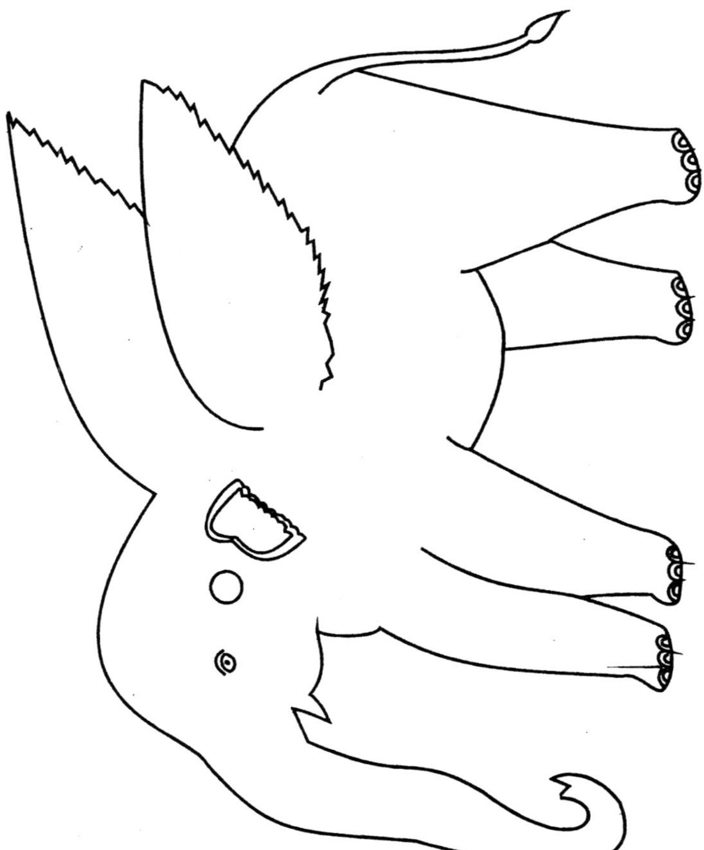

Fig. 16. : शुभ्रदन्ती—Śubhradantī, a female elephant, wife of Sārvabhauma diggaja.

अथ कुमुदाख्यदिग्गजोत्पत्तिः (8)

साम्ना चन्द्रमसेनापि चक्रे पिंगलया सह।
कुमुदं कुमुदप्रख्यं नागं नागवरोपमम्॥

कुमुदशब्दनिरुक्तिः-

कूनां मुदं यः करोति कुमुदः स निगद्यते।
अथवा कुमुदप्रख्यः कुमुदोऽयं प्रकीर्तितः॥

ऐरावतः पुण्डरीकः पुष्पदन्तोऽथ वामनः।
सुप्रतीकोंऽजनः सार्वभौमः कुमुद इत्यपि॥

एते यथाक्रमं प्रोक्ताः पूर्वादीनां दिशां गजाः।
अभ्रमुः कपिला ताम्रकर्णी चाथांगना पुनः॥

तथैवानुपमा चाथांजनवत्येव धेनुका।
शुभ्रदन्ती पिंगला चे[त्ये]ता दिग्गजधेनुकाः॥

इत्यष्टदिग्गजानामुत्पत्तिः॥

व्याख्या—एवंप्रकारेण सार्वभौमाख्यमुत्तमदिग्गजं सृष्ट्वा तदनु स विधाता पूर्ववत् **चन्द्र**मसाख्यं साम गायन् सन् पिंगलाख्यया हस्तिन्या समेतं विकसितसितकुमुदवत् मनोहरश्वेतवर्णच्छुरितांगं नितरां हृष्टमत एव पूर्वोक्तैरावतसार्वभौमगजतुल्यदर्शनं देवादीनामपि नयनानन्दकरं कुमुदाख्यं दिग्गजमपि तस्मात् कपालादेवासृजदिति **लक्षणवाक्यार्थः**। किंच एवंप्रकारेण सृष्टस्य यस्य यस्य पुंगजस्य शरीरे यो यो वर्णक्रमो निगदितः स एव वर्णप्रकरस्तस्य तस्य पत्न्याः करिण्याः शरीरेऽपि भासनशील इति **भावः**। तदानीमेव दिव्यगजदंपत्यौपम्यम्। तस्मादेव पुंगजानां तत्करिणीनां च शरीरवर्णतौल्येऽपि तादृशपुंगजप्रमाणापेक्षया करिण्यस्ताः सर्वा अपि औन्नत्ये किंचिन्न्यूनप्रमाणा एव। अयं च क्रमः उत्तरत्र वक्ष्यमाणमानवकरिणीषु सर्वास्वपि द्रष्टव्य इति **शास्त्रसमयः**। एवं तेषां पुंदिग्गजानां दीर्घमनोहरदन्तचतुष्कप्राप्तिः मनोहरपक्षयुगलमेलनं चाजन्मसिद्धम्। करिणीनां तासां तु नितरां ह्रस्वदन्तप्राप्तिः। तथापि पुंगजानामिव मनोहरपक्षयुगलप्राप्तिश्च आजन्मसिद्धा। एवं भेदे सत्यपि

करिण्यस्ताः सर्वा अपि स्वस्ववल्लभानुगुण- सौशील्यादिसद्गुणचर्यासमेताः मनोहराङ्ग्यः कामरूपाः तैः साकं संचरणशीला एव। एवं तत्त**द्दिक्तटम**वाप्य रेजुरिति व्यवस्था। अपि च-एवं रीत्या कमलासनेन तेन सृष्टिकर्त्रा सामगी-त्युच्चारणपूर्वकं निर्मितेषु गजेष्वष्टसु-

ऐरावतो दिग्गजः	वासवदिशोऽधिपतिरभूत्।
पुण्डरीकाख्यदिग्गजः	वह्निदिशोऽधिपतिरभूत्।
पुष्पदन्ताख्यो दिग्गजः	यमदिशोऽधिपतिरभूत्।
वामनाख्यदिग्गजः	निर्ऋतिदिशोऽधिपतिरभूत्।
सुप्रतीकाख्यदिग्गजः	वरुणदिशोऽधिपतिरभत्।
अंजनाख्यदिग्गजः	वायुदिशोऽधिपतिरभूत्।
सार्वभौमाख्यदिग्गजः	कुबेरदिशोऽधिपतिरभूत्।
कुमुदाख्यदिग्गजः	ईशानदिशोऽधिपतिरभूत्।

अत एव एतेषां दिग्गजव्यवहारो युक्त इति मर्यादा। किंच-एवमत्रोक्ता गजा एव तत्तद्दिङ्मुखसंरक्षकाश्चाभूवन्निति पुराणवचनमप्यंगीकृत्यैव **शास्त्रकारः पालकाप्यो महर्षिः** 'एते यथाक्रमं प्रोक्ताः पूर्वादीनां दिशां गजा' इत्युक्तवान्। तस्मादेतेषु गजोत्तमेषु कस्मिन् वा समये किमर्थं केन वा प्रकारेण तत्तद्दिक्संरक्षणधूरारोपितेति चेत् तत्सर्वमपि **विष्णुपुराणादौ** ज्ञेयम्। विस्तर-भयान्नात्रोच्यत इति।।

Again Brahmā created another elephant, Kumuda-diggaja, with his wife Piṅgalā, white in colour like night-lotus, repeating Candramāsa sāmaveda-hymns.

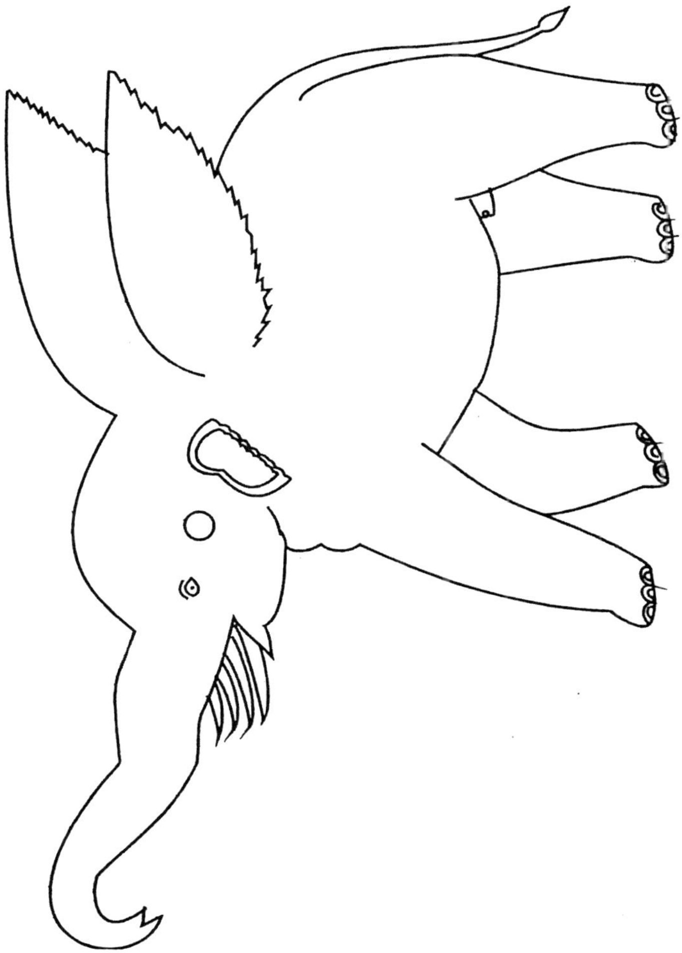

Fig.17 : कुमुद दिग्गज–Kumuda-diggaja, a divine elephant.

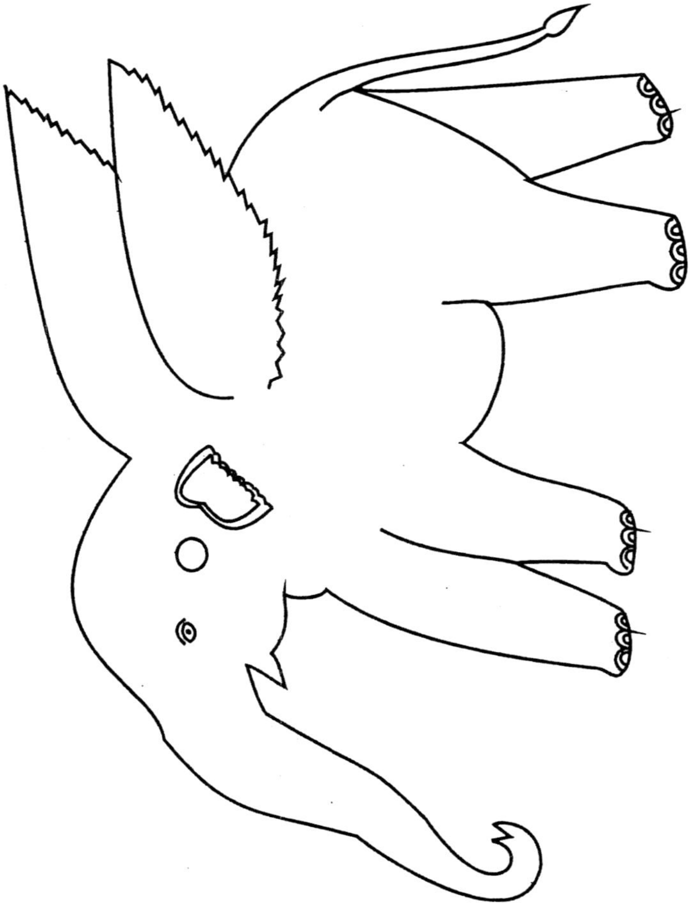

Fig. 18. : पिंगला–Pingalā, a female elephant, wife of Kumuda-diggaja.

अथ-दिग्गजसन्तानोत्पत्तिक्रमः॥

तत्र प्रथमस्य ऐरावतदिग्गजस्य सन्तानोत्पत्तिक्रमः (1)

मूलम्

सपक्षाः कामरूपास्ते विचेरुः पृथिवीतले।
स्थानेषु रमणीयेषु करिणीभिः समन्विताः॥
सर्वलक्षणसंपन्नानष्टौ कैलासवर्चसः।
अभ्रम्व्यां जनयामास पुत्रानैरावतो गजः॥
मेघः पद्मोदरोऽरिष्टश्चपलो रुचिरोंऽगदः।
अरुजः पद्मगुल्फश्च तस्याष्टौ जज्ञिरे सुताः॥
दीर्घशुण्डः सितश्रोत्रदन्तरोमाक्षिवालधिः।
मतंगजो महाकायः सोऽयमैरावतान्वयः॥

व्याख्या—एतावता प्रबन्धेनाष्टानां दिग्गजानां तत्पत्नीनां च सृष्टिक्रम-स्वरूपगुणादिकं प्रतिपाद्याधुना तस्मिन्नेव युगे तादृशदिग्गजेभ्यो जनितानां पुत्रगजानां स्वरूपलक्षणादिकं विशदयति **शास्त्रकारः**-सपक्षा इत्यादिना। पूर्वोक्तरीत्या स्वेच्छानुगुणं संप्राप्तविविधकामगतिशरीरेषु मनोहरपक्षयुगलसमेतेषु तेष्वष्टसु दिशागजेषु मनोहराभिः स्वस्वहस्तिनीभिः साकं वसन्तादिसमय-रमणीयेषु भूतलेषु क्रीडत्सु सत्सु तत्र ऐरावताख्यो गजश्रेष्ठस्तावत् स्वपत्न्याम-भ्रम्व्यामष्टपुत्रानुत्पादयामास। तेषां नामानि यथा— मेघः, (1), पद्मोदरः (2), अरिष्टः (3), चपलः (4), रुचिरः (5), अंगदः (6), अरुजः (7), पद्मगुल्फः (8) इति। एवं नाम्ना भासुरास्ते सर्वेऽप्यष्टौ तनया अत्यन्तं दीर्घशुण्डादण्डोपेताः सर्वेष्वप्यवयवेषु श्वेतवर्णयुता अपि चतुर्षु दन्तेषु अक्षिसमीपतलेषु वालधिप्रदेशेषु च श्वेतिमाधिक्ययुताः स्वपितुरैरावतस्येव मनोहरपक्षयुगलवन्तस्तुंगशरीरा अपि विरेजुरिति **लक्षणवाक्यार्थः**। इदमेव मुख्यं लक्षणं ऐरावतसन्तानगजेषु दृश्यमिति **शास्त्रकारः**॥

॥ अथ द्वितीयस्य पुण्डरीकाख्यदिग्गजस्य सन्तानोत्पत्तिक्रमः (2)॥

मूलम्

पुण्डरीकोऽप्यजनयत् कपिलायां सुतानिमान्।
चतुरो हन्निरित्थं च सुप्रदिष्टं प्रमर्दिनम्॥

जीमूतं चात्मनस्तुल्यानात्मतुल्यपराक्रमान्।
कुब्जरोमा बृहत्कुंभः क्रोधनः सारसेक्षणः।।
अखण्डायतशुण्डोऽयं पुण्डरीकान्वयः करी।

व्याख्या–अथ-द्वितीयस्य पुण्डरीकाख्यदिग्गजस्य कतिपयाः पुत्रा इत्याकांक्षायामाह–पुण्डरीकोऽपीति। पूर्वोक्तलक्षणोपेतः पुण्डरीकाख्यदिग्गजोऽपि कपिलाख्यायां स्वपत्न्यां हन्निरित्थं(1), सुप्रदिष्टं(2), प्रमर्दनं(3), जीमूतं(4), इति नामभाज आहत्य संख्यायां चतुरः पुत्रानुत्पादयामास। एतेऽपि चत्वारः पुण्डरीकदिग्गजपुत्राः स्वजनकस्येव दन्तचतुष्कभाजः शुद्ध- श्वेतवर्णभासुरांगाः गरुद्युगलसमेताः सर्वेष्वप्यवयवेषु क्षुद्रह्रस्वनिबिडरोमयुताः कमलदलवत् रक्तवर्णनयनांचलाः नितरां दीर्घशुण्डाः किंचित्कोपयुताश्च जज्ञिर इति **वाक्यार्थः**। इदमेव मुख्यं लक्षणं पुण्डरीकसन्तानगजेषु दृश्यमिति **भावः**।।

।। अथ तृतीयस्य पुष्पदन्ताख्यदिग्गजस्य सन्तानोत्पत्तिक्रमः (3)।।

मूलम्

पुष्पदन्तस्ताम्रकर्ण्यां तथाजनयदात्मजान्।
विषह्यं साहसं रिक्को विचित्राह्वं विचारिणम्।।
स्थूलबिन्दुधनुर्वंशः कृष्णरोमा कृशोदरः।
पृथुलस्कन्धहस्तोऽयं पुष्पदन्तान्वयोद्भवः।।

व्याख्या–अथ तृतीयस्य पुष्पदन्ताख्यस्य दिग्गजस्य सन्तानलक्षणमाह–पुष्पदन्त इति। पुष्पदन्ताख्यो दिग्गजः ताम्रकर्ण्याख्यायां स्वपत्न्यामीषद्रक्तवर्ण-भासुरांगान् स्थूलबिन्दुपुंजितशुण्डादण्डान् कृष्णवर्णरोमराजियुतान् कृशोद-रानत्यन्तं पृथुलस्कन्धभागान् पंच पुत्रान् जनयामास। तेषां नामानि यथा-विषह्यः (1), साहसः (2), रिक्कः (3), विचित्रः (4), विचारीति (5), तस्मादस्य पुष्पदन्तगजस्य सन्ततिजनितानां सर्वेषामपि गजानां पूर्वोक्त-स्थूलबिन्द्वादिरेव मुख्यं लक्षणमाकलनीयमिति मर्यादा।।

॥ अथ-चतुर्थस्य वामनाख्यदिग्गजस्य सन्तानोत्पत्तिक्रमः (4) ॥

मूलम्

अंगनायामजनयत् वामनोऽपि सुतं गजः।
स्निग्धनीलांबुदप्रख्यं नाम्ना नीलांबुदं नृप॥
जवी जलविहारेच्छुः दीर्घहस्तोऽग्निवर्णयुक्।
विस्तारायामवानेष वारणो वामनान्वयः॥

व्याख्या—अथ चतुर्थस्य वामनाख्यस्य दिग्गजस्य पुत्रलक्षणमाह-अंगनायामिति। वामनाख्यो दिग्गजोऽपि स्वपत्न्यामंगनाख्यायां नीलमेघनामानं पुत्रमेकमजनयत्। एवमुदितो नीलमेघगजस्तावत् पूर्ववत् दन्तचतुष्कसमेतः निबिडनीलवर्णछुरितांगः नितरां गमनवेगवान् जलविहारे बद्धाशयः नितरामायतशुण्डादण्डान्तर्भागे वह्निज्वाले वारुणकान्तियुक् तथैवोत्तुंगायतशरीरश्च रराजेति **वाक्यार्थः**। इदमेव मुख्यं लक्षणमेतदन्वयजातानां गजानामंगेषु दृश्यमिति **व्यवस्था**॥

॥ अथ-पंचमस्य सुप्रतीकाख्यदिग्गजस्य सन्तानोत्पत्तिक्रमः (5) ॥

मूलम्

तथैवानुपमायां च सुप्रतीकात् सुतास्त्रयः।
पृथुश्च संप्रहारी च संपाती च प्रजज्ञिरे॥
कपोताक्षः करोदग्रः कैरवद्युतिरुन्नतः।
सूक्ष्मरोमा सुवीरोऽयं सुप्रतीकान्वयो द्विपः॥

व्याख्या—अथ पंचमस्य सुप्रतीकाख्यदिग्गजस्य पुत्रलक्षणं विशदयति-तथैवेति। सुप्रतीकाख्यो दिग्गजोऽपि स्वपत्न्यामनुपमाख्यायां त्रीन् पुत्रान् उत्पादयामास। तेषां नामानि यथा—पृथु(1), संप्रहारी(2), संपाती चेति(3)। एवमुदितास्त्वेते त्रयः पुत्राः कपोतलोचनसदृशलोचनयुताः दीर्घकराः विकसित-कैरवकान्तितुल्यश्वेतवर्णमण्डितसर्वावयवाः नितरां सूक्ष्मरोमाणश्चासन्। इदमेव मुख्यं लक्षणं एतद्वंश्यानां गजानामपि शरीरेषु दृश्यमिति **भावः**॥

॥ अथ-षष्ठस्यांजनाख्यस्य दिग्गजस्य सन्तानोत्पत्तिक्रमः(6) ॥

मूलम्

अंजनश्चांजनावत्यामंजनाचलसन्निभान्।
दिव्याप्रमेयावरुजः सुषुवे स सुतानिमान्॥

स्निग्धवालधिदन्तोष्ठः श्वेतरोमा सुपुष्करः।
तुंगजंघः कुंजरोऽयमंजनान्वयसंभवः॥

व्याख्या—अथ षष्ठस्यांजनाख्यस्य दिग्गजस्य पुत्रलक्षणमाह–अंजनश्चेति। अंजनाख्यो दिग्गजोऽपि अंजनावत्याख्यायां स्वपत्न्यां नीलपर्वतवत् नितरामुत्तुंगान् पुत्रान् त्रीनुत्पादयामास। तेषां नामानि यथा–दिव्यः(1), अप्रमेयः(2), अवरुक्ः(3), इति। एवमुदिता एते त्रयः पुत्रगजाः नीलवर्णछुरितावयवाः अत्यन्तं स्निग्धवालाः क्वचित् सूक्ष्मश्वेतरोमयुताश्चोत्तुंगजंघाः आसन्। इदमेव मुख्यं लक्षणं एतत्सन्ततिजनितानां सर्वेषामपि गजानां शरीरे दृश्यमिति **क्रमव्यवस्था**॥

॥अथ-सप्तमस्य सार्वभौमाख्यस्य दिग्गजस्य सन्तानोत्पत्तिक्रमः (7)॥

मूलम्

शुभ्रदन्त्यां सार्वभौमः पंचाजनयदात्मजान्।
मेघः पुष्पधरोऽसह्यः सहपद्ममहार्णवौ॥

ह्रस्वस्थूलेक्षणः स्थूलगण्डशुण्डालमस्तकः।
कान्तः पाटलवर्णोऽयं सार्वभौमान्वयो गजः॥

व्याख्या—अथ सप्तमस्य सार्वभौमाख्यस्य दिग्गजस्य पुत्रलक्षणमाह–शुभ्रदन्त्यामिति। सार्वभौमाख्यो दिग्गजोऽपि स्वपत्न्यां शुभ्रदन्त्याख्यायां तनयान् पंच जनयामास। तेषां नामानि यथा– मेघः(1), पुष्पधरः(2), असह्यः(3), सहपद्मः(4), महार्णव(5) इति। एवमुत्पन्ना इमे पुत्रगजाः श्वेतरक्तवर्ण-भूषितांगाः ह्रस्वश्रोत्रयुगलाः ह्रस्वनयनाः स्थूलजंघाः स्थूलगण्डाः स्थूलमस्तकाश्च विरेजिरे। इदमेव लक्षणं एतदन्वयगजानां शरीरे दृश्यमिति पूर्ववत् **व्यवस्था**॥

॥ अथाष्टमस्य कुमुदाख्यस्य दिग्गजस्य सन्तानोत्पत्तिक्रमः (8)॥

मूलम्

पिंगलायां समुत्पन्नौ कुमुदस्यापि दन्तिनः।
तनयावात्मसदृशौ महापद्मोर्मिमालिनौ।
ताम्राक्षस्तुंगदन्तोऽयं कृष्णविस्तीर्णपुष्करः।
कुमुदापाण्डरः कुंभी कुमुदान्वयसंभवः॥

इति दिग्गजपुत्रोत्पत्तिक्रमः

व्याख्या—अथाष्टमस्य कुमुदाख्यस्य दिग्गजस्य पुत्रलक्षणमाह—पिंगलायामिति। कुमुदाख्यो दिग्गजोऽपि पिंगलाख्यायां स्वपत्न्यां महापद्म-मूर्मिमालिनमेतौ द्वौ तनयावजनयत्। एवमुत्पन्नौ गजावेतौ ताम्रवर्णमनोहरलोचनौ नितरामुत्तुंगदन्तचतुष्कौ कृष्णवर्णभासुरशुण्डादण्डौ तदितरेष्ववयवेषु कुमुदकान्तिसदृशश्वेतवर्णभासुरौ विरेजतुरिति **लक्षणवाक्यार्थः**। इदमेव मुख्यं लक्षणमेतदन्वयजनितानां सर्वेषामपि गजानामंगेषु दृश्यमिति **व्यवस्था**। तथा च—एतावता प्रबन्धेन—

ऐरावतगजात् अष्टौ पुत्राः
पुण्डरीकगजात् चत्वारः पुत्राः
पुष्पदन्तगजात् पंच पुत्राः
वामनगजात् एकः पुत्रः
सुप्रतीकगजात् त्रयः पुत्राः
अंजनगजात् त्रयः पुत्राः
सार्वभौमगजात् पञ्च पुत्राः
कुमुदगजात् द्वौ पुत्रौ

आहत्य संख्यायां एकत्रिंशत्संख्यकाः दिग्गजपुत्राः जज्ञिर इति **पूर्वेणान्वयः**। एवमेकत्रिंशत्संख्यकेभ्यो दिग्गजपुत्रेभ्यः असंख्यास्तनयाः करिण्यश्च कालक्रमेण उदिता इति **भावः**। एवमुदितानां सर्वेषामप्येतेषां वारणानां मनोहरपक्षद्वयं चतुर्दन्तप्राप्तिः स्वशरीरेषु स्वस्वजनकस्येव

मनोहरतत्तद्वर्णमेलनं सौशील्यादिकं दीर्घमायुः सुचरितमप्याजन्मसदृश्यानीति **क्रमः**।।

।। अथ-गवावयवदेवनिरूपणम् ।।

मूलम्

गणे देवगणानां तु विस्तारः संप्रचक्षते।
ब्रह्मा मूर्ध्नि गले शक्रः स्कन्धे विष्णुरपि स्थितः।।

अग्निर्नाभौ रविर्दृष्ट्यां मृत्युः पादेषु दन्तिनाम्।
धरा विशाला वक्षस्सु मेढ्रे चाथ प्रजापतिः।।

हस्तेषु नागास्तिष्ठन्ति सर्वलोकधुरंधराः।
गात्रयोरश्विनौ श्रोत्रे दिशो मनसि चन्द्रमाः।।

अंगोपांगेषु वेदांश्च बुद्धौ शंभुर्व्यवस्थितः।
पर्जन्यो हृदि नागानामिति देवगणाः स्मृताः।।

इति पालकाप्यमहर्षिप्रणीते गजशास्त्रे अष्टदिग्गजोत्पत्तिकथनं नाम द्वितीयं प्रकरणम्।।

व्याख्या–एवं रीत्या प्रतिपादितानां सर्वेषामपि गजानां अंगदेवताः का इत्याकांक्षायां तत्तत्स्थानसीमाकथनपूर्वकं तन्नामानि व्यनक्ति गणे देवगणा-नामिति। एवमुक्तानां सर्वेषामपि गजानां–

1.	मूर्ध्नः	ब्रह्माधिपतिः
2.	गलस्य	शक्रोऽधिपतिः
3.	स्कन्धस्य	विष्णुरधिपतिः
4.	नाभेः	अग्निदेवोऽधिपतिः
5.	पादानां	यमदेवोऽधिपतिः
6.	नयनयुगलस्य	सूर्योऽधिपतिः
7.	वक्षसः	भूमिदेव्यधिनेत्री
8.	मेढ्रस्य	प्रजापतिदेवोऽधिपतिः

9. पुष्करस्य सर्पदेवोऽधिपतिः

10. सव्यापसव्याख्योदरपार्श्वतलयोः अश्विनौ देवावधिपौ।

11. श्रोत्रयुगलस्य दिग्देदेवोऽधिपतिः

12. मनसः चन्द्रोऽधिपतिः

13. अंगोपांगानां वेदपुरुषोऽधिपतिः

14. बुद्धेः शंभुरधिपतिः

15. हृदयस्य पर्जन्यदेवोऽधिपतिरभूदिति **तत्क्रमः**।।

तथा च-गजशरीरस्थानेषु एतेषु पंचदशसु ब्रह्माद्या एते पंचदश देवोत्तमाः सन्ततं स्थितिभाज इत्यर्थः। तस्मात् भूपालादिभिः धनिकैः यद्येते वारणाः संमानिताश्चेत् तदा एतादृशांगदेवानां प्रसदनमहिम्ना तेषामैश्वर्याभिवृद्धिं जयाद्यने-कमंगलपरंपरां च ते वारणाः कुर्युरिति **भावः**।।

इत्यनन्तकृष्णभट्टारकविरचितायां भावदर्शिन्याख्यायां
गजशास्त्रव्याख्यायां द्वितीयं प्रकरणम्।।

All the female elephants are a bit shorter than the male. Regarding colour and wings they are same as males but no tusks. However, the female ones have the same nature and conduct and beauty as their males respectively.

The above-said elephants are Lords for eight corners of the world as mentioned below:-

1. Airāvata-diggaja Lord of East
2. Puṇḍarīka-diggaja Lord of South-east
3. Puṣpadanta-diggaja Lord of South.
4. Vāmana-diggaja Lord of South-west
5. Supratīka-diggaja Lord of West.
6. Añjana-diggaja Lord of North-west
7. Sārvabhauma-diggaja Lord of of North
8. Kumuda-diggaja Lord of North-east.

The descendants of Diggajas

The above mentioned eight Lord elephants have given birth

to numberless descendants through their wives as they were enjoying them on moon days in these three worlds.

1. Airāvata-diggaja had 8 sons—[(1) Megha, (2) Padmodara, (3) Ariṣṭa, (4) Capala, (5) Rucira, (6) Aṅgada, (7) Aruja, and (8) Padmagulpha]. The most characteristic features of Irāvata's sons are : Long trunks, big bodies and more white near their eyes and ears.

2. Puṇḍarīka-diggaja had 4 sons—[(1) Hannirittha, (2) Supradiṣṭa, (3) Pramardana, and (4) Jīmūta] who had huge bodies, short hair all over the bodies, red eyes and a little hot temper.

3. Puṣpadanta-diggaja had 5 sons—[(1) Viṣahya, (2) Sāhasa, (3) Rikka, (4) Vicitra and (5) Vicārī] who had reddish colour on their bodies, red dots on their trunks and black hair all over their bodies.

4. Vāmana-diggaja had a son Nīlamegha who was very swift in speed and had a long trunk. He was very fond of playing in water.

5. Supratīka-diggaja had 3 sons—[(1) Pṛthu, (2) Samprahārī and (3) Sampātī] who had pigeonś eyes, thin hair, and long trunk.

6. Añjana-diggaja had 3 sons—[(1) Divya, (2) Aprameya and (3) Avaruk] who had very smooth bodies, beautiful trunks and little higher knees.

7. Sārva-bhuma-diggaja had 5 sons—[(1) Megha, (2) Puṣpadhara, (3) Asahya, (4) Sahapadma and (5) Mahārṇava] who had small ears, eyes, stout knees, big and stout cheeks and heads.

8. Kumuda-diggaja had 2 sons—(1) Mahāpadma and (2) Ūrmimālī who had long and stout tusks, and black trunks. All the 15 main limbs of the elephants are filled with 15 Devas.

तृतीयप्रकरणम्

दिग्गजशापानुग्रहकथनम्

मूलम्

कदाचिदागतं शंपां पालकाप्यं मुनीश्वरम्।
प्रत्युत्थायाभिगम्यार्घ्यपाद्याभ्यां प्रतिपूज्य च॥

अंगराजस्ततो भूयोऽप्यपृच्छन्मुनिपुंगवम्।
कथं द्विदन्तनिर्वृत्तिः कथमल्पायुषश्च ते॥

जिह्वा कथं परावृत्ता स्वेदश्चाभ्यन्तरः कथम्।
कथं नराणां पत्रत्वमन्तर्दाहः कथं भवेत्॥

स्ववीर्यसंपदज्ञानं कथं पंकांबुपांसुभिः।
विहतिश्च कथं मुष्कादर्शनं च तथाभवत्॥

कथं कामचराभावः कथं देवत्वहीनता।
कथं स्वकीयविण्मूत्रे जिघ्रन्त्येते मृगा इति॥

राजपुत्रं प्रसन्नात्मा प्रोवाच वदतां वरः।
ग्रहदोषबलेनैव वारणास्त्वंगभूपते॥

शप्ता अभूवन्मुनिभिस्तस्मात् शापः प्रवक्ष्यते।
ऋषिर्दीर्घतपा नाम तस्याश्रममुपागताः।
दिग्गजाः संगताः सर्वे जघ्नुराश्रमवासिनः॥

व्याख्या—एवंप्रकारेण **पालकाप्यमहर्षि**कथितदिग्गजतत्सुतजन्म-क्रमादिश्रवणेन सन्तुष्टो **रोमपादभूपतिः** पूर्वप्रतिपादितरीत्या चंपानगरसमीपे बद्धानां विविधजातीनां गजानामंगचेष्टास्वभावलक्षणादिकं प्रत्यहं निरीक्ष्य

तद्विषये किंचित् जिज्ञासुरभूत्। अथ कदाचित् यदृच्छया स एव **पालकाप्य-महर्षिस्तस्य** भूपतेरास्थानसभामाजगाम। तथागतं तं मुनिवरं दूरतो निरीक्ष्याभिमुखमागत्य यथाक्रमं प्रणम्य अर्घ्यपाद्यासनदानादिना तस्याध्वखेदमपनीय तदनुज्ञया तदन्तिक एवोपविष्टः सन् भो भगवन् महर्षे भवदुदीरितदिग्गजोत्पत्ति-क्रमादिकं निशम्य नितान्तं सन्तुष्टो धन्यश्चास्मि। तथापि तेभ्य एव दिग्गज-पुत्रसन्तानेभ्यः उदितानामेषां वारणानां चतुर्दन्ताभावः कथमभूत् (1) कथमेते अल्पायुषो जाताः (2) कथमेषां जिह्वा तावत् परावृत्ताभूत् (3) कथमेषामन्तः-शरीरतलेष्वेव स्वेदोद्रेकः (4) कथमेतैर्वारणैः भूपालादीनां वाहनत्वमंगीकृतम्। (5) किं च-एतेषां वारणानां जठरान्तर्भागे दाहशक्तेराधिक्यं कथमभूत्। (6) स्ववीर्यसंप**दज्ञा**नं च कथमभूदेतेषाम् (7) किमर्थमेते मदावलाः पंकपरागादिना क्रीडनं कलयन्ति (8) एतेषां, मुष्कप्रदर्शनाभावः कथमभूत् (9) एवं कामचराभावश्च कथमासीत् (10) देवशक्तिहीनाश्च कदाभूवन् (11) कथमेषां वारणानां स्वकीयविण्मूत्रादिषु प्रीतिरुत्पन्ना (12) इत्येवं द्वादशप्रकारेण सन्देहो मे जायते। एतत्सर्वमपि भवानेव निराकर्तुं प्रभवतीति व्याजहार। एवं महीपालवाणीमाकर्ण्य स **पालकाप्यो महर्षि**स्तथा द्विदन्त-प्राप्त्यादिविषये पूर्वहेतुं व्यक्तीकर्तुमुपचक्रमे ग्रहदोषबलेनैवेत्यादिना। भो महीपाल ग्रहदोषबलात् स्वापराधवशाच्च एतेषु गजेषु बहुविधाः शापाः पूर्वैः प्रेरिताः। कथमिति चेदुच्यते। प्रथमप्रकरणप्रतिपादितरीत्या हिमवतः सानुभागे वटवृक्षः कश्चिन्महानासीत्। तस्याधः स्थले कलिताश्रमः **दीर्घतपा** नाम कश्चिन्मुनिवरश्चिराय तपश्चार। तस्मिन् समये केचित् दिग्गजाः संघीभूय तत्रागत्य मानुषगन्धासहिष्णवः कोपवशात् तत्रत्यानां मुनीनामुटजादिकं भंक्त्वा मुनीन् निरपराधांश्च जघ्नुः।

Chapter-III

Description of the curses given to the elephants

After a short time, the king *Romapāda* visited the place where the elephants were fastened with chains and ropes on the banks of the Champa river and had a suspicion on seeing them changed in their nature, character etc. One day as he was waiting for the opportunity, the sage *Pālakāpya* came to this spot and was welcomed with *Arghya-pādya*. Then the king asked the sage the following 12 questions to clear his doubts.

1. How is it that the descendants of eight lord elephants had two tusks only instead of four?

2. Why should their age be reduced?

3. Why should their tongues be turned from bottom to top (i.e.) the blunt and thick portion outside the mouth and the sharp pointed one inside?

4. Why should be perspiration stop to these elephants?

5. Why should these accept to be the vehicles to the kings and nobles.

6. Why should they feel more hunger (appetite) in their stomachs?

7. Why should they forget their over might?

8. Why should they play with mud and dust and throw them on their own heads?

9. Why should their testicles disappear from sight?

10. Why should they not independently move instead of being controlled?

11. When did the divine power decrease to these elephants?

12. Why should they be fond of their own urine, semen and other nuisances?

To the above questions, the sage *Pālakāpya* began to answer in the followeing ways :—

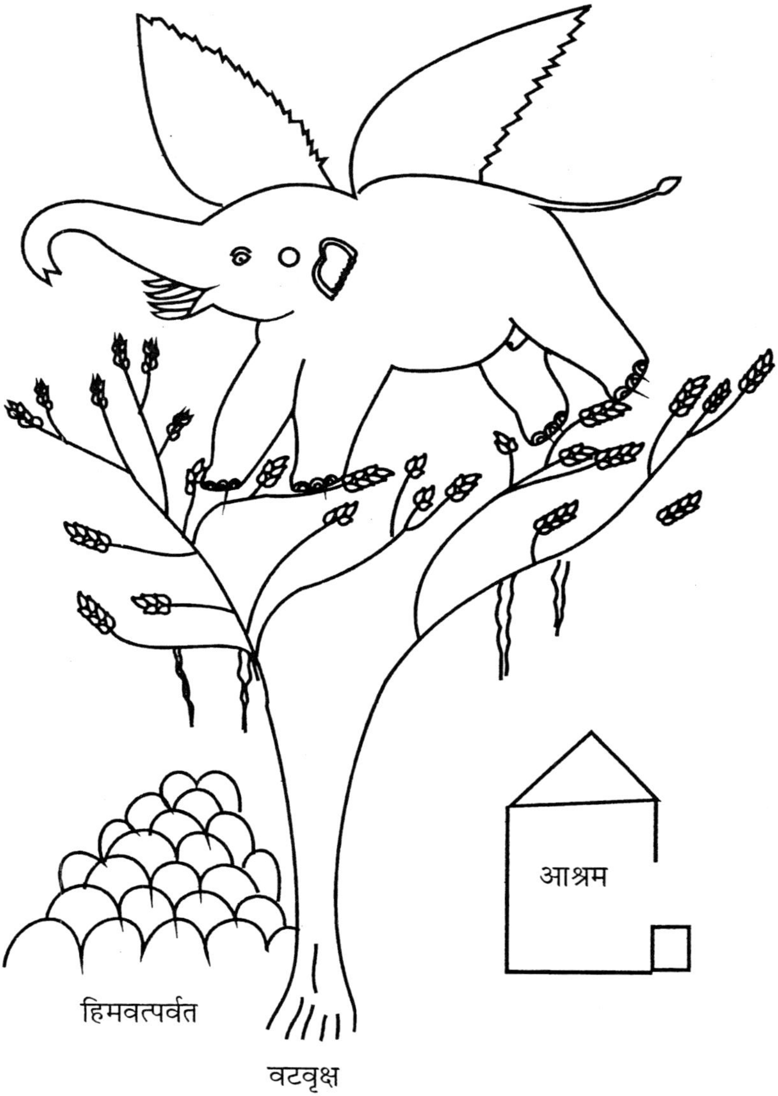

Fig.19 :हिमवतः सानुभागे वटवृक्षस्योपरि दिग्गजानामवरोहणक्रमः

दुष्टदिग्गजकृतमहर्षिवधक्रमः-

मूलम्

क्रुद्धेन तेन शप्तास्ते भविष्यथ न संशयः।
द्विदन्ताः स्वकुलोत्पन्नाः तथैवाल्पायुषश्च ते।।

हीनवीर्यजवोत्कर्षा हीना देवप्रभावतः।
विमुक्ताः कामचारेण भविष्यथ न संशयः।।

नराणां वाहनत्वं च गमिष्यथ च वारणाः।
अद्यप्रभृति भो यूयं पक्षहीना भविष्यथ।।

ऋषिणैवं गजाः शप्ता पक्षहीना महीतले।
नृपाणां वाहनत्वं च प्रापुरंगमहीपते।।

व्याख्या—क्रुद्ध इति। एवमुक्तप्रकारेण गर्वोद्रिक्तैर्दिग्गजैः महर्षीणामाश्रममण्डले ध्वंसिते सति केषुचिन्मुनिषु तेषां दिग्गजानां दन्तप्रहारादिना चूर्णीकृतांगेषु सत्सु तदा तस्याश्रमपदे महान् दीनध्वनिरजृंभत। तस्मात् तत्र महतीमापदमाकलय्य स तु **दीर्घतपाः मुनीन्द्रः** नितरां क्रुद्धः सन् दर्पातिशयात् तस्य पुरत एव स्थितान् तान् दिग्गजान् निरीक्ष्य भो दिग्गजाः यतो यूयं नितरां मदान्धा भूत्वा मुनीनेतान् ताडयथ; तेन हेतुना इतःप्रभृति युष्माकं युष्मत्कुलप्रसूतानां सर्वेषां च गजानां पक्षहानिर्भवतु। तद्द्वारा दिव्यबलशक्तिहानिः देवत्वहानिश्च भविष्यति। किं च-युष्माकं कामचारत्वं च नश्यतु। एवमितः प्रभृति युष्माकं दन्तद्वयप्राप्तिरेवास्तु। किं च-यूयमल्पायुषश्च भूत्वा तत्र तत्र भूलोकादिषु देशेषु भूपालादीनां वशगाः सन्तः तद्वाहनत्वं च प्राप्स्यथेति शशाप। अनेन वाक्येन **रोमपादभूपाल**कृतद्वादशप्रश्नेषु प्रथमाद्वितीयपंचमदशमैकादशप्रश्नानां प्रतिवचनं **पालकाप्यो**क्तं सूक्ष्मया धिया चोह्यम्।।

Long ago there was a sage by name **Dīrghatapas** doing penance in the valley of the Himālayas. The **diggajas** and their descendents went to his hermitage and began to kill the sages at the scent of human beings.

Fig. 20. : दुष्टदिग्गजकृतमहर्षिवधक्रमः

मूलम्

अथ देवा हविर्भागं कदाचिन्नाग्नये ददुः।
ततोऽग्निरभवद्‌गुप्तस्तदन्वेषणतत्परः॥

ब्रह्मा प्रोवाच दिङ्‌नागानग्निमन्वेष्टुमात्मजान्।
गच्छतेति तथा कुर्म इति ते प्राहुरब्जजम्॥

अथ दीर्घारण्यऋषेः सानुगाः सात्मजा गजाः।
गत्वाश्रमं हुताशस्य तस्य पत्नीमकल्मषाम्॥

धर्षयामासुरग्निस्तु गूढो देवात्मनां ततः।
स्वाहायाः क्रन्दितं श्रुत्वा क्रुद्धो दग्धुमुपागमत्॥

तेषां देवप्रभावान्न शक्तो दग्धुमनेकपान्।
शशाप पूर्वं पुरतो ब्रह्मणोऽपि मतंगजाः॥

वयं तथा कुर्म इति प्राहुर्यस्मादशंकिताः।
तस्मादद्यप्रभृत्येव जिह्वैषां परिवर्तिता॥

भवत्वन्तर्दाहयुक्ता अपि नागा भवन्त्वमी।
इत्यन्तर्दाहयुक्तास्ते गजरूपा निनादिनः॥

जहुश्च त्रैदशं रूपमुपतस्थुश्च वेधसम्।
स च तान् वीक्ष्य हस्ताभ्यां परिमृज्याह पद्मभूः॥

कुतो भयं समुत्पन्नं रूपत्यागः कथं कृतः।
अथाग्निशापमुक्त्वा ते स्वापराधं तु नोचिरे॥

ततः क्रुद्धः पद्मयोनिः तान् शशाप यथाहितम्।
गजा दधतु निर्वाणं लुण्ठनात् पंकपांसुषु॥

अनेन ब्रह्मशापेन ततोऽद्यापि मतंगजाः।
नष्टान्तर्दाहदुःखाश्च नीरागाश्च भवन्त्यमी॥

स्वेदप्रक्लिन्नवस्त्रत्वात् देवास्तु शिथिलां युधि।
चलच्च्युतासनाः सर्वे नोत्सहन्ते युधि स्म ते॥
तदाह तान् गजान् पाशी स्वेदो न स्यन्दतां बहिः।

व्याख्या—अथ देवा इति। पुरा कदाचित् वासवाद्याः देवाः स्वस्वयागादिषु अग्निपुरुषाय हविर्भागं न प्रददुः। अतस्तादृशपरिभवमसहिष्णुरग्निदेवः क्वचिन्निलीनोऽभवत्। तथा लीनेऽग्निदेवे विनष्टयागादिः पद्मभूः तदन्वेषणार्थं कांश्चित् देवोत्तमान् प्रथमं प्राहिणोत्। चिराय ते तत्र तत्रान्विष्य अग्निदेवमदृष्ट्वैव प्रतिनिवृत्ताः। तदनु विधाता अतिदेवबलपराक्रमानेतान् गजानाहूय भो भो गजाः अग्निदेवान्वेषणाय यूयं गच्छथेत्यवादीत्। तेऽपि मदान्धास्तथा कुर्म इत्युक्त्वा तथैव नाकोद्यानादिस्थलेषु विविधेष्वन्वेषणमाकलय्य अप्राप्ताग्नि-वृत्तान्ताः सन्तः **दीर्घारण्यमहर्षे**राश्रमपदमवाप्य तत्र स्थितिमतीमग्निभार्यां स्वाहादेवीं विलोक्य भो देवि त्वदन्तिक एव प्रायशोऽग्निर्भवितव्यः। आहोस्वित् कुत्र वा वर्तते। वदस्वेत्यूचिरे। सा तु न प्रत्युत्तरमदात्। तदा एते मूढा गजाः क्रुद्धाः सन्तः स्वशुण्डादण्डं तस्याः स्वाहादेव्या गले संबध्य तां चकर्षुः। सा तु स्वाहादेवी नवं परिभवमसहिष्णुरुच्चैश्चक्रन्द। तदार्तरवमारादाकर्ण्य ससंभ्रमं बहिरागतोऽग्निदेवः तान् दूरतो निरस्य क्रोधाविष्टः सन् शापप्रदानेन स्वकरस्थितविविधायुधैः खण्डनेन च तान् गजान् दग्धुं छेत्तुं च उद्युक्तोऽभूत्। तथा तेषां गजानां देवांशकत्वात् तथा परिभवं कर्तुमग्निर्नैव शशाक। अतो नितरां क्रुद्धः सन् तत्पुरतः स्थित्वा भो मदान्धा गजाः यूयं ब्रह्मणः सदसि अग्नेरन्वेषणं कुर्म इति यतो निःशंकमुक्तवन्तः, तादृशापराधवशादद्यप्रभृति युष्माकं रसना तावत्परावृत्ता भवतु। किं च-युष्माकमुदरभागे दाहाधिक्यं च भवत्विति शशाप। एवमग्निशापहतास्ते गजाः अन्तर्दाहाधिक्ययुताः विकृतशरीराः दुःखान्विताः विधातुः सविधमुपेत्य स्वापराधक्रममनुक्त्वैव अग्निकृत-शापक्रममूचुः। सोऽपि कमलासनः तत्सर्वमपि स्वज्ञानचक्षुषा ज्ञात्वा अद्यप्रभृति वारणा एते मूढाः पंकलुण्ठनपांसुलुण्ठनादिषु प्रीतिं दधत्विति शशाप। अत एवाद्यापि अग्निशापवशादेव मतंगजानामुदरे क्षुद्बाधा भवति। एवं ब्रह्मशापवशादेव मतंगजाः स्वशुण्डादण्डेन स्वोपरि पंकपरागादीन् प्रक्षिपन्तीति **क्रमः**। एतेन **रोमपाद**कृततृतीयषष्ठाष्टमप्रश्नानां प्रत्युत्तरं कृतमिति **भावः**। अथ स्वेद-स्याभ्यन्तरत्वे हेतुमाह-स्वेदप्रक्लिन्नवस्त्रत्वादिति। पूर्वं वासवाद्या देवाः दिग्गजेषु कलितयुद्धासनाः सन्तः समरतलं दैत्यनिरसनाय जग्मुः। तदा एतेषां गजानां शरीरे श्रमवशात् स्वेदप्रस्रावः समजनि। तादृशस्वेदजलप्रसरणेन प्रक्लिन्नवस्त्रकरतलाद्याः देवाः चलच्च्युतासनाः सन्तः युद्धे स्थातुं न

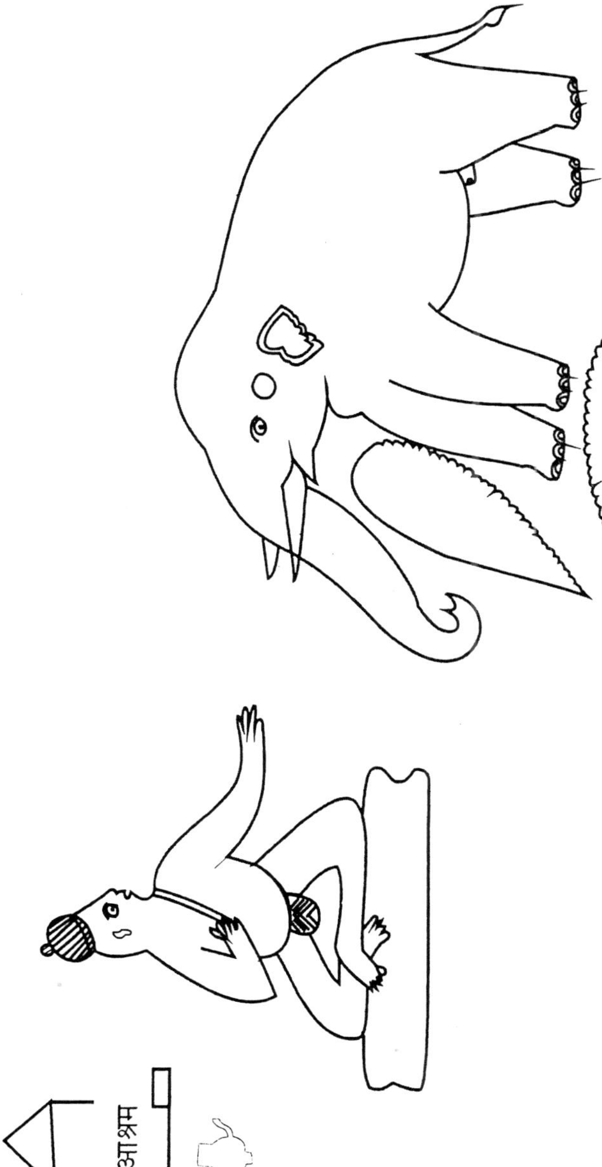

Fig. 21. : दिग्गजानां पक्षपतनं प्रति दीर्घतपोमहर्षिकृतशापक्रमः

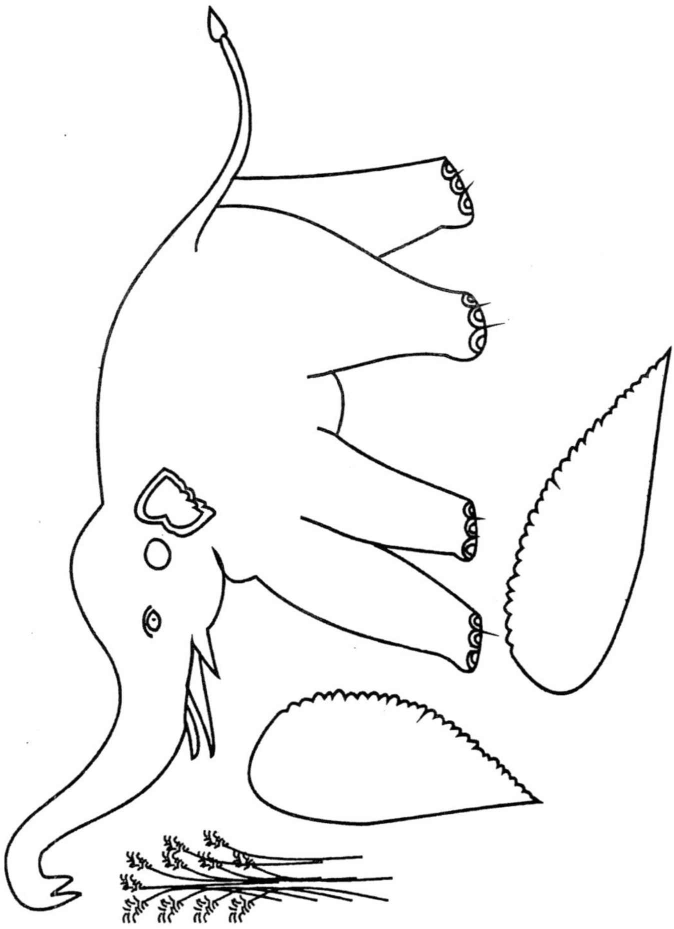

Fig. 22. : महर्षिशापेन दिग्गजानां पक्षयुगलपतनक्रमः

शेकुः। तादृशदुरवस्थां निरीक्ष्य वरुणस्तावत् अद्यप्रभृति सर्वेषामपि गजानां अन्तः शरीरतलेष्वेव स्वेदो भवतु न बहिः स्यन्दतामित्यवददिति। अनेन **रोमपाद**कृतचतुर्थप्रश्नस्य प्रत्युत्तरमुक्तं ज्ञेयम्।

The sage *Dīrghatapas* grew indignant and cursed them that they should have only two tusks instead of four, that their age should be reduced and limited, they should obey the human-beings and be the vehicles for the kings and nobles, they should lose their wings and the power of free-roaming according to their whims and fancy and they should lose the divine power. From these, answers for questions 1, 2, 5, 10 and 11 have been given.

मूलम्

भृगोः कदाचिन्मातंगाः सप्तछदमनोहरम्।
आश्रमं जग्मुरुन्मत्ताः मदगन्धासहिष्णवः॥
अग्नौ मूत्रपुरीषाणि तदा विससृजुश्च ते॥
ततः क्रुद्धो भृगुमुनिः शशापैतान् मतंगजान्।
स्वकीय एव विण्मूत्रे जिघ्रन्त्वेते मृगा इति॥
ततस्त्वेतान् मृगान् दृष्ट्वा जंगमानिव पर्वतान्।
ऋषयो विस्मिताः सर्वे वाक्यमूचुः पितामहम्॥
अतिवीर्या महासत्त्वाः रूपतेजोबलान्विताः।
कथमेते मृगाः क्रुद्धाः न हिंस्युः प्राणिनोऽपरान्॥
अथ ब्रह्मा प्रतीतात्मा तान् मुनीन् प्रत्यभाषत।
स्ववीर्यसंपदं ह्येते न वेत्स्यन्ति मृगा इति॥
ब्रह्मा मृथोपकरणच्युतिकारणाच्च
नागान् शशाप घनकोपनिविष्टचेताः।
गात्रद्वयत्रिगाकसन्धिषु मध्यदेशे
मुष्कस्थितिं विधिरदात्सततं गजस्य॥
अथ ते वारणाः श्रुत्वा शापमात्मापराधजम्।
परं दैन्यमुपागम्य ब्रह्माणमिदमूचिरे॥

मुनिशापविदग्धानां भविष्यति गतिः कथम्।
अस्माकमन्वयानां तु गजानां वनचारिणाम्।
रोगमुक्तिः कथं ब्रह्मन् विषमात्यशनादिभिः॥

इत्थं वाक्यं दिग्गजानां श्रुत्वोवाच पितामहः।
गवार्थे ब्राह्मणार्थे वा संग्रामे भुजजन्मनाम्॥

प्राणान् त्यक्त्वाथ मातंगाः ततः स्वर्गं गमिष्यथ।
उत्पत्स्यते कोऽपि नागाः गजगर्भान्महामुनिः॥

आयुर्वेदस्य वेत्ता वै मत्कृतस्य भविष्यति।
एवमुक्त्वा तु दिङ्नागान् विससर्ज यथासुखम्॥

ततस्ते प्रययुः स्थानं स्वस्थमैरावतादयः।
दिग्वारणान्वयास्ते तु लोकं मानुषमागताः॥

विचरन्तो महीं कृत्स्नां सशैलवनकाननाम्।
शतशो यूथसंख्याभिः प्रवृद्धास्तु सहस्रशः॥

इति पालकाप्यमहर्षिप्रणीते गजशास्त्रे दिग्गजशापानुग्रह-
कथनं नाम तृतीयं प्रकरणम्॥

व्याख्या—अथ गजानां स्वकीयविण्मूत्रे प्रीतिहेतुमाह–भृगोरिति। पुरा कदाचित् ते तु दिग्गजाः संघीभूय सप्तच्छदवृक्षच्छायाभिः मनोहरं **भृगुमहर्षे**-राश्रमपदमागत्य तद्वृक्षमदगन्धासहिष्णवः सन्तः तान् वृक्षान् केचित् दिग्गजा बभंजुः। अन्ये केचित् दिग्गजाः तस्य महर्षेरग्निकुण्डे विण्मूत्रविसर्जनादिकम-कुर्वन्। एवमाश्रमक्षोभमाकलय्य स तु मुनीन्द्रः क्रुद्धः सन्भो गजाः यतोऽत्र वह्निकुण्डे विण्मूत्रक्षेपणं कृतम्, तेनाद्यप्रभृति युष्माकं स्वकीयविण्मूत्ररेतसा-माघ्राणादिविषये प्रीतिर्भवत्विति शशाप। अनेन द्वादशप्रश्नस्य प्रत्युत्तरमाकलितं ज्ञेयम्। स्वबलाज्ञाने हेतुमाह–ततस्त्वेतान् मृगान् दृष्ट्वेति। अस्य **विशदार्थस्तु**-एवं रीत्या कालक्रमेण शतसहस्रयूथसंख्याभिः प्रवृद्धान् जंगमपर्वतानिव स्थितान् गजानेतान् निरीक्ष्य विस्मयं गतास्ते सर्वे आदिमहर्षयः ब्रह्मणः सविधमुपेत्य भगवन्! एवंप्रवृद्धैरतिवीर्यसत्त्वयुक्तैरेतैर्गजैः यदि कदाचित्

प्राणिनां दुर्बलानां हिंसा जनिता चेत् क उपायो भवता चिन्तित इत्यब्रुवन्। तत्साधु मत्वा पद्मासनः एतेषां गजानां स्वबलपराक्रमज्ञानं कदापि नोदेतु इत्युक्तवान्। अनेन दुर्बलेभ्यः प्राणिभ्योऽपि गजानामेतेषां भयप्रसक्तिः लोकहिताय ब्रह्मणा कलितेति **व्यवस्था।** मुष्कादर्शनं प्रति हेतुस्तु–पूर्वं ब्रह्मणः सविधमुपेत्य केचित् देववीरा ऊचुः। यथा–भो भगवन्! इमे दिग्गजोत्तमाः समुष्काः। तस्मात् आयुधादिभारोद्वहने शीघ्रगमनादौ चासमर्था इति। तच्च निशम्य सृष्टिकर्ता स्वसंकल्पवशेन सर्वेषामपि गजानामपर-पादोपरिस्थितत्रिगाख्यपादसन्धितल एव गजमुष्काः निलीनाः भवेयुः। बहिस्तस्य प्रदर्शनं माभूदित्युक्त्वा तथा कारयामासेति **पूर्वेणान्वयः।** अनेन **रोमपाद**कृत-सप्तमनवमद्वादशप्रश्नानां प्रत्युत्तरं कलितं बोध्यम्। तस्मादेवं कालक्रमेण गजानां विविधाः शापाः जनिता इति बोधः। एवं स्वापराधेनैव संचितान् शापानाकलय्य ते सर्वे गजाः कदाचित् संघीभूय विधातुः सन्निधं प्राप्य प्रणम्य भगवन्! एवमस्मदपराधपरंपराभिरेव विविधाः मुनिशापाः अस्मान् दहन्ति। कदा वास्माकमस्मत्कुलजनितानां वारणानां च सद्गतिप्राप्तिः। कथं वा रोगनिवृत्तिरिति प्रार्थयामासुः। स तु विधाता वागीमेतां शुभां ज्ञात्वा भो वारणाः शापानुभवं प्रति मनःक्लेशं त्यजत। युष्माकं भूलोकादिस्थलेषु महीपालादिभिः सत्पुरुषैः संमानननादिकं भविष्यति। तस्मात् यूयमचिरेणैव कालेन गजगर्भात् प्रादुर्भविष्यतः आयुर्वेदवेत्तुः **पालकाप्यमहर्षे**रनुग्रहभूम्ना रोगभयरहिताः सुखभाजः चिरमुषित्वा गवामुपकाराय वा ब्राह्मणपरित्राणाय वा भूपालयुद्धार्थाय वा परित्यक्तप्राणाः सन्तः दिव्यशरीरमवाप्य पुनरपि स्वर्गस्था भवन्त्वित्यनुगृहीतवान्। शेषं स्पष्टम्।।

इति श्रीमदन्तकृष्णभट्टारकविरचितायां भावदर्शिन्याख्यायां गजशास्त्रव्याख्यायां तृतीयं प्रकरणम्।।

Some years back, the Devas did not give the Agni-deva (fire god) any share in *Haviṣ* (fire sacrifice). So he went to a secluded place and hid himself. Brahmā lost some importance in the performance of *Yāga* (fire sacrifice) owing to absence of Agnideva and sent the elephants to find him cut some how or other. Accordingly, they went to the hermitage of sage

Dīrghāraṇya and asked the wife of that firegod Swāhādevī where was her husband. As she did not reply, the foolish elephants grew angry and pulled her collars with their trunks to kill her when she cried for help. Her husband, Agnideva, came out of the *āśrama* and cursed them that their tongues should be turned inside and the blunt thick portion should come out of the mouth as they accepted to search him in the presence of Brahmā and added that they should feel much more hungry (appetite) i.e. fire should be inside their stomachs and burn them with hunger.

After receiving the curse, the elephants went to Brahmā and represented their curse from the fire-god without revealing their mischief, done to his wife.

Brahmā understood the truth of their mischief by the sight of his *Yoga* and cursed them that they should play with dust at all times and throw them on their own heads of their own accord.

On another occasion, the Devas rode on elephants' backs to fight against the *Asuras* and *Rākṣasas*. Owing to the heavy perspiration on their bodies, they could not fight with them as their armours were wet and so, one of the Devas, by name Varuṇa, cursed them (elephants) that their perspiratoin should be inside their bodies in future. Questions, 3, 4, 6 and 8 are answered.

On some other occasion, these foolish elephants went to the hermitage of the sage Mataṅga and spoiled the seven-leaves' trees owing to the dislike of the smell of those trees and passed their urine and dung in the *Homa-kuṇḍa*. On seeing the mischief done by them, the sage Mataṅga grew angry and cursed them that they should be very fond of smelling their own urine, dung and semen.

On some other occasion, the seven *Ṛṣis* went to Brahmā and expressed that the huge mountain-like elephants would very easily smash the smaller ones to pieces if they would become angry; and to which Brahmā cursed that they (elephants) could not know their own might.

On another occasion, Brahmā thought that they could not run fast owing to the heavy and huge testicles and so he cursed them that their testicles should disappear from sight and he intermingled with their nerves. Answers for questions 7, 9 and 12 are given.

As they have been cursed many a time like this they felt much and went to Brahmā. They expressed that they have done wrong on many occasions foolishly and have been entangled in these curses and desired to be happy without generations. To which Brahmā replied that if they would help the Brāhmaṇas, cows or kings in wars, they would have no-generations in future and leave happily in the *swarga-loka*.

Fig. 23. : दुष्टदिग्गजकृताश्रमवृक्षक्षोभक्रमः

Fig. 24. : मतंगमहर्षेः होमकुण्डे दुष्टदिग्गजकृतविष्ठादिपातनक्रमः

चतुर्थं प्रकरणम्

॥ अथ गजवननिरूपणम्॥

मूलम्

पूर्वं नागवनं प्राच्यं ततश्चेदिकरूषकम्।
दशार्णकं ततो विद्यात् ततः स्यादांगरेयिकम्॥
कालिंगकं पंचमं स्यात् षष्ठं स्यादपराजितम्।
सौराष्ट्रकं सप्तमं स्यात् ततः पांचनदं पुनः॥

तत्र प्राच्यवनगजलक्षणम् (1)

लौहित्योदरकाननानि यमुनाभागीरथीसंगमः
शंभोर्मौलिभुजंगमस्तकमणिच्छायारुणा जाह्नवी।
मन्दारोपवनोपविष्टरमणोत्संगस्थविद्याधरी-
गीतापूरितकन्दरः स हिमवान् प्राच्यं वनं दन्तिनाम्॥
शिरः कर्णोष्ठजठररदनोत्संगगण्डकैः।
गलमांसैर्बलकरैः वंशोष्ठीवांसदेशकैः।
विशालांसतलैर्युक्ताः कुनखाः कपिला गजाः।
सरय्वां च चरन्त्येते मालवे विषये तथा।
गोचरे पर्वते चैव अंगदेशे चरन्ति ते॥
तत्रोत्तमांश्च मगधान् पुण्ड्रकाश्मीरकोसलान्।
पांचालदेशं च तथा कलिंगविषयं तथा।
सेवन्ते जाह्नवीं केचित् गोमतीरसवाहिनीम्।
प्राच्येषु पूर्वमथवापि समुद्रवेलां
लौहित्यमब्धिमभितः सुरनिम्नगायाः।

Fig. 25. : प्राच्यवनगजः उत्तमः Prācyavana or Prayāga forest's elephants, superior

पुण्यान् नदीक्षितिधरानपि गोचरादीन्
अंगादिचारुविषयान् विचरन्ति नागाः॥

बृहत्कुंभशिरोष्ठास्यदन्तास्तुंगा महोदराः।
पृथुहस्ताः पृथकटाः महावंशसुपेचकाः॥

कपिलाः कान्तरावाश्च प्राच्यकाननजा गजाः।

व्यासप्रोक्ते गजशास्त्रे-

प्राच्यं गंगाप्रयागस्तुहिनधरणिभृल्लोहितो मध्य एषाम्।
तत्रोद्भूतो गजेन्द्रो बहुतरलवपुः शान्तकोपोऽग्नियुक्तः॥

व्याख्या—एवं प्रकरणत्रये प्रतिपादितेनानेन ग्रन्थेन **गजशास्त्रकारस्य पालकाप्यमहर्षेरु**त्पत्तिक्रमः तदनु दिग्गजानां तत्सुतानां चोत्पत्तिक्रमः ततस्तेषामपराधवशादेवं संजातविविधशापपतनक्रमः ततो ब्रह्मकृतगजानुग्रहप्रकारश्च प्रतिपादित इति **व्यवस्था।** तस्मादेवं प्रकरणत्रयपठनानन्तरं **अस्मिन् चतुर्थे प्रकरणे** उपरितनप्रकरणेषु च पूर्वोक्तप्रकारेणात्र भूलोके विविधेषु प्रदेशेषु स्थितिभाजां मानुषैरेव ग्रहीतुं योग्यानां कलियुगगजानां जातिस्वरूपलक्षणगुणादिकमेव विस्तरशः सुखबोधाय शास्त्रकारेणोपदिश्यत इति **सन्दर्भव्यवस्था। तत्रास्मिन् चतुर्थे प्रकरणे** गजानामुत्पत्तिस्थानानि षोडशवनानि शास्त्रनिर्दिष्टानि। एषु षोडशवनेषु बहवो देशाः अन्तर्गता इति **भावः।** तस्मादद्यापि तेष्वेव प्रदेशेषु गजानामुत्पत्तिबाहुल्यं दृश्यत इति **व्यवस्था।** तस्मात् तेषां षोडशवनानां स्थाननिर्देशपूर्वकं तत्रत्यगजानां स्वरूपगुणादिकं क्रमेण प्रतिपादयतीति बोध्यम् तत्र प्राच्यवनं प्रथमं (1), द्वितीयवनं चेदिकरूषकाख्यम् (2), तृतीयं दाशार्णकवनं (3), चतुर्थमांगरेयिकवनं (4), पंचमं कलिंगवनं (5), षष्ठमपराजितवनं (6), सप्तमं सौराष्ट्रकवनं (7), अष्टमं पांचनदवन (8), मिति क्रमं कृत्वा तत्क्रमेण तत्रत्यगजलक्षणं कथयतीति **क्रमपरिपाटी।** तत्र प्राच्यवनस्य स्थितिः कुत्रेति चेत् तद्विशदयति लौहित्योदरेत्यनेन पद्येन। हिमवन्मध्यभागस्य दक्षिणपार्श्वे परमेश्वरपदकमलविन्यासधन्यः कैलासो नाम पर्वतो भासते। तद्दक्षिणत एव गंगायमुनाख्ययोः प्रसिद्धनद्योरुत्पत्तिः। तस्मात् तादृशकैलासपर्वतसानुतट्यारभ्य

तयोर्गंगायमुनयोः संगमस्थानाख्यप्रयागक्षेत्रपर्यन्तं स्थलस्य तस्योदीच्यं दिशि लौहित्यानदीतटपर्यन्तं द्विशतयोजनविस्तीर्णं स्थलं प्राच्यवनमिति पूर्वनहर्षिभिर्निर्दिष्टम्। तथा चास्मिन् प्राच्यवने तत्र तत्र कुंजगुहादिप्रदेशेषु संजाताः कुंजरा सर्वेऽपि दृढतरमस्तककण्ठरदनाः मस्तकतले निबिडरोमयुताः पृथूदराः विशालगण्डफलकाः पृथुलदीर्घशुण्डादण्डाः किंचित् श्वेतवर्णमिलितकृष्णवर्णछुरितांगाः तुंगाः मृगयासमरभारवहनादिकार्येषु दृढचित्ताः बलपराक्रमसहिताः कुनखोपेताः मधुररींकारध्वनियुताश्च भवन्ति। किं चान्यैश्च शुभलक्षणैरुपेताः एते वारणाः सरयूनदीतीरभूमिषु यमुनागंगयोस्तीरभूमिषु मालवदेशभूमिषु गोचरपर्वतसमीपस्थलेषु अंगदेशभूमिषु मगधदेशभूमिषु पुण्ड्रदेशभूमिषु काश्मीरदेशभूमिषु कोसलदेशभूमिषु पांचालदेशभूनिषु कलिंगदेशभूमिषु गोमतीनदीतीरभूमिषु स्वेच्छासंचारशीलाः अद्यापि दृश्यन्ते। नान्येषु स्थलेष्वेषां यदृच्छाप्रवृत्तिर्भवतीति **भावः। व्यासप्रोक्ते गजशास्त्रे** तु-एतस्मिन् प्राच्यवने जनिताः मदावलाः सर्वेऽपि शीघ्रगतयः कोपहीनाः सततभक्षणनिरताश्च भवन्तीति।।

IV. Chapter

Descriptions of the elephants available in 16 main forests

Having described the authors's life and winged elephants with their descendants completely, the sage *Pālakāpya* began to describe our modern elephants available in 16 main forests both in this and ensuing chapters.

1. Prācyavana-or eastern forest
2. Cedikarūṣaka-forest
3. Daśārṇaka-forest
4. Āṅgareya forest
5. Kaliṅga-forest
6. Aparānta-forest
7. Saurāṣṭra-forest
8. Pañcanada-forest

1. Prācyavana-Elephants.

Prācyavana:- extends from the sources of the Ganges and Jumna in the Himālayas to Prayāga (modern Allahabad) in the east and the Lauhitya river in the north, about 200 *yojanas*. Elephants available in this forest possess strong heads, tusks, good tuft of hair on their bodies and heads, stout stomachs, broad cheeks, long trunks and a little whitish black colour. They are very powerful in war and hunting, very calm, swift, active and intelligent. They are easily controllable. They have shrill cry pleasant to hear.

॥अथ-चेदिकरूषकवनगजलक्षणम् (2)॥

मूलम्

मेखला त्रिपुरी चैव दाशार्णो देश एव च।
उन्मत्तगंगा इत्येषां मध्ये चेदिकरूषकम्॥
पार्श्वोन्नताश्च मध्वाभरदनाः शीघ्रविक्रमाः।
सुगात्राः शुभपादाश्च स्वायत्ताः कपिलास्तथा॥
चण्डा ह्युदग्रपादाश्च क्वचित्केचित् तथा गजाः।

व्याख्या—अथ चेदिकरूषकवने जनितानां गजानां लक्षणमाह-मेखलेति। मेखलानद्याः प्राच्यां दिशि त्रिपुरस्थलस्य दक्षिणस्यां दशार्णदेशस्य प्रतीच्यामुन्मत्तगंगाख्यसरितः उदीच्यां च दिशि यत्स्थलमतिविशालं निर्दिष्टं एतेषां मध्यभागे स्थितिमतस्तस्यैव स्थलस्य चेदिकरूषकवनमिति नामान्तरम्। तस्मान्नानावृक्षजालमेदुरेऽस्मिन् चेदिकरूषकवने जनिता गजाः किंचिद्वामना अपि शुभावयवसंयुताः मधुकान्तियुतदन्तधारिणः उदरपार्श्वभागे दृढमांससमेतास्त्वरितगमनाः मस्तकभागे निबिडरोमयुताः कपिलवर्णछुरितांगाः गजपालकैः सुलभमसाध्याश्च भवन्तीति **लक्षणवाक्यार्थः**।

2. Cedikarūṣaka-forest Elephants

Cedikarūṣaka forest is in the east of Mekhalā river, south of Tripura-sthala, west of Daśārṇa country and north of Unmatta-gaṅgā. The elephants available in this forest are a little short in size, proportionately strong and beautiful, not easily controllable, and whitish black in colour. They are very rapid in movement.

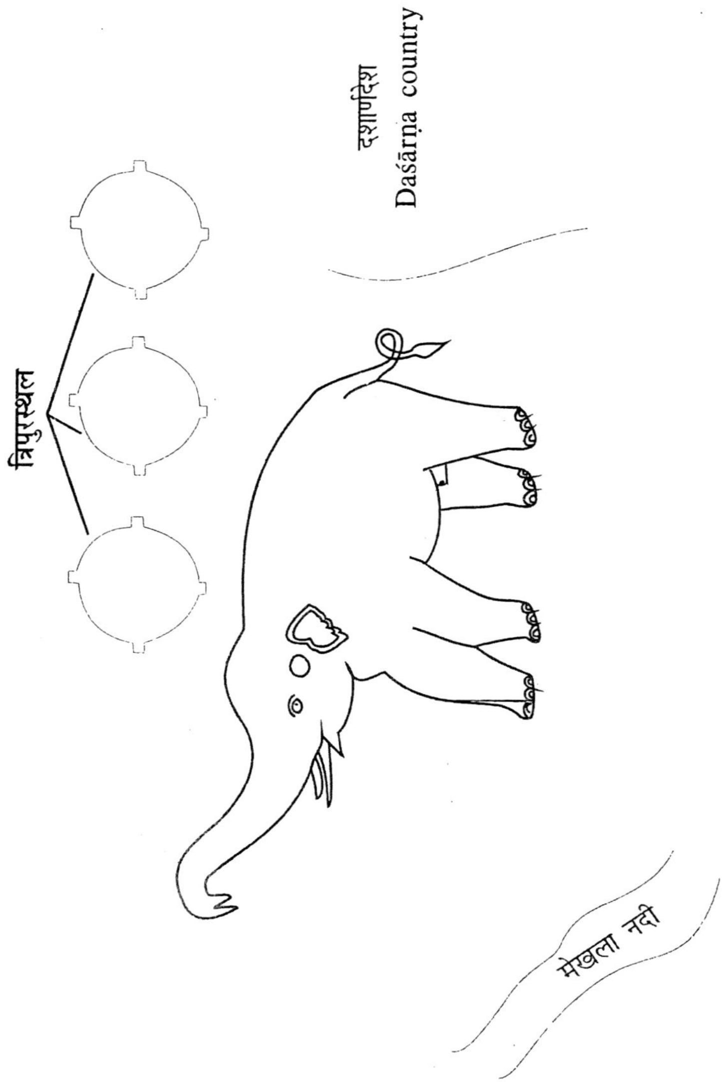

Fig. 26. : चेदिकरूषकवनगजः Cedikarūṣaka-forest's elephants, superior

॥अथ-दशार्णकवनगजलक्षणम् (3)॥

मूलम्

दाशार्णोन्मत्तगंगात्रिपुररसवतीमेखलामध्यमाहुः
चैद्यं तत्र प्रजातः शुभकरणजवो ह्रस्वसर्वांगलक्ष्मीः।
मध्ये श्रीपर्वतश्रीबलधरणिभृतोर्वेत्रवत्या दशार्णं
दाशार्णश्चापि शस्तः बृहदवयवयुक् पिंगलस्तत्र जातः॥

व्याख्या—अथ दशार्णवने जनितानां गजानां लक्षणमाह-दाशार्णेति। अस्मिन् श्लोके पूर्वार्धस्य **एवं व्यवस्था।** यथा इदं तु पूर्वार्धं पूर्वोक्तचैद्यक-रूषकवनजनितमतंगजविषये **व्यासस्य** यो**ऽभिप्राय**स्तं व्यनक्तीति **क्रमः।** तद्विषये तादृशा**शयस्तु**-पूर्वोक्तस्थलचतुष्कमध्यवर्तिनि वने जनिताः वारणाः शुभावयवा अपि ह्रस्वाकारा एव दृश्यन्त इति। अन्यत् **पालकाप्यो**क्तलक्षणानु-सारीति **भावः।** अथ-दशार्णवनगजलक्षणमाह मध्य इति। वेत्रवतीनद्याः प्राच्यां दिशि श्रीपर्वतस्य दक्षिणस्यां दशार्णदेशस्य प्रतीच्यां बलपर्वतस्योत्तरस्यां च यत्स्थलं, एतन्मध्यवर्ति तदेव भूतलं दशार्णवननामभाक्। अत्र वने जनिताः वारणाः तुंगशरीराः सर्वैः शुभलक्षणैरुपेताः पिंगलवर्णभासुराः नितरां श्लाघ्यगुणान्विताः भवन्तीति **भावः।**

3. Daśārṇa-forest Elephants.

Daśārṇa-forest lies in the east of Vetravatī river, south of Śrī-parvata, west of Daśārṇa country and north of Bala-parvata. Elephants available in this forest are very tall, very good natured, very superior in quality, very strong and brown in colour.

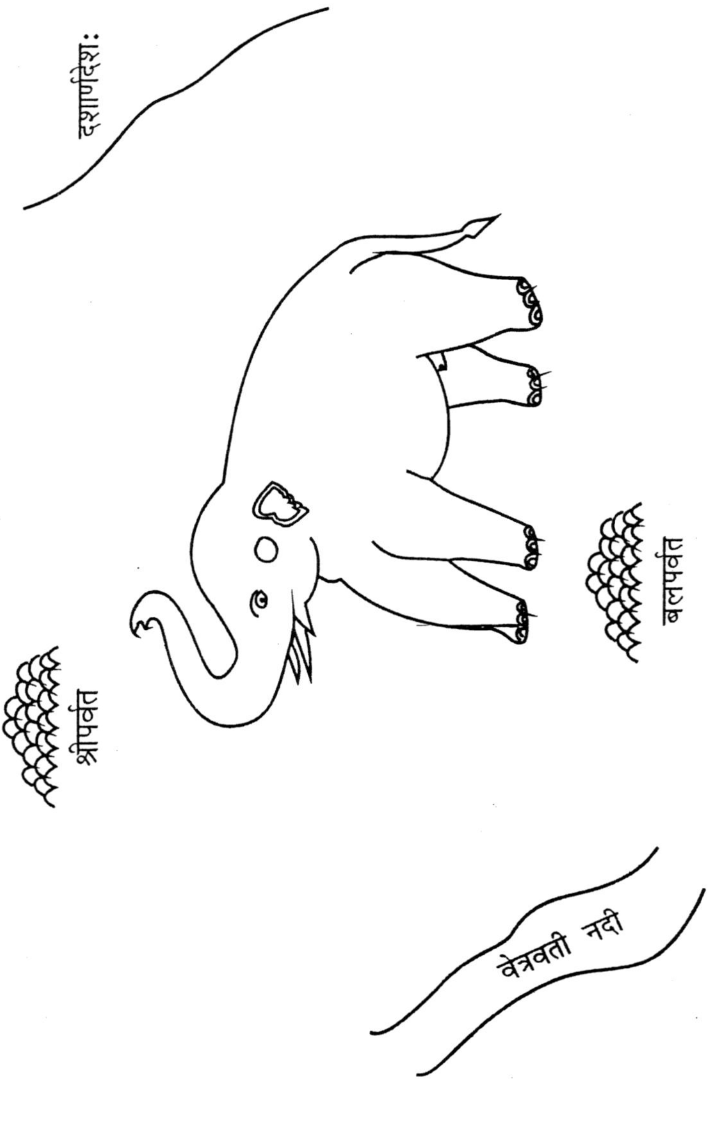

Fig. 27. : दशार्णवनगजः उत्तमः Daśārṇa-forest's elephants, superior

।।अथ-आंगरेयवनगजलक्षणम् (4)।।

मूलम्

रेवायाः पारियात्रक्षितिधरविदिशादेशयोर्ब्रह्मवत्याः।
मध्यं स्यादांगरेयं शुभदृगतिबलस्तत्र जातो मृदुत्वक्ः।।

व्याख्या–अथ-आंगरेयवने जनितानां गजानां लक्षणमाह-रेवाया इति। रेवानद्याः दक्षिणे भागे विदिशादेशस्य प्राच्यां दिशि च पारियात्रभूधरब्रह्मवती-नद्योश्च यत् मध्यस्थलं, तदेव आंगरेयवनमित्युच्यते। तत्र वने जनिता मतंगजाः नितरां कृष्णवर्णछुरितांगाः शुभमनोहरनेत्राः अतीव बलवन्तः सन्ततं स्वशुण्डादण्डं स्वरदनोपरि स्थापनशीलाः मृदुस्पर्शाश्च दृश्यन्ते। अत एते **मूल्याधिक्यार्हा इति भावः।।**

4. Āṅgareya-forest Elephants.

Āṅgareya-forest lies in the south of Revā river, east of Vidiśā-country, and between Pāriyātra hills and the Brahmavatī river. Elephants available in this forest are very dark and beautiful, very tall, strong and very smooth. They have beautiful eyes and always twist their tusks with their trunks. They are worthy of high prices.

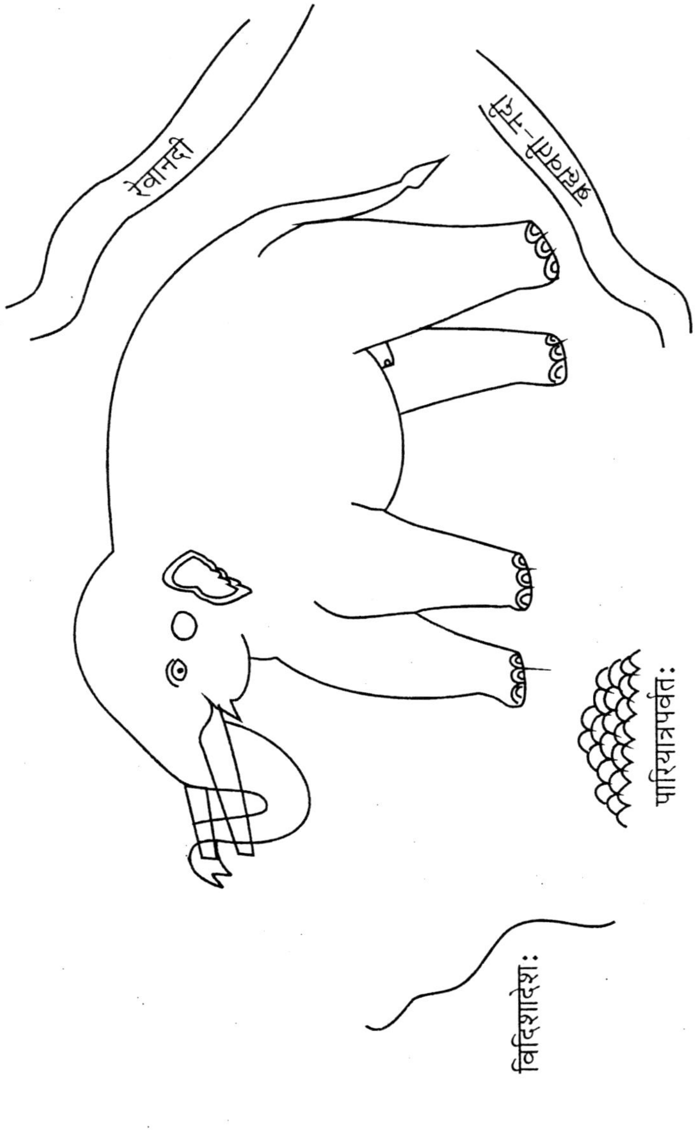

28. : आंगरेयवनगज: उत्तम: Āṅgareya-forest's elephants, superior

॥अथ-कलिंगवनगजलक्षणम् (5)॥

मूलम्

कालिंगं सह्यविन्ध्योत्कलकलशजदिक्वारिधीनां तु मध्यं
तत्रत्यः सूक्ष्मरोमा मधुदृगभिनवो वर्ष्मवान् मन्दचारः।

व्याख्या–अथ कालिंगवने जनितानां गजानां लक्षणमाह–कालिंगमिति। सह्यपर्वतस्य उत्तरस्यां दिशि विन्ध्यपर्वतस्य दक्षिणस्यां महोदधिनामकसमुद्रस्य पश्चिमस्यां दिशि च यत् स्थलं शतयोजनविस्तीर्णं तदेव कालिंगवनमित्युच्यते। दक्षिणापथवनापरपर्यायनामन्यस्मिन् वने संजाता मातंगाः नातितुंगाः नापि ह्रस्वाः नितरां कृष्णवर्णमनोहरांगाः हृष्टा अपि मन्दगतयश्च भवन्तीति **वाक्यार्थक्रमः**॥

5. Kaliṅga-forest Elephants

Kaliṅga-forest lies in the north of the Sahya-mountains, south of the Vindhyas, west of Bay of Bengal and its area 100 *yojanas*. Elephants available in this forest are neither too tall, nor too short, black in colour, strong and stout, with pleasure and slow in movement.

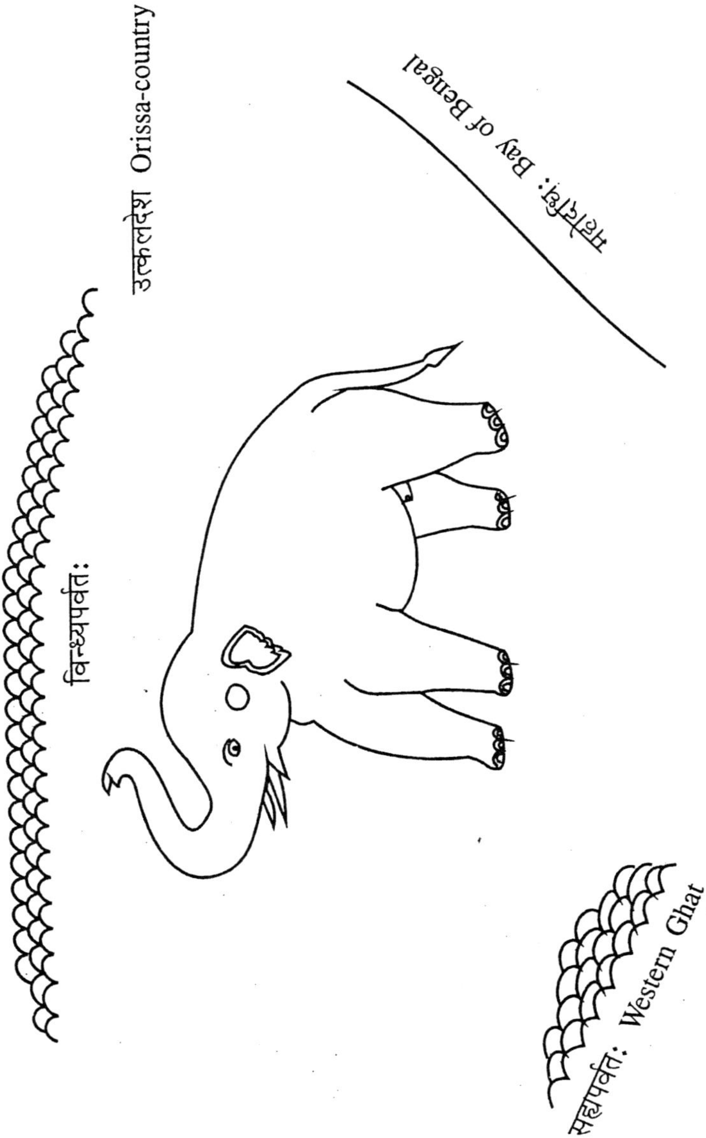

Fig. 29. : कलिंगवनगजः Orissa-forest's elephants, superior

॥अथ-अपरान्तवनगजलक्षणम् (6)॥

मूलम्

रेवाकृष्णाद्रिरंभोनिधिरपि चरमक्ष्माभृतः पूर्वदेशः
तन्मध्यं चापरान्तं सुतनुरतिबलस्तत्र जातो मृदुत्वक्।

व्याख्या–अथ-अपरान्तवने जनितानां वारणानां लक्षणं व्यनक्ति-रेवेति। अस्तमयपर्वतस्य प्राच्यां दिशि रेवानद्याः दक्षिणस्यां नीलगिरेश्च दक्षिणस्यां पूर्वोक्तमहोदध्याख्यस्य समुद्रस्यादिदूरे प्रतीच्यां चापरान्तवनं निर्दिष्टम्। तत्र वने जनिता महाबलाः नितरां दृढमनोहराकृतयः मृदुस्पर्शाः नितरां कृष्ण-वर्णछुरितांगाः मृगयासमरादिकार्येषु अखिन्नमानसाः भवन्ति। अत एव एते **मूल्याधिक्यार्हा इति भावः**॥

6. Aparānta-forest Elephants

Aparānta forest-lies in the east of Astamaya-parvata (sun-set hill) and south of the Revā river and Kṛṣṇagiri. Elephants available in this forest are very strong, beautiful, tall, very smooth, jet black, very bold in war and hunting and worth for more value.

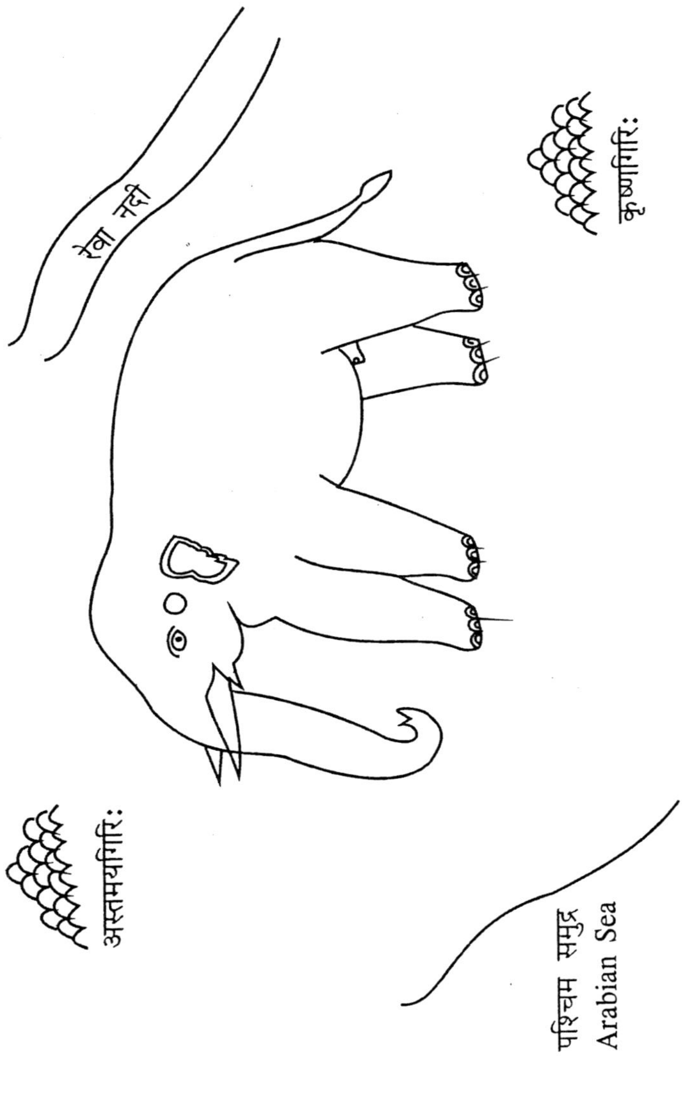

Fig. 30. : अपरान्तवनगजः उत्तमः Aparānta-forest's elephants, superior

॥ अथ-सौराष्ट्रवनगजलक्षणम् (7)॥

मूलम्

रेवावन्त्यर्बुदाख्यप्रमदपुरवरद्वारकानां च मध्यं
सौराष्ट्रं तत्र जातस्तनुनखवदनः तत्त्वतोऽल्पायुरज्ञः।

व्याख्या—अथ सौराष्ट्रवने जनितानां करिणां लक्षणमाह-रेवेति। द्वारवत्याः प्राच्यां दिशि रेवायाः दक्षिणस्यामवन्तिदेशभूमेः प्रमदपुरभूमेश्च दक्षिणस्यां अर्बुदपर्वतस्य प्रतीच्यां च दिशि यत् स्थलं पंचाशद्योजनविस्तीर्णं तत् सौराष्ट्रवनमित्युच्यते। तस्मिन् सौराष्ट्रवने जाता मातंगाः नितरां कृष्णवर्णच्छुरितांगाः मस्तकभागे निबिडरोमराजियुताः ह्रस्वनखाः ह्रस्ववदनाः मूढचेतसः अल्पायुषश्च भवन्ति। अत एते वारणाः **अधमा इति भावः॥**

7. Saurāṣṭra-forest Elephants

Saurāṣṭra-forest lies in the east of Dwārakā, south of the Revā river, Avanti country and Pramadapura, and west of Arbuda-mountains and its area is 50 *yojanas*. Elephants available in this forest are jet black, dull, short in age, and inferior ones. They have thick hair on their heads, narrow faces and small nails.

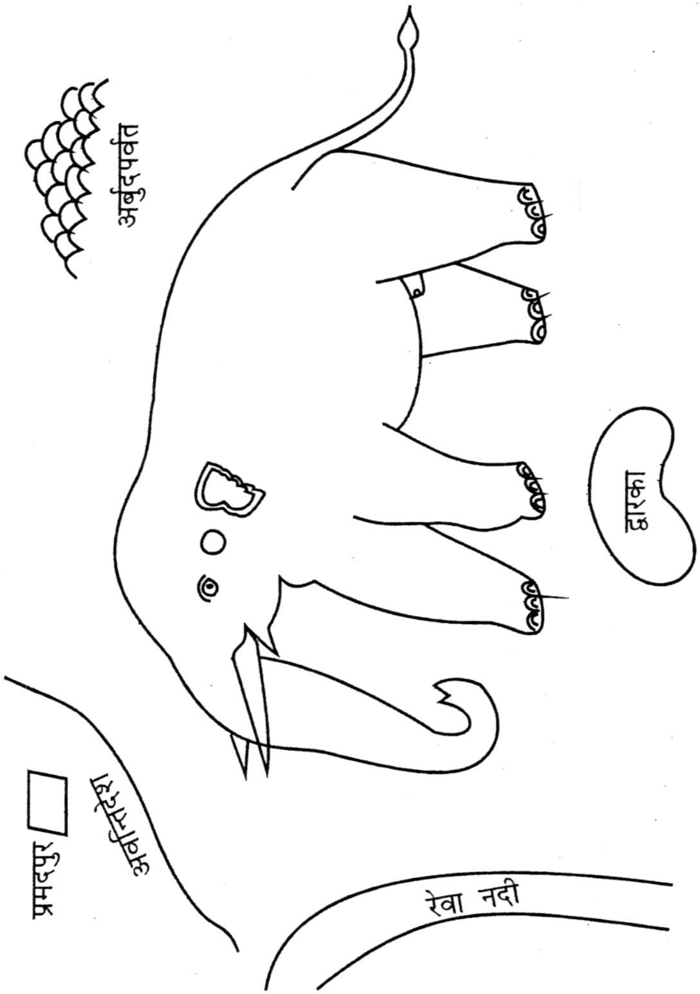

Fig. 31. : सौराष्ट्रवनगजः अधमः Saurashtra-forest's elephants, inferior

॥अथ-पांचनदवनगजलक्षणम् (8)॥

मूलम्

कालेयारण्यसिन्धोस्तुहिनगिरिकुरुक्षेत्रयोरन्तरं स्यात्
कान्तारं चोत्तरं पांचनदमतिबलस्तूत्कटस्तत्र जातः।

इत्येष वननिर्देशो वारणानां महीपते।
रूपाचारवपुर्भिस्तु गजा ज्ञेया वनाश्रिताः॥

प्राच्यं कालिंगकं प्रोक्तमपरान्तं वनोत्तमम्।
चैद्यरूषकदाशार्णमांगरेयं तु मध्यमम्॥

सौराष्ट्रकं पांचनदं जघन्यं वनमुच्यते।

व्याख्या–अथ-पांचनदवने जातानां गजानां लक्षणमाह-कालेयेति। कुरुक्षेत्रस्य प्रतीच्यां हिमालयस्य दक्षिणस्यां सिन्धोरुदीच्यां कालेयवनस्य प्राच्यां च यत् स्थलं द्विशताधिकयोजनविस्तीर्णं निर्दिष्टम्, तत् पांचनद-वनमित्युच्यते। तत्र वने जनिता वारणाः नितरां कृष्णवर्णछुरितशरीराः मस्तके निबिडरोमयुताः यंत्रादिभिः सुलभमसाध्याः कैश्चित् दुर्गुणैरुपेताश्चण्ड-पराक्रमा दृश्यन्ते। एवं रीत्या अष्टौ वनानि अस्मिन् भरतखण्डे निर्दिष्टानि। तस्मादेतेषु वनेषूत्पन्ना गजा रूपाचारशरीरलक्षणैरेवमत्र प्रतिपादितलक्षणैश्च तत्तद्वने जनिताः ज्ञेयाः सूक्ष्मधियेति। किं च-गजानामुत्पत्तिं तद्वननिर्णयादि च बोद्धुं कापि व्यवस्था। यथा-तस्मिन् तस्मिन् वने ये ये सृगालव्याघ्रादयः तैः सदृशध्वनियुता वा इति प्रथमतो (1) गजानां रींकारस्वरलक्षणं परीक्षयेत् ततः शरीरवर्णपरीक्षा, (2) ततः शरीरपरिमाणपरीक्षा (3), ततो गुणपरीक्षा, (4) तदनु बलपरीक्षा (5) चेति परीक्षामेवं पंचधा कलयन्ति **गजशास्त्रलक्षणवेत्तारः प्राचीनाः। एवं परीक्षाकलनेऽपि प्रकारद्वयं ज्ञेयम्।** यथा-यदि गजानां परीक्षाविषये वनलक्षणमंगीक्रियते तदा उत्तरत्र वक्ष्यमाण-भद्रादिलक्षणं न प्रधानं भवति। यदि भद्रादिलक्षणं प्रधानमंगीक्रियते तदा वनलक्षणस्य प्रयोजनं नैव भवति। अत एव लक्षणकारणं न निरर्थकम्। तत्र तत्र देशेषु प्रकारद्वयेनैव परीक्षा करणीयेति **संप्रदायः**। तथापि विशेषतो वनलक्षणेनैव गजा मृग्यन्त इति **प्राचां मतमवलम्ब्यैव शास्त्रकारः**

पालकाप्यः प्रथमतः एव वनलक्षणमेवमत्र प्रतिपादितवानिति **सन्दर्भक्रमशैली।** किं च-एवमत्र प्रतिपादितेष्वष्टसु वनेषु प्राच्यवनं कालिंगवनमपरान्तवनमित्येतानि त्रीणि वनानि नितरामुत्तमानि। एतेषु वनेषु त्रिषु जाता वारणाः उत्तमा एव। चैद्यकरूषकवनं दाशार्णवनमांगरेयकवनमित्येतानि त्रीणि वनानि मध्यमानि। सौराष्ट्रकवनं पांचनदवनमित्येतत् वनद्वयं तु अधमं ज्ञेयम्। एतेषूत्पन्नाः मातंगास्तु मध्यमा अधमा इति च क्रमेण ज्ञेयमिति **परिपाटी॥**

8. Pāñcanada-forest elephants

Pāñcanada-forest lies in the east of Kurukṣetra (Delhi), south of the Himālayas, north of Indus river and west of Kāleya-forest and its area is about 200 *yojanas*. Elephants available in this forest are very dark, not easily controllable, very strong in physic, though they have some bad qualities in them. They have thick tuft of hair on their heads and huge bodies.

These are five main points to test the qualities of the elephants available in these eight main forests and the adjoining forests and jungles mentioned above.

1. Test of cry.
2. Test of colour.
3. Test in size and measurements.
4. Test of nature and conducts.
5. Test of strength.

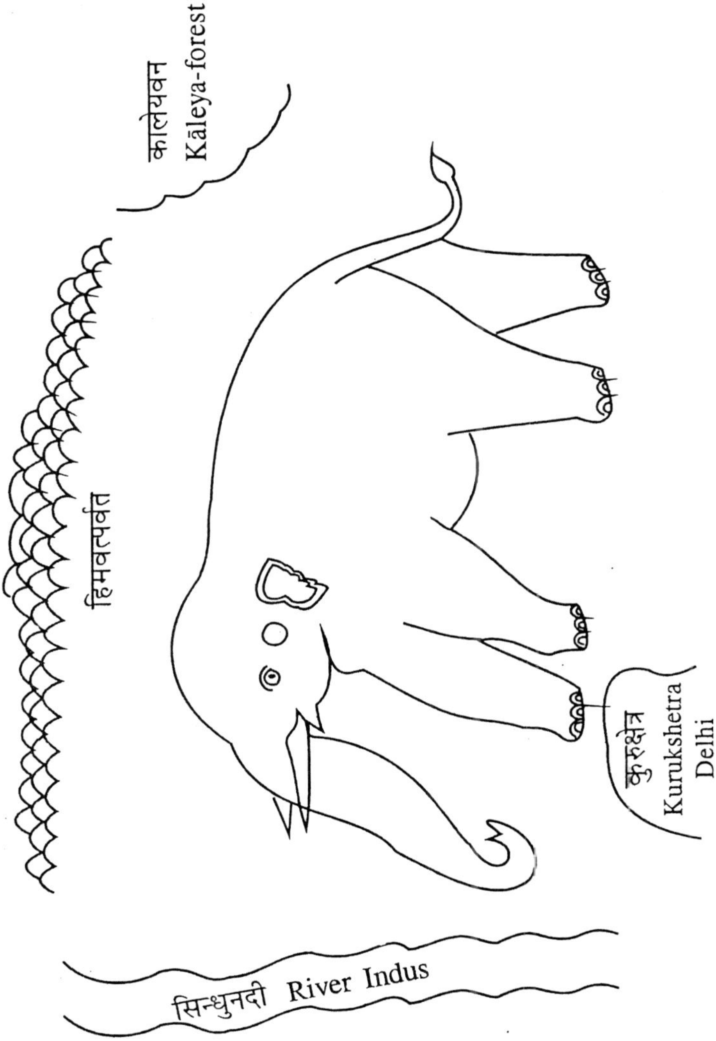

Fig. 32. : पांचनदवनगजः उत्तमः Punjab country-elephants, superior

॥अथ-पूर्वोपवनगजलक्षणम् (1)॥

मूलम्

उपपूर्ववनान्यष्टौ भवन्तीह महीपते।
वक्ष्यामि तत्त्वतस्तेषां लक्षणान्यनुपूर्वशः॥

किरातविषयो नाम पूर्वेण हिमभूभृतः।
तत्रोत्पन्नाश्च विकृताः दुर्विज्ञेयाश्च वारणाः॥

व्याख्या–एतावता प्रबन्धेन विशेषतो गजोत्पत्तेः गजवृन्दसंचारस्य च हेतुभूतान्यष्टौ वनानि निर्दिश्याधुना **शास्त्रकार**स्तावत् हिमवतः सर्वास्वपि दिक्षु अतिसमीपस्थले स्थितिभाजामन्येषामुपवनाख्यानामष्टानामधमवनानां स्थाननिर्देशपूर्वकं तत्र जनितानां मातंगानां च लक्षणं विशदयति–उपपूर्ववना-नीत्यादिना। हिमालयस्य प्राच्यां दिशि नातिदूरे किरातदेशो वर्तते। तस्मिन् देशे तत्समीपारण्यभूमिषु पूर्वोपवनाख्यासु संजाता वारणाः विकृतशरीराः ह्रस्वशुण्डादण्डाः मृगयाकारव्याधादीनां वशमप्राप्ताः कुंजगुहादिष्वेव प्रायशो वासभाजो भवन्ति। अत एते वारणाः क्रियानर्हाः। न स्वीकार्या **इत्युपदेशः**। किं च-किरातवने जनिता वारणाः सर्वेष्वप्यवयवेषु अशुभस्वरूपदीर्घरेखान्वि-ताश्च भवन्तीति **नवीनाः**॥

There are also eight more inferior forests surrounding the Himālayas on eight directions.

There is a country by name Kirāta inhabited by the barbarians in the east of the Himālayas. Elephants available in these forests are very ugly both in colour and in bodies. There are bad stripes on their bodies. They have too short trunks. They are uncontrollable and uncapturable even to the hill tribes men. They will be always hiding in bushes and caves. They shirk work and are not enterprising.

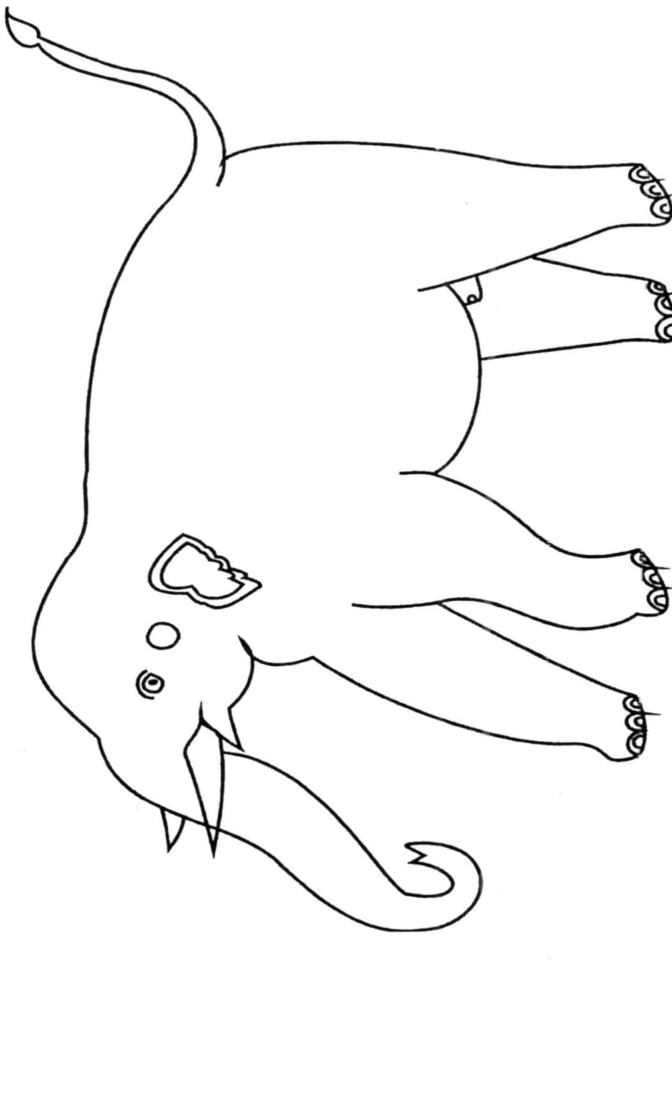

Fig. 33. : पूर्वोपवनगजः अधमः Himālaya's Eastern-forests' elephants. Inferior

।।अथ-आग्नेयोपवनगजलक्षणम् (2)।।

मूलम्

पूर्वदक्षिणतस्तस्य लीलाख्यो नाम पर्वतः।
तत्रत्या ह्रस्ववदनाः विषयाश्चापि वारणाः।।

व्याख्या–अथ–आग्नेयोपवने जातानां गजानां लक्षणमाह–पूर्वदक्षिणत इति। हिमवतो महागिरेराग्नेयभागे लीलाख्यः पर्वतो वर्तते। तस्य गिरेः प्रान्ततलेषु आग्नेयोपवननामधेयेषु जनिता वारणाः सर्वेऽपि ह्रस्वमुखाः स्थूलशरीराः दुर्गुणान्विताः दुष्टकार्यकरणलोलुपाः सुलभेन मानुषवशमप्राप्ता भवन्ति। अत एते मतंगजाः कार्यानर्हाः। न स्वीकार्या इति **भावः**।।

(2) South-east forest

In the south-east of the Himālayas there is a mountain called Līla. Elephants available in this hill and its surrounding forests are small-faced and huge-bodied, unfit for work, uncontrollable and uncapturable.

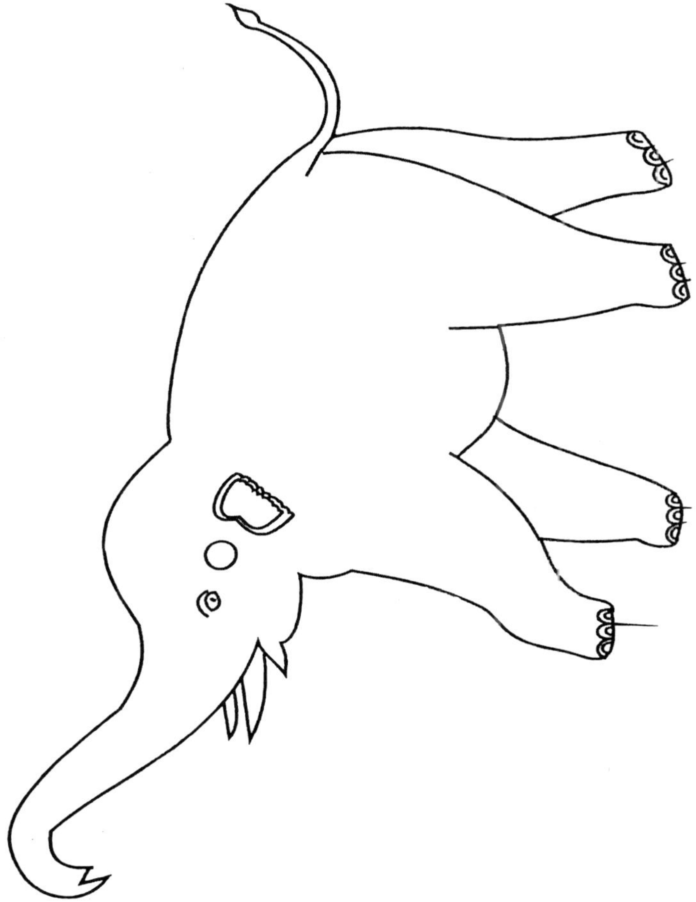

Fig. 34. : आग्नेयोपवनगजः अधमः South-eastern forest's elephants, Inferior

॥अथ-दक्षिणोपवनगजलक्षणम् (3) ॥

मूलम् .

विशालद्वीपमित्यस्य दक्षिणे राक्षसा गजाः।
ह्रस्वाकारा विरूपाश्च विकृताश्च भवन्ति ते॥

व्याख्या–अथ-दक्षिणोपवने जनितानां गजानां लक्षणमाह-विशालद्वीपमिति। पूर्वोक्तस्य तस्य हिमवतः दक्षिणे भागे विशालद्वीपमिति नामभाक् किंचित् स्थलं प्रसिद्धम्। तत्रोत्पन्नाः मातंगाः सर्वेऽपि कृष्णवर्णाः निबिडरोमयुतमस्तकोपेताः ह्रस्वप्रमाणाः विकृतशरीरवन्तः यंत्रादिभिः निर्दिष्टकार्याण्यकुर्वाणाः मानुषधेनुहरिणादिसत्त्वहिंसने निरताः अत एव राक्षसगुणोपेता भवन्ति। अत एते दूरतो वर्ज्या इति **भावः**॥

(3) South-forest—There is a secluded island called Viśāladwīpa in the south of the Himālayas. Elephants available in this forest are not proportionate in their shape, though black in colour. They are fond of killing human beings, cows, deer etc. As they have bad qualities they are termed after Rākṣasas.

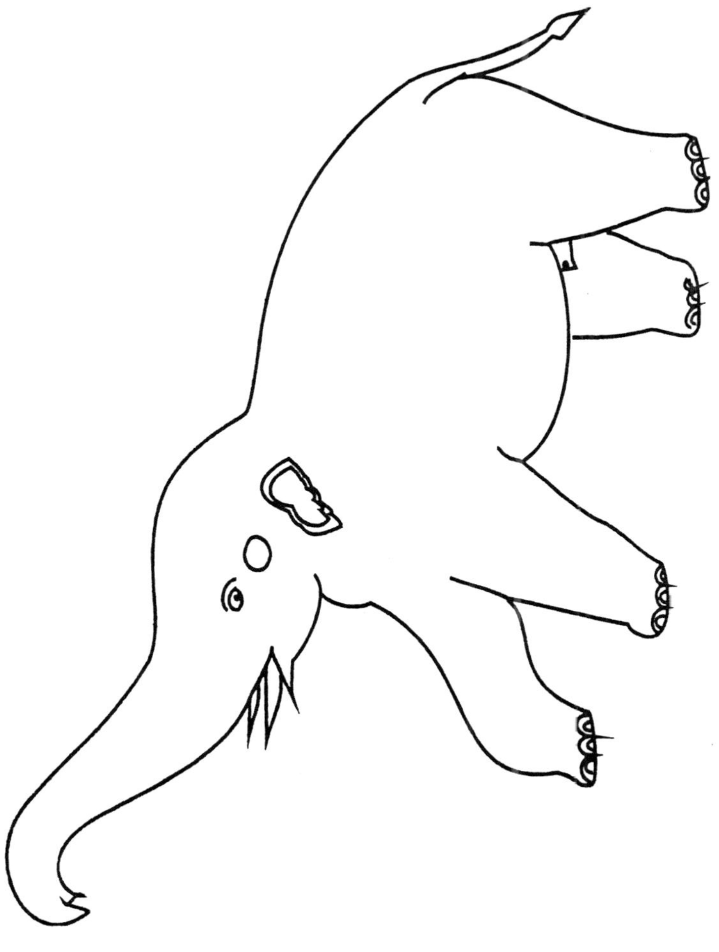

Fig. 35. : दक्षिणोपवनगजः Southern-forest's elephants, Inferior

॥अथ-नैर्ऋत्योपवनगजलक्षणम् (4)॥

मूलम्

बर्बराह्वयदेशस्तु गिरेर्दक्षिणपश्चिमे।
ह्रस्वाश्च ह्रस्वदन्ताश्च तत्रोद्भूता मतंगजाः॥

व्याख्या–अथ-नैर्ऋत्योपवने जनितानां गजानां गुणादीन् विशदयति-बर्बराह्वयदेशस्त्विति। हिमालयस्य निर्ऋतिभागे नातिदूरस्थले बर्बरनामको देशः। तस्य देशस्यारण्येषु निर्ऋत्युपवनाख्येषु उत्पन्नाः वारणाः सर्वेऽपि ह्रस्वप्रमाणाः ह्रस्ववदनाः बलपराक्रमतेजोहीनाः दुर्गुणोपेताश्च भवन्ति। अत एतेऽपि वारणाः न प्रशस्ता इति **भावः**।

(4) South-western forest—There is a country called Barbara. Elephants in these parts are very small in size, not strong and bad natured. They have small tusks and shirk work.

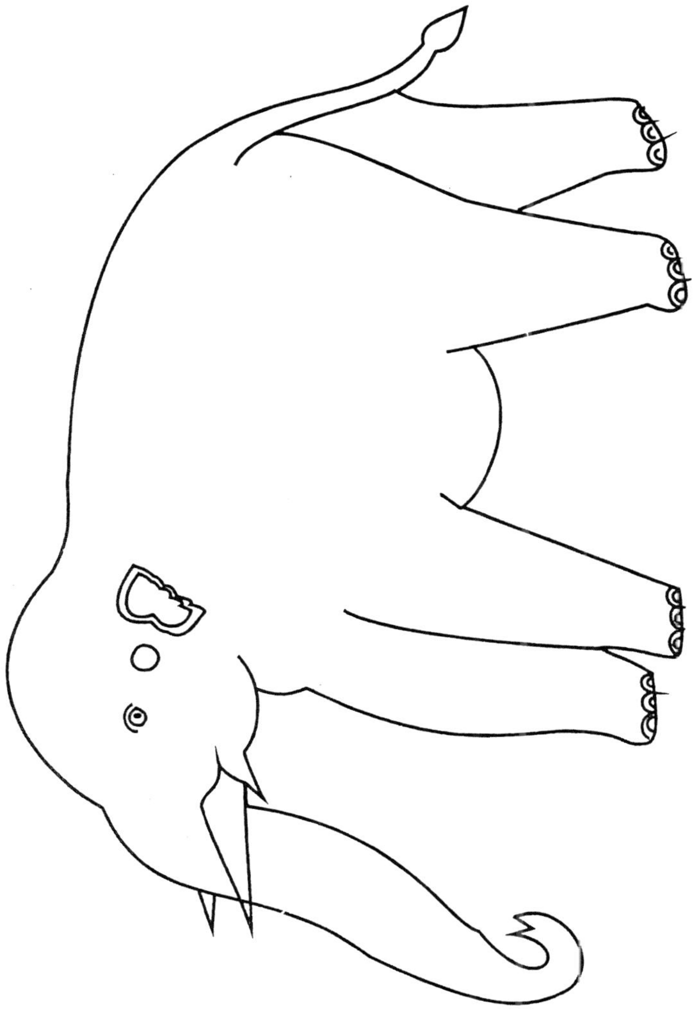

Fig. 36. : नैर्ऋत्योपवनगजः अधमः South-western forest's elephants, Inferior

॥अथ-पश्चिमोपवनगजलक्षणम् (5)॥

मूलम्

गिरेश्च पश्चिमे भागे विह्वलो नाम पर्वतः।
तत्रोत्पन्नाः ह्रस्वकराः दीर्घपादाश्च वारणाः॥

व्याख्या–अथ पश्चिमोपवने जनितानां गजानां स्वरूपलक्षणादिकं विशदयति-गिरेस्त्विति। पूर्वोक्तरीत्या हिमवतः प्रतीच्यां दिशि विह्वलो नाम पर्वतः। तस्य पर्वतस्य समीपारण्यभूमिषु पश्चिमोपवनाख्यासु संजाताः स्तंबेरमाः नितरां ह्रस्वशुण्डादण्डाः दीर्घपादाः सल्लक्षणहीनाश्च भवन्ति। अत एतेऽपि दूरतो वर्ज्या **इत्युपदेशः**।

(5) West forest–There is a mountain called Vihwala in the west of the Himālayas. Elephants available in this forest possess small tusks, heads and long legs and have many bad qualities.

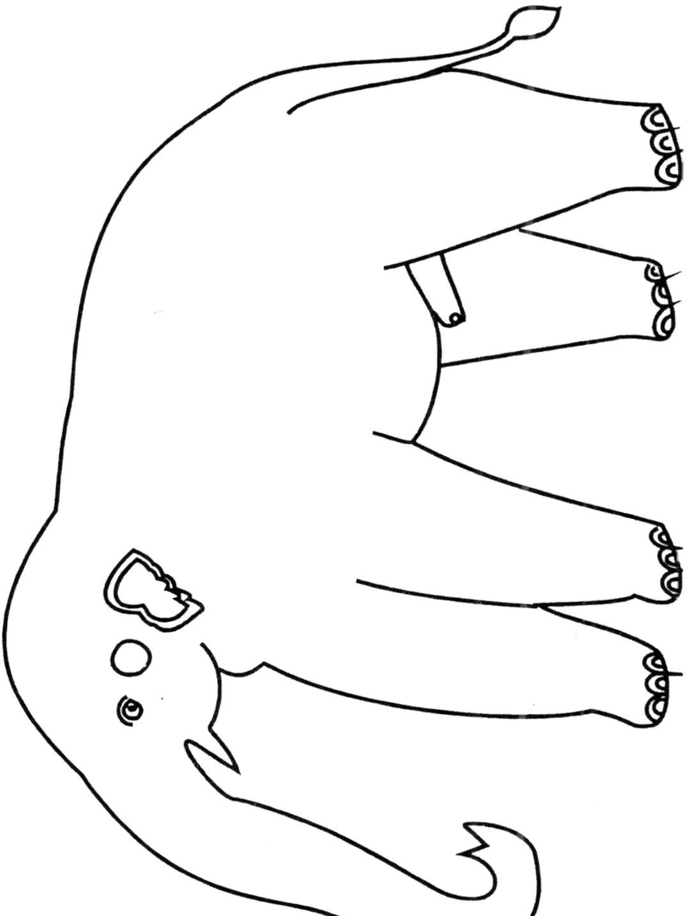

Fig. 37. : पश्चिमोपवनगजः अधमः Western forest-elephants, Inferior

॥अथ-वायव्योपवनगजलक्षणम् (6)॥

मूलम्

गिरेर्वायव्यदेशे तु वातिकाख्यः शिलोच्चयः।
तत्रोत्पन्नाः कृशांगाश्च वर्णतो धूसरा गजाः॥

व्याख्या—अथ वायव्योपवने जनितानां गजानां लक्षणमाह-गिरेरिति। पूर्वोक्तरीत्या हिमवतो वायव्यभागे नातिदूरे स्थले वातिकाख्यः पर्वतो वर्तते। तस्य गिरेः समीपारण्यतलेषु वायव्योपवनाख्येषु जनिताः करिणः अत्यन्तं कृशदेहाः धूमवर्णछुरितांगाः भवन्ति। अतो दुर्बला एते कार्यानर्हा इति व्यवस्था॥

(6) North-west forest—There is a mountain called Vātika in the north-east of the Himālayas. Elephants in this tract are very tall, very weak, long and gray in colour.

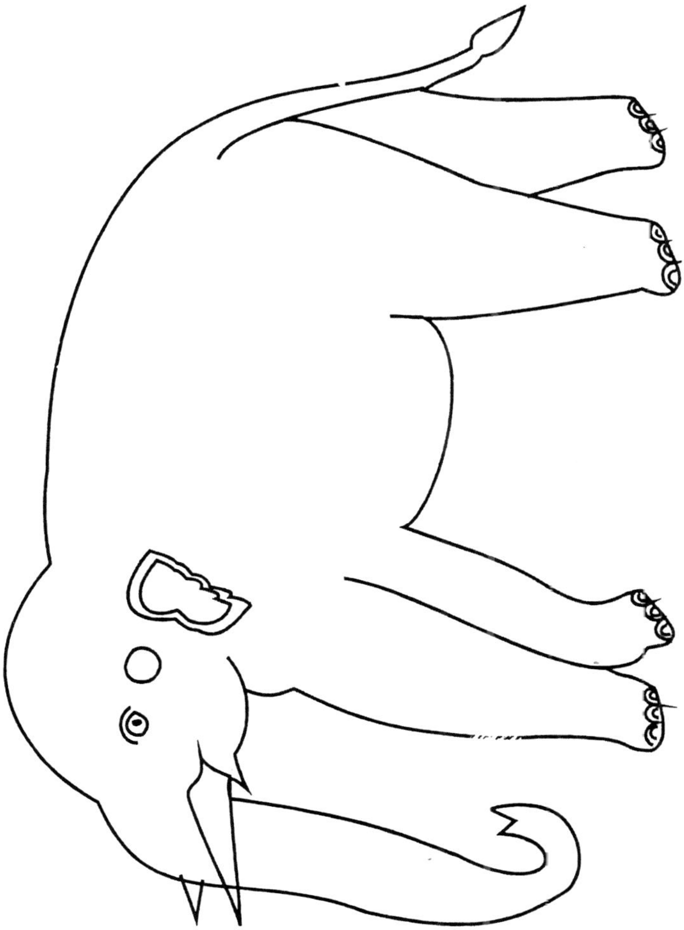

Fig. 38. : वायव्योपवनगजः अधमः North western forest elephants, Inferior

॥अथ- उत्तरोपवनगजलक्षणम् (7)॥

मूलम्

तदुत्तरे पार्वतीयाः म्लेच्छजातिगुणान्विताः।
अज्ञानात्म्लेच्छजातित्वादल्पायुष्या न संशयः॥

व्याख्या–अथ-उत्तरोपवने जनितानां गजानां लक्षणमाह-तदुत्तर इति। हिमवतस्तस्योत्तरभागे नितरां विशालान्यरण्यतलानि बहूनि सन्ति। तेषु वनभागेषु उत्तरोपवनाख्येषु तत्र तत्र जनिताः इभाः सर्वेऽपि स्पष्टांगा अपि अज्ञानिन एव यजमानादिनिर्दिष्टकार्यादीनि कृच्छ्रेणापि ज्ञातुमसमर्थाः। परन्तु-म्लेच्छा इव विविधदुर्गुणोपेताः सुरास्वादननिरताः सुलभकोपाः अल्पायुषाश्च भवन्ति। अत एतेऽपि मदाविलकटाः करटिनो दूरतस्त्याज्या इति **भावः**।

(7) North forest—There are many big mountains in the north of the Himālayas. Elephants in these forests are drunkards of palmyra and cocoanut toddy. Though they are strong, they are dull and foolish. They are very short in age. They have inferior qualities and nature like the Mlecchas (Mohammadans).

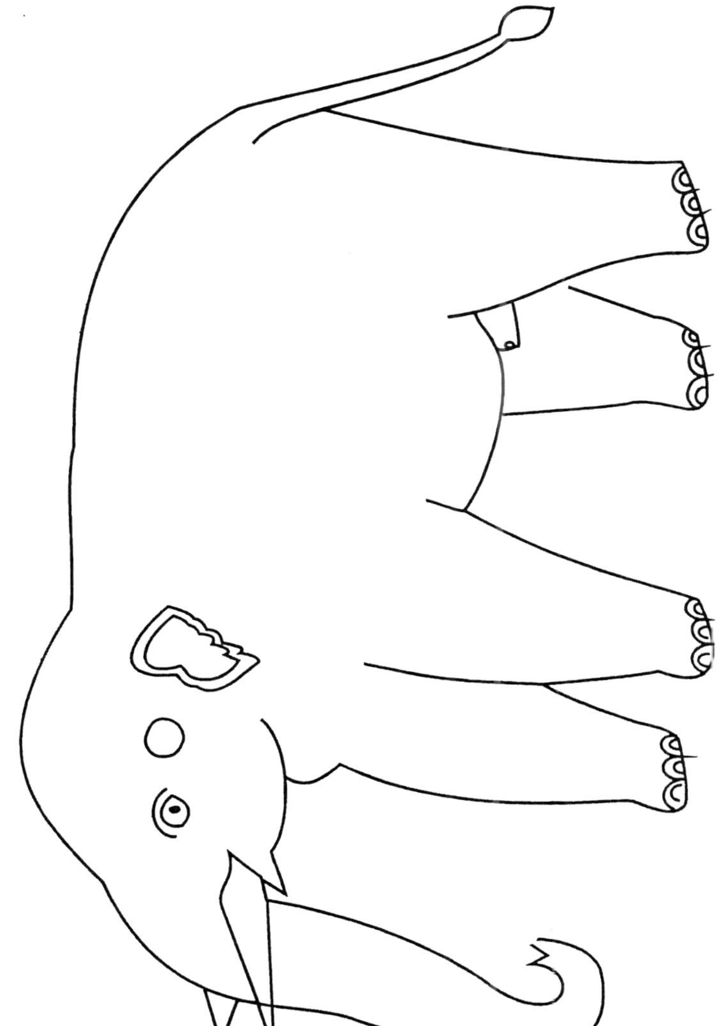

Fig. 39. : उत्तरोपवनगजः अधमः North-western forest's elephants, Inferior

॥अथ-ऐशानोपवनगजलक्षणम् (8)॥

मूलम्

ततश्चोत्तरपूर्वायां भूधरेन्द्रे तु वारणाः।
पैशाचका भस्मवर्णाः सर्वकर्मसु गर्हिताः॥

इति पालकाप्यमहर्षिप्रणीते गजशास्त्रे गजवननिरूपणं नाम चतुर्थं प्रकरणम्॥

व्याख्या–अथ-ऐशानोपवने जनितानां गजानां लक्षणमाह-ततश्चेति। तस्य हिमभूभृतः ऐशान्यां दिशि बहवः शिलोच्चया वर्तन्ते। तेषां पर्वतानां समीपारण्यतलेषु ऐशानोपवनाख्येषु जनिताः वारणाः सर्वेऽपि कृशदेहाः भस्मवर्णाः क्रूरहृदयाः पिशाचा इव बालकादीन्निरीक्ष्य तज्जिघांसया ससंभ्रममुपसर्पणशीलाः यजमाननिर्दिष्टकार्यादीननादृत्य स्वेच्छागमनशीलाः कृच्छ्रेणापि साधयितुमयोग्याः मानुषस्नेहविध्वंसकाश्च भवन्ति। अत अते वारणा अवश्यं परिहरणीया **एवेत्यर्थः**। एवं प्रतिपादितेष्वेतेषु उपवनाष्टकस्थलेषु संजाता वारणाः सर्वैरपि न स्वीकार्याः। एतैर्न किमपि प्रयोजनमिति **भावः**। क्वचित्समये हिंसाकारिणश्च। अतो न क्रेतव्या **इत्युपदेशः**॥

इतिश्रीमदनन्तकृष्णभट्टारकविरचितायां भावदर्शिन्याख्यायां गजशास्त्रव्याख्यायां चतुर्थं प्रकरणम्॥

(8) North-east forest—There are very big mountains in the north-east of the Himālayas. Elephants born in these forests are ash-colourd, treacherous in character, like devils and ghosts, very cruel and uncapturable. These elephants in these eight forests are very bad charactered. They are unfit for any work as hunting, lifting heavy loads and war. They are not advisable for purchase.

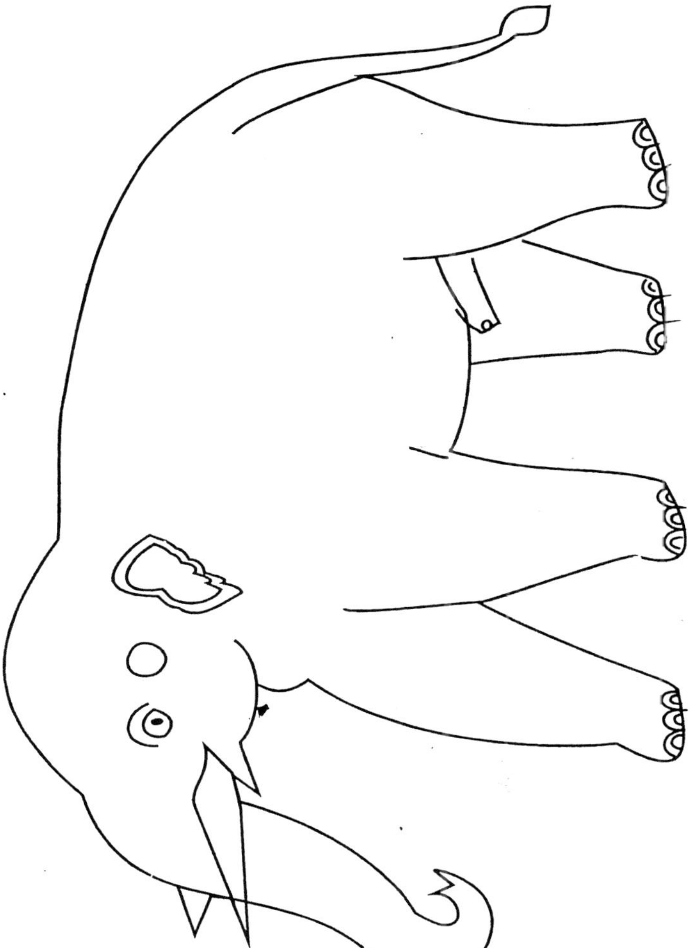

Fig.40. : ऐशानोपवनगजः, अधमः, North-eastern forest elephants (8) Inferior.

पंचमं प्रकरणम्

कालीयगजलक्षणनिरूपणम्

मूलम्

अथातः संप्रवक्ष्यामि वयोज्ञानं महीपते।
यो न वेत्ति स्तन्यजातं जाते मासे पिबन् शिशुः॥

व्यासप्रोक्ते गजशास्त्रे–

मासजो विक्लवो व्यग्रः स्तन्यं पातुं न वेत्ति च।

व्याख्या–पूर्वस्मिन् **प्रकरणे चतुर्थे** भरतखण्डेऽस्मिन् षोडशवनानि गजोत्पत्तिकारणानि तत्तत्स्थानसीमाकथनपूर्वकं निर्दिष्टानि। तेषु वनेषूत्पन्नानां गजानामुत्तममध्यमाधमस्वरूपगुणलक्षणादिकं क्रमेण प्रतिपादितम्। अस्मिंस्तु **पंचमे प्रकरणे** तेषु वनेषु तदन्तिकगिरिगुहासानुभागादिस्थलेषु प्रसूतानां गजानां वयो ज्ञातुं तदर्हलक्षणादिकमुच्यत इति **पूर्वकथाप्रसंगः**। तत्र **शास्त्रकार**स्तावत् विंशत्युत्तरशतसंवत्सरकाल एव करिणां परमावधिवयःकाल इति **पठितवान्**। अयमेव वयःकालः **शालिहोत्रादि**भिः सर्वैरप्यंगीकृत एव। तस्मात् तादृशपरमावधिकालपर्यन्तं तस्मिन् तस्मिन् वयसि गजानां गुणचर्यादिकमत्र क्रमेण प्रतिपाद्यत इति **व्यवस्था** ज्ञेया। तत्र नवप्रसूतो गजशावकः प्रथमे मासि जनन्याः स्तन्यं पातुमपि न वेत्ति। अतोऽयं शिशुरिति नामभाक् भवतीति **शास्त्रकारः पालकाप्यो महर्षिः। व्यास**स्तु–प्रथममासगलनपर्यन्तं जातस्य तस्य शावकस्य विक्लव इति नाम **व्यवहृत-वानिति पूर्वव्यवस्था।**

Chapter-V

Description of the age of elephants

After describing the nature and qualities of various elephants in 16 main forests in India in the previous chapter, the sage

Fig. 41. : प्रथममासवयस्कगजः 1st month elephants with their mothers

Pālakāpya began to describe them from their birth to the end of their life. The utmost age for the elephants is determined to be 120 years.

Nature and quality of the 1st month elephants

The young elephants in their first month do not regularly open their eyes and they do not know even to drink their mother's milk. They will be always morose and lying by the side of their mothers.

द्विमासको रक्तवर्णः हंसः पंकप्रियो गजः।

व्यासप्रोक्ते गजशास्त्रे

स्तनं पिबेद्द्विमासस्तु पंकेप्सुर्मण्डको मृदुः॥

व्याख्या–द्विमासक इति। मासद्वयवयस्को गजशावकः पुष्कराग्र-मुखनयनांचलादिषु रक्तवर्णभाक् सन् पंकपरागक्रीडनासक्तो भवेत्। सोऽयं गजशावकः हंसक इति नामभाक् भवेदिति **शास्त्रकारः पालकाप्यमहर्षिः।** **व्यासस्तु**–मासद्वयवयस्को गजशावकः मृदुस्पर्शः सन् प्रत्यहं दशवारं षोडशवारं वा मातुः स्तन्यं पिबेत्। स्तन्यपानानन्तरमितस्ततो गत्वा जनन्या अदूर एव पंकपरागादिषु खेलनपरो गच्छेत्। एवंभूतस्य गजशावकस्य मण्डक इति नाम विदुरार्या इति **पूर्वकालीनव्यवस्था।**

The elephants in their 2nd month have red colour in the corners of their eyes, faces and end of their trunks. They drink milk about 10 or 15 times a day. They begin to play in mud and dust. The author named this sort of elephants as ''Hamsa'' while the sage *Vyāsa* as "Maṇḍaka".

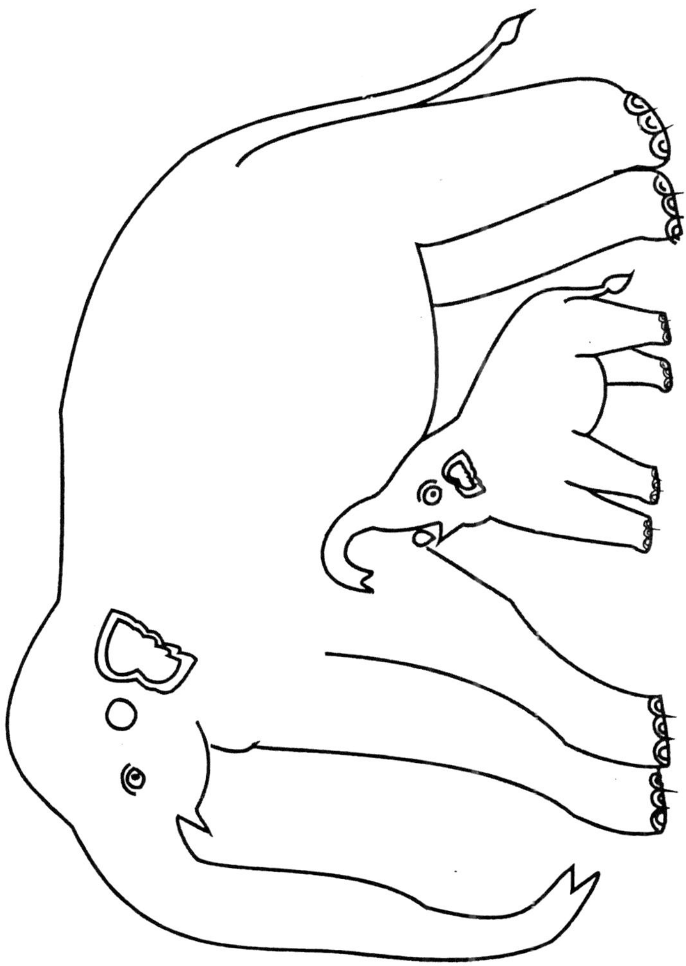

Fig. 42. : द्वितीयमासवयस्कगजः 2nd month elephants

त्रिमासो यूथनिष्क्रामी जलदुग्धप्रियो गजः।

व्यासप्रोक्ते गजशास्त्रे–

त्रिमासो यूथनिष्क्रामी जलकामी च दुग्धपः॥

व्याख्या–त्रिमास इति। जननानन्तरं मासत्रयवयस्को गजशावकः प्रातर्मध्यं सायंतने च नियमेन मातुः स्तन्यपाननिरतो भवेत्। समयान्तरेषु किंचित् जलपानासक्तः शश्वत् स्वकरतलेन जलास्फालनादिक्रीडासुखं चानुभवन् सन् यदृच्छया गजयूथे स्वाभिमुखमागते सति तैर्गजैः साकं स्वयमपि गन्तुमभिलाषी च भवेदिति **पालकाप्यो महर्षिः। भगवान् व्यास**स्तु–एवं-लक्षणोपेतस्यास्य गजशावकस्य मासत्रयवयस्कस्य यूथनिष्क्रामीति नाम दत्तवानिति।

3rd month elephants

They drink their mother's milk regularly and punctually three times a day (i.e) morning, midday and evening. At other times they are irregular in doing so. At times they drink water too. They go to ponds or channels if they are near to play. They follow their aged ones if they come in front. The sage *Vyāsa* called these (3rd month elephants) "Yūthaniṣkrāmī."

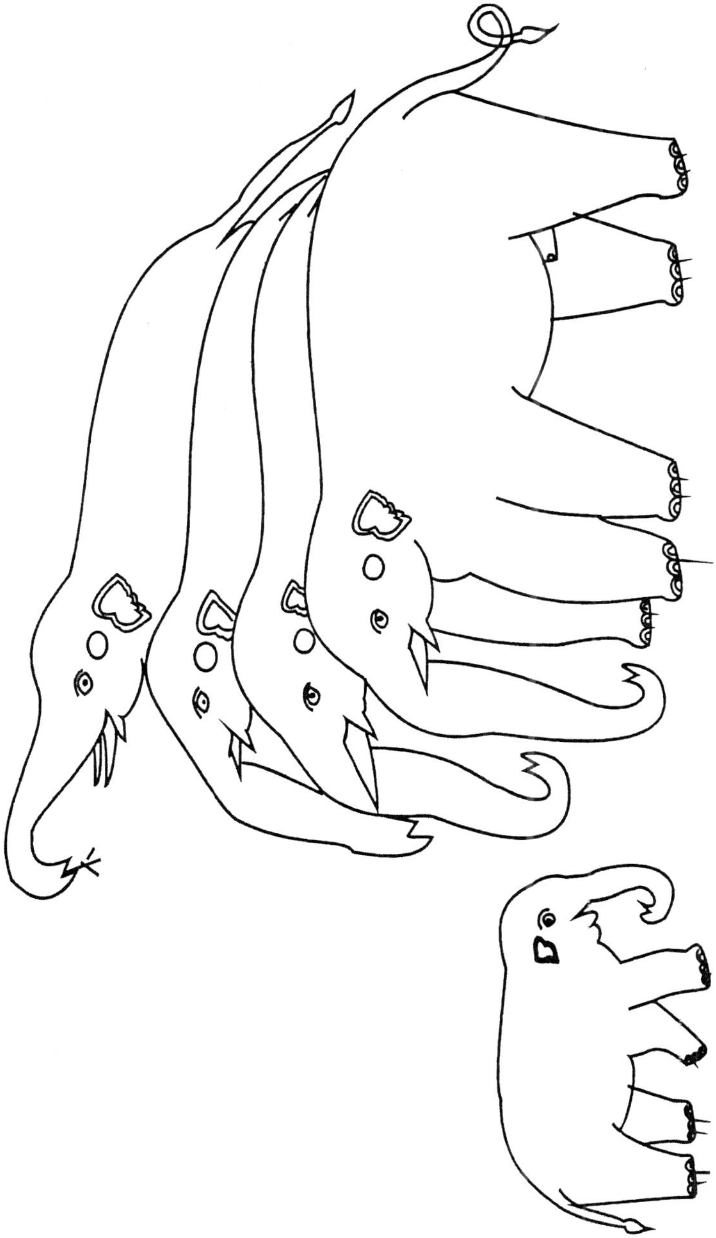

Fig. 43. : तृतीयमासवयस्कगजः 3rd month elephants

चतुर्थे चपलांगः स्यात् सर्वत्र परिधावति।

व्यासप्रोक्ते गजशास्त्रे-

चतुर्थे चपलांगः स्यात् गजो गर्वेण धावति॥

व्याख्या—चतुर्थ इति। चतुर्थमासवयस्को गजशावकश्चपलांग इतस्ततो गच्छन् सन् क्वचित् निम्नोन्नतस्थलनिबिडकुंजादिस्थलस्वरूपमजानन् सन् झडिति परिधावनशीलो भवेत्। एवंप्रकारेण स्वल्पकालं स्वमातुः सविधं विहाय स्थलान्तरभागपि तत्क्षणादेव पुनः प्रतिनिवृत्त्य स्वमातुरन्तिकस्थो भवतीति **भावः। भगवान् व्यासस्तु**—मासचतुष्कवयस्को गजशावकः भीतिमजानन् किंचित् गर्वयुतः सन् स्वावासमीपस्थतरुसमीपं वा इतस्ततो वा स्वशुण्डाप्रसारणपूर्वकं परिधावनशीलो भवेदिति।

They will wander here without understanding the elevations and depression in the ground. Though they run about, they will come and join their mothers very shortly. *Vyāsa* says that they will project their trunks to catch-hold of the twigs to eat with a little pride. But they are incapable of grazing.

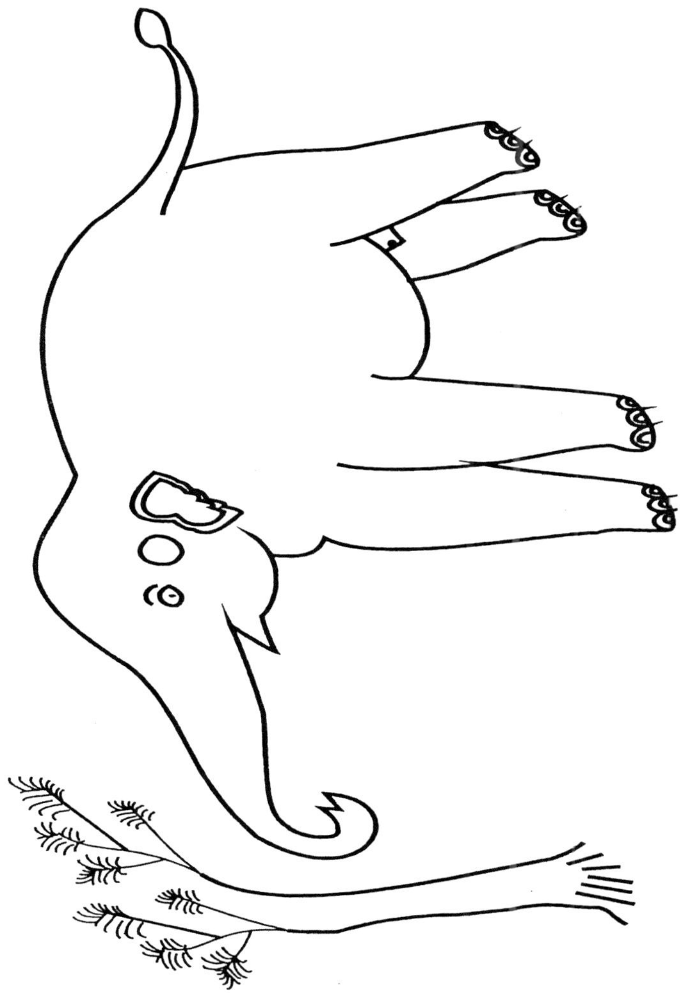

Fig. 44. : चतुर्थमासवयस्कगजः 4th month elephants

पंचमे विक्लवाक्षश्च संघातात् पार्श्ववान् भवेत्।

व्यासप्रोक्ते गजशास्त्रे-

पंचमे विक्लवाक्षश्च जग्ध्वा मृदु च पल्लवम्।।
सल्लकीं खदिरं चैव कर्णिकारं च खादति।
व्यक्तसंस्थानदेहश्च वृत्तकुंभमुखो गजः।।

व्याख्या–पंचम इति। पंचममासवयस्को गजशावकः प्रातः सायं-समये च स्वजनन्याः सविधं विहाय गजान्तरमध्यगतः सन् कुतूहलात् तैः साकं किंचित् दूरं गमनशीलो भवेत्। तथापि तस्मात् स्थलात् झडिति प्रति-निवृत्य स्वमातुः निकटतटमेवाश्रयेदिति **पालकाप्यः। व्यास**स्तु-पंचममासवयस्को गजशिशुः स्वावासस्थलात् किंचित् दूरं गत्वा तत्रत्यस्थलान्तराणि वृक्षान्तरादींश्च निरीक्ष्य चकितलोचनः सन् प्रतिनिवृर्तत। समयान्तरे स्वजनन्या साकं प्रस्थितः सन् वृक्षसमीपं गत्वा कर्णिकारपल्लवसल्लकीपल्लवखदिरकिसलयजालादीनि च स्वशुण्डादण्डेन ग्रहीत्वा शश्वन्निरीक्ष्य मृदु भक्षयेत्। एतादृशगुणान्वितोऽयं गजः पंचमे मासि तत्तदवयवेषु सम्यक् पुष्टिमवाप्य मनोहरमुखो वृत्तकुंभद्वयश्च भवेदिति।

They will go and play for some time with the other elephants both morning and evening and then some join their mothers. *Vyāsa* says that they will fear to see the adjacent sceneries and they will eat the slender leaves of the twigs and branches. They will have a beautiful formation of their bodies in dimensions.

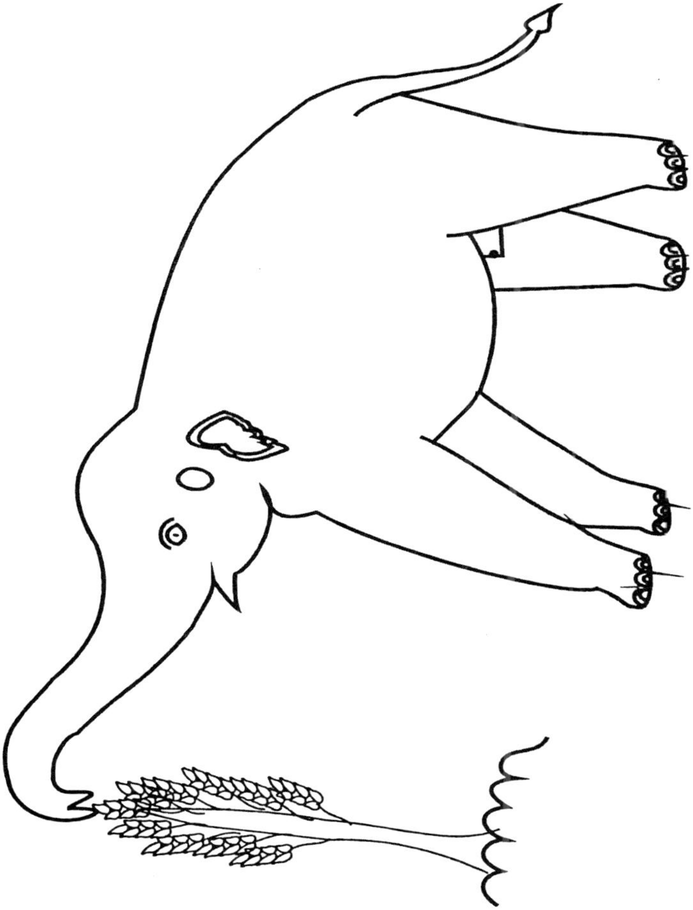

Fig. 45. : पंचममासवयस्कगज: 5th month elephants

षष्ठे लक्ष्योपदन्तश्च दृष्टमंभश्च धावति।

व्याख्या–षष्ठ इति। षष्ठमासवयस्को गजशावकः किंचिल्लक्ष्योपदन्तद्वयो भवेत्। किं चायं गजशावकः स्वावासस्थलस्य नातिदूरस्थितान् पल्वलतटाकह्रदादीन् प्रति जलावगाहनजलपानादिकार्यासक्तः सन् झडिति धावनशीलो भवेत्। किं च-ग्रीष्मादिसमयेषु आतपक्लेशमसहिष्णुः सान्द्रछायं तरुतलमाश्रयेदिति **क्रमः**।

They will stoop to play in ponds or channels near to them. They will have the growth of inner-tusks to a very little extant. They will not tolerate the heat of the sun and will be in the shelter of the trees.

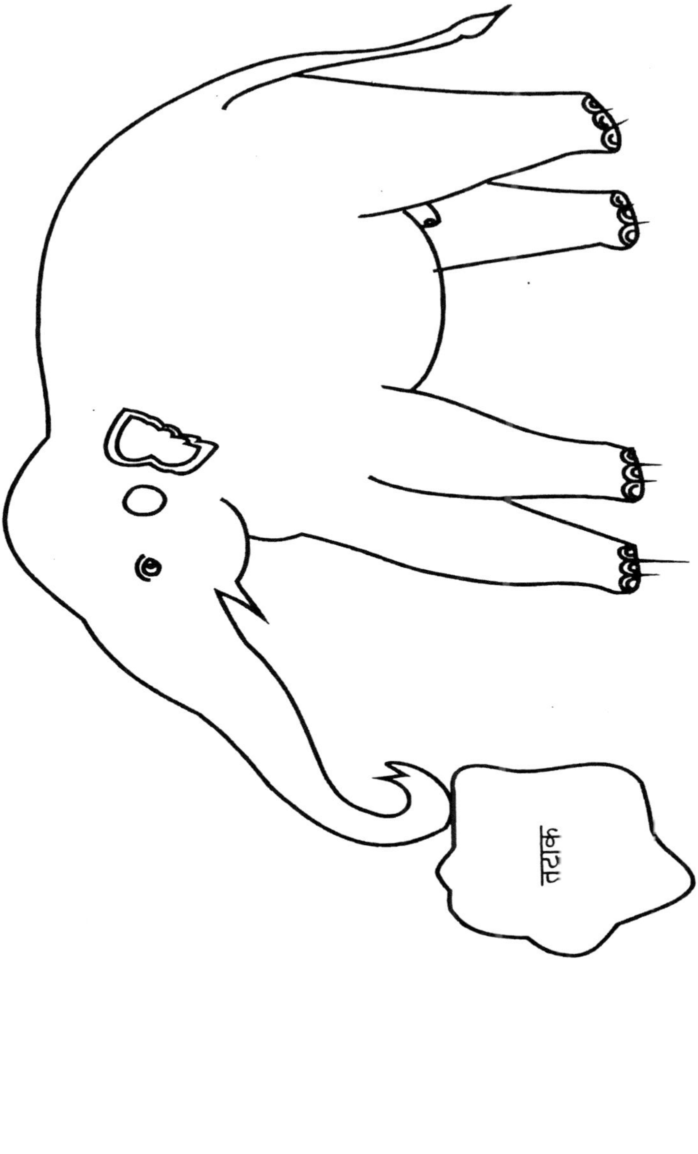

Fig. 46. : षष्ठमासवयस्कगज: 6th month elephants

सप्तमे तृणखादी स्याल्लण्डभक्षश्च जायते।
पदैस्तु न विरोधः स्यात् तद्वयश्चेति निश्चयः॥

व्यासप्रोक्ते गजशास्त्रे-

सप्तमे खादति तृणं लण्डभक्षो विशेषतः।

व्याख्या–सप्तम इति। सप्तममासवयस्को गजशावकः नवमृदुतृण-खादनपरो भवेत्। समयान्तरे लण्डभक्षकश्च भवतीति **प्रसिद्धिः।** लण्डो नामातिमृदुपल्लवसल्लकीवृक्षविशेष इति **प्रांचः**। किं चायं सप्तममासवयस्को गजशावको गमनसमये स्खलितपदो न भवेदेव। इतः पूर्वं मासषट्कगलनपर्यन्तं गमनसमये गजशिशोः पदविन्यासस्खालित्यमिति **भावः**। अन्यत् स्पष्टमेव।

They will eat green grass and slender leaves. They will regularly run without trembling their feet. They will become stout.

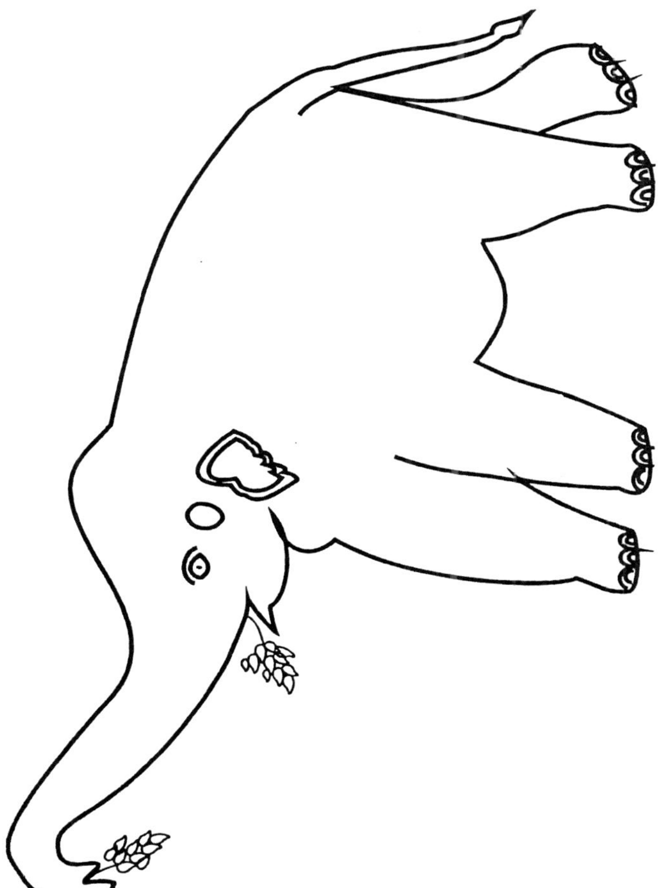

Fig. 47. : सप्तममासवयस्कगजः 7th month elephants

अष्टमे चपलो गन्ता

व्यासप्रोक्ते गजशास्त्रे।

अष्टमे चपलो गन्ता प्रबोधश्च विशेषतः॥

व्याख्या–अष्टम इति। अष्टममासवयस्को गजशावकः करचरणकार्येषु नितरां संभ्रमयुक्तः सन् इतस्ततो मुहुर्मुहुर्धावनशीलो भवेदिति **पालकाप्यः। व्यास**स्तु–अष्टममासवयस्को गजशावकः दिवासमये एकत्र न स्थिरो भवेत्। रात्रिकाले तादृशनिद्रया विमुक्तः सन् दीर्घकालं जागरणपरो भवेदिति। तस्मात् सर्वेषामपि गजशिशूनां प्रथममासप्रभृति सप्तममासपर्यन्तं निशासु विशेषतो निद्राप्राप्तिरिति **भावः**। अष्टममासप्रभृत्येव नक्तं निद्रायाः संकोच इति **क्रमः**। मृगान्तरापेक्षया नक्तं तुरगाणां निद्रासांकोच्यम्। तदपेक्षया नक्तं करिणां निद्रासांकोच्यमिति **प्रसिद्धा व्यवस्था** बोध्या॥

They will be very hasty in movements. *Vyāsa* says that they will not remain in one and the same place during day times. They will keep awake for a long time during nights even more than horses, which sleep for a shorter period than all the animals.

Fig. 48. : अष्टममासवयस्कगजः 8th month elephants

नवमे निद्रयाधिकः

व्यासप्रोक्ते गजशास्त्रे-

नवमे क्रोधनश्चापि जिघत्सन् पल्लवानपि।

व्याख्या–नवम इति। जननानन्तरमष्टममासे गते सति गजशावकः स्तन्यपानजलपानपल्लवादिभक्षणानन्तरं किंचित् श्रान्त इव प्रतिमूहूर्तं स्वल्पनिद्रापरो भवेदिति **पालकाप्यः। व्यास**स्तु–नवममासवयस्को गजशावकः प्रातः मातुः स्तन्यपानानन्तरं स्वावासस्थलसमीपस्थिततरुलतादिनिकटमवाप्य स्वशुण्डां प्रसारयित्वा तदीयपल्लवकिसलयादीन् गृह्णीयात्। समयान्तरे स्वल्पकोपं चावाप्य तदीयदृढशाखां भङ्क्तुमपि यत्नवान् भवेत्। एवं प्रबलसाध्यं कार्यं प्रति प्रयतनशीलो भवेदिति।

After drinking their mother's milk and water and eating slender-leaves, they will take rest for some time. *Vyāsa* says that they will be very persistent and angry. They will try to bend the strong branches of the trees while eating the leaves, but, if they can not do it, owing to lack of strength, they will become angry and persistent in doing so.

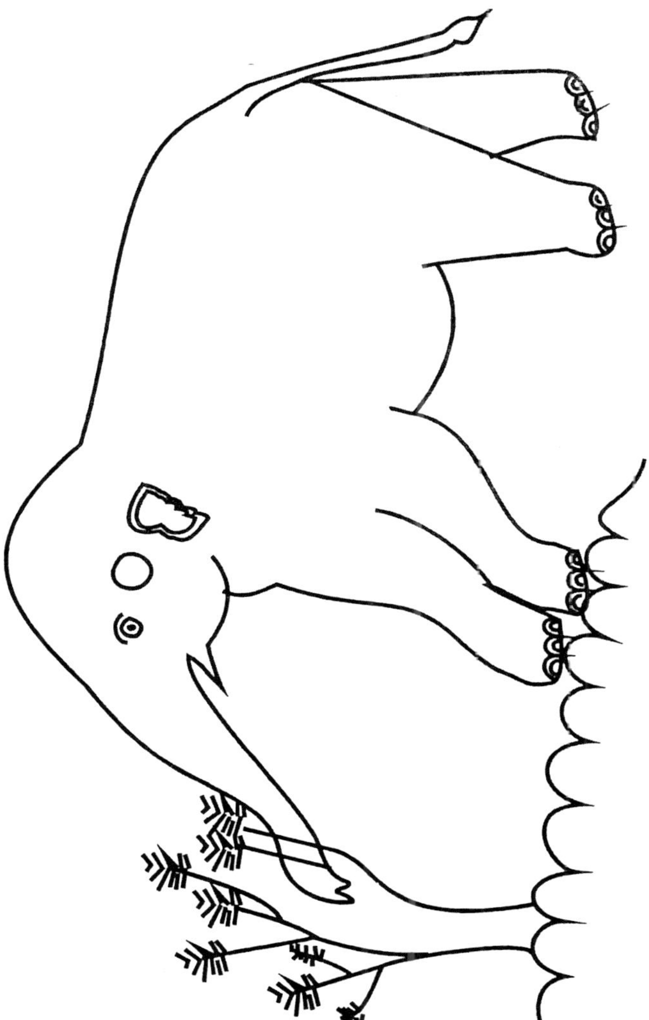

Fig. 49. : नवममासवयस्कगजः 9th month elephants

॥अथ दशममासवयस्कस्य गजस्य लक्षणम्॥

दशमे भक्षणासक्तः सततं मातृवत्सलः।

व्यासप्रोक्ते गजशास्त्रे-

दशमे च पिबेत्स्तन्यमजस्त्रं मातृवत्सलः॥

व्याख्या—दशम इति। दशममासवयस्को गजशावकः किंचित् क्षुदाधिक्ययुतः सन् शश्वन्मातुः स्तन्यं पिबेत्। तदनु मुहूर्तान्तरे जलपानपरस्तृणखादनपरश्च भवेदिति **क्रमव्यवस्था।** किं च दिवा नक्तं प्रायशः स्वमातुर्निकट एव स्थितिभाक् भवेदिति **पालकाप्यः। व्यासस्तु**-दशममासवयस्को गजः मातुः स्तन्यं पिबन् तदन्तिक एव स्वबाल्यचेष्टादिकं प्रदर्शयेदिति।

They will feel more hungry and drink their mother's milk often. They will often eat grass and leaves. *Vyāsa* says that they will exhibit their skill in playing always with their mothers.

Fig. 50. : दशममासवयस्कगजः 10th month elephants

अथ-एकादशमासवयस्कस्य गजस्य लक्षणम्॥

एकादशे व्यक्ततालुः

व्याख्या—एकादश इति। एकादशमासवयस्को गजः स्पष्टं दृश्यतालुप्रदेशः किंचित् पुष्टांगः प्रातरादिकालत्रयेऽपि नवतृणादिखादनपरः झडित्येव भक्षितस्य जीर्णशक्तियुतश्च भवेदिति।

They have the power of digesting any thing eaten very shortly. They become very stout and beautiful.

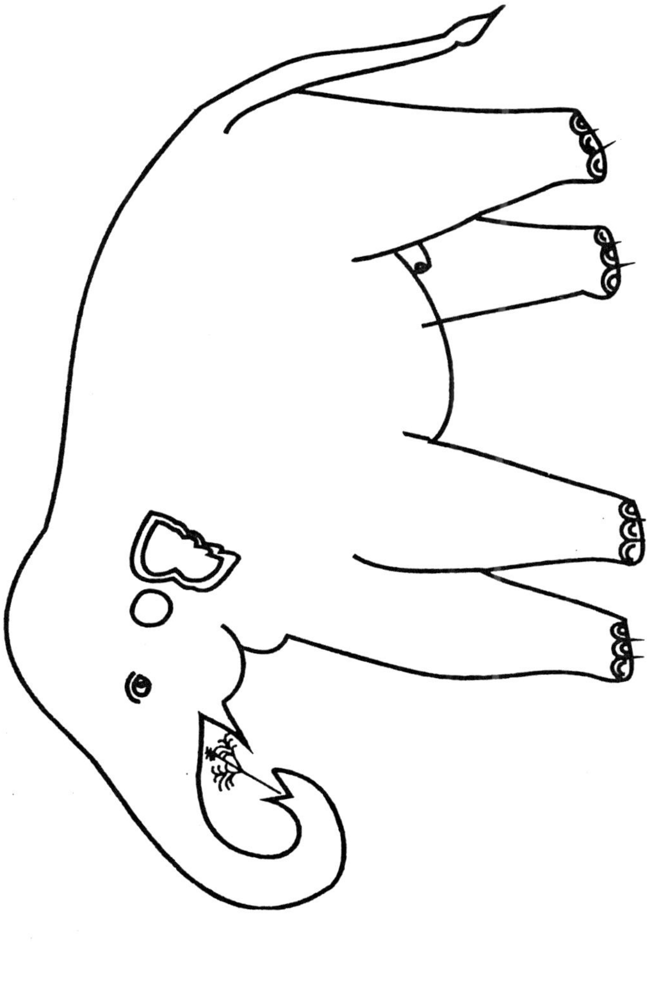

Fig. 51. : एकादशमासवयस्कगजः 11th month elephants

॥अथ-द्वादशमासवयस्कस्य गजस्य लक्षणम्॥

विनिद्रो द्वादशे भवेत्।
ताम्रजिह्वोष्ठरदनश्रवणः स्निग्धपार्ष्णिकः।
व्यक्तकृष्णास्यतालुः स्यादनुपादनखस्तथा॥
मृदुश्रवणरोमा च जातवर्षश्च लक्ष्यते।

व्यासप्रोक्ते गजशास्त्रे-

वर्षी द्वादशमासस्तु मन्दछिन्नकुशांकुरः॥

व्याख्या—ताम्रेति। द्वादशमासवयस्को गजः दिवास्वापं दूरतो निरस्य नक्तमपि मुहूर्तकालमेव निद्रामंगीकरोति। किं चास्य एकवर्षवयस्कगजस्य जिह्वायामोष्ठयोः रदने श्रवणतले च किंचित् रक्तवर्णशोभा दृश्या भवेत्। उदरतलस्य पार्श्वयोरुभयोरपि मसृणिमशाली। एवमस्य गजस्य वदनतलं तालुभागश्च कृष्णवर्णभाक् भवति। पादेषु चतुर्ष्वपि नखपंक्तिः स्वच्छश्वेतवर्णयुता भवेत्। श्रवणतले रोमराजिः मृदुस्पर्शश्च भवेदिति **पालकाप्यः। व्यासस्तु**-एकवर्षवयस्को गजस्तु वर्षीयगज इति नामभाक् सन् मन्दं कुशांकुरादीन् छित्त्वा स्वकरे तत् धृत्वा भक्षितुं वा त्यक्तुं वा नेच्छावान् भवतीति।

They will never sleep in day times. Their lips, tongues and ears will become red and their ribs and sides will become very soft and smooth. There will be a very beautiful black colour on their faces. Their nails will become big and white. There will be growth of hair in their ears. We should understand that they are one year old if they possess the above symptoms (signs) and qualities. In this way we should understand their peculiar age according to their symptoms (signs) and qualities. All the elephants available in any forest till one year in the whole world will have the same tendency described above, like the children of human-beings, as crying, playing, drinking etc.

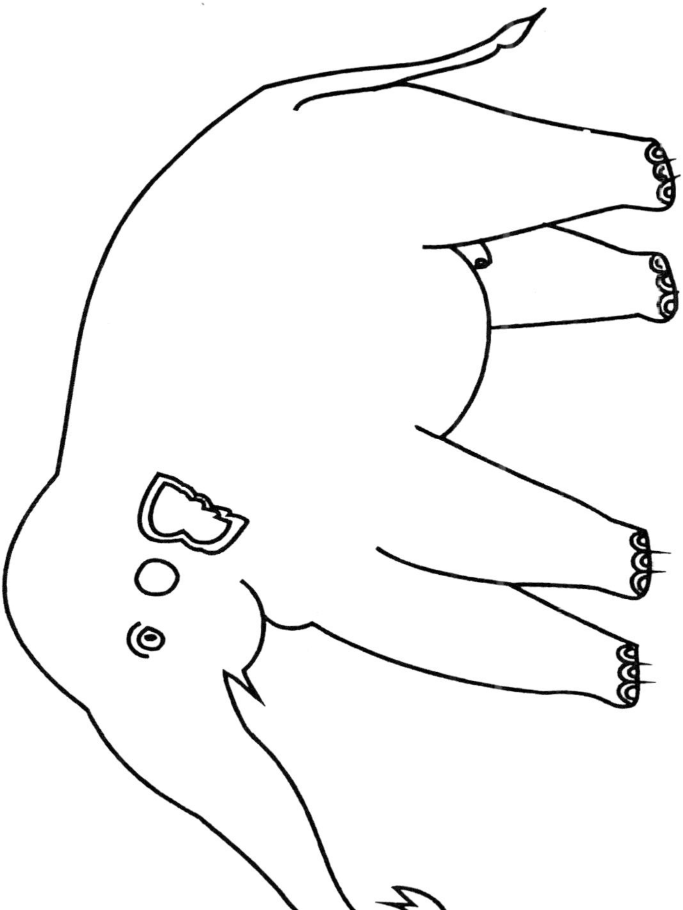

Fig. 52. : द्वादशमासवयस्कगजः 12th month elephants

॥अथ-वर्षद्वयवयस्कस्य गजस्य लक्षणम्॥

विरज्यमानजिह्वोष्ठः सान्द्रत्वक् सर्वसन्धिषु।
मृद्वत्ति यवसं भक्ष्यं सदास्विन्ननखांकुरः॥

रक्तछविर्भवेद्दन्ती वर्षद्वितयसंमितः।
बिन्द्वंचिताग्रकर्णः स्यात्सोऽयं चूचुक ईरितः॥

व्यासप्रोक्ते गजशास्त्रे-

किंचित्सान्द्रनखोऽतिरागरसनोष्ठादिः पयोऽल्पं पिबेत्
किंचिद्वल्लितृणादिखादितुमना गात्रान्तरे लोहितः।
निर्धावत्यनिमित्तमेव मुदितः प्रायो भृशं मीलितः
नम्राक्षो नयनप्रमादकृतये वर्षद्वये चूचुकः॥

पुराणनीरं बहुकोमलांगो
घासानि भुंक्ते बहुदुःखचित्तः।
द्विवत्सरोऽयं शिशुघोषभीरुः
स चूचुकोऽतः सितदन्तपंक्तिः॥

व्याख्या—एवं प्रकारेण प्रथममासप्रभृति द्वादशमासपर्यन्तं गजशिशोर्यः गुणचेष्टास्वभावादिः स निगदित इति **भावः**। एवमत्रोक्तक्रमस्तावत् सर्वेष्वपि देशेषु सर्वेष्वपि वनेषु सर्वेष्वपि गिरिगह्वरादिप्रदेशेषु च जातानां सर्वेषामपि गजशिशूनां निरीक्षणीय इति **भावः शास्त्रकारस्य**। यथा वा मानुषशिशोः प्रथममासप्रभृति क्रन्दनखेलनस्तन्यपानादिकः सर्वेष्वपि देशेषु तुल्यप्रकारो दृश्यते; तेनैव प्रकारेण सर्वेष्वपि देशेषु सर्वेषामपि गजशिशूनां तुल्यबालक्रीड-नादिकमिति **विशदार्थः**। एवंरीत्या प्रथमसंवत्सरपर्यन्तं गजशिशोर्लक्षणक्रीडादिकं क्रमशो निरूप्याधुना **शास्त्रकारः** वर्षद्वयवयस्कवर्षत्रयवयस्कादीनां गजानां गुणचेष्टाकार्यादिकं विस्तरेण प्रतिपादयितुमारब्धवानिति **सन्दर्भार्थक्रमः**। तत्र वर्षद्वयवयस्को गजः जिह्वायामोष्ठयोः किंचित् रक्तवर्णाधिक्ययुतः सन् करोरुपादादिसन्धिस्थलेषु विशेषतः सान्द्रत्वक् बलयुक्तो भवेत्। एवं भक्षणीय-सल्लकीपल्लवानि तृणानि गुडादीनि च मृदु भक्षयेत्। नखारंभतले सततं स्वेदयुक्तः सन् कर्णाग्रभागे क्वचिन्मुखमध्यभागे च रक्तवर्णबिन्दुवृन्दभासुरो

भवेत्। एवं लक्षणोपेतस्यास्य चूचुक इति नाम प्रसिद्धमिति **पालकाप्यः**। **व्यासस्तु**-चूचुकाख्योऽयं द्विवर्षगजः सान्द्रीभूतनखः नितरामरुणरसनोष्ठापर-गात्रारंभतलभागश्च भूत्वा प्रतिदिनमेकवारमेव पयःपानाय सक्तियुतो भवेत्। समयान्तरे विविधवल्लीतृणादिखादनपरश्च भवेत्। कारणं विनैव मुदितः सन् इतस्ततः प्लुतगतिमंगीकृत्य शश्वत् धावनशीलो भवेत्। किं च-क्षुच्छान्त्यनन्तरं किंचिन्मीलितनेत्रो भूत्वा पुनरपि नयनोन्मीलनसमये किंचिदा-लस्ययुक्तश्च भवेत्। अपि च-मृदुस्पर्शांगोऽयं द्विवर्षगजः पुराणजलपान-विषये घासभक्षणविषये च किंचिद्दुःखितमानसः सन् अन्यस्य बालगजस्य रींकाररवमाकर्ण्य किंचित् भीतश्च भवेत्। किं च एवंलक्षणोपेतस्यास्य चूचुकगजस्य बालदन्तप्रादुर्भावश्च भवेत् नखाश्च स्वच्छसितछायायुक्ता भवेयुरिति।

The epidermis of the elephants in their 2nd year become very strong and thick. Usual red colour comes in their tongues. Their nails even begin to perspire. There will be a few red or white dots on their ears and faces. *Vyāsa* says that their nails too become strong. They occasionally drink milk. They will sumptuously eat the leaves and branches. They will always unreasonabaly play with hops. After taking food they will close their eyes sitting for some time.

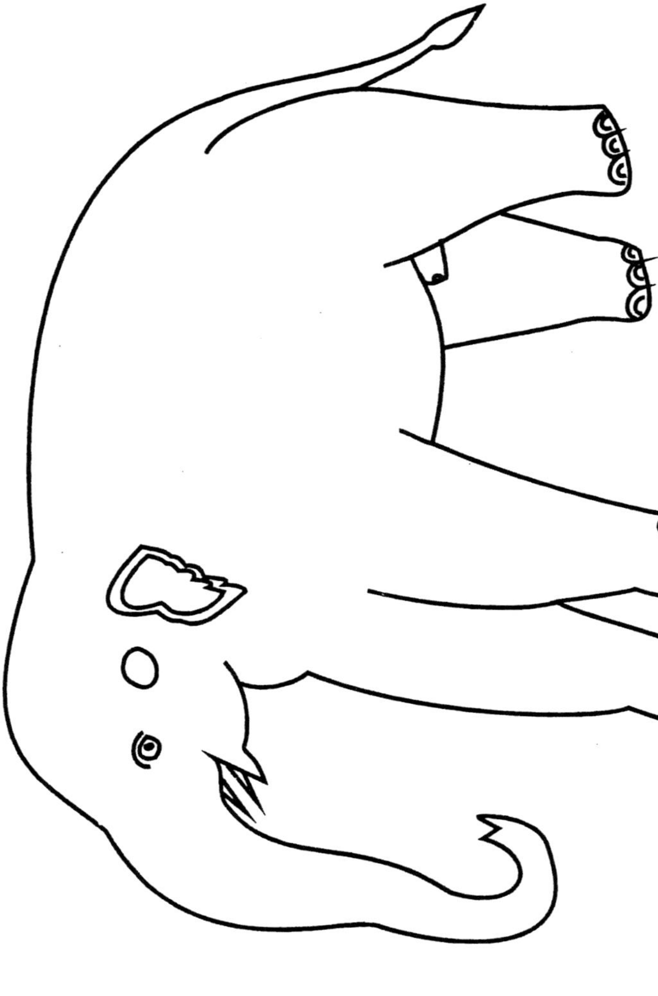

Fig. 53. : द्विवर्षवयस्कगजः 2nd year elephants

।।अथ-त्रिवर्षवयस्कस्य गजस्य लक्षणम्।।

बिन्द्वंचिताग्रकर्णः स्यात्तथा रोमशचूलिकः।
भक्ष्यादः क्षीरदन्तश्च त्रिवर्षः स भवेन्नृप।।

व्यासप्रोक्ते गजशास्त्रे-तृतीये अपसर्पश्च।

स्फुटनखविधुसन्धिः श्रोत्रदन्तप्रविष्ट-
छविरुरसि सबिन्दुः कर्णपिंगूषयोश्च।
भवति शिरसि केशी नम्रशीर्षस्तृणादी
दृढतरपदपंक्तिः सोऽपसर्पस्तृतीये।।

व्याख्या—बिन्द्वंचितेति। वर्षत्रयवयस्को गजः कर्णयोरुभयोरप्यग्रभागे रक्तवर्णबिन्दुजालपरिवृतो भवेत्। एवमस्य गजस्य मौलिभागे रोमराजिर्दृश्या भवेत्। किं चायं गजबालकः मातुः स्तन्यपानविरक्तो भूत्वा भक्ष्यद्रव्याणि तृणपल्लवादीनि भक्षयितुं सल्लकीशाखादीन् भङ्क्तुमपि यतेत। किं च-स्फुटं दृश्यदन्तयुगलो भवेत्। किं च-रोमशचूलिकश्च भवतीति **पालकाप्यः**। रोमशचूलिकः निबिडरोममस्तकवानित्यर्थः। **व्यास**स्तु-वर्षत्रयवयस्को गजः श्वेतवर्णभासुरनखयुक्तः सन् दृढपादसन्धियुतो भवेत्। एवं मस्तकस्याधोभागे श्रोत्रप्रान्ते दन्तस्योपरि त्वग्भागे पिंगूषस्थाने वक्षसि च रक्तवर्णबिन्दुयुतः सन् मस्तकभागे रोमवान् भवेत्। एवं तृणपल्लवभक्षणनिरतः। किं चास्य गजस्य गमनसमये सैकतपरागादिषु प्रदेशेषु पदविन्यासरेखादिकं च व्यक्तं दृश्येत। अतोऽयं बलवानिति।

There will be many red or white dots on their ears, chest and upper lips. There will be full growth of hair on their heads. There will be growth of tusks in their jaws visible to a little extent. *Vyāsa* says that there will be strength in their joints. They are fond of suger-canes, sallakī-leaves and they will pull them down at times with roots.

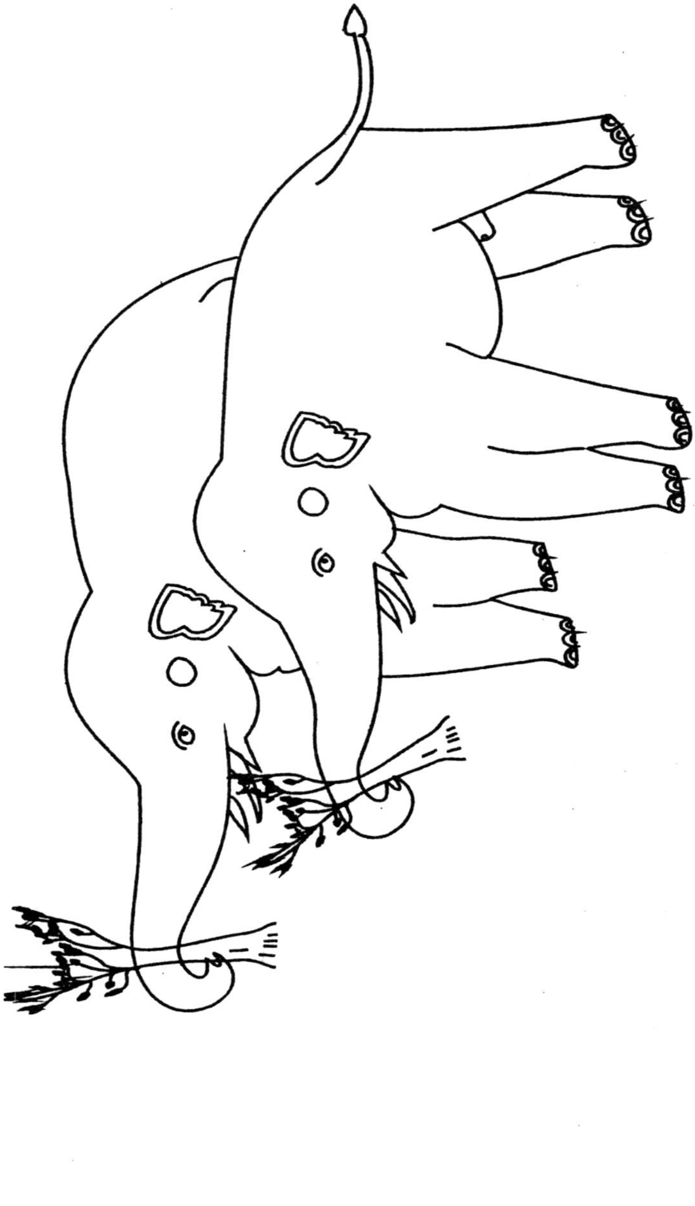

Fig. 54. : तृतीयवर्षवयस्कगजः 3rd year elephants

अथ-चतुर्वर्षवयस्कस्य गजस्य लक्षण्।।

चतुर्थेऽब्दे तु बर्बरः।।

चतुरब्दः स्थिरदन्तः चलचित्तः स्थूलजंघावलिशेफः।
बहुनिद्रः स्फुटरोमा सितबिन्दुर्बर्बरोऽयमलिशोभः।।
चोद्यमानस्ततो यंत्रा समारूढो विशेषतः।
यातायातस्य वेत्ता च दन्तयोरपि निर्गमः।।

व्याख्या–चतुर्वर्षगजविषये **व्यासस्या**शयमाह **शास्त्रकारः**-चतुर्थेऽब्दे तु बर्बर इति। चतुर्वर्षवयस्को गजः बर्बरनामभाक् भवतीति **प्रांचः**। अतोऽयं गजः दृढबहिरागतदन्तयुगलयुतः सन् पृथुशेफमवाप्य जंघातले किंचित् स्थौल्ययुतश्च भवेत्। किं चायं गजः यजमाननिर्दिष्टकार्यकरणसमये क्षणं चलचित्तश्च भवेत्। निशायां मुहूर्तत्रयकालनिद्रापरश्च भवेत्। किं च एवंगुणसमेतस्यास्य गजस्य शरीरावयवेषु सर्वेष्वपि भ्रमरवत् कृष्णवर्णप्राप्तिः। कर्णमुखादिस्थलेऽपि किंचित्कृष्णवर्णबिन्दुप्राप्तिः। सर्वांगेष्वपि सूक्ष्म-रोमावलिव्याप्तिश्च भवेदिति। **पालकाप्यस्तु**-चतुर्वर्षगजः बहिरागतदृढदन्त-युगलसमेतः सन् स्कन्धभागे यन्तारं वहन् सन् तेन प्रचोदितो गमनशीलो भवेत्। किं चायं गजः गतागतमार्गस्य स्वरूपं स्वकृतकार्यस्य स्वरूपादिकं च ज्ञात्वा पुनरपि तत्करणे अभिलाषयुक्तो भवेदिति।

Their tusks, legs and penis become strong. There will be a little growth of hair on the whole of their bodies. There will be development of red or white spots round the eyes, on their ears and faces. There will be spread of beautiful black colour throughout their bodies. This is the proper time for them to learn teaching of work from their *mahout* on their backs. They are fickle-minded at the time of teaching and childish. They will now and then begin to sleep to the teaching by the *mahouts*. They will understand clearly what they have learnt and worked.

Fig. 55. : चतुर्थवर्षवयस्कगजः 4th year elephants

।।अथ-पंचवर्षवयस्कस्य गजस्य लक्षणम्।।

पंचमे त्वल्पनिद्रः स्याद्वत्सरे हृष्टमेढ्कः।

व्यासप्रोक्ते गजशास्त्रे-

पंचमे कलभो नाम-

काष्ठत्वक् तृणसेवनस्तनुकचः पंकाम्बुपांसुप्रियः
स्वल्पं हृष्यति कोपमेति च सुखं दुःखं यतो बुध्यति।
शब्दादीनपि वेत्ति यंतृवशगो ह्युत्थानवित्प्रोल्लसन्
स्वच्छावग्रहदन्त एष कलभः प्राप्तः समां पंचमीम्।।

व्याख्या–पंचमवर्षवयस्कगजः दृढस्थूलबहिरागमनशीलमेढ्रयुतः सन् निशायां मुहूर्तनिद्रापर एव भवेदिति **पालकाप्यः। व्यासस्तु**–पंचमवर्षगजः कलभ इति नामभाक् भवति। अयं तु कलभः सल्लकीखदिरवटादीनां क्षुद्रकाष्ठमृदुत्वग्भक्षणशीलः तत्पलाशभक्षणशीलः तृणादिभक्षणशीलश्च भवेत्। गजस्यास्य शरीरे तनुरोमराजिरेव दृश्या भवेत्। किं चायं गजः पंकपरागजल-क्रीडासक्तो भूत्वा निशायामर्धमुहूर्तकालं निद्रावशगो भवेत्। यजमाननिर्दिष्ट-कार्यकरणसमये स्वस्य सुखदुःखप्राप्तिं ज्ञात्वा श्रमातिरेकात् स्वल्पकोपं च प्राप्नोति। पार्श्वतस्ताडितभेरीकाहलीतूर्यादिवाद्यनिनदस्वारस्य च वेत्ता। यजमाननिर्दिष्टकार्याणि अविलंबेन निर्वहणशीलः। स्वच्छावदातबहिरागतदन्त-युगलश्चेति।।

They can easily eat the slender-branches, coconuts, grass, sugar-canes etc. and digest them easily. They are very fond of playing in water often. They can well understand the difficulties and enjoyments, sorrows and happinsss at the time of instruction given by the *mahouts*. They get strength for animal passion. The white tusks come out fully.

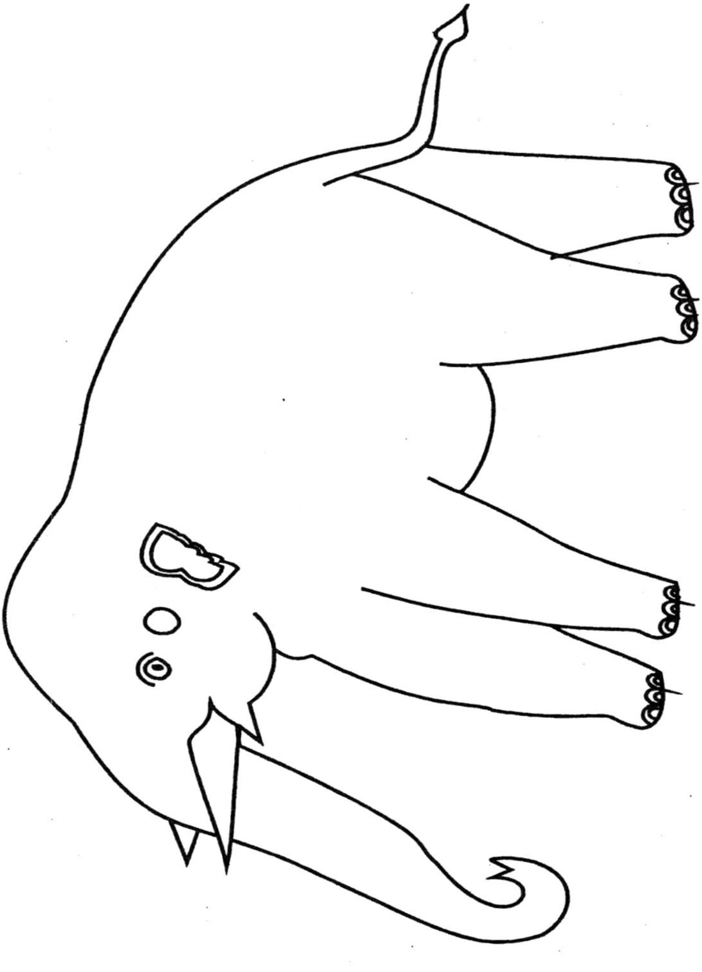

Fig. 56. : पंचवर्षवयस्कगाजः 5th year elephants

।।अथ-षट्वर्षवयस्कस्य गजस्य लक्षणम्।।

सृक्वाग्रे कर्णयोश्चापि कटयोरक्षिकूटयोः।
प्रतिमाने च पिंगूषे बिन्दुभिर्व्यक्तविग्रहः।।
षट्वर्षः स तु विज्ञेयो विज्ञाता सुखदुःखयोः।

व्यासप्रोक्ते गजशास्त्रे-षष्ठे वैकारिकः स्मृतः-

पिंगूषकर्णकटसृक्विविलासनेत्र-
कूटास्यकर्णयुगलप्रतिमानदेशे।
यः सान्द्रबिन्दुसुभगो वलिहीनवर्ष्मा
वैकारिकं तमिह षट्सममामनंति।।

व्याख्या—सृक्वाग्र इति। षष्ठवर्षवयस्को गजः सृक्विभागे कर्णान्तिकतले कटयोः लोचनयोः प्रान्ततले प्रतिमानाख्यगण्डस्थले पिंगूषाख्ये कर्णपुरस्तले च रक्तवर्णबिन्दुभिरुपेतो भवेत्। किं चास्मिन्नेव षष्ठे वयसि अंगोपांगानां पुष्टत्वं तथा मनोहरत्वं च भवेत्। एतादृशमनोहरांगैरुपेतो गजः स्वस्य सुखस्य दुःखस्य च विज्ञाता भवेदिति **पालकाप्यः। व्यासस्तु पालकाप्योक्तं** लक्षणं सर्वमप्यंगीकृत्य विशेषमाह-यथा षष्ठवर्षगजस्य कण्ठस्थाने उदरसमीपतलेषु च वलिस्तावत् निलीना भवेत्। कुतः। तथा पुष्टत्वात्। किं चायं गजः वैकारिकनामभाक् च भवतीति।

There will be many white or red spots round their temples, eyes, mouth, in and out of their ears and on the trunks. They get more strength than the 5th year. *Vyāsa* names these elephants at the 6th year as Vaikārika. They will never shirk work.

Fig. 57. : षट्वर्षवयस्कगजः 6th year elephants

।।अथ-सप्तवर्षवयस्कस्य गजस्य लक्षणम्।।

वलयः कण्ठभागे स्युर्नखानां चापि सान्द्रता।
वृत्तेऽर्धेऽपि च संस्कारात् हन्तुं दन्तेन हृष्यति।
स्निग्धपुष्करवालश्च सप्तवर्षो मतंगजः।

व्यासप्रोक्ते गजशास्त्रे-सप्तमाब्दे शिशुः प्रोक्तः-

घननखतलसन्धिप्रोथसन्धानचिक्का-
बलिकरपृथुशीर्षो दन्तखादी सकण्डुः।।
स्फुटचरणजवावस्कारवान् सप्तवर्षः
शिशुरिति कथितोऽसौ स्निग्धदोः पुष्कराग्रः।।

व्याख्या-वलय इति। सप्तमवर्षवयस्कस्य गजस्य कण्ठभागे वलयो दृश्या भवेयुः। तत्र हेतुस्तु-तस्मिन् सप्तमे वयसि गजानां शरीरपुष्टिप्राप्तिरेवेति। एवमस्मिन् वयसि नखा अपि विशदाः सान्द्राश्च भवेयुः। किं च-तेषां शुण्डादण्डे वाले पूर्ववयस्युद्भूतकर्कशरोमावलिविगलनात् मासृण्यं चोद्भवति। तस्मादेवं लक्षणोपेतो गजः बहिर्निर्गतमनोहरदन्तयुगलः सन् यजनाननिर्दिष्ट-कार्यादिके स्वेन निर्वर्तितेऽपि तदा कार्यावसाने मदावेशात् तादृशकार्यं प्रति स्वल्पकोपं कौतूहलं चावाप्य दन्तशुण्डावालप्रसारणादिकमाकलयेदिति **पालकाप्यः।** **व्यास**स्तु-सप्तमवर्षवयस्को गजः दृढनखसन्धिसमेतः दृढपाद-दृढशुण्डादण्डः मस्तकभागे व्यक्तं दृश्यकुंभद्वयसमेतश्च दीर्घदन्तयुगलोपेतश्च भवति। कदाचित् कण्डूवेदनां चावाप्य दन्तखादी च भवेत्। किं चास्मिन् सप्तमे वयसि गजानां चरणचतुष्के वेगाधिक्यं दृश्यते। किं चायं मदावलः स्वशुण्डादण्डेन शश्वत् पंकपरागादिकमुद्धृत्य स्वमस्तकाद्यूर्ध्वशरीरे तद्बीजनशीलश्च भवेत्। किं चास्मिन् वयस्ययं गजः शिशुरिति निगद्यत इति। स्पष्टमन्यत्।।

There will be growth of flesh around their necks owing to the stoutness. Their nails and tusks become much stronger and smoother than before. They can walk very swiftly. Their skulls will become stout and they will sometimes bite their teeth (tusks) owing to sensation.

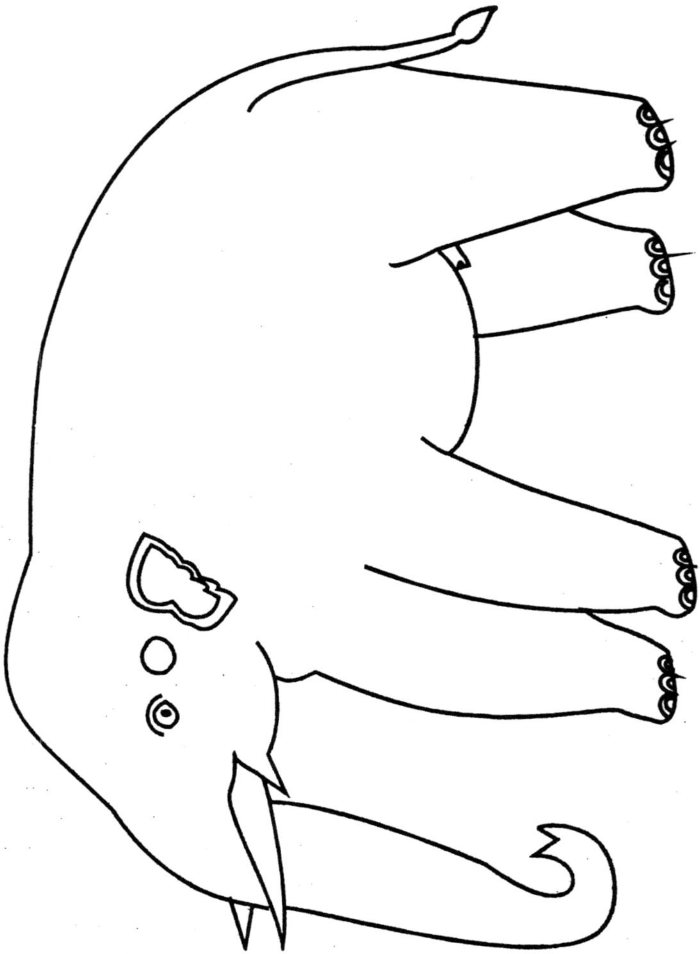

Fig. 58. : सप्तवर्षवयस्कगजः 7th year elephants

॥अथ-अष्टवर्षवयस्कस्य गजस्य लक्षणम्॥

मन्दक्रोधो मंदहर्षश्चलदन्तरदन्तयुक्।
हृष्टमेढ्रश्च सततं बहुभिर्बिन्दुभिर्वृतः॥
समं हृष्टैश्च नागैश्च रमते धेनुकामनाः।
सुचिकित्सव्रणश्चापि अष्टवर्षो मतंगजः॥

व्यासप्रोक्ते गजशास्त्रे-अष्टमे वत्सरेंऽजनः।

नवनखतलसन्धिक्षेपजातव्रणौघो
मृदुतरयवसाशी चंचला दन्तपंक्तिः।
चपलगतिरजस्त्रं दानवर्षी प्रहर्षी
प्रहरणमृदुकोशो ह्यष्टमेऽब्देंऽजनाख्यः॥

व्याख्या—मन्दक्रोध इति। अष्टमवर्षवयस्को वारणः यजमाननिर्दिष्टकार्यकरणे स्वल्पकोपयुतो भवेत्। सल्लकीपल्लवादिभक्षणानन्तरं स्वल्पकौतूहलमप्यवाप्य स्वशुण्डां दन्तोपरि पातयेत्। मुहुश्चर्वणवशात् दन्तचांचल्ययुतो भवेत्। किं चायमष्टवर्षगजः पूर्वोक्तसृक्विकटपिंगूषादिस्थलेषु स्फुटदृश्यव्यक्तवर्णबिन्दुभिरुपेतश्च भवति। अपि चास्मिन्नेव वयसि पुंगजानां मेढ्रवृद्धिः। तदुद्रेकश्च। तस्मादयं गजः हृष्टैरन्यैर्वारणैः सहितः सन् करिणीमनुसरति। किं चास्मिन्नष्टमे वयसि गजानां विशेषतः कण्डूत्पत्तिः। अतस्तादृशकण्डूनिवारणार्थं कण्डूयितपादादिस्थलेषु पादान्तरशुण्डाघर्षणादिना व्रणादिकं च भवति। किं चायं गजोऽस्मिन्नेव वयसि अंजन इति नामभाक् सन् मृदुतमतृणखादी भवेत्। नाधिकजलपायी। किं चास्य गजस्य तत्र तत्र चपलगतेर्दन्तयुगलं च तरुस्तंभादिषु घर्षणादिना किंचित् शिथिलं भवेत्। किं चास्मिन्नेव वयसि कटतले दानस्रावश्च भवेत्। अतोऽयं वारणः युद्धाय न निवेश्य इति। स्पष्टमन्यत्॥

Their temper will be serene at work both in peace and danger. They will have erection of penis often. They will play with their equals. They will go and stand by the side of the female elephants often. There will be much increase of white or red spots around the temples, eyes and ears. They will not at all be attacked with any disease at this age and if at all they are, they will be in no minute (=time) cured. Owing to the sensation they will scratch their trunks, legs etc. and wounds will be formed, which will also be cured in no minute (=time no). Ruttish-water will be oozing at this age. They are quite fit for all works except elephant-war.

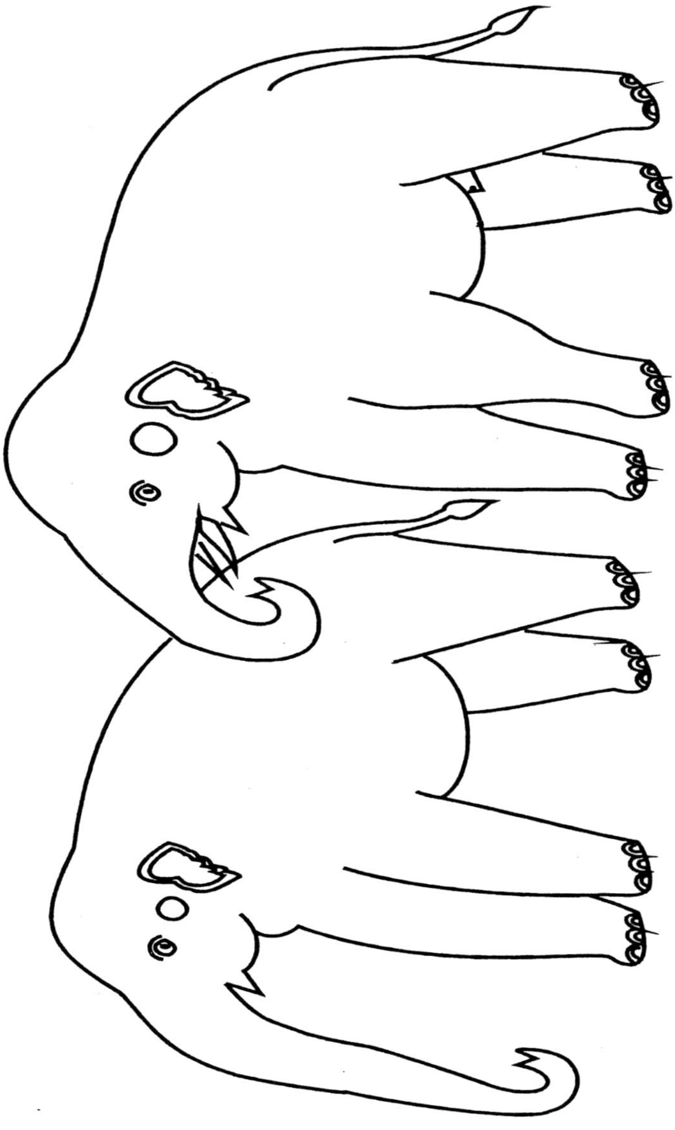

Fig. 59. : अष्टवर्षवयस्कगजः 8th year elephants

॥अथ-नववर्षवयस्कस्य गजस्य लक्षणम्॥

अजातशुक्लः सान्द्रत्वक् शीर्षरोमा मतंगजः।
उत्साहवान् सत्त्वयुक्तो नवमेऽब्दे प्रकीर्तितः॥

व्यासप्रोक्ते गजशास्त्रे—नवमे प्रभवः प्रोक्तः-

शुक्लेक्षणः प्लवति धेनुममुक्तशुक्लः
स्निग्धच्छविर्निबिडदन्ततटः पृथूराः।
यो रन्ध्रसन्धिषु घनः सुदृढप्रहारी
दन्तारुणो नवसमं प्रभवं वदन्ति॥

व्याख्या—अजातशुक्ल इति। नववर्षवयस्को गजः सर्वेष्वप्यवयवेषु नितरां कठिनसान्द्रत्वक्समेतः मस्तकतले केशयुतश्च भवेत्। किं च-यंत्रादिभिः श्रमसाध्यकार्ये निर्दिष्टेऽपि तत्क्षणादेव तत्कर्तुं नितरामुद्युक्तो बलाढ्यश्च भवेदिति **पालकाप्यः। व्यासस्तु**-सर्वेऽपि वारणाः नवमे वयसि किंचित् शुक्लवर्णमनोहरनेत्रयुगलाः गात्रान्तरेषु मासृण्ययुक्ताः मनोहरशरीरकान्तयः दृढतरदन्तदृढतरगण्डपृथुलघनोदरसहिताश्च भवेयुः। किं चास्मिन् नवमे वयसि गजानां युद्धप्रवीणता। दन्तयोः किंचिदारुण्यं च दृश्यते। तस्मादेवं लक्षणोपेताः हृष्टाः पुष्टांगाः नवमवयस्का गजाः करिणीमवलोक्य कामवशात् स्वकीयमेढ्रं बहिः कुर्वाणाः तत्सुरताभिलाषात् तदन्तिकोपसर्पणशीलाश्च भवन्ति। किं चैते वारणा अस्मिन् वयसि प्रभव इति नामान्तरभाजश्चेति।

There will be full growth of hair on their heads. Their limbs, nerves, flesh etc. will become very strong and mascular. They will try to do any hard work with zeal. They will often go with the female elephants and begin to enjoy with them, if they happen to meet them. Their stomachs become more stout and beautiful, than the previous years. There will be slight appearance of white or red spots on their eyes. They are now fit for war and hunting.

Fig. 60. : नवमवर्षवयस्कगजः : 9th year elephants

॥अथ-दशमवर्षवयस्कस्य गजस्य लक्षणम्॥

एवं तु दशमे वर्षे गजो व्यक्तघनछविः।
बलवान् व्यक्तदेहश्च बहुलो व्यक्तदीधितिः॥

संप्राप्तशुक्लमेढ्रश्च यूथानामपि हर्षितः।
सान्द्रहस्तः सदोत्साही स्थिराः सर्वत्र संधयः॥

व्यासप्रोक्ते गजशास्त्रे—विक्कः स्यात् दशमेऽब्दके॥

कृष्णांबुदाभो बलवान् शुभाक्षः स्निग्धांसगण्डप्रपदप्रदेशः।
सुव्यक्तदन्तः प्रथमां दशां तु प्राप्तः करीन्द्रः स्थिरसर्वसन्धिः॥

संजातशुक्लः प्लवति स्थिरांगः प्रहृष्टमेढ्रः स्थिरजातदन्तः।
तेजोबलाढ्यो दशमे तु वर्षे युद्धे निदर्शः कथितः स विक्कः॥

व्याख्या—एवमिति। पूर्वं नवमवयसि गजानां ये ये गुणस्वरूपादयः प्रतिपादिताः त एव गुणादयो दशमे वयस्यपि लक्ष्या भवेयुः। तथापि तदपेक्षयास्मिन् दशमे वयसि बलाधिक्यं विशेषतेजःप्राप्तिः संपूर्णदेहवृद्धिश्च भवेत्। किं चास्मिन् वयसि स्थिता गजाः संजातशुक्ला अत एव दृढतरमेढ्रयुताः मैथुननिरताश्च। किं च-युद्धार्हाश्चेति **पालकाप्यः। व्यासस्तु**-अस्मिन्नेव दशमे वयसि गजशरीरे कृष्णवर्णाधिक्यं भवेत्। पूर्णबलसमृद्धिः। मनोहर-नेत्रविलासः मनोहरशरीरद्युतिश्च। किं च-पुष्कलशुक्लोत्पत्तिवशात् मैथुनेच्छा-समृद्धिश्चेति। किं चास्मिन् वयसि गजाः विक्का इति नामभाजो भवन्तीति। स्पष्टमन्यत्॥

They are much stronger. There will be brightness and shining in their bodies like clouds. They are very fond of fighting in war and fond of going with the bigger elephants if they happen to meet them. They have eager desire for intercourse as their penes become full of semen and erect.

Fig. 61. : दशमवर्षवयस्कगजः 10th year elephants

॥अथ-द्वितीयदशावयस्कस्य गजस्य लक्षणम्॥

दशायां तु द्वितीयायां मुखरोमा मतंगजः।
जवनः स्थिरमांसश्च तेजस्वी ग्रहणे तथा॥

वारणायोधने चैव युक्तस्तुस्येषु दर्पितः।
समस्तैर्धातुदोषैश्च मुक्तोऽखिलगुणान्वितः॥

व्यासप्रोक्ते गजशास्त्रे-

परतो दशवर्षेभ्यः विंशतेः कलभः स्मृतः।
दशां द्वितीयां तु गतः करीन्द्रः तेजोबलस्थैर्यविशेषयुक्तः।
आयोधने तुल्यगजेषु दृप्तः गुणैः समस्तैरपि संप्रतीतः॥

उत्साही स्फुटगात्रसन्धिवमथुर्गर्भप्रदो दुर्गभित्
संग्रामादिबली घनप्रहरणः पीताभदन्तान्वितः।
सूनानाभिसितः सुवृत्तजघनोऽवस्कारकर्णांचलः
प्रोताख्यः शरविक्रमबलो याति द्वितीयां दशाम्॥

व्याख्या—एतावता प्रबन्धेन सर्वेषामपि करिणां करिणीनां च मासक्रम-वर्षक्रमवयस्सु स्वरूपगुणादिकं प्रतिपादितम्। अधुना दशवर्षप्रभृति विंशत्युत्तर-शतवर्षाख्यपरमायुष्कालपर्यन्तं गजानां ये ये गुणस्वरूपादयः स्पष्टं दृश्याः भवेयुः तत् विस्तेरण दर्शयितुमारब्धवानिति **सन्दर्भव्यवस्था**। तत्रेयं परिपाटी च ज्ञेया। यथा-एकादशवर्षप्रभृति विंशतिवर्षपर्यन्तं गजानां द्वितीया दशा। एकविंशतिवर्षप्रभृति त्रिंशद्वर्षपर्यन्तं तृतीया दशा चेत्येवं क्रमेण दशवर्षकाल-गणितदशाद्वादशकं निर्णीय तदनुसारेणैवाधुना गजानां द्वितीयदशागुणादिक-माह-दशायां तु द्वितीयायामिति। अस्य **विशदार्थस्तु**-दशायामस्यां द्वितीयायां सर्वेषामपि वारणानां मुखे कर्णसमीपे लोचनकूटतले च रोमावल्याधिक्यम्। गात्रान्तरेषु मितरोमप्राप्तिश्च। किं चास्यां द्वितीयदशायामेव करिणां निरर्गल-जवनगतिर्भवेत्। एवं स्थिरमांसप्राप्तिश्च। सर्वविधधातुदोषविमुक्तिपूर्वकं सद्गुणप्राप्तिश्च। अतोऽस्यां दशायामेव गजाः ग्राह्या **इत्युपदेशः**। किं च-एतद्दशायुता गजाः स्वसदृशबलयुतैरन्यैर्गजैः साकं समराकलनतत्पराश्चेति

पालकाप्यः। व्यासस्तु—अस्यामेव द्वितीयदशायां सर्वे वारणाः कलभा इति नामभाजो भवन्ति। सर्वकार्यनिर्वहणशक्तियुताः स्फुटविभक्तदेहाः करिणीनां गर्भप्रदानशीलाश्च राजन्ते। किं च–दृढतरदुर्गभित्तिभेदनार्हपूर्णबलसमेताः समरोत्सुकाः पीतवर्णदृढदन्तयुगलाः दृढघट्टनशीलाः विश्रान्तिसमयेषु स्वकीयमस्तकादिभागेषु परागावस्करादिप्रक्षेपकाः शरप्रसारवदतिवेगगतियुताश्च भवेयुरिति। स्पष्टमन्यत्॥

The author has described the age of elephants from their birth to twelve months regularly month by month and then from the **1st** year to 10 years regularly year by year. Since he has described them, we will have to understand the age of the elephants according to their nature, quality, action etc. He has divided their whole age into 12 *daśās* or periods (each 10 years). Now first period has been clearly mentioned.

2nd period. 11-20 years

Elephants at this period will have small hair on their faces. They will run very swiftly like an arrow. They will become stronger than the previous period. There will be a bright appearance in their bodies. They are very fond of fighting with each other in the wars. After training, their nature and characters will be changed. They are capable of giving pregnancy to the female elephants. They can break down even the fort-walls if they dash against them.

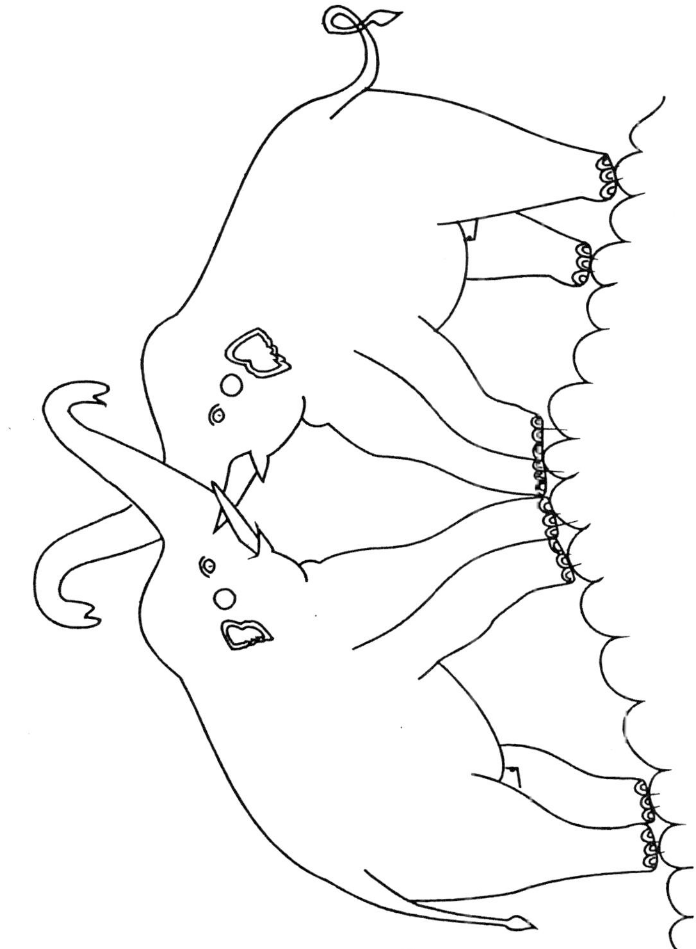

Fig. 62. : : द्वितीयदशावयस्कगजः 2nd period—11-20 years old

Fighting Elephants

॥अथ-तृतीयदशावयस्कस्य गजस्य लक्षणम्॥

तृतीयायां दशायां तु हन्तुमिच्छति कोपनः।
तैश्चापि लक्षणैर्युक्तः सन्धानप्रोथसन्धिषु॥

सान्द्रहस्तः सदोत्साही स्थिराः सर्वत्र सन्धयः।
बहुलाश्च स्थिराश्चैव वलयस्तु त्रिसन्धयः॥

तेष्वेव तु प्रदेशेषु क्वचित् छिन्नवलिस्तथा।

व्यासप्रोक्ते गजशास्त्रे-

तृतीयायां दशायां तु जवनः परिकीर्तितः।
संपूर्णमातंगबलः सुतेजाः मेधान्वितः कामजवान्वितश्च।
कूलंकषः सुस्थिरसन्धिदेशो दशामुपेतः करिराट् तृतीयाम्॥

तत्तन्मानविभक्तकर्णदशनोत्संगादिरुद्यन्मद-
घ्राणः सर्वगुणान्वितो रणदृढः सुस्निग्धरोमछविः।
क्लीबाक्षः प्रियदर्शनोच्चविचलद्वृद्धिः सुधीः कोपनः
हन्ता धातुसमः स एष जवनो याति तृतीयां दशाम्॥

व्याख्या–पूर्वोक्तरीत्या एकविंशतितमवय आरभ्य त्रिंशद्वयःपर्यन्तं तृतीया दशा। एतादृशतृतीयां दशां प्राप्तः गजस्तावत् निरपराधाय स्वस्मै अपराधं कुर्वते पुरुषाय प्राणिने वा कोपाधिक्ययुतः सन् तं हन्तुमपि यतेत। किं च-पूर्वप्रतिपादितरीत्या सर्वावयवेष्वपि दृढसन्धिबलाधिक्यमप्युपेत्य दृढकरः सन् विविधकार्यकरणपरो भवति। किं च-कण्ठे चोदरे वलित्रययुतश्च भवेत्। प्रदेशान्तरेषु क्वचित् त्रुटितवलियुतश्चेति **पालकाप्यः। व्यास**स्तु-अस्यामेव तृतीयदशायां सर्वेषामपि गजानां संपूर्णबलोदयः शरीरसौन्दर्यं शिक्षणादिविषये बुद्धिपाटवं चोद्भवति। करिणीं प्रति कामाधिक्यं च जायते। किं चायं गजो दशायामस्यामेव विशेषमदयुक्तः सन् समरपरश्च भवति। अपि च-मस्तकशुण्डादन्तादिषु जायमानकण्डूनिवारणाय नदीकूलंकषः तरुस्कन्धघर्षणपरः दृढभित्तिभेदनपरश्चेति। किं च-इमां तृतीयां दशां उपेयुषां वारणानां संपूर्णौन्नत्यादिप्राप्तिरिति। एतद्दशागलनानन्तरं न शरीरवृद्धिरिति

भावः। एवंलक्षणोपेताः तृतीयादशायां स्थिता इमे गजाः जवननामभाजः कीर्त्यन्ते।।

If any one were to meddle with them they are keeping quiet. They will try to kill him or it with great fury at this period. Their trunks will become much stronger to pull down the trees or anything else with roots. They can lift and load, work hard and fight well in the elephants-war without difficulty. They are very intelligent and have much passion. There will be much oozing out of ruttish-water from their temples.

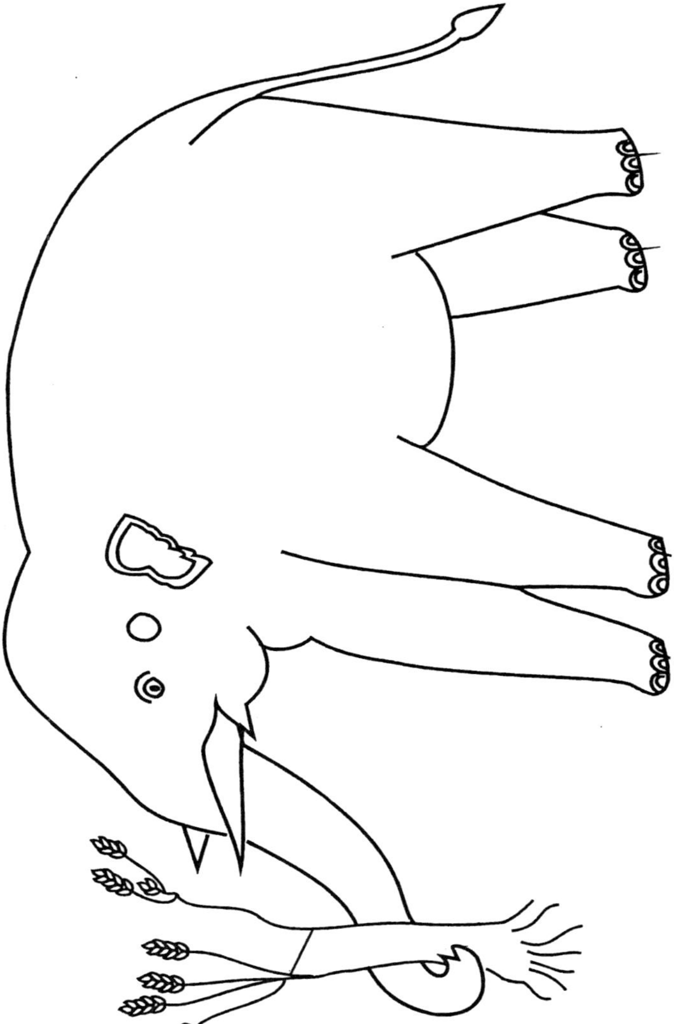

Fig. 63. : तृतीयदशावयस्कगजः 3rd period—20-30 years old

॥अथ-चतुर्थदशावयस्कस्य गजस्य लक्षणम्॥

चतुर्थ्यां तु दशायां स्यात्करिणो लक्षणं तथा।
चारणीयप्रदेशेषु सरूपीष्वेव कामवान्॥
पदयोश्चापि कटयोः कर्णयोरपि दानवान्।

व्यासप्रोक्ते गजशास्त्रे-चतुर्थ्यामपि कल्याणः-

निराकरिष्णुर्गजबद्धवैरं संजातदर्पो बलसंप्रयुक्तः।
संपूर्णसंस्थानबलः स्थिरांगो वृक्षान् विभिन्द्यात्सरलान् चतुर्थ्याम्॥
सन्धानादिषु जातसुस्थिरबली गृह्णाति युक्तं मदं
निद्रालुः प्रतिदन्तिवैरिमनसा प्रीतः कराधूननात्।
केशोर्ध्वश्चपलश्च सन्धिषु युवा यूथप्रयोगाश्रयः
कल्याणाह्वयमेति वारण इह प्राप्तश्चतुर्थी दशाम्॥

व्याख्या—चतुर्थ्यामिति। पूर्वोक्तरीत्या एकत्रिंशत्तमवयःप्रभृति चत्वारिंशत्तमवयःपर्यन्तं चतुर्थी दशा निर्दिष्टा। तामिमां चतुर्थी दशां प्रविष्टो गजस्तावत् पूर्वदशोक्तलक्षणादियुत एव भवति। तथापि दशायामस्यां कामाधिक्ययुतः सन् स्वगुणसदृशगुणवतीषु करिणीष्वेव रन्तुं कृतप्रयत्नो भवेत्। किं चास्यां दशायां गजस्याक्षिकूटयोः गण्डयोः कर्णप्रांततले च मदजलप्रसारणस्याधिक्यं भवतीति **पालकाप्यः। भगवान् व्यास**स्तु-चतुर्थीदशामिमां प्राप्तः गजराजस्तावत् बलदर्पाधिक्यमवाप्य स्वसमानबलेषु प्रतिपक्षगजेषु वैरं बद्ध्वा तादृशवैरनिरसनाय तैः साकमायोधनलंपटश्च भवेत्। किं च-एवं कालक्रमेण संपूर्णशक्तिमवाप्य मदावेशात् सल्लकादिवृक्षविपाटने च बद्धाशयो भवेत्। अपि च-मदावेशात् नेत्रनिमीलनपूर्वकं स्वल्पकालसुषुप्तिकालेऽपि प्रतिवैरिगजमर्दनाय स्वशुण्डामदूरे प्रसारणशीलो भवति। अनेनास्य मदाधिक्यमुक्तम्। अत एवायं युवागज इति। तस्मादयं युवावारणः संपूर्णसन्धिबन्धकलशौर्यादियुतः सन् मस्तके पृष्ठोपरि च मृदुलकेशी भूत्वा कल्याणगज इति च व्यवहारपात्रं भवतीति॥

The elephants will have the same qualities at this period as the previous period. They will try to be always with the female ones. There will be more oozing of ruttish-water from their temples. They will find opportunity to fight and defeat their enemies with vigour and pride. They are named as Kalyāṇa-elephants.

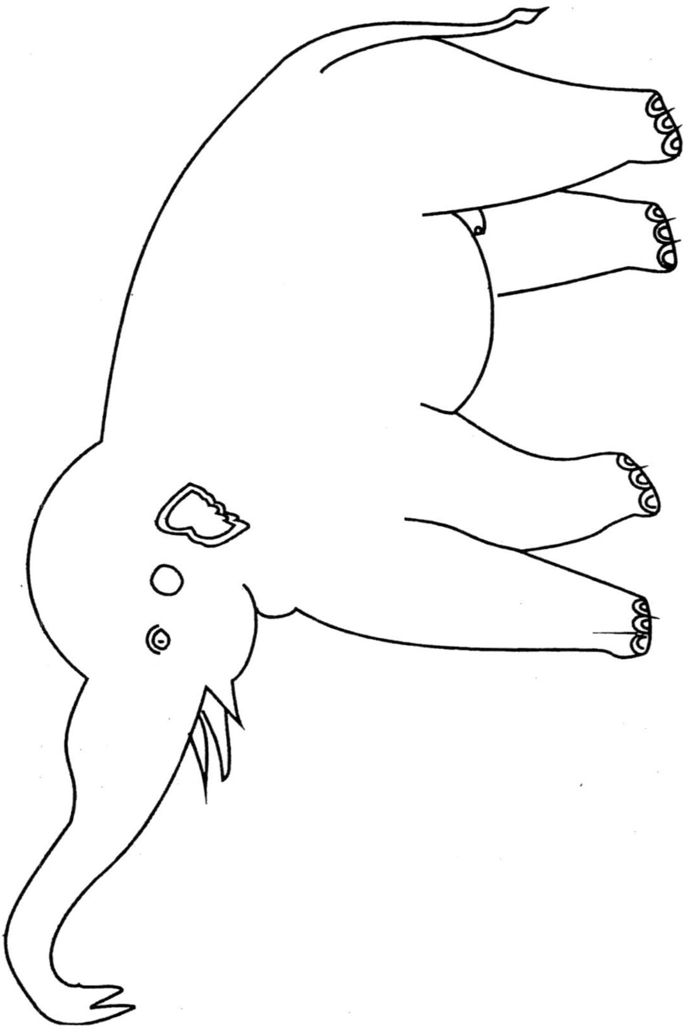

Fig. 64. : चतुर्थदशावयस्कगजः 4th period—30-40 years old

॥अथ-पंचमदशावयस्कस्य गजस्य लक्षणम्॥

पंचम्यां तु दशायां स्यात्करिणो लक्षणं त्विदम्।
सकचस्त्वग्भवेनापि संबद्धोऽतिमदेन च॥
दुःखमात्मकृतं चान्यकृतं च सहते सदा।
क्षुत्पिपासेऽपि सहते तेजस्वित्वं प्रपद्यते॥
प्राप्नोति चोद्यमं तीक्ष्णं वीर्यं चाधिकमुच्यते।
व्यावृत्तदन्तवेष्टश्च शब्दभीरुर्मदान्वितः॥
कर्णे कटान्ते वेष्टे च पिंगूषे मस्तकेऽपि च।
दानवर्षी च सततं वारणस्तु मदान्वितः।

व्यासप्रोक्ते गजशास्त्रे-पंचम्यां यूथ उच्यते।

अतीव सम्बद्धमदश्च शूरः सन्धानवान् यंतृवचोऽनुयायी।
पूर्णछविर्व्युत्सहनः सुवीर्यः करेणुगामी किल पंचमीगः॥
सन्धानप्रभृतिप्रदेशविगलद्दानान्वितोद्यद्वली
सान्द्रः कर्णकटाक्षकेऽपि सहजामायाति च श्रेष्ठताम्।
निद्रामेत्यनिमित्तमेव मुदितः शूरोऽपि सर्वंसहः
यूथो नाम सदा मदाविलकटः प्राप्तो दशां पंचमीम्॥

व्याख्या—पंचम्यामिति। एवंचत्वारिंशत्तमवय आरभ्य पंचाशद्वयः-कालपर्यन्तं पंचमी दशा। तादृशपंचमीं दशां प्राप्तो वारणः सर्वेष्वप्यवय-वेष्वधिकवलियुतः सन् त्वचि नितरां काठिन्यमवाप्य निबिडसूक्ष्मरोमावृतसर्वांगो दृश्यो भवति। किं चायं गजो मदाधिक्यवान् सन् स्वकृतदुःखं स्वस्कन्धतो-पविष्टयंत्रादिभिर्जनितदुःखादिकं च वोढा भवति। एवं क्षुत्पिपासातपवर्षादि-श्रमसहनशीलश्च भवेत्। अपि च-गजान्तरसहायं विना दुःसाध्यकार्याणि स्वयमेक एव साधयितुमुद्युक्तः सन् तादृशबलाधिक्यवीर्याधिक्ययुतश्च भवेत्। किं चास्यां पंचम्यां दशायां मदोत्पत्तेराधिक्यात् स्वकीयहस्तमितस्ततश्चालयित्वा दन्तयोस्तं शश्वत्पातयेत्। एवं करणमेव वयस्यस्मिन् तस्य विलासाय भवतीति **व्यवस्था।** किं च-एतां पंचमीं दशामापन्नो वारणः भेरीताडन-जनितोच्चैर्निनादात् भीतिं चाप्नोति। अयं तु **क्रमः** वनचरगजविषयक इति

भावः। किं चास्य गजस्य कर्णसमीपतले पिंगूषस्थाने नेत्रान्ते गण्डस्थाने च दानस्रावो भवेदिति **पालकाप्यः। व्यास**स्तु-पंचमीं दशामापन्नो मदावलो यूथः यूथानामग्रगण्यो भवति। किं चायं वारणो मदाधिक्यबलाधिक्यसमेतः सन् यजमाननिर्दिष्टकार्यादच्युतो भवति। एवं युद्धादिविविधकार्यकरणे उत्साहयुतः समुचितसमयेषु करेणुसंयोगमप्याकलयेत्। अपि चास्यामेव दशायां गजानां नैसर्गिकतेजोबलसौन्दर्यादिप्राप्तिः। तथाप्यकाले स्वल्पनिद्रापरः सन् कार्यनिर्वहणे असहायशूरो भवतीति। **स्पष्टमन्यत्॥**

At this period all parts of their bodies are well be filled with hair. They will be very fond of their prime youth and strength. They can withstand all kinds of difficulties as sun's heat, rain, cold, hunger, thirst and their *mahouts* instructions however hard they may be. They can try to accomplish 5 or 6 elephants' work at a time. They will be always waving their trunks and at times twist their tusks with them. They will try to please their masters by completing satisfactorily the work given to them. They will at times desire to be along with the female ones.

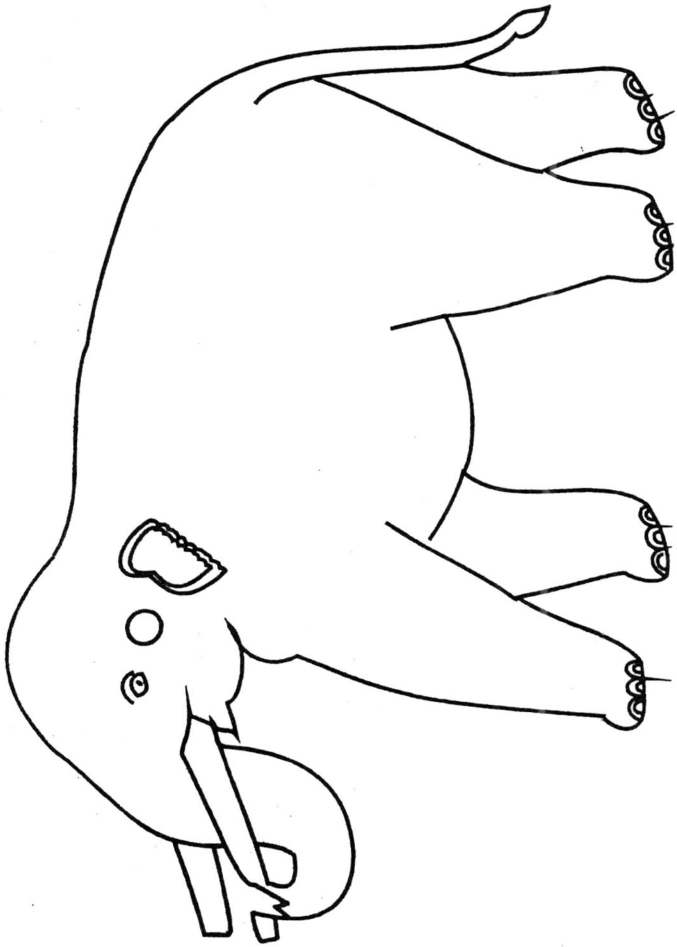

Fig. 65. : पंचमदशावयस्कगजः 5th period 40-50 years old

॥अथ-षष्ठदशावयस्कस्य गजस्य लक्षणम्॥

षष्ठ्यामिदं दशायां तु करिणो लक्षणं त्विदम्।
स्पष्टरोमावलिश्चापि कचभिन्नवपुस्तथा॥

हीयमानेन्द्रियग्रामस्तथा भिन्नवलिर्गजः।
तनुधातुचयश्चापि पतदुत्कर्षकस्तथा॥

व्यासप्रोक्ते गजशास्त्रे-षष्ट्यां विवृतदन्तः स्यात्।

ऊर्ध्वं विनिर्भिन्नवलिप्रदेशः किंचिद्विहीनेन्द्रियधातुतेजाः।
पृष्ठोष्ठकर्णादिषु जातरोमो षष्ठ्यां करी निस्सृतदन्तमूलः॥

व्याख्या—षष्ठ्यामिति। एकपंचाशत्तमवय आरभ्य षष्टिवर्षकालपर्यन्तं षष्ठी दशा निर्णीता। एतादृशषष्ठीं दशां प्राप्तः करीन्द्रस्तावत् सर्वेष्वप्यवयवेषु रोमपाल्याधिक्ययुतः सन् कण्ठजठरादिस्थलेषु संप्राप्तानेकवलिः सन् स्वल्पबलहानिमप्यवाप्य किंचित् हीनेन्द्रियशक्तिः विनष्टनाडीपुष्टिः किंचित्स्खलितगतिश्च भवतीति **पालकाप्यः। व्यास**स्तु-षष्ठ्यां दशायां तु शरीरोर्ध्वभागे वलिरेखा बह्व्यो भवन्ति। **लक्षणान्तराणि तु पालकाप्य-निर्दिष्टरीत्यनुसारीणीति।**

They will be at this period robust and strong with loose hanging muscles. They will have long hair on their bodies. There will be a slight decrease of strength, might in some of their limbs. They will have a slight shake when they walk. There will not be any more growth of hair and tusks here-after.

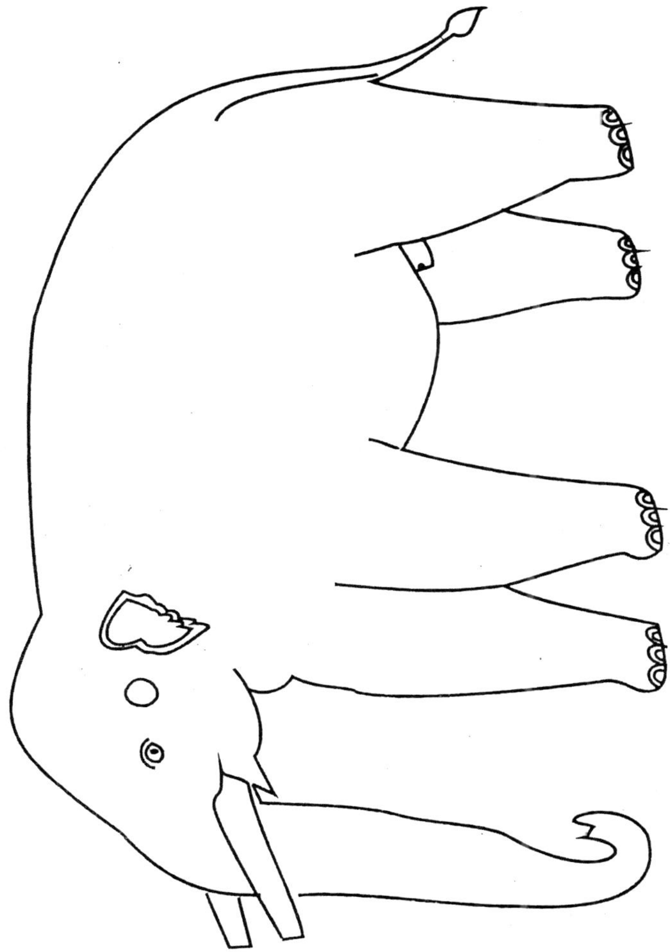

Fig. 66. : षष्ठदशावयस्कगजः 6th period—50-60 years old

॥अथ-सप्तमदशावयस्कस्य गजस्य लक्षणम्॥

सप्तम्यां तु दशायां स्यात्करिणो लक्षणं त्विदम्।
कचाविलाखिलांगश्च।

व्यासप्रोक्ते गजशास्त्रे-सप्तम्यां तु विकर्णकः-

अल्पाग्निपित्तो बहु मातरिश्वा
स्तब्धांगयुक्तः परुषछविश्च।
अल्पांगचेष्टो विकलो विवर्णः
प्राप्तः करी साप्तमिकां दशां स्यात्॥

व्याख्या—सप्तम्यामिति। एकषष्ठितमवय आरभ्य सप्ततिवर्षपर्यन्तं सप्तमी दशा पूर्वोक्तरीत्या निर्णीता। तादृशसप्तमीदशासमेतो वारणस्तावत् सर्वेष्वप्यवयवेषु प्रवृद्धनिबिडदीर्घरोमावल्या दूरीकृतसौन्दर्यो भवतीति **पालकाप्यः। व्यास**स्तु-सप्तम्या दशया समेतो गजः विकर्णक इति नामान्तरभाक्। अयं तु गजो मन्दीभूतजाठराग्निः मन्दपित्तप्रसारः किंचिदधोमुखो भवति। स्वल्पाहारश्च। किं चास्यामेव दशायां गजानां श्रमातिरेकात् शश्वन्निश्वासाधिक्यम्। कार्यानर्हता च। अपि च-करचरणादिमंजुलचेष्टाहीनो विकृततनुरल्पकार्यकरणेऽपि मन्दोत्साहः शिथिलधातुवर्गश्च भवतीति।

At this period, the elephants will have complete growth of hair throughout their bodies and they will loss beauty. Vyāsa says that there will be a slight decrease of hunger (appetite). They will be much tiresome. There will be a decrease of sight, hearing, strength etc. These are called Vikarṇakas.

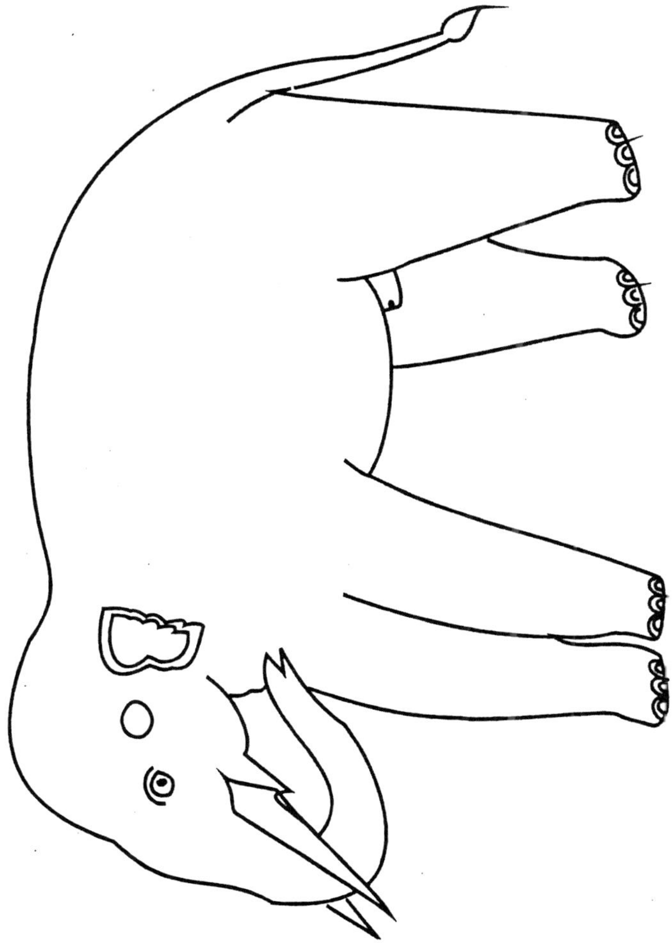

Fig. 67. : सप्तमदशावयस्कगजः 7th period—60-70 years old

॥अथाष्टमदशावयस्कस्य गजस्य लक्षण्॥

युद्धादौ सश्रमस्तथा।

व्यासप्रोक्ते गजशास्त्रे-अष्टम्यां बीरबीत्युक्तः-

कचाविलांगोऽपि विवर्णकायः कृच्छ्रव्रणो मुक्तविषाणमूलम्।
अदन्तवृद्धिर्जलपूर्णनेत्रः नागोऽष्टमीं प्राप्य दशां न रम्यः॥
निद्रालुः सततं करस्त्रुतकफः दुर्वर्णरूक्षछविः
भीत्या यूथबहिश्चरन् श्लथधिया दंताभिवृद्ध्युज्झितः।
निर्वीर्यः सततोपदग्धनयनः पादप्ररोहः क्षणं
प्राप्तः स्यात्स्थिरभीर्गजोऽष्टमदशां संभिन्नरोमावलिः॥

व्याख्या—युद्धादाविति। एकसप्ततितमवय आरभ्याशीतिवर्षपर्यन्तं अष्टमी दशा कथिता। तादृशाष्टमीं दशामवाप्य गजाः सर्वेऽपि विगलितबलपराक्रमाः श्रमयुताः युद्धकार्यभारवहनादिकार्यपराङ्मुखाश्च भवन्ति। किं च-कृच्छ्रसाध्य-मूलरोगादिविविधरोगपीडिताः जनरहितगुहादिस्थलसेवनपराश्चेति **पालकाप्यः।** **व्यासस्तु**-अष्टम्यां दशायामस्यां गजानामवयवेषु रोमपाल**स्या**धिक्यमंगवैवर्ण्यम्। दुःसाध्यरोगोत्पत्तिः। कदाचित् दन्तपतनं च भवेत्। तथा दन्तपतनाभावे दन्तचलनं वा भवेत्। दन्तवृद्धिहानिश्चेति। तथा च—सर्वेषामपि गजानां चतुर्थवयः-कालमारभ्य सप्ततिवर्षपर्यन्तमेव दन्ताभिवृद्धिरिति **व्यवस्था।** किं चास्यां दशायां गजानां नेत्राणि जलपूर्णानि। किंचिन्मालिन्यवन्ति च। किं चैते वारणाः कचावृतांगाः शश्वत् श्रान्ताः अधोमुखाः अकालनिद्रापराः पुष्कराग्र-गलितकजलस्त्रावाः विकृतकान्तयः गजान्तराद्भीताः एकान्तस्थलवासपराः बुद्धिभ्रंशयुताः गलितवीर्याः कदाचित् ज्वलितनेत्राश्च भवन्तीति। **स्पष्टमन्यत्॥**

They will be much afraid of any hard work, such as hunting, war, lifting heavy weights etc. They will be physically very weak. The disease will not be easily cured if it comes at this period. They will not like to be in the midst of other elephants or people and they will like loneliness. The tusks will either fall down or shake. They will have short-sight and hence ruttish-water will begin to ooze out. Their faces will be bent down and they will have untimely sleep. The cold water (bronchite) from their trunks will ooze always. They will have shock in their brains.

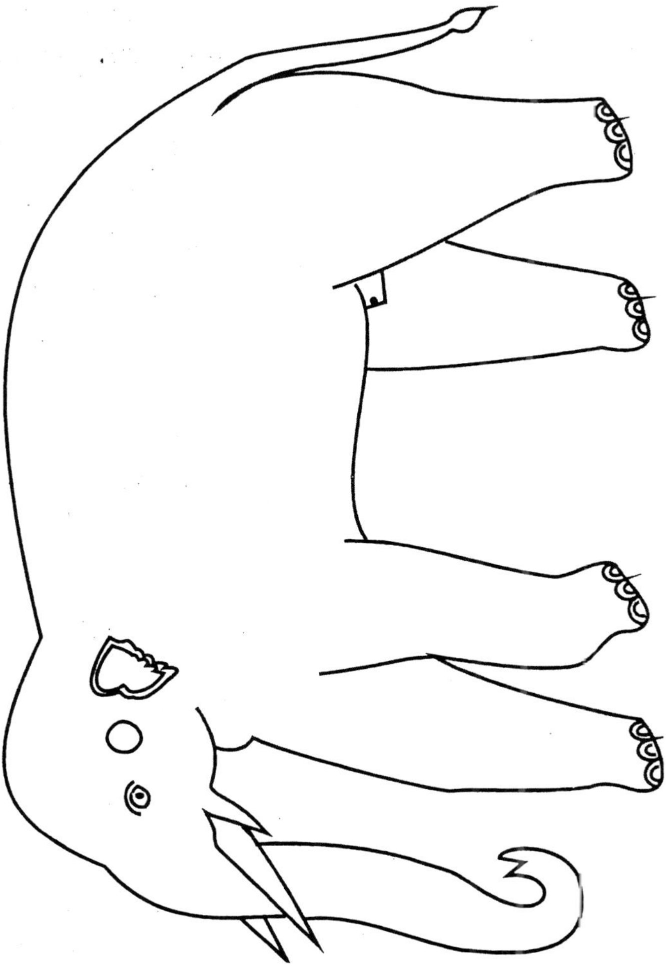

Fig. 68. : अष्टमदशावयस्कगजः 8th period—70-80 years old

।।अथ-नवमदशावयस्कस्य गजस्य लक्षणम्।।

वलीभिश्छादितांगश्च मृदुभक्ष्यं च सेवते।
दुर्गाणि वर्जयंश्चापि दन्तरोगी भवत्यपि।।
न च रागाद्भयाद्वापि क्रोधाद्वा ताडितो भृशम्।
पृष्ठग्रीवांसदेशेषु नवम्यां च समश्नुते।।

व्यासप्रोक्ते गजशास्त्रे-पुराणो नवमीं गतः-

कचाविलांगः शिथिलाक्षियुग्मः गुहाशयो गर्हितयूथचारः।
विमुक्तदुर्गः शिथिलांगसन्धिः दशां प्रपन्नो नवमीं गजः स्यात्।।

स्रस्तग्रीवः प्रचलदशनो यूथपर्यन्तसेवी
दंष्ट्राहीनो मृदुयवसभुक् दुर्गदूरः श्लथांगः।
रूक्षछायो वलियुततनुः मन्दगो मन्दनादः
निर्मेदोऽयं स्वपिति विषमं स्यात्पुराणो नवम्याम्।।

व्याख्या-वलीभिरिति। एकाशीतितमवय आरभ्य नवतिवर्षपर्यन्तं नवमी दशा। तादृशनवमीं दशामापन्नस्य गजस्य शरीरं तावत् श्लथितबहुवलीकं भवेत्। अतो बलहीनांगोऽयं गजः मृदुतृणयवसादिकमपि मन्दं भक्षयेत् । दुर्गभेदनभारवहनादिकार्येषु पराङ्मुखो भूत्वा कदाचित् दन्तरोगान्वितश्च भवति। किं च-कदाचित् क्रोधभयरागादिना नुन्नहृदयोऽपि मन्दगतिरेव स्यात्। न जवनगतिमश्नुते। पृष्ठदेशे ग्रीवायामंसतले च सन्धिबन्धशैथिल्य-प्रसक्तिरिति **पालकाप्यः**। **व्यास**स्तु-प्राप्तनवमीदशाकः कुंजरः रोमावलिप्रवृद्ध्या सन्धिबन्धशैथिल्यादिना च विकृतशरीरश्चञ्चलदृष्टिः गुहाद्येकान्तस्थलसेवनपरः गजान्तरैः साकं संचारविमुखश्च भवेत्। एवं बलहीनो नमितकन्धरश्चलद्दन्तः मन्दगमनश्चर्वणशक्तिहीनो भूत्वा मृदुतृणादीनि स्वल्पान्येव भक्षयति। भूमौ मन्दं निषण्णपरः स्वपिति। मन्दरव इति। **स्पष्टमन्यत्।**

There will be still more growth of hair throughout their bodies and their muscles will be bent down. Their eating and digesting power will be decreased. They can not run even if they are forced and beaten. They will very slowly lie-down and sleep. They can not cry aloud and are unfit for any work. Their heads will be bent down. Their bones are quite visible.

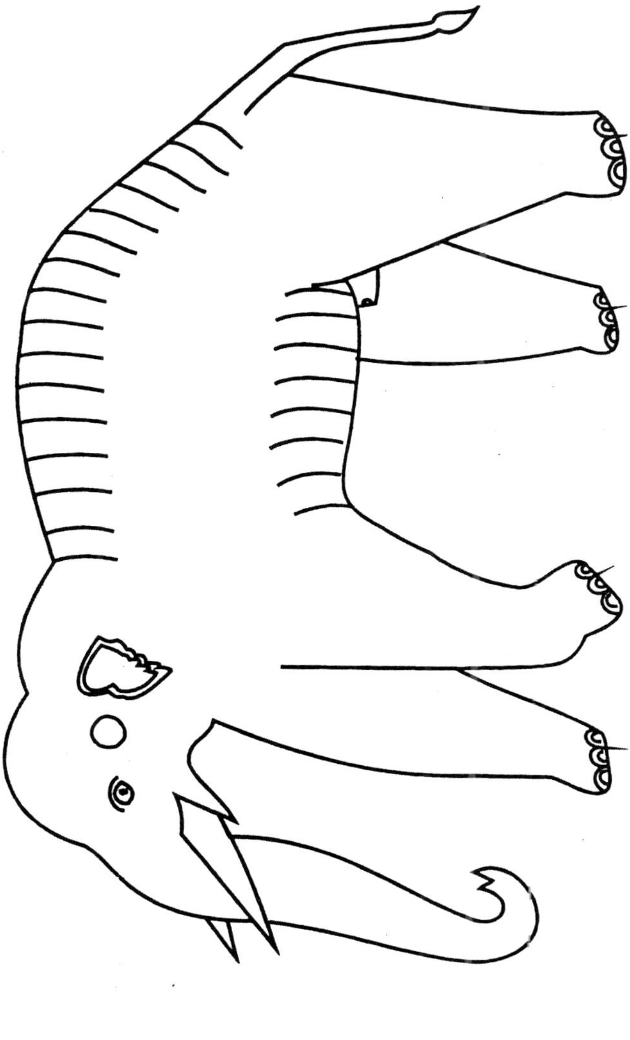

Fig. 69. : नवमदशावयस्कगजः 9th period—80-90 years old

॥अथ-दशमदशावयस्कस्य गजस्य लक्षणम्॥

किंचित्पार्ष्णितले चापि स्त्रस्तभावोऽस्ति हस्तिनः।
न चोर्ध्वं हरते किंचित् स्कन्धे च न निषेवते॥
अल्पाहारश्च भवति न च मेढ्ः प्रहृष्यति।
केशवालाक्षिकक्ष्यान्तैः स्थूलैर्मूत्रपुरीषवान्॥
ईदृग्लक्षणसंपन्नो शतवर्षो भवेद्गजः॥

व्यासप्रोक्ते गजशास्त्रे-दशम्यां स्थविरो ज्ञेयः।

विशीर्णरोमांगविषाणकृच्छ्रमूत्रारतिः स्वल्पगतिः प्रखिन्नः।
कृच्छ्रात्प्रयातः परितः श्लथांगः प्राप्तः करी स्याद्दशमीं दशां ताम्॥
शीर्यन्ते दशनाः क्षयी च विगलत्सर्वांगरोमा चल-
द्दन्तो मांसबलक्षयी चलतनुः प्रस्त्रस्तमेदोऽल्पभुक्।
रूक्षांगः पटली सिरांचिततनुः कृच्छ्राच्च विण्मूत्रकृत्
तृष्णालुः कृमिजालभक्षितनखो वृद्धो दशम्यां स्मृतः॥

व्याख्या-किंचिदिति। एकनवतितमवय आरभ्य शतवर्षपर्यन्तं दशमी दशा। दशामेतां प्राप्ताः कुंजराः पृष्ठभागे पार्श्वयोः स्कन्धभागस्योपरि च यंत्रारोहणभारयोजनादिकं दूरीकुर्वन्ति। अत इमे विगलितबलाः निरिन्द्रियाश्च भूत्वा स्वल्पाहाराः नितरां कृशशरीराः स्थूलाक्षिस्थूलकुंभाः कृच्छ्रेण पुरीषमूत्र-विसर्जनकारिणश्च भवन्तीति **पालकाप्यः। व्यास**स्तु-दशमीं दशामुपेतः स्थविराख्यो गजः शीर्णदन्तो गलितरोमावलिः क्षामशरीरः अत एव स्पष्टं दृश्यान्तर्नाडीपुंजः क्षयरोगभाक् गलितमदः तृष्णावान् कृमिजालभक्षित-पादनखश्च भवेदिति। शेषं **स्पष्टम्।**

10th Period—90-100 years

They can not endure even the *Mahout's* sitting on their backs. Their whole bodies will look very ugly and lose their beauty thoroughly. Their heads will be swollen. Their physical strength will utterly be lost. Their bones will be very distinctly visible. They will feel difficult to pass urine and dung. Their nails will be rotten and worms and insects will be eating them. They will have more thirst and they will try to quench their thirst very often. There will be various diseases at this period. They will relish very little food. They will feel very difficult both to lie down and stand up.

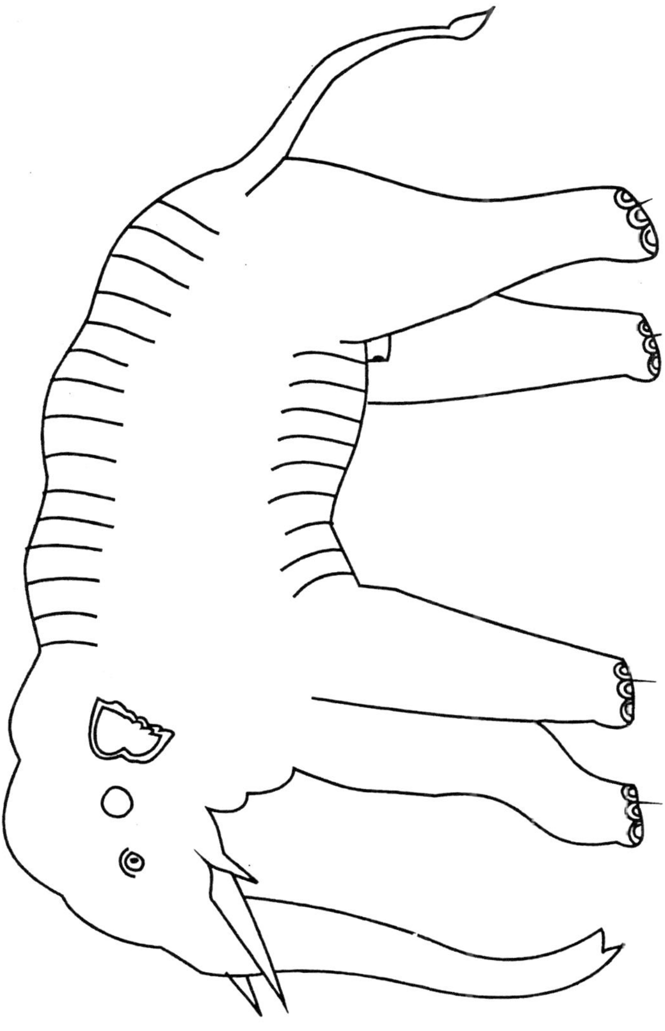

Fig. 70. : दशमदशावयस्कगज: 10th period—90-100 years old

।।अथ-एकादशदशावयस्कस्य गजस्य लक्षणम्।।

वलिभिन्नकचश्चापि क्रोशन्मूत्रोल्पचेष्टितः।
स तु संवर्धितो हस्ती रोमशो बहुलछविः।।
महाकुंभो महाकर्णश्चैकादशदशांगतः।

व्यासप्रोक्ते गजशास्त्रे—एकादश्यां तु पूर्वकः।।

सप्ररूढक्षतो रूक्षः सृक्वास्थिप्रोथसन्धिषु।
एकादशदशः सोऽयं पूर्वको नाम वारणः।।

व्याख्या—अथ-पूर्वोक्तरीत्या एकादशदशां प्राप्तः करी वलिभिन्नमस्तको भूत्वा नितरां क्रोशनपूर्वकं मूत्रपुरीषोत्सर्जनकारी अत्यन्ताल्पचेष्टः नितरामुत्तुंगो महाकर्णः पृथुकुंभयुतश्च भवतीति **पालकाप्यः। व्यास**स्तु-एकादशदशां प्राप्तः पूर्वकनामा गजः कदाचित् सृक्विप्रोथादिस्थलेषु व्रणयुतो भवेत्। नितरां कृशदेहः दृश्यनाडीजालः अल्पभुक् च भवतीति। लक्षणान्तराणि तु पूर्वदशाया-मुक्तप्रकारानुसारीणीति।।

They will be much hunch-backed with ugly figures. They will appear to be very tall. They will feel much more difficulty to eat their food. Their heads will be much hung down. Their bones will be much more distinctly visible. They will feel much pain when they pass urine and dung. Their ears will be much widened. There will be many wounds and diseases in their bodies.

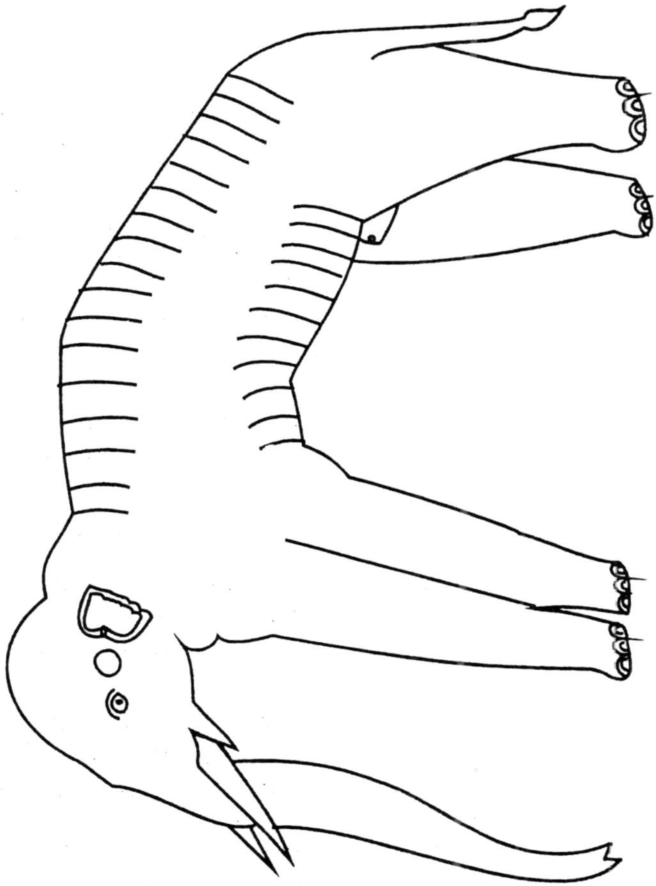

Fig. 71. : एकादशदशावयस्कगजः : 11th period 100-110 years old

॥अथ-द्वादशदशावयस्कस्य गजस्य लक्षणम्॥

समाहितः स्थिरमनाः सुदीर्घांगुलिपुष्करः।
स विंशतिर्वर्षशतं समं जीवति वारणः॥

व्यासप्रोक्ते गजशास्त्रे-

द्वादश्यां स्यादयोग्यस्तु नैव ज्ञेया तु पद्धतिः।
आयुर्ज्ञानं वयोज्ञानं गर्भिणीज्ञानमेव च॥
मुनयोऽपि च मुह्यन्ति किं पुनर्मांसचक्षुषः।

व्याख्या—समाहित इति। लोके सर्वेऽपि वारणाः पूर्वोक्तरीत्या दशादशक-पर्यन्तवयस्का एव प्रायशो भवेयुः। यदि केषांचित् गजानां दीर्घमायुस्तदा तेषां गजानामेकादशदशालक्षणं पूर्वोक्तरीत्या ज्ञेयम् यदि कदाचित् तेषु गजेषु केषांचित् गजानां द्वादशदशाप्राप्तिः तदा तादृशवारणाः नितरां वृद्धा सर्वकार्यानर्हाः। अयोग्या इति निर्दिश्यन्ते। किं च-तादृशाः द्वादशदशावयस्काः दीर्घायुष्य-प्राप्तिवशात् स्थिरमानसाः दृढस्मरणयुक्ताः नितरां दीर्घकरसमेताश्च भवन्तीति **प्रसिद्धिः**। तस्मादेतावता प्रबन्धेन तत्तद्वयःक्रमानुगुणं निर्दिष्टानि विविधानि लक्षणानि सम्यक् निरीक्ष्यैव गजानां वयोनिर्णयः कार्यः। तत्र आयुर्ज्ञानविषये वयोज्ञानविषये गर्भिणीज्ञानविषये च मुनयोऽपि मुह्यन्ति। किमुत मानवाः। अत एवमुक्तलक्षणैरन्यैश्च लिंगैः गुणचर्यादिभिश्च गजानां वयोनिर्णयः कृच्छ्रेण सूक्ष्मया धिया कार्य इति **भावः**।

Most of the elephants will die in their 100th year. Some may live till 110 years. Very few will live up to 120 years. These elephants will be blind, deaf, very weak, hunch-backed and quite unable to take their food even. Their bones and nerves will be worn out and quite visible.

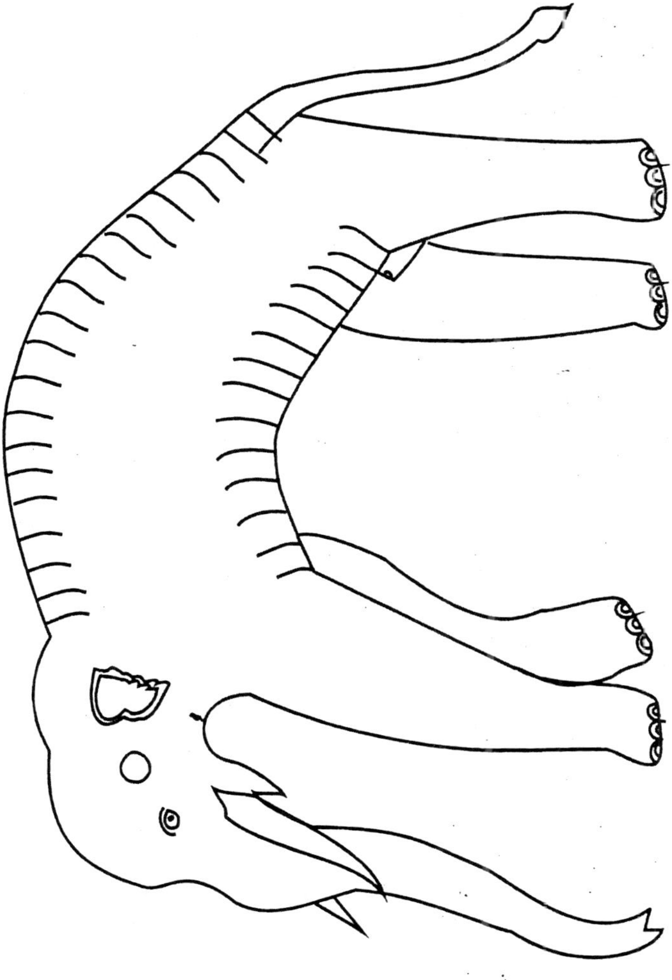

Fig. 72. : द्वादशदशावयस्कगजः 12th period—110-120 years old

॥अथ-गजानामुत्तममध्यमाधमवयोविभागक्रमः॥

दशसंवत्सरादूर्ध्वमाचतुर्दशमुत्तमम्।
चतुर्दशाब्दात् द्वात्रिंशन्मध्यमं वय उच्यते॥

तस्मात्संवत्सरादूर्ध्वं यावत्सप्ततिवत्सराः।
अधमं तद्वयः प्रोक्तं ततो वृद्धोऽबलो गजः॥

अथ-वयोविभागफलकथनम्-

वयसि प्रथमे तस्य सर्वशिक्षाक्रमः स्मृतः।
मध्ये वयसि नागानां युद्धमेकं प्रशस्यते॥
अन्ते वयसि राजेन्द्र गजान् कर्मसु योजयेत्।

इति पालकाप्ये वयोज्ञानम्-

अथ-वैशंपायनीये वयोज्ञानम्

भद्रनामयुता ये तु नागास्तु चिरजीविनः।
तत्पादहीनशरदो मन्दास्तेभ्योऽर्धवत्सराः॥

मृगजातिगजाः सर्वे विंशत्यग्रशतं द्विपाः।
संकीर्णानां वयो वेदविदो जानन्ति च क्रमात्॥

वृष्टिमायुर्वयो गर्भं कल्याणं वासवध्वनिम्।
जानन्ति मुनयो नैव जानन्ते मानवाः कथम्॥

भद्रमन्दमृगाणां तु वयो ज्ञातुं न शक्यते।
तथापि लक्षणाद्भेदात् संकीर्णकरिणां वयः॥

चिह्नतस्तद्विजानीयुः योगिनश्च कथंचन।

देशप्रभेदवलिवर्णरदस्वभाव-
सारांशदन्तजवमानतनूरुहाणि।
कर्णौ मणीन् वनचरांश्च बुधा विचार्य
कृच्छ्रादिदं गजवयः कथयन्ति दक्षाः॥

जन्मवृत्तं वारणानां विदुर्वेदविदो वयः।
विज्ञातुमनलं कृच्छ्रादन्यं विकलबुद्धयः॥
स्तन्यैकपानाः प्रथमे वत्सरे गजशावकाः।
चतुरंगुलमानाश्च बाला अष्टादशाब्दतः॥
कथितैषामियं वृद्धिः चतुरंगुलसंयुता।
द्वात्रिंशदब्दपर्यन्तं देहवृद्धिश्च दन्तयोः॥
स्थौल्यं चत्वारिंशदब्दपर्यन्तं दीर्घतापि च।
मध्याधमोत्तमवयः क्रमात् तज्ज्ञेयमीरितम्॥
भेदनिर्मार्तृकं ज्ञेयं गजानामुत्तमं वयः॥

ततस्त्रिंशद्वत्सरान्तं—मध्यमं त्रिंशदब्दतः।

दशावस्थान्तमधमं विंशत्युत्तरकं शतम्॥
निष्फलास्तत्परं ज्ञेयाः विंशाद्बाल्ये मदावलाः।
सर्वकर्मक्रियायोग्याः युद्धवर्ज्याश्च केवलम्॥
उत्तमं मध्यमं चान्त्यं वयस्तद्वत्क्रमात् बलम्।
दशोपरिदशावीर्यं विद्यादेवं च सर्वशः॥
स्वपेच्च मन्दं प्रमृशेच्च यायात्
चलत्करो यश्चलकर्णवालः।
प्रस्त्रस्तगात्रः परवानजस्त्रं
स द्वादशीं प्राप्य दशां करीन्द्रः॥

इति पालकाप्यमहर्षिप्रणीते गजशास्त्रे
कालीयगजलक्षणनिरूपणं नाम पंचमं प्रकरणम्॥

व्याख्या—एतावता प्रबन्धेन सर्वेषामपि गजानां प्रथममासप्रभृति आविंशत्युत्तरशतवर्षं परमाविधिकजीवितकालं कलयित्वा तादृशवयसि तस्मिन् तस्मिन् गजानां शरीरलक्षणगुणस्वरूपादिकं प्रतिपाद्याधुना तादृशवयःकार्यफला-दिकमाह-दशसंवत्सरादित्यादिना। अतः पूर्वोक्तशरीरलक्षणगुणप्राप्त्यादिभिरेव

गजानां वयोनिर्णयः कार्यः। तत्र च तत्तद्वयःकालानुगुणमेव शिक्षाविधिर्गजेष्वारोपणीय इति **व्यवस्था।** तस्मात्तदर्थं तादृशवयःकालस्त्रिधा विभक्तः। यथा-उत्तमं वयः मध्यमं वयः अधमं वयश्चेति। तत्र सर्वेषामपि गजानां दशवर्षप्रभृति आचतुर्दशवत्सरमुत्तमं वयः। पंचदशवर्षप्रभृति द्वात्रिंद्वर्षपर्यन्तं मध्यमं वयः। ततस्त्रियस्त्रिंशत्तमवत्सरप्रभृति सप्ततितमवर्षपर्यन्तमधमं वयः। तदूर्ध्वमुत्तममध्यमाधमवयःकाल इति। किं च-एवं प्रकारेण द्वितीयवर्षप्रभृति नवमवर्षपर्यन्तं बाल्यवय इति च **क्रमो बोध्यः**। किं च-पूर्वोक्तप्रकारेण सर्वेषामपि गजानां द्वितीयतृतीयचतुर्थाद्यानवमवर्षपर्यन्तं कालक्रमेण सकलशिक्षाविधिरापादनीयः। (1) **शिक्षाप्रकारस्तु** आलानबंधनं स्वदत्ताहारस्वीकरण एवाभिलाषबन्धनम् (2) कोपनीचीकरणं (3) भारवहनादिकार्यकरणसमयजनितश्रमसहनं (4) निर्दिष्टमार्गेणैव गमनागमनं (5) पुरुषान्तरप्राण्यन्तरादीन् प्रति तर्जनादिविरतिः (6) यंतृवचोऽनुकरणं (7) युद्धादिसाहसकार्येष्वभीतत्व(8)मित्यादिकः। तस्मादेतादृशशिक्षाक्रमस्वीकरणतत्पाटवप्राप्त्यनन्तरं गजानां वयोदशकं भवितव्यम्। तादृशदशमवर्षप्रभृति द्वात्रिंशद्वर्षपर्यन्तं युद्धाद्युत्तमकर्मसु गजाः योजनीयाः। अतः परमधमवयसि भारवहनादिकार्येषु गजाः नियोक्तव्या इति **क्रमव्यवस्था।** अतः परं वृद्धा गजाः न नैव कार्यार्हाः। एवंकरणमेव तेषां सौख्यबलाद्यभिवर्धनाय। **नान्यथेत्युपदेशः शास्त्रकारस्य पालकाप्यमहर्षेः। वैशंपायनीये ग्रन्थे** गजवयःक्रमस्तु-एवम्। यथा-उत्तरत्र वक्ष्यमाणशैल्या भद्रजातीनां गजोत्तमानां वयःकालस्तावत् शतद्वयवत्सरपरिमितः। मन्दजातिनां गजानां तु पंचाशदुत्तरशतवर्षकालपरिमितः। एवं मृगजातिनां गजानां वयस्तु-**पालकाप्योक्तरीत्या** विंशत्युत्तरशतवर्षकालपरिमितमिति। **संकीर्णजातिगजानां वयस्तु-गजायुर्वेदविद्भिः पण्डितैरपि न निर्णेतुं शक्यमिति।** कुतः। वयोज्ञानं वयःप्रमाणं वृष्ट्याविर्भावसमयं गर्भप्राप्तिसमयं शुभप्राप्तिसमयादिकं च दिव्यचक्षुषो मुनयोऽपि न विदन्ति। कथं नु मानवाः शक्यन्ते। अत एवंप्रतिपादितरीत्या तत्तल्लक्षणैः जातिभेदक्रमैः देशभेदभूसारादिभेदक्रमैश्च गजवयःकालो निर्णेतव्यः। किं च-गजानामंगे जायमानरक्तवर्णबिन्दुकर्णमणिरेखावल्यादिनिरीक्षणेन बलपरीक्षया दन्तवर्णपरीक्षया जवादिपरीक्षया प्रकारान्तरैरपि गजवयो निर्णेतव्यम्। किं च-भद्रजातिगजाः मन्दजातिगजाः मृगजातिगजाः संकीर्णजातिगजाश्च सर्वेऽपि प्रथममासप्रभृति

दशममासपर्यन्तं मातुः स्तन्यपाननिरताः तदन्तिकोपसर्पणपराः तया साकं संचारपराश्च भवन्ति। तस्मिन् दशमे वयसि गजानां यात्रदौन्नत्यं दृश्यते; तदपेक्षया अष्टादशांगुलौन्नत्यं विंशतिवयसि दृश्यं भवेत्। तदपेक्षया अष्टादशांगुलौन्नत्यं द्वात्रिंशद्वयसि भवेत्। तथा दशवर्षगमनानन्तरं प्रतिवर्षं चतुरंगुलौन्नत्यप्राप्तिद्वारा द्वात्रिंशद्वयःकालपर्यन्तं देहवृद्धिः गजानाम्। तथा दन्तवृद्धिश्च। एवं चत्वारिंशद्वर्षपर्यन्तं गजशरीरे स्थौल्यप्राप्तिश्च। नातः परमेतेषां वृद्धिरिति व्यवस्था। तस्मादेवमत्र निर्दिष्टेषु वयःकालेषु उत्तमवयःकालानुगुणं उत्तमबलोत्तमतेजःप्राप्तिः। मध्यमवयःकालानुगुण-मधमवयःकालानुगुणं च तत्प्राप्तिः। अत एवं क्रमेणैव तत्तद्वयःकालानुगुणं कार्यादिकमपि योजनीयमिति व्यवस्था च ज्ञेया। **स्पष्टमन्यत्।**

इति श्रीमदन्तकृष्णभट्टारकविरचितायां गजशास्त्रव्याख्यायां कालीयगजलक्षणनिरूपणं नाम पंचमं प्रकरणम्।।

We can not exactly say the proper and limited age to the end of their life, as it is impossible even to the sages to say clearly and definitely the exact present age and the age limited to death and the pregnancy of females. Therefore, we have to determine roughly the age of elephants born in the various forests in India and neighbouring countries as by months, years and periods as per above mentioned points.

1-10 years—The young age for the elephants is from 1-10 years, when all kinds of training is given and they will be well up in grasping everything.

10-20 years—The best age for all of them is from 10-20 years, when they carry out all kinds of training given to them.

20-32 years—The prime youth for all of them is from 20-32 years when they are able to produce young ones. They are fit for war, hunting, lifting heavy weights, carrying loads and doing other kinds of work.

32-70 years—Inferior age. They are not fit for any important work as hunting, war etc. but they are only fit for carrying heavy loads or burdens. Above 70 years most inferior age.

They are quite unable to do any kind of work. Therefore, classes of elephants as Bhadra. Manda, Mṛga and Saṅkīrṇa (Mixed breed)

(1) Bhadra-elephants—It is superior most class of elephants. They live till 200 years.

(2) Manda-elephants—It is superior class or second. They live till 150 years.

(3) Mṛga-elephants—It is the inferior class of elephants. They live till 120 years.

(4) Saṅkīrṇa-elephants—It is the 4th class of elephants. Their age cannot be determined.

All elephants will grow 4 inch in height every year till 32 years from their birth height. They will grow in stoutness till 40 years from their birth. Some may be very tall and stout even in their youth. Therefore, they should not be called as old ones. Their age is determined by seeing their nature, quality, traced, birth-place, speed, strength, growth of hair, tusks in length, colour of tusks etc.

षष्ठं प्रकरणम्

देशभेदगजलक्षणनिरूपणम्

पालकाप्य उवाच-

देशभेदविभक्तेन गजानां लक्षणं शृणु।

कांभोजलाटपुरसिन्धुवनायुजांग-
जाता विनीतसितकुंभनखांकदन्ताः।
ह्रस्वांगवालमृदुदीर्घकराण्डकोशाः
नागा रजोगुणपरीतशरीरभावाः॥

व्याख्या—पूर्वस्मिन् **पंचमे प्रकरणे** वनवासिनां तदितर-नगरादिस्थलवासिनां च सर्वेषां गजानां प्रथममासप्रभृति आविंशत्युत्तरशतवयःकालं दृश्यगुणस्वरूपलक्षणादिकं प्रतिपाद्याधुनास्मिन् **षष्ठे प्रकरणे** कांभोजलाटादिषु देशेष्वनेकेषु जातानां गजानां शरीरलक्षणस्वरूपगुणादिकं संग्रहेण व्यक्तीकर्तुमारब्धवान् **शास्त्रकारः**-कांभोजेत्यादिना। तत्र कांभोजदेशस्थिता गजाः लाटपुरदेशस्थिता गजाः सिन्धुदेशस्थिता गजाः वनायुदेशस्थिता गजाः अंगदेशस्थिता गजाश्चैते सर्वेऽपि विशेषतो नीलवर्णछुरितांगाः किंचिच्छ्वेत-वर्णरोमयुतमस्तककुंभाः किंचिच्छ्वेतनखदन्तोपेताः ह्रस्वरोमाणो मृदुदीर्घकराः मृदुलमेढ्राश्च भवन्ति। किं चैते गजाः उत्तमाः। रजोगुणाधिक्ययुताः। अत एव कामाधिक्यवन्तश्चेति **भावः**॥

Chapter VI

Descriptions of Elephants of various countries in India.

The elephants born in the following countries and adjoining ones have a good blue colour throughout their bodies, a whitish hair on their heads, nails and tusks. They have long trunks.

They are very smooth when sweared and they possess good nature and conduct. They are moderate in size.

1. Kāmbhoja—Hindu Koosh-mountains and so near Tibet.
2. Lāṭapura—West of Narmada-river including the forest of Broach, Ahmadabad and Baroḍa Rājya.
3. Sindhu—Upper Indus including the forest of Chambā, Jind, Kapartala, Patiala and Suket Rājya.
4. Vanāyuja—Or Pārasīka-Persian forests.
5. Aṅga—The forests of modern Bhagalpur (in Bihar and Orissa).

Fig. 73. : कांभोजादिदेशगजः उत्तमः Superior elephants

पुलिन्दबंगालसुमन्दहूणनेपालकावन्तिविदर्भजाताः।
शोणांकवृत्ताननकायनेत्राः शूराः कफोद्रिक्तसुशान्तचित्ताः॥

व्याख्या–अथ-पुलिन्दादिदेशसंजातानां गजानां लक्षणमाह–पुलिन्देति। पुलिन्ददेशजाताः गजाः बंगालदेशजाता गजाः सुमन्ददेशजाता गजाः हूणदेशजाता गजाः नेपालकदेशजाता गजाः अवन्तिदेशजनिताः गजाः विदर्भदेशजाता गजाश्च एते सर्वेऽपि मनोहरदृढगात्राः कर्णतालस्थाने पिंगूषस्थाने कराग्रभागे नेत्रसमीपे च शोणवर्णबिन्दुजालसहिताः वृत्ताकारमस्तकाः तथैव वृत्तकायाः सुवृत्तनेत्राश्च भवन्ति। किं चैते वारणाः युद्धादिविविधकार्यनिर्वहणार्हपूर्णशौर्योपेताः। अपि च-सुतरां शान्तचित्ताः दुर्गुणहीनाः किंचित्कफस्वरूपयुताश्च भवन्तीति **प्रसिद्धिः**। एते उत्तमगजा इति **भावः**॥

The elephants born in the following and adjoining countries have red spots on the end of their trunks, in the ears, round their eyes and over their temples. They are moderate in height, very strong, powerful, and very hard-working without losing temper. They have other good qualities also, as obedience etc. At times they have more bronchite.

1. Pulinda—
2. Bangāla—Eastern Bengal, including Tippera and Cooch Bihar forests.
3. Sumanda—
4. Hūṇa—
5. Nepālaka—All forests of Nepal Rājya.
6. Avanti—North of Narmada forests, including, Dhar, Malwa, Alwar, Bharatpur, Bikaner, Bundi, Jaipur, Jodhpur, Krishnagarh,Udaipur, Partapgarh forests.
7. Vidarbha—Modern Berar forests including Bidar forests.

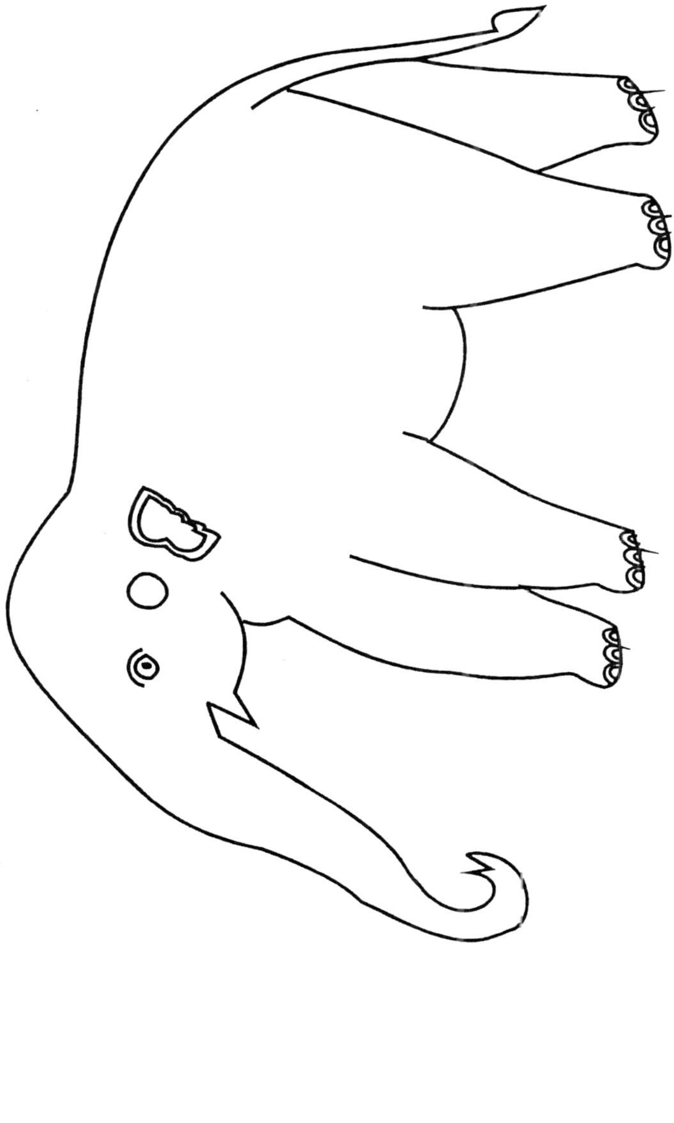

Fig. 74. : पुलिन्द्बंगालादिदेशगजः उत्तमः Superior elephants

सौराष्ट्रगूर्जरकलिंगयवन्तवत्स-
काश्मीरजाः सितमुखाः सितगण्डदेशाः।
श्वेताण्डजाश्च पवनाशनतामसास्ते
कन्दर्पगन्धतनुभिन्ननखांकदन्ताः॥

व्याख्या—अथ—सौराष्ट्रादिदेशजनितानां वारणानां लक्षणमाह—सौराष्ट्रेति। सौराष्ट्रदेशसंजाता गजाः गूर्जरदेशजाता गजाः कलिंगदेशजाता गजाः यवन्त-देशजाता गजाः वत्सदेशसंजाता गजाः काश्मीरदेशजाता गजाश्चैते सर्वेऽपि अवयवान्तरेषु कृष्णवर्णभासुरा अपि मुखमध्यभागे गण्डद्वयमध्यस्थाने च किंचिच्छ्वेतवर्णयुता एव भवेयुः। किं च-एतेषां गजानां अण्डकोशश्च ईषच्छ्वेतरोमावलियुत एव। अपि चैषां गजानां पंचवर्षानन्तरं यौवनारंभसमये मदनमदातिरेकात् पादनखाः दन्तयुगलं च किंचित् स्फुटितमेव भवेत्। तथापि न शैथिल्यप्रसक्तिः। अत एते गजाः भुजगवत् तामसगुणान्विताश्चेति। एते मध्यमगजा इति **भावः**।

The elephants born in the following and adjoining countries have white dots on their faces and temples though they are completely black. They are tall and stout. There are stripes on their nails and tusks at the time of their youth (from 5th year). They are a little dull-natured, however good their nature is.

1. Saurāṣṭra—Kathiawar forests, including the forest of Raivataka or Girnar hill, Rajkot, Dharampur, Navnagar.
2. Ghūrgara—Guzarat forests.
3. Kaliṅga—Orissa forests including the forests of Rajamandri, Cuttack and Puri.
4. Yavanta—Kabul forests.
5. Vatsa—
6. Kāśmīra—all forests of Ḳashmir Rājya.

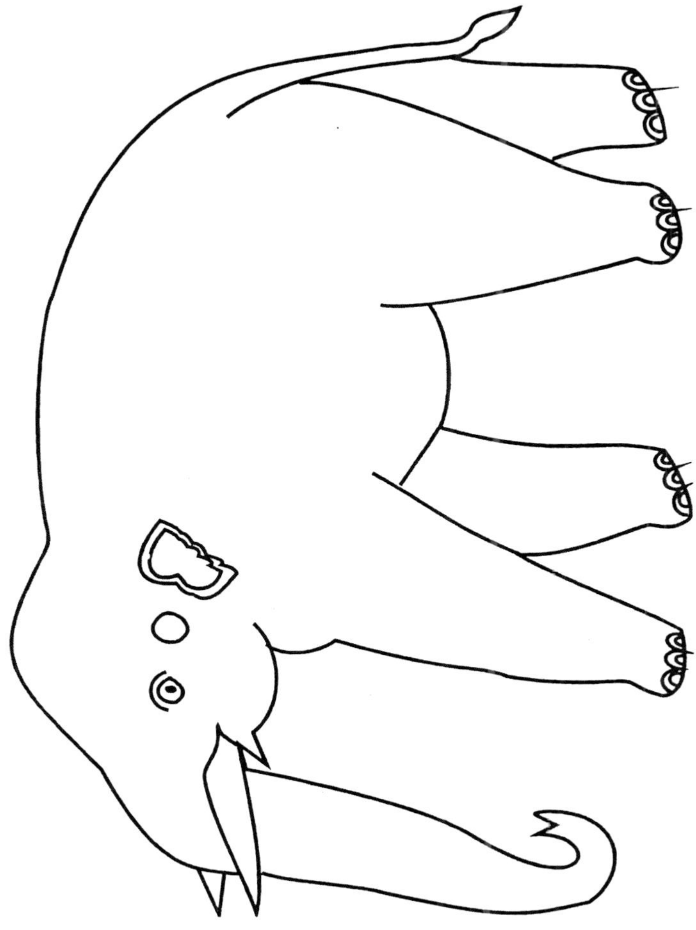

Fig. 75. : सौराष्ट्रगुर्जरादिदेशगजः मध्यमः — Middle class or 2nd class elephants

मत्स्यबर्बरत्रिगर्तमालवाश्मन्तजाः पवनभक्षतामसाः।
पीतलोचननखांकपुष्कराः श्वेतवामनरदान्तमेहनाः॥

व्याख्या–अथ–मत्स्यादिदेशजातानां करिणां लक्षणमाह–मत्स्येति। मत्स्यदेशजाता गजाः बर्बरदेशजाताः गजाः त्रिगर्तदेशजाता गजाः मालवदेशजाता गजाः अश्मन्तदेशजाता गजाश्चैते सर्वेऽपि पुष्टांगाः शौर्ययुताः हस्तिपकयजमाना–दीनामधीनसद्गुणोपेताः भुजगवत् तामसगुणोपेताः कृष्णवर्णशरीरयुता अपि लोचनभागे नखेषु पुष्करे च किंचित् रक्तवर्णयुताः ह्रस्वश्वेतदन्तयुगलोपेताः ह्रस्वमेढ्राः कामाधिक्यहीना भवन्ति। अत एते गजाः उत्तमा इति **भावः।**

The elephants born in the following and adjoining countries are robust and very tall. They are good-natured and very obedient to their masters. They possess red dots or colour on their trunks, around their eyes, very short and white tusks. Though they have small penis they are very passionate.

1. Matsya or Virāṭa—Western forests of Dholpur Rājya, including the forests of Jeypore Rājya.
2. Barbara—
3. Trigarta—Loodiyana forests.
4. Mālawa—Bundelkhand forests, including the forests of Bhopal, Devas, Gwalior, Indore, Greechha, Rewa and other nearer Rājyas.
5. Aśmanta—all forests of Travancore State.

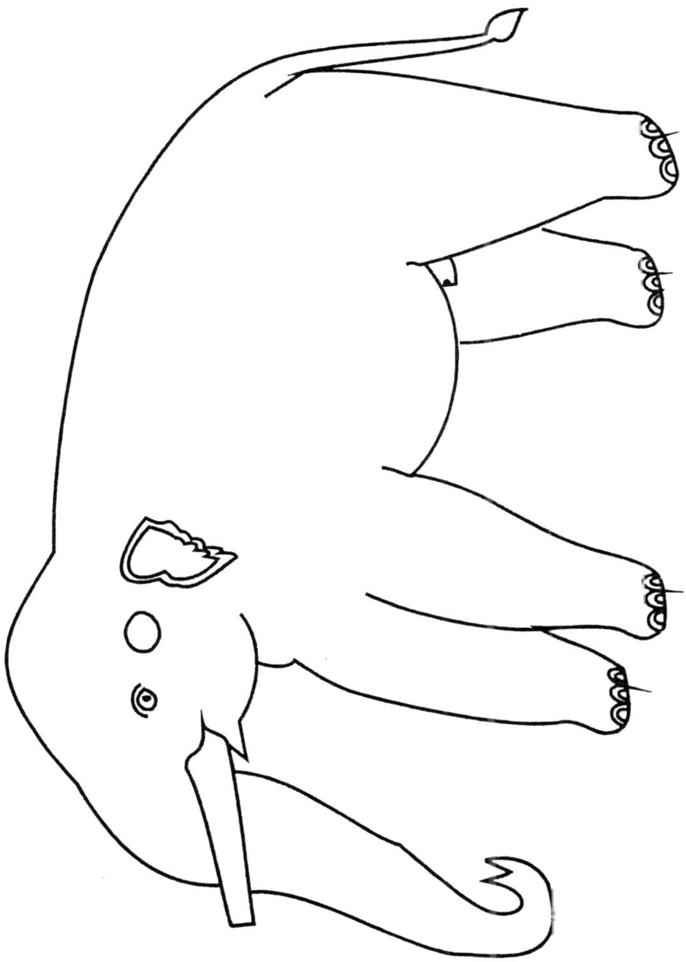

Fig. 76. : मत्स्यबर्बरादिदेशगजः उत्तमः Superior elephants

सौवीरबाह्लीकदशार्णदेशजातास्तु कालागरुतुल्यगन्धाः।
कडाररोमाननदन्तमूलाः कफोज्ज्वलाः प्रोद्धतयुद्धवीराः॥

व्याख्या—अथ-सौवीरादिदेशजातानां दन्तावलानां लक्षणमाह-सौवीरेति। सौवीरदेशजाता गजाः बाह्लीकदेशजाता गजाः दशार्णदेशजाता गजाश्च कृष्णागरुधूमवासनातुल्यशरीरगन्धाः भवेयुः। अत एते अत्युत्तमाः मूल्याधिक्यार्हा गजा इति **भावः।** किं च-एतेषां वारणानामाननं कडारवर्णयुतरोमराजियुतं भवति। दन्तयुगलं च कपिलवर्णयुतमेव। अपि च-एते कफाधिक्यवन्तोऽपि प्रचण्डयुद्धाद्युत्तमकार्येषु असहायशूराः मनोहराश्च भवेयुरिति **भावः।**

The elephants born in the following and adjoining countries are very robust and tall. They have brown hair throughout their bodies, especially in faces. They are very keen in war and hunting. They have a kind of Kālāgaru's smell in their bodies. They are worth much.

1. Sauvīra—Thaneshwar forests and other nearest ones.
2. Bālhīka—Eastern forests in Punjab.
3. Daśārṇa—

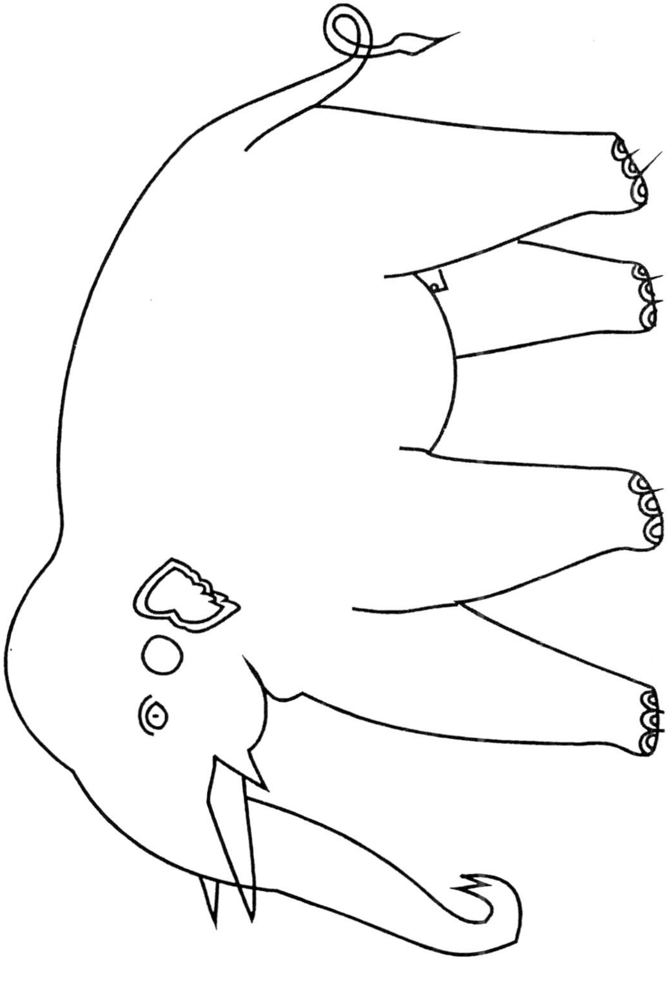

Fig. 77. : सौवीरबाह्लीकादिदेशगजः उत्तमः Superior elephants

गीर्वाणबाहुकमरालतहारिदेश-
जाता विचित्रतनुभिन्नरदा भवन्ति।
शोणाण्डपुष्करविनीलनखाश्च पीत-
देहाश्च कोमलरजोगुणकर्बुरांगाः॥

व्याख्या–अथ–गीर्वाणादिदेशजातगजलक्षणमाह–गीर्वाणेति। गीर्वाणदेशजाता गजाः बाहुकदेशजाता गजाः मरालदेशजनिताः गजाः तहारिदेशजनिता गजाश्च रक्तवर्णमिलितकृष्णवर्णछुरितांगाः शुद्धशोणवर्णयुतपुष्कराः शोणमेढ्राश्च भवन्ति। किं च-एतेषां गजानां दन्तयुगलं तावत् ह्रस्वाकारं बाल्ये श्वेतवर्णयुतं यौवने ईषद्रक्तवर्णमिश्रितश्वेतवर्णोपेतमन्त्ये वयसि किंचित् कृष्णवर्णमिश्रितश्वेतवर्णयुतं च दृश्यते। किं च-एतेषां गजानां पादनखपंक्तिस्तावत् सर्वदा नीलवर्णछुरितैव किं च-एते गजाः रजोगुणयुताः। अत एव कामाधिक्यवन्तश्च तथापि कार्यसमयेषु उत्तमगुणान्विता एवेति **भावः**।

The elephants born in the following and adjoining countries have a mixed colour of black and red throughout their bodies and they are moderate in height. Their nails are a little blackish in colour. Their trunks are filled with red spots. They will never fail in any hard work. There will be a change of colour in tusks as white in their younger period, a mixed colour of red and white in their youth and black and white in their old-age.

1. Gīrvāṇa
2. Bāhuka
3. Marāla
4. Taḥāri—modern Tehri Garhwal state forests, including northern forests of Delhi.

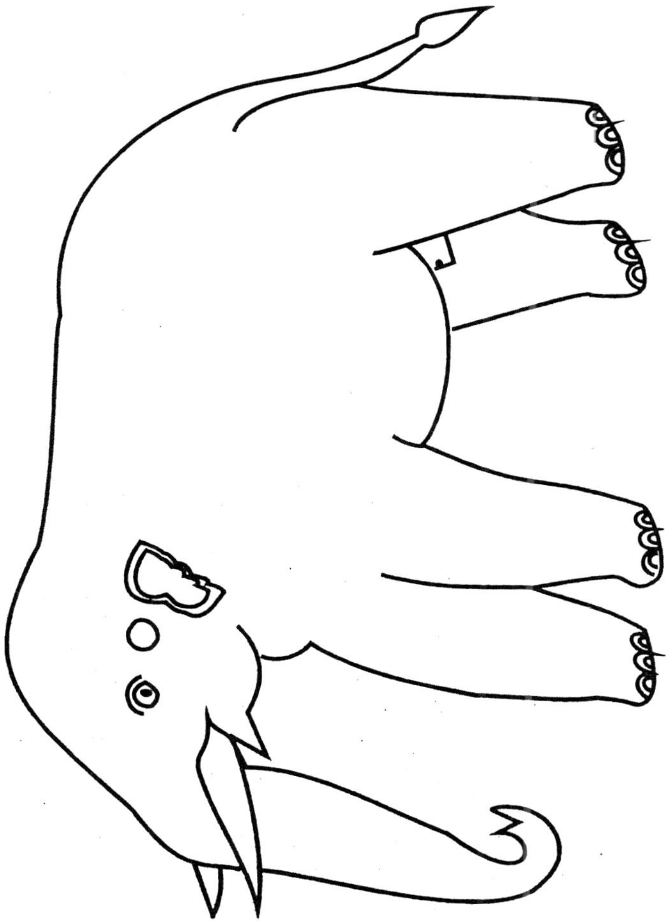

Fig. 78. : गीर्वाणबाह्कादिदेशगजः उत्तमः Superior elephants

मत्स्यराष्ट्रकरहाटकभोटदेशसंभवगजास्तिलगन्धाः।
जिह्मनीलिममनोजवशीलाः दीर्घपुष्कररदास्तनुदेहाः।।

व्याख्या–अथ–मत्स्यादिदेशजनितानां गजानां लक्षणमाह–मत्स्येति। मत्स्यदेशजाता वारणाः राष्ट्रकरदेशोद्भवा वारणाः हाटकदेशजाता गजाः भोटदेशजाता गजाश्च तिलगन्धवन्मनोहरशरीरगन्धाः। अत एवोत्तमाः। मूल्याधिक्यार्हा इति **भावः**। किं च–एते गजाः नितरां दीर्घशुण्डाः दीर्घरदनाः किंचित् ह्रस्वशरीराश्च दृश्यन्ते। किं चैते कृष्णवक्रमेढ्रवन्तश्च।।

The elephants born in the following and adjoining countries are a little bit stout in size. They have long trunks and tusks. They are black and beautiful. Their smell is like of gingili-seeds.

1. Matsya—Western Rajaputana-forests.
2. Rashtrakara—
3. Hāṭaka—
4. Bhoṭa—All forests of Bhutan.

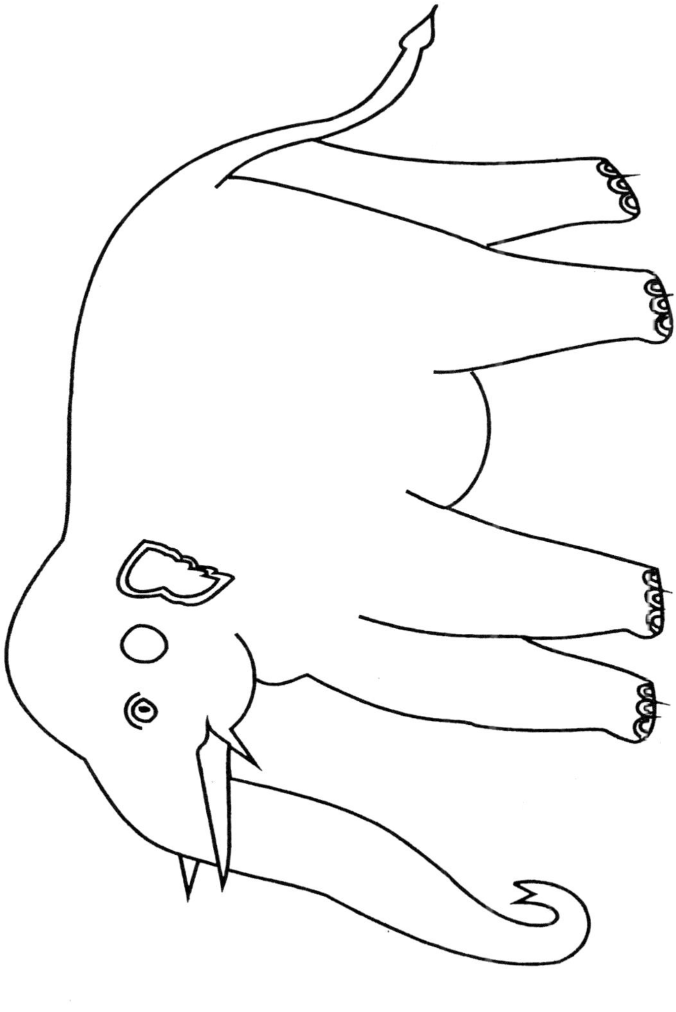

Fig. 79. : मत्स्यादिदेशगजः उत्तमः Superior elephants

कर्णाटकान्ध्रमलयालविकुन्तपाण्ड्य-
पाश्चात्यतौलवकोंकणगौडजाताः।
नीलांकशुभ्ररदनांकनखाश्च शूराः
तान्नैकधा किल वदन्ति गजज्ञवृद्धाः॥

व्याख्या–अथ-कर्णाटादिदेशजातानां करिणां लक्षणमाह-कर्णाटेति। कर्णाटदेशजाता गजाः आन्ध्रदेशजनिता गजाः मलयालदेशजाता गजाः विकुन्तदेशजाता गजाः पाण्ड्यदेशजाता गजाः पाश्चात्यदेशजाता गजाः तुलुदेशजनिता गजाः कोंकणदेशजाता गजाः गौडदेशजाता गजाश्चैते सर्वेऽपि विशेषतो मनोहरनीलवर्णछुरितांगाः शुद्धश्वेतवर्णरदनयुगलनखपंक्तिसहिताः भारवहनमृगयादिकार्येषु विशेषशौर्ययुताश्च नातितुंगाः नापि ह्रस्वाश्च भवन्ति। किं च एतेषु देशेषु जनितानां गजानां गुणादिकं तु तत्तद्वयःकालानुगुणं विविधस्वरूपं भवति। अतस्तान्नैकधा किल वदन्तीत्युक्तम्॥

The elephants born in the following countries and adjacent jungles have a beautiful blue colour on their bodies. Their nails and tusks will be milky white. They are very mighty and powerful and moderate in size. Their nature and characters change according to stage of age.

1. Karṇāṭaka—all forests of Mysore state.
2. Āndhra—all forests between Krishna and Godavari rivers.
3. Malayāla—all forests of Western ghats.
4. Vikunta—all forests of South and North Canara Dts.
5. Pāṇḍya—Madura forests and its adjoining forest.
6. Pāścātya—Mangalore Dts forests.
7. Tuluva—Near Goa forest.
8. Koṅkaṇa—Western forests of Hyderabad (Deccan).
9. Gauḍa—Benares forest and Western forests of Bengal.

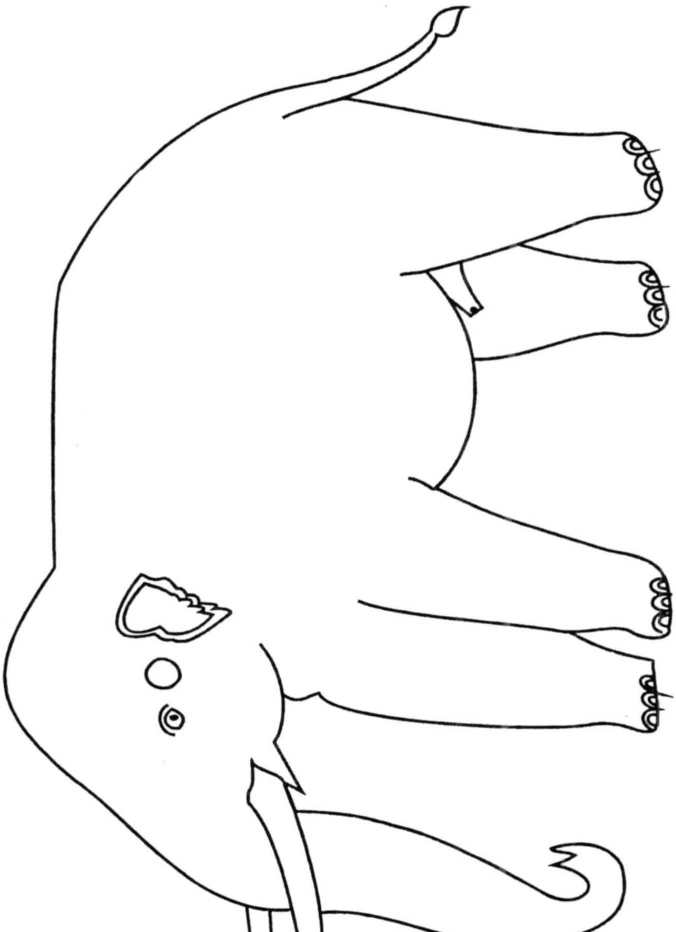

Fig. 80. : कर्णाटकान्ध्रादिदेशगजः उत्तमः Superior elephants

सूक्ष्मबिन्दुरुचिराननकर्णाः स्निग्धताम्रनयनास्तनुदन्ताः।
चेतसो हितकराः किल शूराः केरलान्तविषयोद्भवनागाः॥

व्याख्या—अथ-केरलदेशजनितानां गजानां लक्षणमाह-सूक्ष्मेति। केरल-देशसंजाता गजाः सर्वेऽपि कृष्णवर्णछुरितांगाः दोषहीनमनोहरावयवाः हस्तिपक-यजमानेच्छाधीनकार्यवन्तः सत्त्वगुणयुता अत एव चेतसः प्रीतिदायिनो भवन्ति। किं च-एते केरलदेशजनिता गजाः नातितुंगाः नातिनीचाः वदनमध्यभागे कर्णतालमध्यभागे च सूक्ष्मरक्तवर्णबिन्दुभिरनेकैः भासुराः ईषद्रक्तवर्ण-मनोहरनयनाः तनुदन्तयुगला भवन्ति। कार्यकाले शौर्यवन्तश्च।

The elephants born in the Kerala country (Cochin) and its adjacent jungles are a little stout in size and very attractive in appearance. They are capable of turning out any kind of work however difficult in may be. There will be many red spots both on their faces and ears. They have a beautiful black colour on their bodies like Jumbu fruits. Their tusks will be small. They have many good qualities as obedience etc.

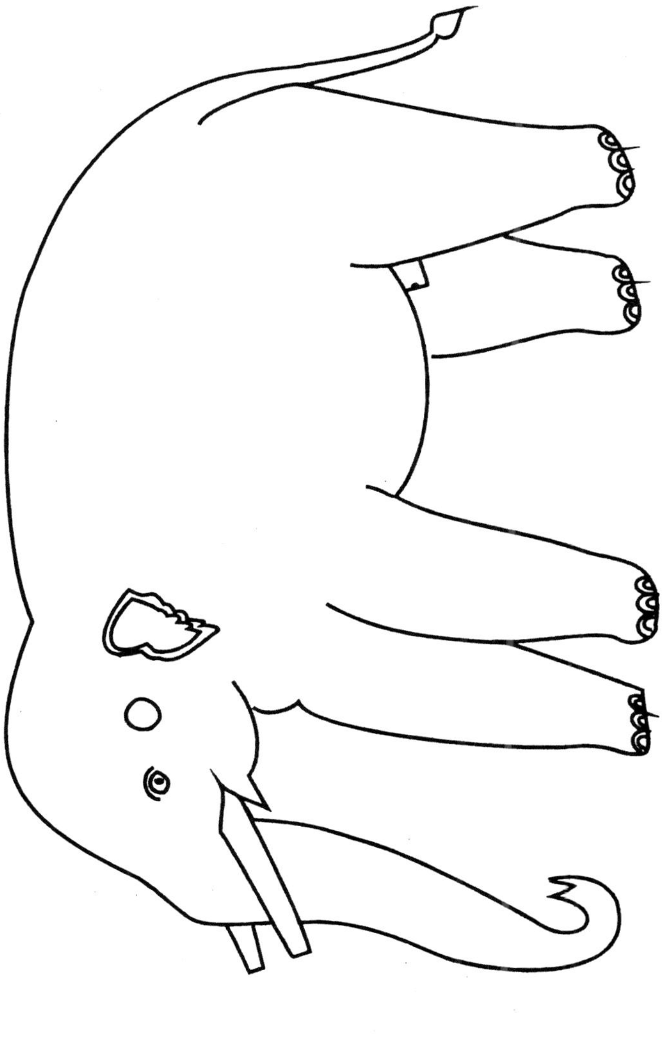

Fig. 81. : केरलदेशगजः उत्तमः Cochin-country elephants

तैलाह्वयाहिरलसह्यकशाल्वलेषु
ये चोद्भवन्ति शितशीतनखांककायाः।
हय्यंगवीनरुचिरा अतिसात्त्विकास्ते
जंबूफलाभतनवः शुभरोमदन्ताः॥

नीलवालमहाराष्ट्रगुर्जराष्ट्रभवाः पुनः।
श्वेताश्च नखदन्तेषु चंचुमल्लसमुद्भवाः॥

कार्णकौशा दीर्घकेशाः भिन्नदन्तान्तराः कृशाः।
स्वस्थानयुद्धवीरास्ते कृपणा मदसंस्थिताः॥

संगरे चकितास्ते तु नागाः स्युर्नीरसप्रभाः।
कुरुदेश्याः शौरसेनाः कुकुरे संभवाः समाः॥

महाजवबलाः शूराः सदा रोषोत्तरा गजाः।
ते च जांगलजाः शूराः शितदीर्घकचाः स्मृताः॥
अनूपजाः पित्तदेहाः ह्रस्वाश्चामदमेहनाः॥

व्याख्या—एतावता प्रबन्धेन कांभोजादिप्रसिद्धदेशजनितानां गजानां लक्षणादिकं प्रतिपाद्याधुना सह्यगिरिसानुभागादिषु स्थलान्तरेष्वपि जनितानां गजानां स्वरूपादिकं विशदयति—तैलेति। तैलगिरिः अहिरलगिरिः सह्यगिरिरेते प्रसिद्धाः। एतेषु पर्वतेषु एतत्सानुतटारण्यपल्वलकुंजादिस्थलेषु च जाता गजाः क्षुद्रप्रमाणा अपि हय्यंगवीनवत् सत्त्वगुणान्विताः अत एव मूल्याधिक्यार्हाः। स्वच्छश्वेतनखाः पक्वजंबूफलवन्नीलकान्तिमनोहरशरीराः सूक्ष्मरोमाणश्च भवन्ति। एवं नीलवालदेशः महाराष्ट्रदेशः गुर्जराष्ट्रदेशः प्रसिद्धाः। एषु देशेषु जनिता गजाः श्वेतनखदन्तयुताः चंचुमल्लाख्यप्रसिद्धगजवंशसंभूताः नातितुंगा नापि नीचाः कार्यसमर्थाश्च भवन्ति। एवं कर्णकुमाख्यदेशजाताः गजाः दीर्घरोमावलीभिरावृतशरीराः परुषभिन्नदन्ताः कृशदेहाः स्वल्पमदाः स्वदेश-युद्धादिकार्येष्वेव शूराश्च भवन्ति। तस्मादेवमुक्ताः नीलवादिस्थलजाता गजाः सर्वेऽपि देशान्तरयुद्धादिसाहसकार्यचकिताः चंडपराक्रमहीनाः परुषवर्णाश्च। किं च—कुरुदेशजनिता गजाः शूरसेनदेशजनिता गजाः कुक्कुरदेशजनिता गजाश्च जलहीनकठिनवनस्थलजाता गजाश्च महावेगगतयः बलसंयुक्ताः

सन्ततं रोषाधिक्ययुताः मस्तकादिस्थलेषु दीर्घरोमराजियुताश्च भवन्ति। एवमति-सलिलदेशजनिता वारणास्तु बलहीनाः ह्रस्वप्रमाणाः पित्तशरीराः मदहीनाश्च भवन्ति। इति **वाक्यार्थक्रमः**। एवमस्मिन् भरतखण्डे कांभोजादिविविधदेशेषु जनितानां गजानां लक्षणादीन् संक्षेपेण प्रतिपाद्य एवं निर्दिष्टेषु देशेष्वेतेषु के वा गजा उत्तमाः के वा मध्यमाः के वा वारणा अधमा इत्याकांक्षायां तन्निरूपयति तरन्तलसरवाहेत्यादिना। तत्रैवं कापि **व्यवस्था**। यथा-तरन्तरादिदेशे वा तरन्तलादिवने वा जाता गजाः तरंतलादिकुलजा इति **गजकुल-व्यवहरणक्रमः**। तस्मात् तरन्तलादिकुलजा गजाः सर्वेऽपि **उत्तमाः**। **सरवाह**कादिकुलजा गजाः **मध्यमाः**। गान्धारभोटादिकुलजनिता गजाः **अधमाः**। अश्मन्तमालवादिकुलजनिता गजाः संकरकुलगजाश्च **मध्यमा** एवेति **गजकुलव्यवस्था शास्त्रकारनिर्दिष्टा बोध्या**।

उत्तमकुलजा गजाः (32)

1. तरन्तलकुलजा गजाः
2. सरवाहकुलजा गजाः
3. प्रज्ञापयोधरकुलजा गजाः
4. यवनकुलजा गजाः
5. सुसुल्लासकुलजा गजाः
6. सुतखण्डकुलजा गजाः
7. शाल्वलकुलजा गजाः
8. शैलूककुलजा गजाः
9. अहिरलकुलजा गजाः
10. सुसह्यककुलजा गजाः
11. चिंचुलकुलजा गजाः
12. बाहबकुलजा गजाः
13. गुर्जरकुलजा गजाः
14. केरलकुलजा गजाः
15. दशार्णकुलजा गजाः
16. बाह्लीककुलजा गजाः
17. सुखदलकुलजा गजाः

18. सौवीरकुलजा गजा:
19. विदर्भकुलजा गजा:
20. अवन्तिकुलजा गजा:
21. नेपालकुलजा गजा:
22. हूणकुलजा गजा:
23. सुमन्दकुलजा गजा:
24. बंगालकुलजा गजा:
25. पुलिन्दकुलजा गजा:
26. प्राग्ज्योतिषकुलजा गजा:
27. पौण्ड्रकुलजा गजा:
28. सिन्धुकुलजा गजा:
29. युगन्धरकुलजा गजा:
30. कोसलकुलजा गजा:
31. पांचालकुलजा गजा:
32. जांगलकुलजा गजाश्चेति।।

मध्यमकुलजा गजा: (10)

1. तहारिकुलजा गजा:
2. बाहुककुलजा गजा:
3. गीर्वाणकुलजा गजा:
4. मरालकुलजा गजा:
5. अंगकुलजा गजा:
6. वनायुजकुलजा गजा:
7. वरसिन्धुकुलजा गजा:
8. लाटकुलजा गजा:
9. कांभोजकुलजा गजा:
10. अनूपकुलजा गजाश्चेति।।

अधमकुलजा गजा: (16)

1. गान्धारकुलजा गजा:
2. भोटकुलजा गजा:

3. करहाटकुलजा गजा:
4. मत्स्यराष्ट्रकुलजा गजा:
5. शूपवर्मकुलजा गजा:
6. कुरुकुलजा गजा:
7. कुक्कुरकुलजा गजा:
8. शूरसेनकुलजा गजा:
9. कार्णकौमकुलजा गजा:
10. पारसीककुलजा गजा:
11. चंचुमल्लकुलजा गजा:
12. कनोपकुलजा गजा:
13. बहुदानकुलजा गजा:
14. गुर्जराष्ट्रकुलजा गजा:
15. नीलवालकुजला गजा:
16. महाराष्ट्रकुलजा गजाश्चेति।

संकरकुलजा गजा: (40)

1. अश्मन्तकुलजा गजा:
2. मालवकुलजा गजा:
3. त्रिगर्तकुलजा गजा:
4. बर्बरकुलजा गजा:
5. मत्स्यकुलजा गजा:
6. काश्मीरकुलजा गजा:
7. यवन्तकुलजा गजा:
8. वत्सकुलजा गजा:
9. कलिंगकुलजा गजा:
10. घूर्णिककुलजा गजा:
11. सौराष्ट्रकुलजा गजा:
12. गौरकुलजा गजा:
13. आरट्टकुलजा गजा:
14. सुसुमल्लकुलजा गजा:

15. शूरसेनकुलजा गजा:
16. चौर्यकुलजा गजा:
17. वंगकुलजा गजा:
18. विदेहकुलजा गजा:
19. सुधेष्णकुलजा गजा:
20. कोंकणकुलजा गजा:
21. समुद्रकुलजा गजा:
22. चौरजीवकुलजा गजा:
23. गौरमकुलजा गजा:
24. जालूककुलजा गजा:
25. केकयकुलजा गजा:
26. खचरकुलजा गजा:
27. यवरलकुलजा गजा:
28. विकुन्तकुलजा गजा:
29. पाण्ड्यकुलजा गजा:
30. पाश्चात्यकुलजा गजा:
31. आन्ध्रकुलजा गजा:
32. कर्णाटकुलजा गजा:
33. मलयालकुलजा गजा:
34. तौलवकुलजा गजा:
35. टंकणकुलजा गजा:
36. गौडकुलजा गजा:
37. सगरकुलजा गजा:
38. मगधकुलजा गजा:
39. चेकितानकुलजा गजा:
40. कालेयकुलजा गजाश्चेति।।

इत्यनन्तकृष्णभट्टारकविरचितायां भावसंदर्शिन्याख्यायां गजशास्त्रव्याख्यायां षष्ठं प्रकरणम्।।

Elephants born in the Taila hills, Ahirala hills and Sahya mountains (Western ghats) are small in size, and very good natured, shine in beautiful blue colour. They have marble-white tusks. Though they are born in Nīlavāla, Maharashtra and Gujarashtra countries, they belong to Chanchumalla breed and they would work hard and fight well in elephant-war in their native countries alone, but, they are not bold enough to go out to fight out in the war and hunting.

Though the elephants of Kukkura, Sūrasena, and Kuru-countries are capable of turning out any hard work as obedience to their masters, hunting and fighting in the elephant-wars, they are very hot and bad tempered.

1. Elephants born in the following 32 countries and forests are the best of all the other ones.

   (1) Tarantala, (2) Saravāha, (3) Prajñāpayodhara, (4) Yavana, (5) Susullāsa, (6) Sutakhaṇḍa, (7) Śālwala, (8) Ahirala, (9) Susahyaka, (10) Chinchula, (11) Bāhaba, (12) Śailūka, (13) Gurjara, (14) Kerala, (15) Daśārṇa, (16) Bāhlīka, (17) Sukhadala, (18) Sauvīra, (19) Vidarbha, (2) Avanti, (21) Nepāla, (22) Hūṇa, (23) Sumanda, (24) Vaṅgāla, (25) Pulinda, (26) Prāgjyotiṣa, (27) Pauṇḍraka, (28) Sindhu, (29) Yughandhara, (30) Kosala, (31) Pāñchāla and (32) Jāṅgala.

2. Elephants born in the following 10 countries are the middle-class ones.

   (1) Tehri, (2) Bāhuka, (3) Gīrvāṇa, (4) Marāla, (5) Aṅga, (6) Vanāyu, (7) Varasindhu, (8) Lāṭa, (9) Kāmbhoja and (10) Anūpa.

3. Elephants born in the following 16 countries are the inferior-class ones.

   (1) Gāndhāra, (2) Bhoṭa, (3) Karahāṭa, (4) Matsyarashtra, (5) Śūpavarma, (6) Kuru, (7) Kukkura, (8) Śūrasena, (9) Kārṇa-kauma, (10) Pārasīka, (11) Chanchumalla, (12) Kanopa, (13) Bahudāna, (14) Gurjarashtra, (15) Nīlavāla and (16) Maharashtra.

4. Elephants born in the following 40 countries are the mixed-class.

(1) Aśmanta, (2) Mālava, (3) Trigarta, (4) Barbara, (5) Matsya, (6) Kāśmīra, (7) Yavanta, (8) Vatsa, (9) Kaliṅga, (10) Ghūrṇika, (11) Saurāṣṭra, (12) Gaura, (13) Āraṭṭa, (14) Susumalla, (15) Śūrasena, (16) Chaurya, (17) Vaṅga, (18) Videha, (19) Sudheṣṇa, (20) Koṅkaṇa, (21) Samudra, (22) Chaurajīva, (23) Gaurama, (24) Jālūka, (25) Kekaya, (26) Khachara, (27) Yavarala, (28) Vikunta, (29) Pāṇḍya, (30) Pāscātya, (31) Āndhra, (32) Karṇāta, (33) Malayāla, (34) Taulava, (35) Ṭaṅkaṇa, (36) Gauḍa, (37) Sagara, (38) Magadha, (39) Cekitāna and (40) Kāleya.

सप्तमं प्रकरणम्

गजग्रहणप्रकारकथनम्

करिणो मूत्रशकृता लिप्तांगैरटवीचरैः।
अरुष्करदलछन्नैः जानीयाद्गजयूथकम्।।

पादप्रचारलिंगैश्च तदाघातहतद्रुमैः।
बुध्यन्ते शयनस्थानैर्गजास्तद्बृंहितैरपि।।

इत्याह भगवान् व्यासो गजानां मार्गलक्षणम्।
करिणस्तुरगारूढैर्मंत्रिभिर्बहुभिर्वृतः।।

परिकर्मयुतः पादपाशजालैः समन्वितः।।
समादिष्टः क्षितीशेन करिलक्ष्मविचक्षणः।
द्विरदान् धारयेत् ग्रीष्मे यत्नतो लक्षणान्वितान्।।

धारयेत् त्रिविधैर्बन्धैः द्विपान् हस्तिपकादिभिः।
पार्थिवेन विधातव्यः पुरुषैर्बन्धवेदिभिः।।

वारिबन्धो वशाबन्धः बन्धश्चानुगतः परः।
उत्तमस्त्रिप्रकारः स्यात् बन्धः करटिनामयम्।।

आपातश्चावपातश्च द्वौ बन्धौ निन्दितौ मतौ।
विनश्यन्ति गजा यस्मात् तस्मात् तौ परिवर्जयेत्।
वारिस्थानं समालोक्य घासं हृद्यं ततः क्षिपेत्।।

सल्लकीकदलीदण्डान् इक्षुदण्डान् सुधासमान्।
नलिनीकन्दकान् मृष्टान् प्रियालान् पिप्पलानपि।।

द्विपो यूथैः समागच्छेदागच्छेत् घासलंपटः।
प्रत्यहं दृश्यते तत्र तदा मार्गो निरुध्यते।।

क्रोशमात्रायतां भूमिं विस्तारेण च तत्समाम्।
वृक्षैः परिधया वापि समन्तात्परिवेष्टयेत्।।

द्वारं तत्र प्रकुर्वीत निवर्तनमहीमितम्।
कुंजराणां प्रवेशार्थं वारिबन्धं विचक्षणः।।

प्रविष्टान् द्विरदान् तत्र सम्यगालोच्य बुद्धिमान्।
वारिद्वारं निरुन्धीत महावृक्षैस्तिरस्कृतम्।।

अन्तःस्थान् बन्धयेन्नागान् सर्वलक्षणसंयुतान्।
ईदृग्विधस्तु यो बन्धः वारिबन्धः स उच्यते।।

इत्याह भगवान् व्यासो वारिबन्धविचक्षणः।।

व्याख्या–एवं पूर्वस्मिन् प्रकरणे निर्दिष्टाः कांभोजलाटादिदेशजाता मातंगाः वनचरमातंगाश्च केन वा प्रकारेण ग्राह्याः। कथं ते स्वमौर्ख्यं विहाय हस्तिपकादीनामाज्ञावशगा भवेयुरित्याकांक्षायां तदर्थमस्मिन् **सप्तमे प्रकरणे** गजग्रहणप्रकारमाह–करिण इति। गजमूत्रजलेन गजानां शुष्कशकृत्पुंजं मेलयित्वा तच्च सम्यक् पिष्ट्वा तादृशशकृल्लिप्तसर्वावयवा वनचरभटा एव तेषां वनगजानां प्रलोभनसमर्था भवन्तीति **व्यवस्था। इत्याद्यः प्रकारः**। एवं गजशकृल्लिप्तदेहान् मानुषान् निरीक्ष्य मदान्धास्ते वारणाः स्वयूथशावकान् मत्वा प्रीत्या तदन्तिकमुपेत्य तादृशनिर्भयवीरभटहस्तप्रसारितदृढपाशदृढशृंख-लादिना सुलभं बद्धा भवेयुरिति **भावः। द्वितीयप्रकारो यथा**–अरुष्करः कृष्णवर्णबृहत्पत्रवनवृक्षविशेषः। तादृशारुष्करवृक्षपत्रसमाच्छादितसर्वावयवाः पूर्वोक्तवीरभटाः तादृशमदान्धगजग्रहणप्रलोभनादये प्रभवन्तीति। तस्मादेव-मुक्तप्रकारद्वयेन वनमध्यसंचरणशीलान् गजान् जानीयात्। वक्ष्यमाणरीत्या बन्धस्थले गृह्णीयादिति **चोपदेशः**। तथा च–मातंगानां मदाविर्भावकाल एव सुलभग्रहणमिति **भावः**। स च कालः गजानां वयश्चतुष्कप्रभृति आविंशतिवर्षः परिकलित इति। किं चारण्यभागे यस्मिन् यस्मिन् स्थले प्रत्यहं गजपादरेखा दृश्यते, यत्र यत्र वृक्षशाखादयस्तादृशवनगजत्रुटिताः खण्डिताश्च दृश्यन्ते, तत्रैव स्थले बन्धः (Keddah) कार्य इति **व्यासस्योपदेशः**। अपि च–वनमध्यतले मदान्धगजबन्धनक्रिया तावत् साहसिकी किल; अतो धीरा

एव पुरुषाः दृढकवचच्छादितांगाः वक्ष्यमाणगुप्तिस्थानेष्वेव स्थितिभाजः दृढशृंखलापाशखड्गाद्यायुधधारिणः सन्तः ग्रीष्मकाल एव वनमध्यमवाप्य सल्लक्षणयुक्तान् द्विरदान् बन्धयेयुः। तस्मिन्नेव ग्रीष्मकाले ते तु वनगजाः सुलभग्राह्याः। नान्येषु समयेष्विति **क्रमः**। तस्मादेतादृशसमये गजग्रहणार्थं करणीय**बन्धस्तावत्त्रिविधो महर्षिभिर्निर्दिष्टः**। एकेन बन्धेन कदाचित् गजग्रहणसिद्धिर्न भवेद्यदि तदा बन्धान्तरेण तच्च साध्यमिति **व्यवस्था**। तादृश- **गजबन्धो यथा-वारिबन्धः वशाबन्धः अनुगतबन्धश्चेति। एते बन्धास्त्रयोऽपि उत्तमाः**। कुतः। एते बन्धाः गजानां सजीवग्रहणे समर्था भवन्तीति। **आपातबन्धाख्यः अवपातबन्धाख्यः द्वावन्यौ बन्धौ निन्द्यौ। वर्ज्यौ। न कदापि प्रयोजयेदिति भावः**। एतयोर्बन्धयोर्मतंगास्ते प्रायेण प्राणवियुक्ता भवन्तीति। अत उत्तमं वारिबन्धस्थानं पूर्वोक्तरीत्या गजसंचा-रार्हस्थले स्थापनीयम्। यथा-पूर्वप्रतिपादितरीत्या पूर्वरात्रिषु कालान्तरे चागतानां गजानां पदपंक्तिं विलोक्य वा तत्त्रुटितशाखापतनादिकलक्ष्म निरीक्ष्य वा तेषां रींकारनिनदं श्रुत्वा वा तत्स्थलं गजग्रहणार्थं निश्चित्य तत्र तं बन्धं प्रकल्पयेदिति **व्यवस्था। अस्य विशदार्थस्तु**-क्रोशप्रमाणवैशाल्ययुतां वा तदधिकवैशाल्यप्रमाणोपेतां वा तावद्दैर्घ्यप्रमाणमानितां च भूमिं तादृशवनमध्यतले स्वीकृत्य तस्याः भूमेः समन्ततः परिखाखननं कारयित्वा तासु परिखासु सलिलकर्दमादिकं पूरयित्वा स्थलस्य तस्यैकस्मिन् कोणे गजागमनप्रवेशार्ह-महामार्गं तादृशपरिघादिहीनं प्रकल्पयित्वा (=प्रकल्प्य) तस्यादूरे दृढछाय-वृक्षषण्डमेदुरे स्थले गजग्रहणकार्यव्यापृतवीरभटादीनां गुप्तिस्थानं निरीक्षिणग्रगृहं च (watching house) दृढकपाटार्गलादियुतं प्रकल्पयेत्। एवं कल्पन-निर्माणानन्तरं पूर्वोक्तस्य परिघामध्यस्थितस्य वारिबन्धाख्यस्य स्थलस्यान्तर्भागे चतुर्ष्वपि दिग्भागेषु मध्यतलेषु च तत्र तत्र इक्षुकदलीसल्लकीपिप्पलीप्रमुखानि गजप्रियाणि लतादीनि च वर्धयित्वा एकवर्षकालपर्यन्तं तद्रक्षणे कलिते सति कदाचित् तत्र तथा वर्धितानामिक्षुकदलीदण्डादीनां भक्षणाशया संघशो वनचरमातंगाः पूर्वोक्तपरिघारहितविवृतद्वारमार्गेणागच्छेयुः। एवं तत्रागतान् तदन्तःप्रविष्टान् गजान् तद्ब्रह्मितादिना सूक्ष्मतो निश्चित्य तावदेव झडिति पूर्वोक्तविवृतद्वारस्थलं दृढवृक्षखण्डादिना शृंखलादिना चाच्छाद्य तदन्तस्थल एव भ्रमणशीलान् वनचरान् तान् गजान् एकमासकालपर्यन्तमाहारहीनान्

कारयेत्। एवं कृते सति तदन्तस्थले बन्धभाजः आहारहीनास्ते सर्वे वनगजाः यावत् तान्ताः किंचित् बलहीनाश्च दृश्यन्ते; तावदेव स्ववशवर्तिनः वश्यान् गजान् दश पंचदश वा तदधिकान् वा तादृशवनगजसंख्यानुगुणं तत्र प्रवेशयित्वा तैः स्वकीयवारणैरावृतान् तान् वन्यवारणान् तद्द्वारा तेषां वन्यवारणानां पादेषु गले पार्श्वयोश्च दृढशृंखलापाशादिभिः बन्धनं हस्तिपकादिभिः वीरपुरुषैः कारयित्वा स्वदेशमानयेदिति। एवंप्रकारेण गजानां व्रणादिहीनं सजीवग्रहणमेव वारिबन्धप्राप्यमुक्तमिति **भावः।**

Fig. 82. : वारिबन्धः: Moat keddah or capturing keddah

॥अथ-वशाबन्धप्रकार:(2)॥

सप्ताष्टौ वा वशावश्याः महाकाया महाजवाः।
आरूढाः पत्रसंच्छन्नाः पाशहस्ताश्च हस्तिपाः॥

करिणीनां करे पाशान् हस्तिबन्धाय दापयेत्।
प्रबध्य कुंजरान् राजा तेषां रक्षणमादिशेत्॥

व्याख्या—एवंरीत्या वारिबन्धक्रमं प्रतिपाद्याधुना वशाबन्धक्रममाह-सप्ताष्टाविति। स्ववशवर्तिनीनां महाबलवतीनां सप्तानामष्टानां वा करिणीनां करे दृढपाशशृंखलादीन् दत्त्वा पूर्वोक्तस्थले समागतस्य तस्य मदान्धस्य कामपरवशस्य वनगजस्य पादादिषु ताभिः करिणीभिरेव पूर्वोक्तशृंखलादिना बन्धनां कारयित्वा स्ववशमानयेत्। एवंकरणमेव वशाबन्ध इति **व्यवस्था।**

How to capture the elephants in Keddah

The King Romapāda asked the sage Pālakāpya how to capture the elephants from their rudeness, obstinate nature etc. To which he replied thus-There are five kinds of Keddah to capture them as—

1. Vāribandha—or digging trenches and capturing them.
2. Vaśā-bandha—or capturing them by introducing tamed lady elephants.
3. Anugata-bandha—or make one coming close to the female elephants in love and passion.
4. Āpāta-bandha—or capturing them in shallow pits.
5. Avapāta-bandha—or capturing them in deep pits.

We should understand the place and determine to keep the Keddah Department for capturing the elephants in the following ways (1) by tracing the footpath (=prints) of elephants in their frequent sauntering (2) by tracing the broken trees and branches where the footpath (=foot-prints) can not be traced or by tracing the places of their beds, enjoyments, their urine and dung, their crying etc.

Vāri-bandha—1st class Keddah.

Generally elephants come in herds. Very big and broad

trenches should be dug on all sides except a furlong or two in width; it should be left for the entrance of elephants in a big plot of ground about 3 square miles. Sugar-cane, plantains, green-grass, bamboos, Tippalees, paddy etc. should be cultivated in that plot for about a year. Watch-houses (polling stations) should be built on the big trees around the trenches for the capturers. The main big gate should be closed by trees, stones, chains etc. when the elephants enter that plot of ground in herds to eat those sugar-cane etc. and it should not be opened till these elephants get themselves quite tired and till their provisions are over. After a month or two when they are wearied with hunger and thirst, tamed elephants double the captured in number should be taken through the gate to that ground and captured by taking oaths from the captured by the tamed. This kind of Keddah is the best of all the others for none is injured in any way.

Tamed female elephants should be taken to wild ones in the forest with chain, ropes etc. when the latter are in extreme animal passion. The former will bind the latter with chains etc. Then the capturers enter inside and capture them carefully.

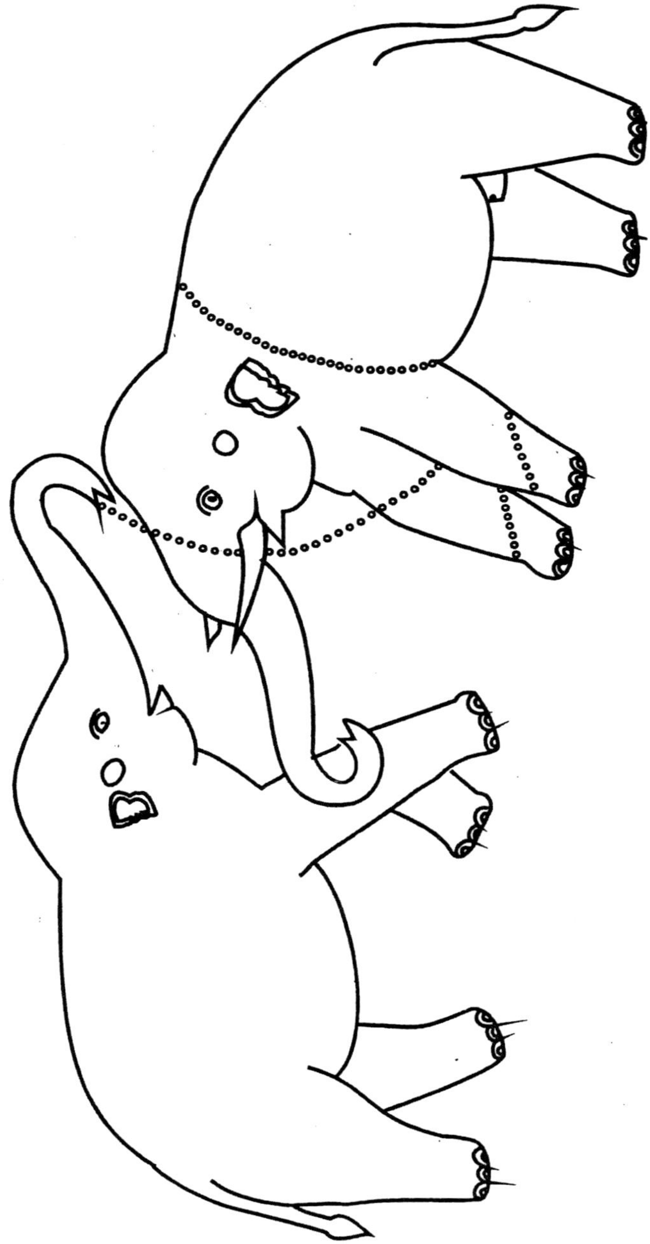

Fig. 83. : वशाबन्धः : Or Female elephants keddah-2

॥अथ-अनुगतबन्धप्रकारः (3)॥

वशां यत्रानुयाति स्म करी मोहसमन्वितः।
बन्धः सोऽनुगतो ज्ञेयः गजबन्धविचक्षणैः।

॥अथ-आपातावपातबन्धयोः प्रकारः (4-5)

आपात ईषत्पातस्तु सल्लकीकदलीयुते।
अवपातस्तु तत्रैव गजस्यात्यन्तपातनम्॥
निन्दितौ द्वाविमौ बन्धौ तस्मात्तौ परिवर्तयेत्॥

॥अथ-आलानबन्धनमंत्रक्रमः॥

आलानीयस्ततः स्तंभे मंत्रेणानेन वारणः।
अथापूर्वं स्वशालायां कीर्तिशौर्यप्रतापवान्।
अनिरुद्धप्रवेशस्त्वं स्तंभे तिष्ठ शरच्छतम्।
आरोग्यबलवान् भूत्वा राज्ञश्च विजयावहः॥

इति पालकाप्यमहर्षिप्रणीते गजशास्त्रे सप्तमं प्रकरणम्॥

व्याख्या—एवं वशाबन्धक्रमं प्रतिपाद्याधुना अनुगतबन्धक्रममाह-वशामिति। संपूर्णयौवनभाजः अत एव मदान्धाः कामाधिक्ययुताः वनगजास्तावदटवीषु यस्मिन् स्थले वशां निरीक्ष्य तन्मोहग्रस्ताः तदन्तिकोपसर्पणपराः आसन्, तत्र स्थले वीरभटादयः स्ववशवर्तिनीः करिणीः प्रेषयित्वा मोहवशात् तत्रागतं तादृशवनगजं तादृशस्वकरिणीकरप्रसारितशृंखलादिना बन्धयेदिति। एवं प्रसिद्धबन्धत्रयप्रकारं प्रतिपाद्याधुना बन्धान्तरक्रमं विशदयति-आपात इति। स्वल्पागाधस्य अवटस्य निर्माणमापातबन्ध इत्युच्यते। अत्यन्तागाधस्य अवटस्य निर्माणमवपातबन्ध इति। अस्य **विशदार्थस्तु**-दण्डद्वयवैशाल्ययुतं वा तदधिकवैशाल्ययुतं वा दण्डत्रयाधिकदैर्घ्ययुतं हस्तपंचकागाधोपेतमवटं खात्वा तदुपरितलं वैणवदण्डवृक्षपलाशादिभिराच्छादितं कारयित्वा तत्स्थलं परितः पुण्ड्रेक्षुकदलीसल्लकसस्यादीनि वर्धयेत्। एवं तत्र कल्पिते सति तद्भक्षणाशया वनगजास्तदन्तिकं संसभ्रममुपसृत्य तद्भक्षपसमये तस्मिन्नवटे पतिता भवेयुः। तत्रैवं गजपतनं दूरादेव निरीक्ष्य हस्तिपकादयस्तदवटसमीपमा-

गत्य स्ववशवर्तिभिः द्विपैरवटपतितान् दीनान् वनगजान् तर्जयित्वा दिनदशक-पर्यन्तमवटपतितं गजं निराहारं च कल्पयित्वा तदनु तस्मिन्नवटे क्रमशः मृत्खण्डशिलाखण्डादिप्रपूरणेन तं गजमुत्कूलितं कारयित्वा स्ववशमानयेदिति। एवमवपातबन्धक्रमेऽपि कार्यशैली तुल्यैव। तथापि द्वाविमौ बन्धौ तु गजानां सजीवग्रहणे न प्रभवतः। कुतः। तया रीत्या अवटे पतितस्य गजस्योत्क्षेपणं तु अशक्यम्। किं चावटे पतनानन्तरं तेषु गजेषु केचित् गजाः नितरां भीता भग्नाशयास्तत्रैव प्राणवियुक्ताश्च भवन्तीति **प्राचां महर्षीणामाशयः। नवीनास्तु**-बन्धाविमौ द्वावपि गजानां सजीवग्रहणाय प्रभवत इति। एवमत्र प्रकारपंचककथितस्य गजबन्धस्य कार्यादिकं सर्वमपि तत्र तत्र देशेषु महीपालसचिवहस्तिपकादिभिः परंपरागतस्वदेशाचारमनतिक्रम्यैव कलनीयमिति **वयम्।** तस्मादेवमुक्तरीत्या वनगजग्रहणानन्तरं तान् सर्वान् स्वनगरस्थ-गजशालामालानस्तंभे बन्धयेत्। तस्मिन् समये अनिरुद्धप्रवेशस्त्वमित्येतन्मंत्रं समुच्चारयन् तानाबध्य तद्रक्षणादिकं यथाक्रमं कलयेदि**त्युपदेशः॥**

इत्यनन्तकृष्णभट्टारकविरचितायां गजशास्त्रव्याख्यायां सप्तमं प्रकरणम्॥

Anugatabandha—3rd class Keddah

The female elephants should be threatened and driven out suddenly from the males when the latter are in extreme love with passion. This place should be well-guarded. When the female ones are driven out, the male will be stunned and will never *stir* out of that place. At that time they should be easily fastened with chains and ropes.

Āpāta-bandha and Avapāta-bandha (or 4th and 5th class Keddah) pit fall

Pits about 20-25 feet deep, 40-50 feet wide and 25-30 feet long should be dug, which (that place) should be generally frequented by the elephants. The pits should be closely covered with thin and little bamboos and over the bamboos mud and sand should be spread and levelled. Over and around the pits, plantains, sugarcanes, bamboo trees etc. should be cultivated and grown for about one year. The elephants in rut, thinking that they are naturally grown, begin to come and eat them. When they step over the pits they will suddenly fall into them. The capturers after watching them falling down into the pits, should try to get the tamed ones after a fortnight or two when they are fully terrified and hungry and threaten them by taking oaths from them. After doing this the pits should be levelled with sand. Then the wild ones will come out of the pits when they should be well fastened with chains and ropes.

The sage says that this kind of Keddah is inferior to the other Keddahs, because, the elephants, when they suddenly fall down into the pits, will be thunderstruck and got terrified. When it is so, some may also die owing to extreme fear and broken heart.

The modern scholars say that this kind of Keddah too is a better one if they are carefully captured.

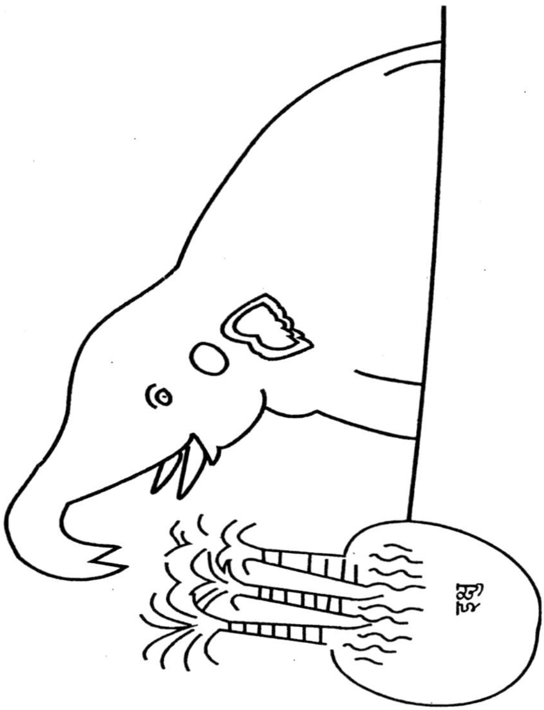

Fig. 84. : आपातबन्धः: Shallow pits

Fig. 85. : अवपातबन्धः: Deep pits

अष्टमं प्रकरणम्

भद्रमन्दमृगसंकीर्णजातिगजलक्षणनिरूपणम्

धैर्यं शौर्यं पटुत्वं च विनीतत्वं सुकर्मता।
अन्वर्थवेदिता चैव भयरूपेष्वमूढता॥

सुभगत्वं च वीरत्वं भद्रस्यैते गुणाः स्मृता।
तेजांशकत्वाद्भद्रस्य नवपूगफलप्रभः॥

कृते कामप्रचारास्तु कामरूपधरा गजाः।
त्रेतायां द्वापरेऽन्यत्र वाहनत्वेन योजिताः॥

त्रेतायां तद्गुणे किंचिन्मन्दत्वान्मन्द उच्यते।
द्वापरे तु युगे सर्वे मृगतां प्राप्य संस्थिताः॥

कलौ तद्गुणसांकर्यात्संकीर्ण इति कथ्यते।
कृते भद्रगुणाः सर्वे भवन्ति करिणां यतः॥

ततस्तत्र समुद्भूतो भद्र इत्यभिधीयते।

भद्रप्रकृतिर्यथा–

जायते समदोद्गारः भद्रनामा मतंगजः।

भद्रादिप्रमाणं यथा–

नवाष्टसप्त चायामो सप्तषट्पंच चोच्छ्रयः।

व्यासप्रोक्ते गजशास्त्रे–

नाहे दश नवाष्टौ च भद्रमन्दमृगक्रमात्॥
अत्युन्नतः स्थूलसुवृत्तकुंभः विस्तीर्णकर्णः कलविंकनेत्रः।
स्निग्धच्छविर्वक्त्रकरोरुदन्तो रक्तोत्पलाकारकरांगुलीकः॥

कोदण्डसंस्थाननिमग्नवंशो विशालवालः सुविभक्तकायः।
वराहजंघो द्विगुणीकृतार्थहस्ताग्रसंस्पृष्टमहीतलश्च॥
आताम्रतालुः पृथुपीनकण्ठः घनाकृतिर्बिन्दुविचित्रवक्त्रः।
दक्षो बली कर्कश उत्तमांगसंरक्ततातुंगवपुर्विनीतः॥
संपूर्णसन्धिः पृथुपुष्कराक्षः समुन्नतः स्थूलतरस्तरस्वी।
प्रतिद्विपालोकनदृश्यमानदानस्रवो भद्रमतंगजः स्यात्॥

अनुभद्रजातिलक्षणम् (1)-

न कृशा न चोपदिग्धाः मधुनिभदन्तेक्षणा धनुर्वंशाः।
समवृत्तगात्रसुभगाः ह्यनुभद्रास्ते गजा ज्ञेयाः॥
गात्रापरं करः पुच्छं न स्थूलं न भवेत्समम्।
विशालमुन्नतं वक्षो धनुराकारवंशकः॥
अत्युन्नतस्थूलकुंभौ कटौ चापि प्रवेशकौ।
स्थूलदन्ता भवन्तीह विपुलं चरणासनम्॥
वराहजघनश्चैव छागकुक्षिर्मनोहरः।
समाः स्निग्धा नखा दन्ताः लोचने मधुपिंगले॥
गौरवर्णो ह्युदग्रश्च लब्धबिन्दुविराजितः।
आतालुताम्रजिह्वोष्ठः एतद्भद्रस्य लक्षणम्॥
वनयूथस्य पुरतो यात्याहारविहारयोः।
मेघभेरीस्वराद्भीतिं नैति गच्छत्यनाकुलम्॥
समानीतो वनात्कर्मकाले सोऽत्यर्थवेदिनः।
आशुग्राही सुशीलश्च न विस्मरति शिक्षितम्॥
कर्मशूरः स्वयं शूरः भूपलक्षणसंयुतः।
ईदृशो भद्रजातिः स्यात्कुंजरो विजयावहः॥

व्याख्या—अथास्मिन्नष्टमे **प्रकरणे** भद्रमन्दमृगसंकीर्णाख्यगजजाति-चतुष्कस्वरूपलक्षणादिकं विशदयति-धैर्यं शौर्यमित्यादिना। धैर्यशौर्यकार्यपाटव-विनीतत्वभयराहित्यादिकं सर्वमपि सल्लक्षणं भद्रजातिगजानामाजन्मसिद्धं भातीति **क्रमः**। पूर्वं कृतयुगे भद्रजातिगजा एव सर्वे। **ते चापि** स्वेच्छागृहीत-विविधरूपाः सर्वत्र संचरणशीलाः पूर्वोक्तसकलसद्गुणसंपन्नाश्चासन्। तदनु

त्रेतायुगे गजास्तादृशसद्गुणेभ्यः किंचित् हीना आसन्। अत एव तेषां मन्दगजाः इति नामव्यवहारक्रमः। किं चैते द्वापरयुगगजाः सर्वेऽपि तेभ्योऽपि सद्गुणेभ्यः किंचिच्च्युताः मृगस्वरूपतामवापुः। अस्मिन् तु कलौ युगे तेभ्योऽपि गुणेभ्यः प्रच्युता एव सर्वे गजाः। किं च पूर्वोक्तानां तेषां तेषां भद्रजातिमन्दजातिमृगजातिस्वरूपसांकर्यवन्तश्च। अत एव कलियुगजाता गजाः प्रायशः संकीर्णगजस्वरूपयुता अपि कोसलकाश्मीरतहारिवंगांगकलिंगादिषु उत्तमदेशेषु जनिताः केचित् गजाः भद्रजातिस्वरूपाः। अन्ये गजास्तु मन्दजातयः। परे तु मृगजातयश्च सन्दृश्यन्ते। अत एव एतेषां भद्रमन्दमृगसंकीर्णाख्यजाति-चतुष्कजनितानां गजानां लक्षणस्वरूपादिकमस्मिन्नष्टमे **प्रकरणे** व्यक्तं प्रतिपादयति **शास्त्रकार** इति **व्यवस्था** बोध्या।।

तस्मात्तेषां गजानां प्रमाणं **पालकाप्योक्तं** यथा-

भद्रजातिगजाः सर्वेऽपि हस्तनवकायामयुताः (Length) करसप्त-कोच्छ्राययुताः (Height)

मन्दजातिगजाः सर्वेऽपि हस्ताष्टकायामयुताः (Length) करषट्-कोच्छ्राययुताः (Height)

मृगजातिगजाः सर्वेऽपि हस्तसप्तकायामयुताः (Length) करपंच-कोच्छ्राययुताः (Height) इति।।

व्यासस्तु-भद्रजातिगजानां हस्तदशकायामं मन्दजातिगजानां हस्तनवकायामं मृगजातिगजानामष्टकरायामं चोक्तवान्। किं चैते-भद्रजातिगजाः सर्वेऽपि गजान्तरापेक्षया अत्युन्नताः अत्युन्नतस्थूलवृत्ताकारमस्तककुंभयुगलोपेताः विशालकर्णाश्च भवंति। लक्षणान्तरादिकं तु मूलत एव पुराणशैल्या स्पष्टं ज्ञेयम्। अनुभद्रजातयो गजास्तु-एतादृशभद्रजातिगजस्वरूपात् किंचित् हीना एव। तथाप्युत्तमा एव। अत एवानुभद्रगजा इति **व्यवहारः**। किं चैते अनुभद्रगजाः भद्रगजाश्च स्थूलदन्ताः रक्तवर्णबिन्दुविराजितमुखकर्णतलोपेताः मेघगर्जितात् भेरीरवादिकाच्च नैव भयं प्राप्नुवन्ति। सूक्ष्मबुद्धयः। हस्तिपकादि-निर्दिष्टकार्यादीनि आशु बुध्यन्ति। शिक्षितं न विस्मरन्ति। यजमानवात्सल्य-वन्तश्च। नितरां बलपराक्रमसौन्दर्यसद्गुणादिभिरुपेताश्च। अत एव इमे भद्रजातिगजाः भूपालानां सामन्तस्य चक्रवर्तेर्युवराजस्य च पट्टाभिषेकसमय-सेवार्हाः। समरादिषु विजयप्रदाश्च भवन्तीति। अत एतेषां मूल्याधिक्यमप्या-कलयन्ति **प्राचीनाः**।।

Description of the 4 main classes of Elephants

1. Bhadra-gajas—or 1st class elephants.
2. Mandagajas—or 2nd class elephants.
3. Mṛga-gajas—or inferior class of elephants.
4. Saṅkīrṇa-gajas—(middle=mixed) class elephants.

1. There are 4 kinds of Yugas mentioned in ancient Purāṇas, as Kṛtayuga, Tretāyuga, Dwāparayuga and Kaliyuga. Elephants in Kṛtayuga were all Bhadra-class, having two wings, four tusks etc., moving from place to place according to their wishes and fancy as prescribed in the 2nd chapter. Elephants of this kind belong to Bhadra-class.
2. The elephants in Tretāyuga were still all in decreased powers owing to the curse of sages, as prescribed in the 3rd chapter. Elephants of this kind belong to Manda-class.
3. The elephants in Dwāparayuga were still more powerful. Elephants of this kind belong to the Mṛga-class.
4. The elephants in Kaliyuga belong to a Saṅkīrṇa-class or mixed-breed. Yet a few of the first 3 classes of elephants too are being born in the modern days.

1. Special description of Bhadra-gaja or 1st class elephants.

These elephants possess very strong and robust bodies, long tails, long, stout and white tusks, very long and stout trunks, hanging over the ground (i.e. even longer than their legs). They are uniformly stout and very tall. They are more courageous. They have very big and stout heads, broad and big ears, beautiful eyes and smooth bodies. The ends of their trunks are red. They have white or red spots on their foreheads and quick movements. The ruttish water will begin to flow from their temples when they happen to see their enemies (elephant-foes). They can very easily grasp anything and everything said by their masters. They have many other good qualities and nature. They will improve the prosperity and long life of the kings and nobles.

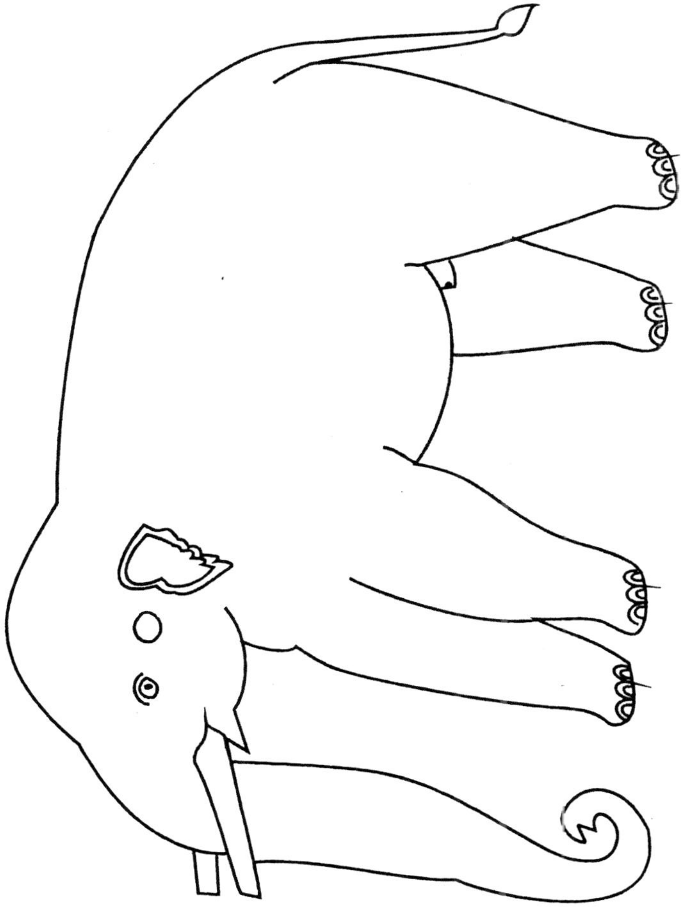

Fig. 86. : भद्रगजः उत्तमः Bhadra elephants superior

॥अथ-मन्दजातिगजलक्षणम् (2)॥

विपुलकरकर्णवदनाः महोदराः स्थूलपेचकविषाणाः।
बहुलबललंबमांसाः हर्यक्षाः कुंजराः मन्दाः॥

व्यासप्रोक्ते गजशास्त्रे-

स्थूलगात्राः दृढश्रोत्रहस्तदन्तनखोदराः।
बलप्रलंबसंभूतमांसाः सिंहावलोकनाः॥

दौर्मनस्यं तथालस्यं निद्रालुत्वं च मूढता।
गंभीरवेदिता चैवं दुष्टत्वं च तमोगुणाः॥

मन्दं यानं मतं सर्वं शुभकर्मसुपूजितम्।
आरोहणं मन्दनाम्नो मातंगस्य मनोहरम्॥

तरुणांबुदसंकाशः रूक्षकृष्णकचाविलः।
श्लेष्मसंसृष्टपित्तासृक्मिथुनप्रभवो गजः॥

उरोमुखं तथा कर्णौ विशालानि भवन्ति हि।
वालधिः पृष्ठवंशश्च विशालो वक्ष एव च॥

भवन्त्येतानि दीर्घाणि लंबमेढ्रः सुकोशकः।
भेककुक्षिसमाकुक्षिः लोचने कपिले शुभे॥

कृष्णमेघनिभो वर्णः सर्वांगोपरि पीनता।
जाड्यं च बलबाहुल्यमिदं मन्दस्य लक्षणं॥

वनेषु वसतस्यस्य शशादेर्यद्भयं भवेत्।
न हृष्यति भवत्येको निद्रालुः सततं भवेत्॥

शिक्षाकाले च तस्यैतल्लक्षणं परिदृश्यते।
गंभीरवेदनं तस्य कर्मशीघ्रं प्रदृश्यते॥

शिक्षितं विस्मरत्याशु मत्तः स्मरति शिक्षितम्।
मन्दकोपो गतौ स्तब्धः मन्दो मातंग ईदृशः॥

स्निग्धछविः सिंहसमानदृष्टिः नवांबुदश्यामसदुत्तमांगः।
अधोमुखः स्थूलबृहत्सुदंतो लंबोदरो दीर्घललाटपट्टः॥

व्याख्या–अथ–द्वितीयस्य मन्दजातिगजस्य लक्षणमाह–विपुलेत्यादिना। मन्दजातिजनिताः सर्वेऽपि मतंगजाः विशालकर्णोपेताः विशालवदनाः पृथुदीर्घकराः बृहदुदरभागाः नितरां स्थूलदन्तास्तथैव नितरां स्थूलपेचकाख्य-कर्णाधःप्रदेशाः बहुमांसमेदुरांगाः सिंहस्येव गभीरनेत्रयुगलाश्च भवन्तीति **पालकाप्यः। व्यास**स्तु मन्दजातिजनिताः मातंगाः स्थूलगात्राः स्थूलोदराः अतिबलाढ्याश्च भवन्ति। किं च–हस्तिपकादिनिर्दिष्टकार्यं प्रति प्रथमतः किंचिद्दौर्मनस्यमालस्यं च प्राप्नुवन्ति। भक्षणानन्तरं निद्रालवः। किं च मन्दजातिगजस्तावत् दीर्घकालेनैव कार्यादिवेत्ता। भद्रगजापेक्षया किंचिद्-दुष्टस्वभावः। मन्दगमनादिश्च भवतीति मन्दजातिगजगुणः। अस्य वर्णस्तु-सजलमेघवन्मनोहरनीलवर्ण एव। सर्वेष्वप्यवयवेषु सूक्ष्मरोमावलियुतश्च। एवं श्लेष्मप्रसारसंयुक्तपित्तसंपर्कादेवायं गज एवं भवतीति **व्यवस्था**। इति गजस्यास्य प्रकृतिर्ज्ञेया। किं चास्य मन्दजातिगजस्य वक्षो वदनं कर्णयुगलं चातिविशालं भवति। हस्तः पृष्ठभागो वालधिश्च वैशाल्यदैर्घ्ययुत एव। बलाधिक्यवशात् सततं लंबमेढ्रयुतश्च दृश्यते। अपि चायं गजो नितरां तोषं भयं दुःखं च प्राप्नोतीति **व्यवस्था**। किं चात्र श्लोकगुंभे **व्यासप्रोक्तं** मन्दजातिगजस्यास्य गुणान्तराणि तु पुराणशैल्या स्पष्टार्थकान्येव। अतो न व्याख्या कलितेति **परिपाटी**॥

2. Manda-gaja or 2nd class elephants.

Though less than Bhadra-gaja, these Manda-elephants have stout and heavy bodies, broad faces and ears, stout stomachs full of strong muscles over the bodies and lion's eyes. They will feel difficult to some extent when they begin to work. They are lazy and dull to some extent. They will walk slowly. Their colour will be beautiful blue for appearance. Owing to more strength there will be often erection of penis. They are morose. They will not appear to be happy. They will suddenly forget anything and remember at once when they are pierced by the spears etc. by the *mahouts*. They are calm in temper. They will have their face lowered down to a little extent. They have beautiful and strong tusks.

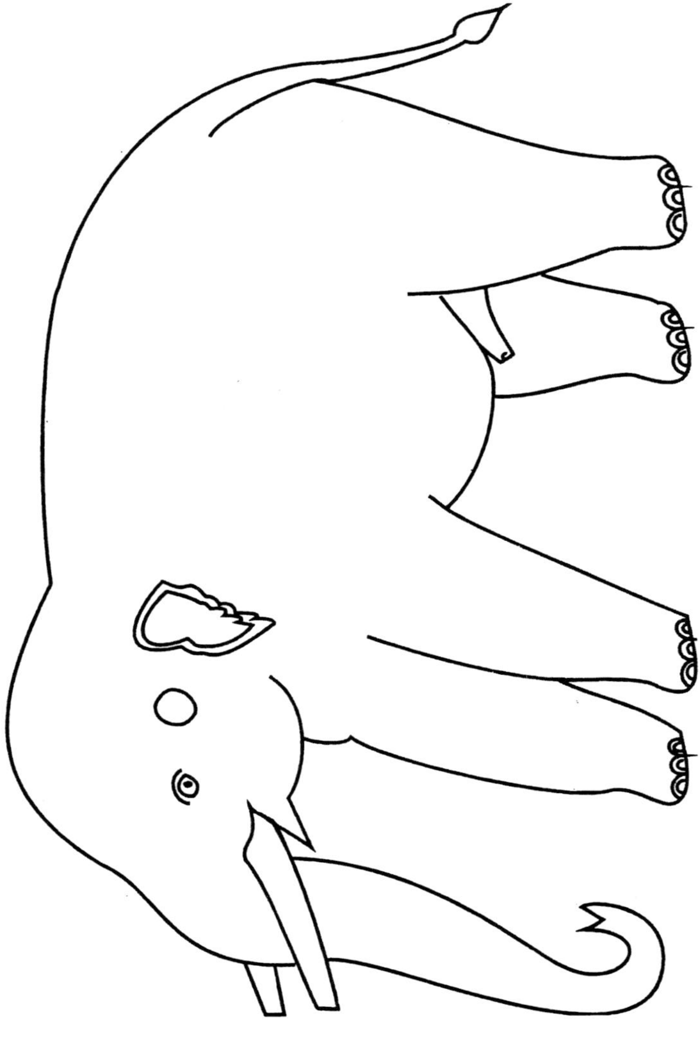

Fig. 87. : मन्दगज: मध्यम: Manda-elephant Middle class elephants

॥अथ-मृगजातिगजस्य लक्षणम् (3)॥

कृशकरचरणग्रीवाः स्थूलाक्षाः ह्रस्ववालमेढ्रोष्ठाः।
संक्षिप्तपृष्ठवंशाः तनुमृगदन्ता मृगा ज्ञेयाः।
नाहायामप्रहीणः कृशनिखिलतनुः धूसरच्छायदेहः।
जिह्मो ह्युत्तानवेदी चपलगतिमतिः क्रोधनः सिन्धुचारी।
स्थूलाक्षो द्वापरस्थः शुभगतिरलसः राजसो ह्रस्ववालः
चण्डः पित्तप्रधानो मृग इति कथितो दीर्घदन्तः सुगात्रः॥

व्यासप्रोक्ते गजशास्त्रे-

तेजस्विता च चण्डत्वं चपलत्वं तथैव च।
शीघ्रता तीक्ष्णसत्त्वं च तथैवोत्तानवेदिता॥

मलिनांबरसंकाशः रूक्षताम्रतनूरुहः।
मृगजाः पित्तसंसृष्टशुक्लशोणितसंभवाः॥

कृशांगुलिर्वालधिमुक्तमेढ्रो लघूदरः क्षामकपोतकण्ठः।
विस्तीर्णकर्णस्तनुदीर्घदन्तः स्थूलेक्षणो यः स गजो मृगाख्यः॥

गात्रपादनखा दन्तौ कोशो मध्यकरोंऽगुलिः।
तनून्येतानि दीर्घाणि शीर्षं पृष्ठं च वालधिः॥

कपोलौ चुबुकं चैव ह्रस्वानि च भवन्ति हि।
समदौ च कटौ कुक्षिकर्णौ च तनुकौ भृशम्॥

अंगुलीहनुकेशाश्च वक्षः कुब्जं प्रदृश्यते।
यस्य श्यामो भवेद्वर्णः स्वच्छे स्थूले च लोचने॥

आकार ईदृशः प्रोक्तः वनचारस्तु कथ्यते।
एकाकी प्रचरत्येव गोप्रचारं च गच्छति॥

पथानुवर्ती भीरुश्च चलचित्तो वने मृगः।
धृतस्य कर्मकाले तु भवेदुत्तानवेदिता।
दुःशीलता च चापल्यं लक्षयेन्मृगदंतिनः॥

व्याख्या–अथ तृतीयस्य मृगजातिगजस्य लक्षणमाह–कृशकरचरणग्रीवा इत्यादिना। पूर्वोक्तरीत्या मृगजातिसंभूताः गजाः सर्वेऽपि पूर्वोक्तभद्रमन्दगजापेक्षया कृशकराः कृशपादाः कृशग्रीवाद्यवयवाः नात्युन्नताः नापि नीचाः धूसरवर्णयुत-छायायुतशरीराः चपलगतयश्चपलबुद्धयः कार्यकालेषु समयान्तरेषु च किंचित्कोपयुताश्च दृश्यन्ते। किं च–मृगजातिगजा एते सर्वेऽपि जलावगाहन-तत्पराः स्थूलाक्षाः राक्षसगुणोपेताः पित्तप्रकृतयः दीर्घदन्तयुता अपि किं-चित्सौन्दर्ययुतावयवोपेताः भवन्तीति **पालकाप्यः। व्यासस्तु** पित्ताधिक्य-संयुक्तशुक्लशोणितसंयोगेनैव एतादृशाः मृगजातिगजाः जनिताः। एते मृगगजाः कृशशरीरा अपि किंचित्तेजोविशेषयुताः कार्यं प्रति पाटवोपेताः नितरां चपलाः शीघ्रगतयश्चा उदग्रसत्त्वं च **स्वभावसिद्धम्।** किं चैषां गजानां कर्णतलं तावत् विस्तीर्णमेव। एवमेतेषां गजानां कटस्थानयोः सन्ततं मदजलप्रसारश्च भवति। किं च–मृगजातिजनितो गजः वनेषु एकाकी सन्नेव सञ्चारशीलः। किं च गोवृषभाजप्रभृतिभिः साकं संचारशीलश्च। गजान्तरपथानुग एव। न पुरोगमनशीलः। एव **मृगजातिव्यवहारो युक्त एवेति।** किं चास्य गजस्य कार्यकाले स्वल्पभीरुत्वं चलचित्तत्वं चाजन्मसिद्धमेवेति। शेषं स्पष्टम्।

3. Mṛga-gaja or inferior elephants.

The elephants of this class have very lean legs, tusks, trunks, and necks, legs, eyes, stout tails, lean lips and lean penis. The hinder portions of their bodies appear to be as if lowered down. Ash-colour is visible in the midst of the black. They are fickle-minded. Their walk is very irregular. They have hot temper and small temples and stomachs. They will be never enterprising for any kind of work. They are cowardice. They will work with reluctance.

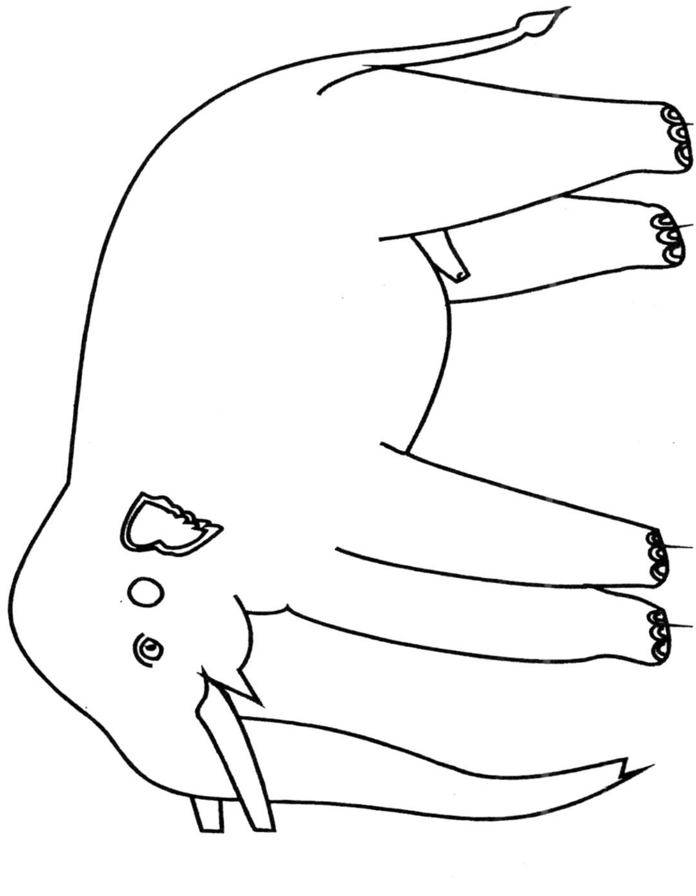

Fig. 88. : मृगगजः अधमः Inferior elephants

।।अथ-संकीर्णगजलक्षणम् (4)।।

व्यासप्रोक्ते गजशास्त्रे-

मिश्रस्तूभयसंयोगः संकीर्णस्त्रिगुणो मतः।
धृतो धावति चात्यर्थं प्रेरितोऽपि न गच्छति।।

प्रत्यर्थवेदी विज्ञेयो व्यालो मिश्रगजो मतः।
भद्रमन्दो भद्रमृगो मन्दभद्रस्तथा परः।।

मन्दो मृगो मृगो मन्दो मृगभद्रश्च मिश्रकः।
भद्रमन्दमृगश्चैको मन्दो वा मृगभद्रयोः।।

मृगो भद्रश्च मन्दश्च संकीर्णाः कीर्तिता गजाः।
ऊर्ध्वाधःकायभेदेन तत्पुनर्भिद्यते द्विधा।।

एवमष्टादशविधं कीर्तितं मृगलक्षणम्।
राजन् कलियुगे नित्यं मिश्रा एव मतंगजाः।।

शुभाशुभविभागेन सांप्रतं निगदाम्यहम्।
गुणाधिक्येन वाप्येषां वर्णाद्वा मुखलक्षणात्।।

मिश्रसंकीर्णजातीनां नाम लक्षणमीदृशम्।
मिश्राणां मिश्रचारस्तु संकीर्णानां तथाह्वयः।
शुद्धसंकीर्णमिश्राणां नाम तादृशमीरितम्।।

।।तत्र प्रथमस्य भद्रमन्दमिश्रगजस्य लक्षणम् (1)।।

भद्रजातिर्महाकायो राजन् भवति दन्तिनाम्।
महान् मन्दो यतो येन संयुक्तो भवति द्विपः।।

भद्रेण पूर्वकायेन मन्देनापरकेन च।
उत्तमस्तु गजानां हि भद्रमन्दो भवेद्गजः।।

व्याख्या—एतावता प्रबन्धेन भद्रमन्दरमृगाख्यानां केवलशुद्धजातिजनितानां गजानां लक्षणं प्रतिपाद्याधुना **शास्त्रकार**स्तावत् मिश्रसंकीर्णगजलक्षणमाह—

मिश्रस्त्वित्यादिना। तत्र उभयप्रकृतिसंयोगः मिश्रनामकः। प्रकृतित्रयसंयोगः संकीर्णनामकश्च भवतीति **व्यवस्था।** अस्य विशदार्थस्तु-केचित् गजाः हस्तिपकादिभिः प्रेरिताः सन्तस्तत्क्षणादेव झडिति यान्ति। अन्ये तु गजाः हस्तिपकादिना प्रेरिता अपि न गच्छन्त्येव। एवं विधाद्वयगजाः शुद्धजातिजनिता इति **व्यवस्था।** एवं हस्तिपकादिना धृतोऽपि यो गजो धावनशीलः एवं हस्तिपकादिना प्रेरितोऽपि यो गजो न गच्छति; एवंविधगुणोपेता एव गजाः मिश्रगजाः इत्युच्यन्ते। **विशेषस्तूत्तरत्र।** एवं संकीर्णगजानामपि लक्षणमूह्यम्। तत्र मिश्रप्रकृतिगजाः संकीर्णप्रकृतिगजाश्च अष्टादशविधा भवन्ति यथा-

1. भद्रमन्दमिश्रगजः
2. भद्रमृगमिश्रगजः
3. मन्दभद्रमिश्रगजः
4. मन्दमृगमिश्रगजः
5. मृगमन्दमिश्रगजः
6. मृगभद्रमिश्रगजः
7. भद्रमन्दमृगसंकीर्णगजः
8. मन्दमृगभद्रसंकीर्णगजः
9. मृगभद्रमन्दसंकीर्णगजः
10. ऊर्ध्वं भद्ररूपाधो मन्दरूपमिश्रगजः
11. ऊर्ध्वं भद्ररूपाधो मृगरूपमिश्रगजः
12. ऊर्ध्वं मन्दरूपाधो भद्ररूपमिश्रगजः
13. ऊर्ध्वं मन्दरूपाधो मृगरूपमिश्रगजः
14. ऊर्ध्वं मृगरूपाधो मन्दरूपमिश्रगजः
15. ऊर्ध्वं मृगरूपाधो भद्ररूपमिश्रगजः
16. ऊर्ध्वं भद्ररूपाधो मन्दमृगरूपसंकीर्णगजः
17. ऊर्ध्वं मन्दरूपाधो मृगभद्ररूपसंकीर्णगजः
18. ऊर्ध्वं मृगरूपाधो भद्रमन्दरूपसंकीर्णगजः इति।।

एवमत्राष्टादशभेदेन विभक्ताः मिश्रप्रकृतिगजाः संकीर्णप्रकृतिगजाश्च

पृथक्पृथक् वक्ष्यमाणलक्षणवाक्येन मुखादितत्तदवयवनिरीक्षणेन वर्णलक्षणादिना च इमे मिश्रगजाः इमे संकीर्णगजा इति सूक्ष्मं ज्ञेयमित्युपदेशः। किं चात्र मिश्रगजानां मिश्रगुणसंपर्कः। संकीर्णगजानां संकीर्णगुणसंपर्कश्च भवेदिति **क्रमपरिपाटी।** एवमत्रोक्तेषु गजेष्वष्टादशविधेषु केचित् गजाः शुभदाः। शुभलक्षणापेताः केचित्तु-अशुभप्रदाः। अशुभलक्षणोपेताश्चेति। **तत्सर्वमप्यत्र शास्त्रकारः क्रमेण विशदयति।** तत्राद्यो भद्रमन्दमिश्रगजस्तावत् एवं ज्ञेयः। यथा-भद्रजातिगजानामंगानि तु महान्ति। मन्दजातिगजानां तु स्थूलांगप्राप्तिरेव। एतदुभयसंयोगश्च यस्य भवेत्, स गजः भद्रमन्दनामभागिति। अस्य विशदार्थ-स्तु-यस्य गजस्य पूर्वकायः, भद्रजातिगजलक्षणयुतः; अपरकायस्तु-मन्दजाति-गजलक्षणयुतश्च भवति; स तु भद्रमन्दनामभाक् भवतीति। किं चास्य भद्रमन्दमिश्रगजस्य हस्ते पिंगूषस्थाने च रक्तवर्णबिन्दुश्रेणी स्फुटं दृश्येति **प्रांचः॥**

4. Saṅkīrṇa-gaja or middle class elephants

There are two varieties in this class as Miśra and Śaṅkīrṇa. Miśra means a mixed breed of two classes only, whereas Saṅkīrṇa is a mixed breed of three classes only.

Bhadra-plus Manda
Manda-plus Mṛga } Miśra Class
Bhadra plus Mṛga

Bhadra plus Manda plus and Mṛga plus-Śaṅkīrṇa-class. There are 18 varieties in these two classes of Miśra and Saṅkīrṇa as described below. Bhadra-class elephants always have huge and strong bodies, whereas Manda-class elephants stout and short and Mṛga lean. This data should be adopted carefully in determining the 18 classes of elephants.

(1) Those elephants which have Bhadra-gajā's qualities and appearance in front of their bodies and Manda-gaja's in rear are the best class. They will give prosperity and long life to their masters.

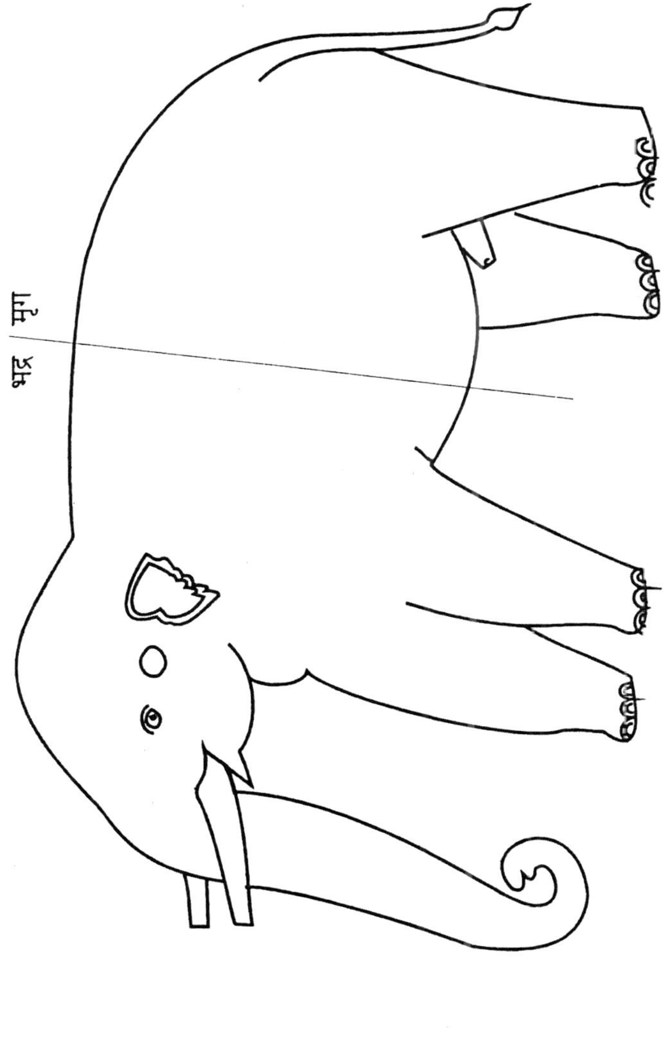

Fig. 89. : भद्रमन्द्गजः उत्तमः First class elephants

॥अथ द्वितीयस्य भद्रमृगमिश्रगजस्य लक्षणम् (2)॥

मृगस्यापि हि रूपेण किंचित्साम्यगतेन वा।
अशुभत्वं न भद्रस्य जायते शुभदो हि सः॥
कायेन यो भवेद्भद्रो मन्दो वापि मतंगजः।
मृगगात्रापरश्चैव स भवेद्वेगवान् गजः॥
लोचनानां प्रधानत्वं यस्मात् शास्त्रेषु कीर्तितम्।
तस्मान्मृगाक्षिसंयुक्तो भद्रोऽपि हि न शस्यते॥

व्याख्या—अथ द्वितीयस्य भद्रमृगमिश्रगजस्य लक्षणमाह–मृगस्यापीति। यस्य गजस्य पूर्वार्धशरीरं भद्रजातिगजलक्षणयुक्तं अपरार्धशरीरं मृगजातिगज-लक्षणयुक्तं च दृश्यते, स तु गजः भद्रमृगमिश्रनामको निगद्यत इति। किं चायं गज उत्तम एव। अपि च-एवं रीत्या यस्य गजस्य लोचनयुगलं तावन्मृगजातिगजाक्षिसाम्ययुक्तं दृश्यते, स तु गर्ह्य एव। न स्वीकार्य **इत्यर्थः**। तस्मात् गजस्वीकरणात्पूर्वमेव तल्लोचनपरीक्षा च कार्येति **सूचितम्।** अतो मृगाक्षिसंयुक्तो गजो भद्रगजतुल्यशरीरभासुरोऽपि न प्रशस्त **इत्युपदेशः॥**

(2) Those elephants which have Bhadra-gaja's qualities and appearance in front of their bodies and Mṛga-gaja's in rear are the best class. They will have very swift walk and they will give prosperity to their masters. Though they have Bhadra-gaja's qualities and appearance in front of their bodies, they are considered to be very inferior if they have Mṛga-gaja's eyes (big-eyes).

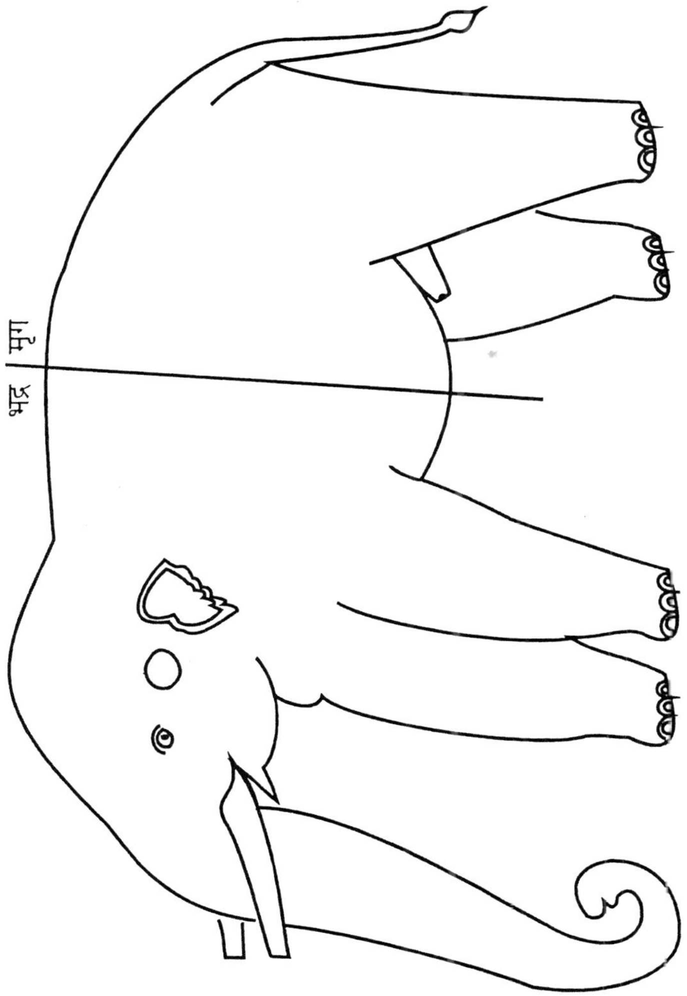

Fig. 90. : भद्रमृगगजः उत्तमः First class elephants

।।अथ-तृतीयस्य मन्दभद्रमिश्रगजस्य लक्षणम् (3)।।

अनेनैव हि रूपेण विपर्यस्तेन यो द्विपः।
सोऽपि शोभन एव स्यान्मन्दभद्र इति स्मृतः।।

व्याख्या–अथ तृतीयस्य मन्दभद्रमिश्रगजस्य लक्षणमाह–अनेनैवेति। यस्य गजस्य पूर्वार्धशरीरं तावत् मन्दजातिगजलक्षणयुक्तमपरगात्रं तु भद्रजातिगजलक्षणयुक्तं च भवति, स तु गजः मंदभद्रमिश्रगजः। **उत्तम एव कीर्त्यत इति।।**

(3) The elephants which have Manda-gaja's qualities and appearance in front of their bodies and Bhadra-gaja's in rear, are the best class.

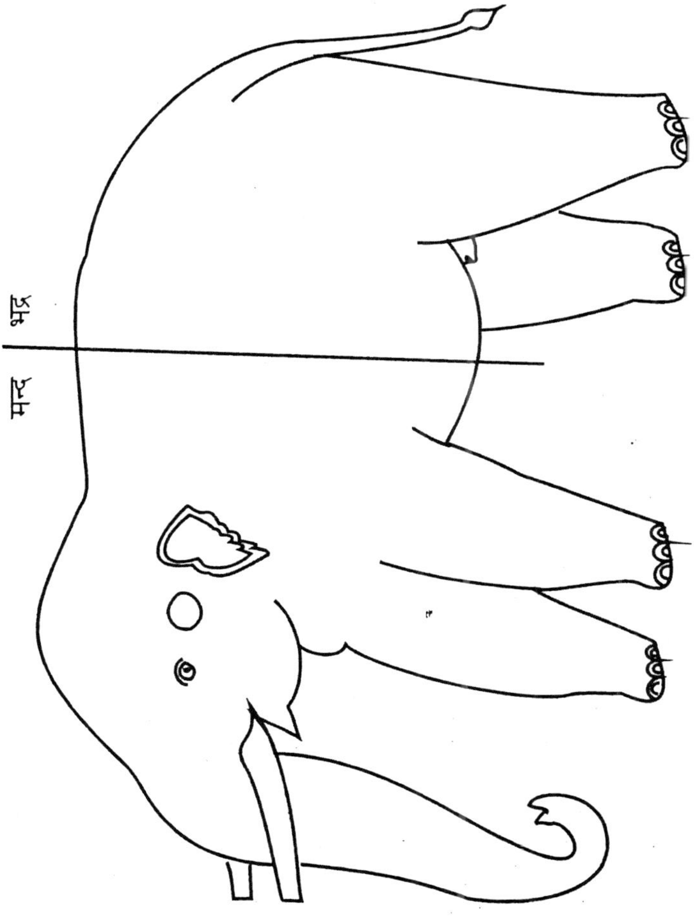

Fig. 91. : मन्दभद्रगजः उत्तमः First class elephants

॥अथ-चतुर्थस्य मन्दमृगमिश्रगजस्य लक्षणम् (4)॥

मन्दावयवबाहुल्ये मृगरूपस्य लेशतः।
भद्रावयवनिर्मुक्तो मध्यमः स गजो भवेत्॥

व्याख्या–अथ-चतुर्थस्य मन्दमृगमिश्रगजस्य लक्षणमाह–मन्देति। यस्य गजस्य पूर्वार्धशरीरं तावत् मन्दजातिगजलक्षणोपेतमपरगात्रं तु मृगजातिगजलक्षणोपेतं च विलोक्यते; स गजः मन्दमृगगज इति व्यवह्रियते। अयं तु **मध्यमगज** एव॥

(4) The elephants which have Manda-gaja's qualities and appearance in front of their bodies and Mṛga-gaja's in rear, are the middle class or the 2nd class ones.

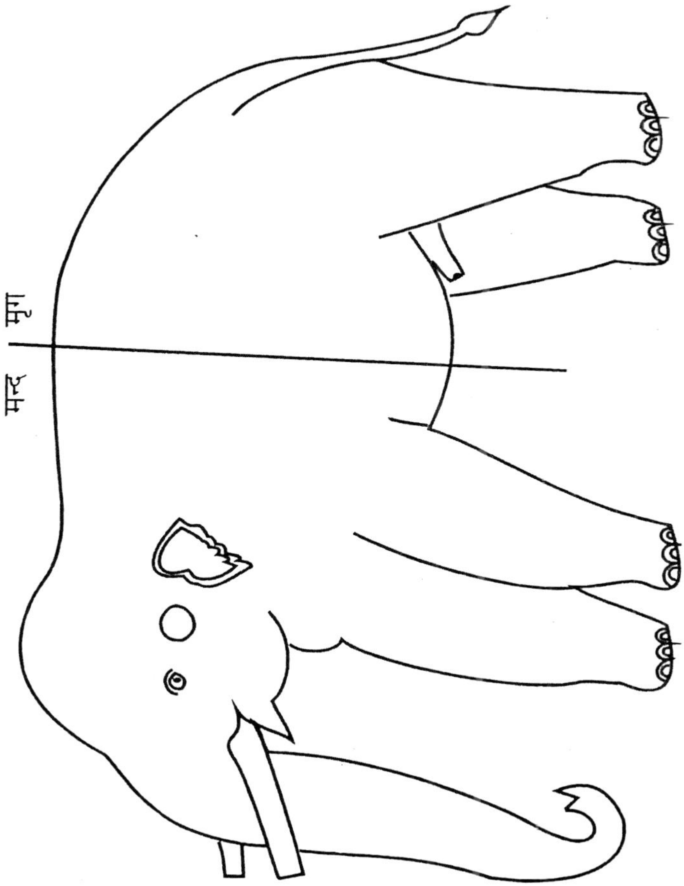

Fig. 92. : मन्दमृगगजः मध्यमः Middle class elephants

॥अथ-पंचमस्य मृगमन्दमिश्रगजस्य लक्षणम् (5)॥

मृगरूपादिसत्त्वं च दृश्यते यस्य हस्तिनः।
अधमस्तु स विज्ञेयः सत्त्वशक्तिविवर्जितः॥
भद्रमन्दो भवेत् श्रेष्ठः मृगमन्दस्तथाधमः।

व्याख्या—अथ पंचमस्य मृगमन्दमिश्रगजस्य लक्षणमाह-मृगेति। यस्य गजस्य पूर्वार्धशरीरं मृगजातिगजलक्षणोपेतमपरगात्रं तु मन्दजातिगजलक्षणयुतं च भवति; स गजः मृगमन्दनामकः। **अधम** एव। कुतः। एवंलक्षणोपेतोऽयं गजः प्रायशः सत्त्वबलशक्तिहीन एवेति॥

(5) The elephants which have Mṛga-gaja's qualities and appearance in front and Manda-gaja's in rear are inferior-class. They are useless in work.

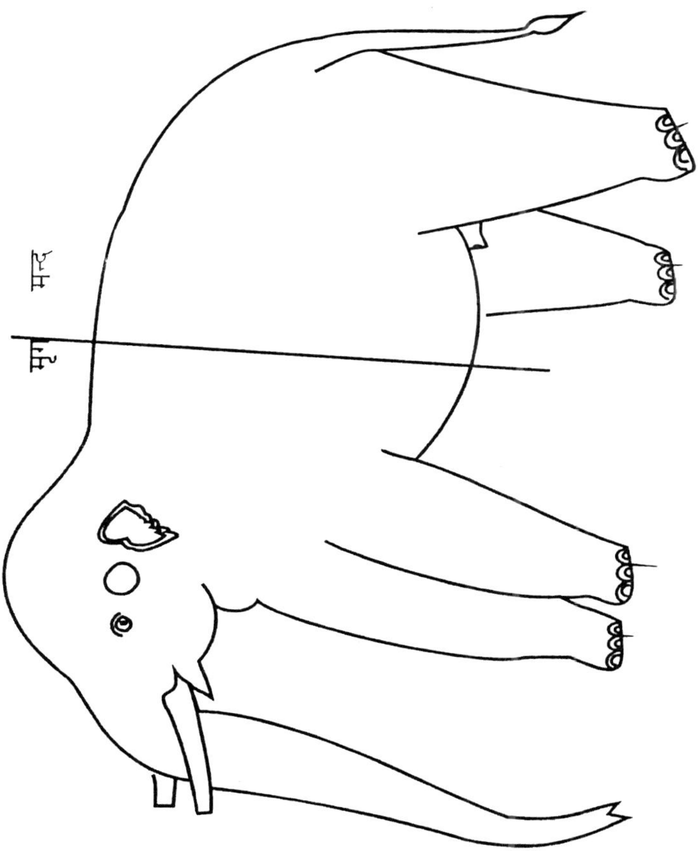

Fig. 93. : मृगभद्रगज: अधम: Inferior elephants

॥अथ-षष्ठस्य मृगभद्रमिश्रगजस्य लक्षणम् (6)॥

तथैव मृगभद्रोऽपि हीन एव न संशयः।
करदन्ताक्षिकुंभैस्तु यो मृगो ज्ञायते गजः॥
शेषावयवभद्रोऽपि हीन एव भवेदसौ।

व्याख्या—अथ षष्ठस्य मृगभद्रमिश्रगजस्य लक्षणं विशदयति-तथैवेति। यस्य गजस्य पूर्वार्धशरीरं मृगजातिगजलक्षणयुक्तं भवति, एवमपरार्धशरीरं तु भद्रजातिगजलक्षणयुक्तं च विलोक्यते; सोऽयं गजः मृगभद्रनामको निगद्यते। अत्र कापि **व्यवस्था**। यथा-यस्य गजस्य करः दंतयुगलमक्षिद्वयं मस्तकभागश्चैते मृगलक्षणयुक्ताश्चेत् अंगान्तरेषु भद्रलक्षणवानपि सोऽयं गज **अधम एव। न शुभद** इति॥

(6) The elephants which have Mṛga-gaja's qualities and appearance in front and Bhadra-gaja's in rear are also inferior as per figure No. 94; if they have Mṛga-gaja's qualities in front -i.e. heads, eyes, trunks and tusks, they are undoubtedly of inferior class. This is the main principle.

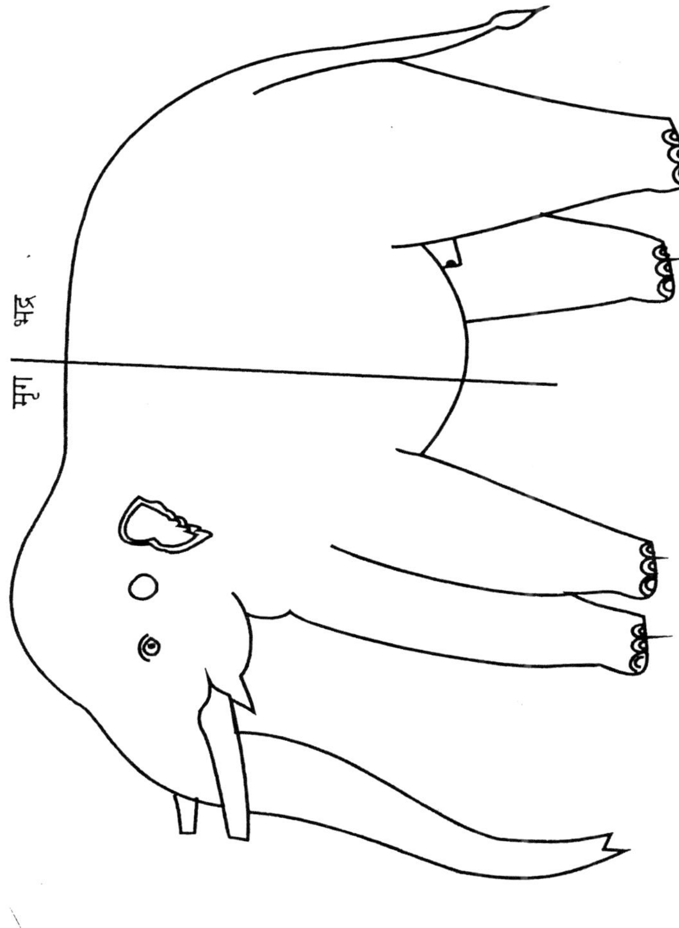

Fig. 94. : मृगभद्रगज: अधम: Inferior elephants

।।अथ सप्तमस्य भद्रमन्दमृगसंकीर्णगजस्य लक्षणम् (7)।।

भद्रमन्दमृगाकारसंयुक्तो मध्यमो भवेत्।
कायेन यो भवेद्भद्रो मन्दोऽपि च मतंगजः।।
मृगगात्रापरश्चैव स भवेद्वेगवान् गजः।।

व्याख्या–अथ सप्तमस्य भद्रमन्दमृगसंकीर्णगजस्य लक्षणमाह–भद्रेति। यस्य किल वारणस्य पूर्वशरीरे भद्रजातिगजलक्षणं मध्यशरीरे मन्दजातिगज–लक्षणमन्त्यशरीरे मृगजातिगजलक्षणं च एवं क्रमेण मिलितं भाति; स गजो भद्रमन्दमृगसंकीर्णप्रकृतियुतः। वेगवांश्च भवति। **उत्तम एवेति।।**

(7) Those elephants which have Bhadra-gaja's qualities and appearance in front, Manda-gaja's in the middle and Mṛga-gaja's in rear, *are the best ones.* They are very swift in walk.

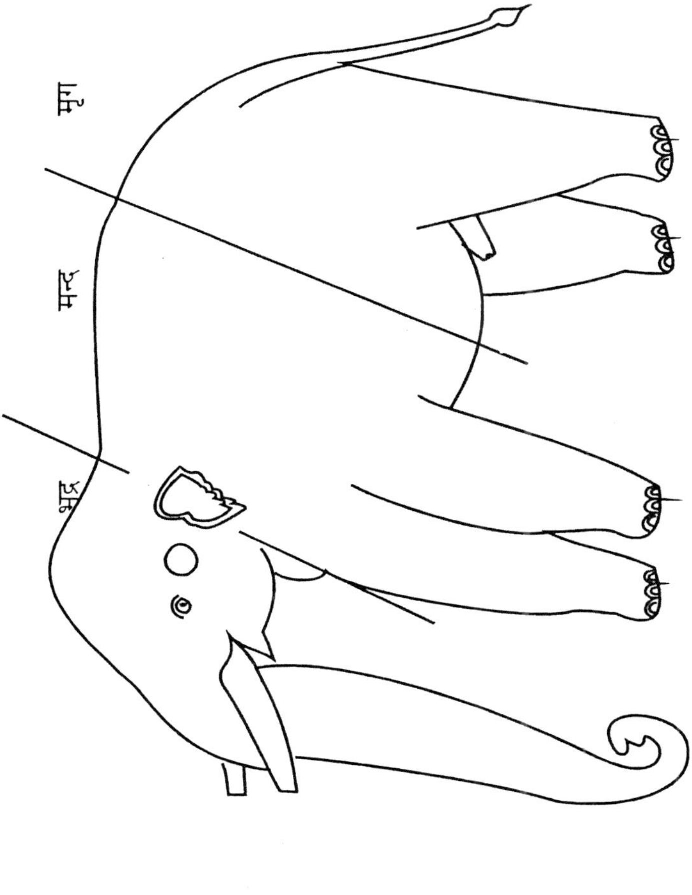

Fig. 95. : भद्रमन्दमृगगजः उत्तमः The best elephant

॥अथाष्टमस्य मन्दमृगभद्रसंकीर्णगजस्य लक्षणम् (8)॥

मन्दावयवबाहुल्यं मृगरूपस्य चैकतः।
भद्रावयवसंयुक्तो मध्यमः स गजो भवेत्॥

व्याख्या–अथाष्टमस्य मन्दमृगभद्रसंकीर्णगजस्य लक्षणमाह–मन्देति। यस्य किल गजस्य पूर्वशरीरे मन्दजातिगजलक्षणं मध्यशरीरे मृगजातिगज-लक्षणमन्त्यशरीरे भद्रजातिगजलक्षणं च क्रमादेवं लक्ष्यते; सोऽयं गजः मन्दमृगभद्रसंकीर्णप्रकृतिनामको भवति। अयं तु **मध्यमगज** एवेति **व्यवस्था।**

(8) Those elephants which have Manda-gaja's qualities and appearance in front, Mṛga-gaja's in the middle and Bhadra-gaja's in rear, *are the middle-class.*

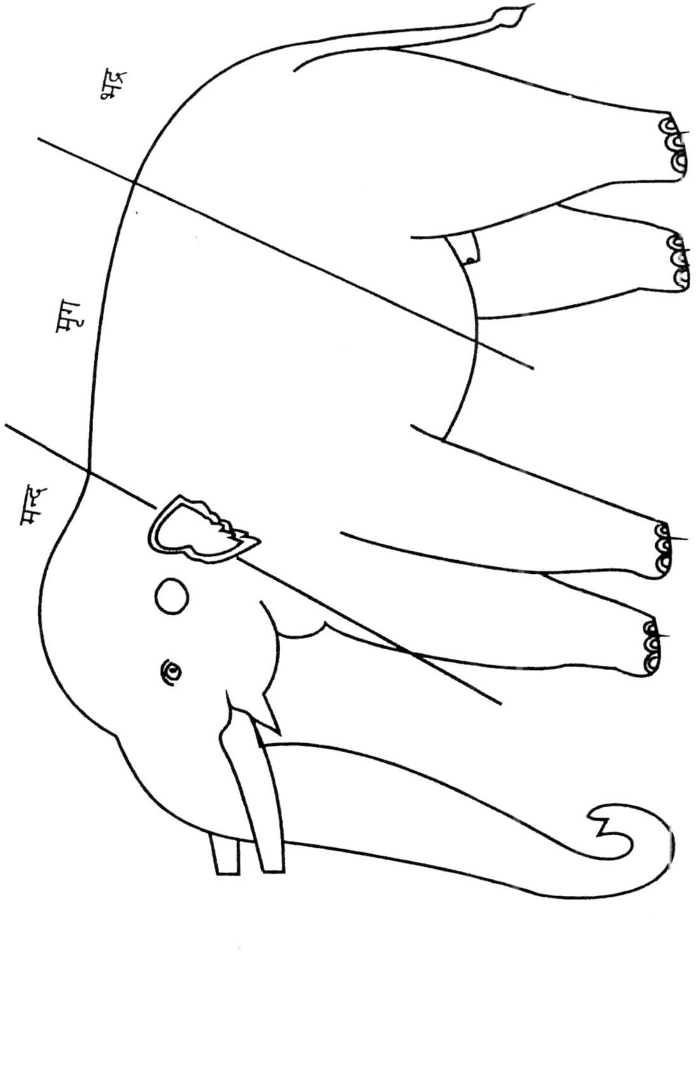

Fig. 96. : मन्दमृगभद्रगजः मध्यमः A middle-class elephant

॥अथ नवमस्य मृगभद्रमन्दसंकीर्णगजस्य लक्षणम् (9) ॥

मृगरूपादिसत्त्वं च दृश्यते यस्य हस्तिनः।
अधमस्तु स विज्ञेयः सत्त्वशक्तिविवर्जितः॥

करदन्ताक्षिकुंभैस्तु यो मृगो ज्ञायते गजः।
शेषावयवभद्रोऽपि हीन एव भवेदसौ॥

व्याख्या–अथ नवमस्य मृगभद्रमन्दसंकीर्णगजस्य लक्षणं विशदयति–मृगेति। यस्य किल मातंगस्य पूर्वशरीरं मृगजातिगजलक्षणयुक्तं मध्यशरीरं भद्रजातिगजलक्षणोपेतमन्त्यशरीरं तु मन्दजातिगजलक्षणोपेतं च क्रमादेवं विलोक्यते; स गजः मृगभद्रमन्दसंकीर्णप्रकृतियुक्तो निगद्यत इति। अयं तु गजः **अधम एव। न स्वीकर्तव्य इति भावः॥**

(9) Those elephants which have Mṛga-gaja's qualities and appearance in front, Bhadra-gaja's in the middle and Manda-gaja's in rear, are of very *inferior class*. They are very weak.

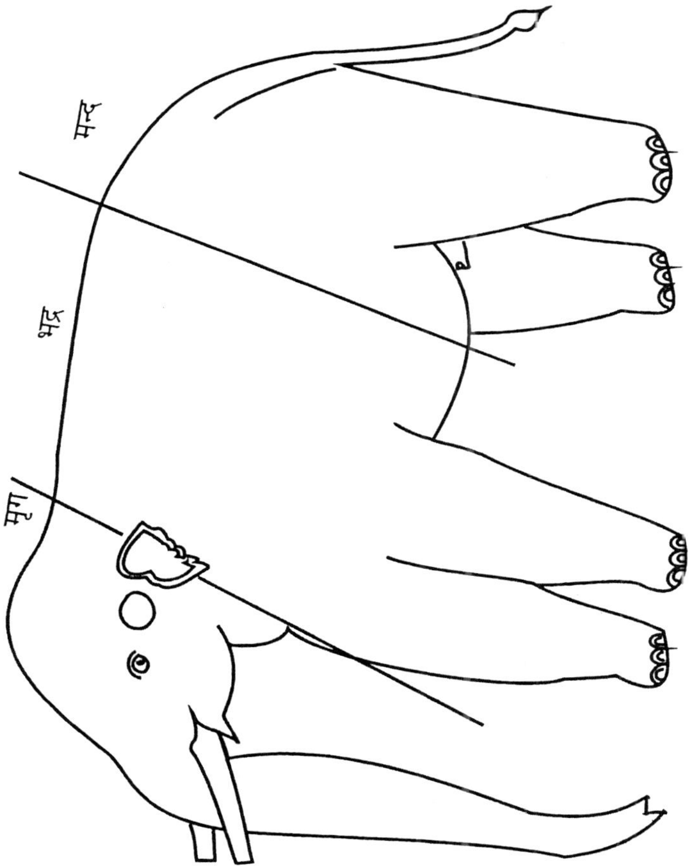

Fig. 97. : मृगभद्रमन्दसंकीर्णगजः अधमः Inferior class elephants

।।अथ-दशमस्य ऊर्ध्वं भद्ररूपाधो मन्दरूपमिश्रगजस्य लक्षणम् (10)।।

भद्रजातिर्महाकायो राजन् भवति दन्तिनाम्।
महान् मन्दो यतो येन संयुक्तो भवति द्विपः।।
भद्रेणोपरिकायेन मन्देनाधोगतेन च।
उत्तमस्तु गजानां हि भद्रमन्दो भवेत् गजः।।

व्याख्या–अथ दशमस्य ऊर्ध्वं भद्ररूपाधो मन्दरूपमिश्रगजस्य लक्षणमाह–भद्रजातिरिति। पूर्वोक्तरीत्या भद्रजातिगजशरीरं तु महदेव। मन्दजातिगजशरीरं च स्थूलमेव। तस्मात् यस्य किल गजस्य उपरिभागशरीरं तावत् भद्रजातिगजलक्षणोपेतमधोभागशरीरं तु मन्दजातिगजलक्षणोपेतं च भवति, अयं तु गज उत्तम एव।।

(10) The elephants which have Bhadra-gaja's qualities and appearance in upper portion of their bodies and Manda-gaja's in the lower, are *the best class*.

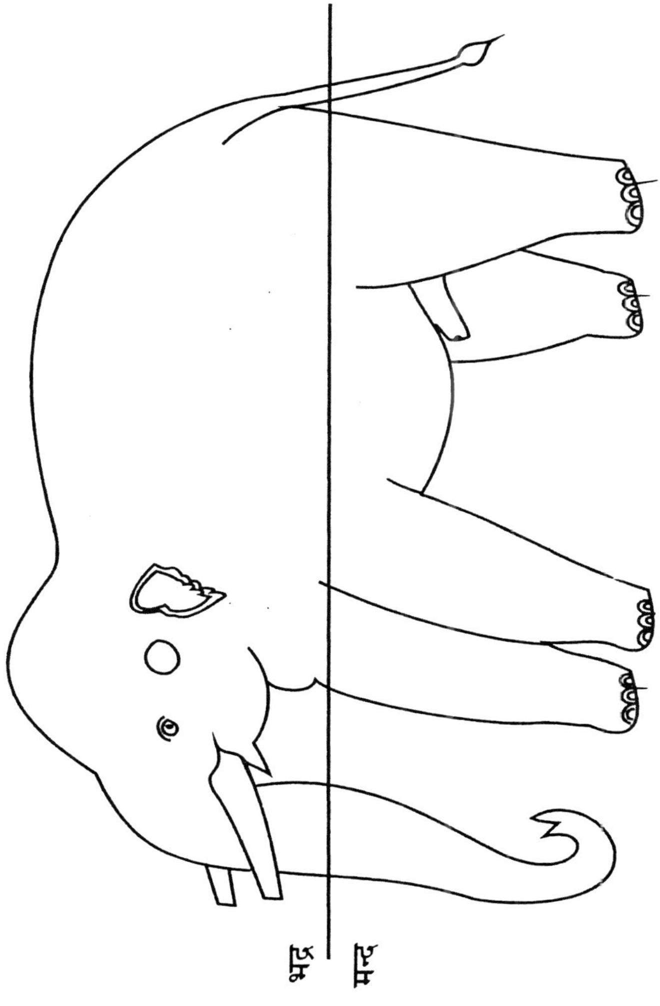

Fig. 98. : भद्रमन्दगजः उत्तमः First class elephants

॥अथैकादशस्य ऊर्ध्वं भद्ररूपाधो मृगरूपमिश्रगजस्य लक्षणम्॥11॥

मृगस्यापि हि रूपेण किंचित्साम्यगतेन वा।
अशुभत्वं न भद्रस्य जायते शुभदो हि सः॥

व्याख्या—अथैकादशस्य ऊर्ध्वं भद्ररूपाधो मृगरूपमिश्रगजस्य लक्षणमाह—मृगस्यापीति। यस्य किल वारणस्य ऊर्ध्वं शरीरं तावत् भद्रजातिगजलक्षणोपेतमधःशरीरं तु मृगजातिगजलक्षणोपेतं च विलोक्यते; अयं च **गजः उत्तम एवेति व्यवस्था॥**

(11) The elephants which have Bhadra-gaja's qualities and appearance in upper portion of their bodies and Mṛga-gaja's in the lower, *are the best class.*

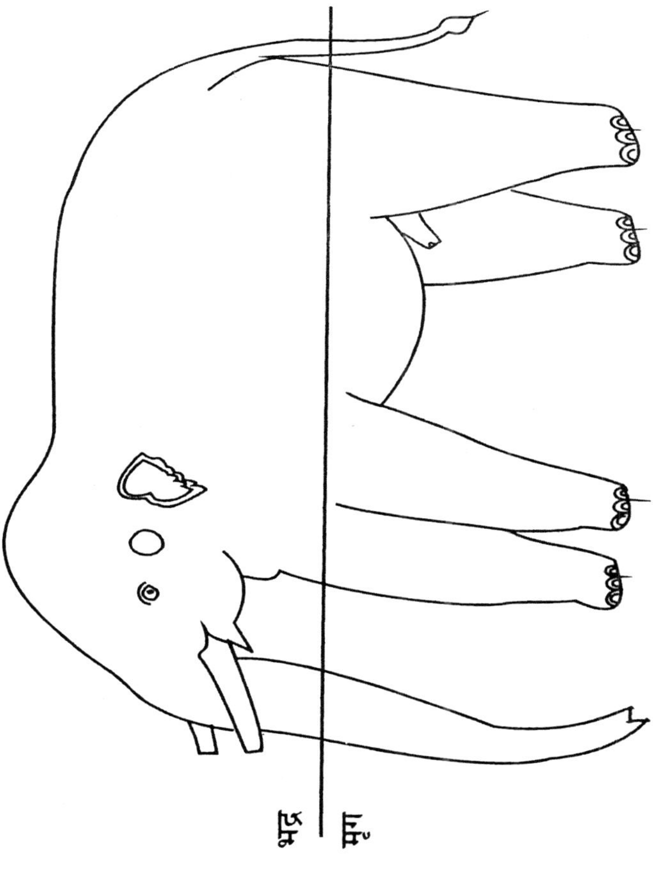

Fig. 99. : भद्रमृगगजः उत्तमः First class elephants

॥अथ-द्वादशस्य ऊर्ध्वं मन्दरूपाधो भद्ररूपमिश्रगजस्य लक्षणम् (12)॥

अनेनैव हि रूपेण विपर्यस्तेन वा द्विपः।
सोऽपि शोभन एव स्यान्मन्दभद्र इति स्मृतः॥

व्याख्या—अथ द्वादशस्य ऊर्ध्वं मन्दरूपाधो भद्ररूपमिश्रगजस्य लक्षण-माह-अनेनैवेति। यः किल वारणः ऊर्ध्वशरीरे मन्दजातिगजलक्षणोपेतः अधःशरीरे भद्रजातिगजलक्षणसहितश्च विलोक्यते; अयं तु **गजः उत्तम एव। यजमानस्य शुभप्रद एव। अतः क्रेतव्य इति भावः॥**

(12) The elephants which have Manda-gaja's qualities and appearance in upper portion of their bodies and Bhadra-gaja's in the lower, *are of the better class*.

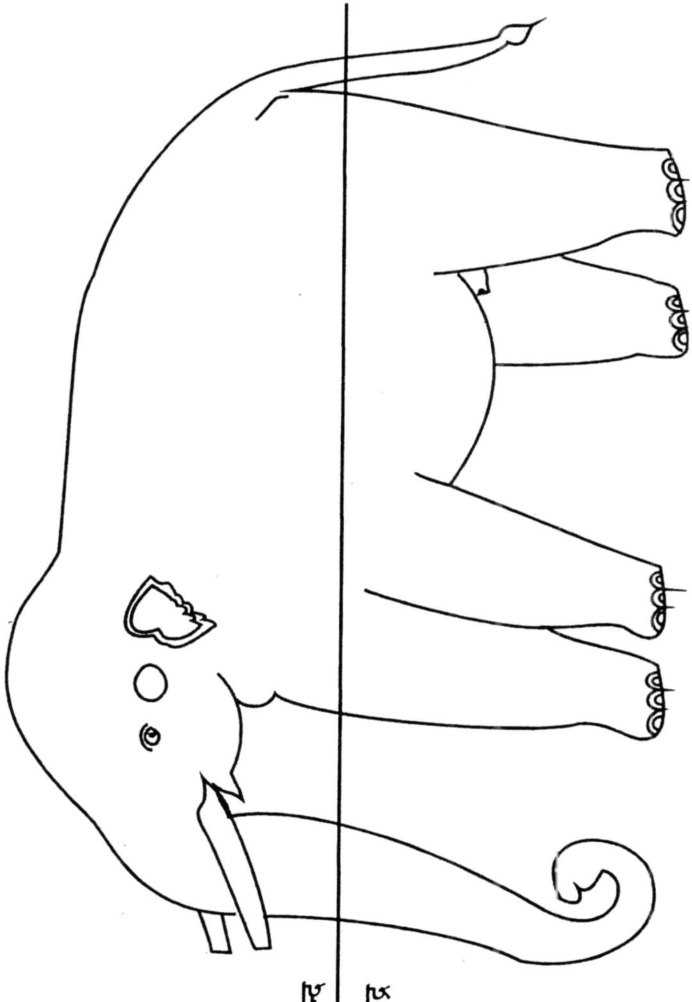

Fig. 100. : मन्दभद्रगजः मध्यमः: First class elephants

॥अथ-त्रयोदशस्य ऊर्ध्वं मन्दरूपाधो मृगरूपमिश्रगजस्य लक्षणम् (13)॥

मन्दावयवबाहुल्ये मृगरूपस्य लेशतः।
भद्रावयवनिर्मुक्तो मध्यमः स गजो भवेत्॥

व्याख्या–अथ त्रयोदशस्य ऊर्ध्वं मन्दरूपाधो मृगरूपमिश्रगजस्य लक्षण-माह–मन्देति। यस्य किल गजस्य ऊर्ध्वं शरीरं तावत् मन्दजातिगजलक्षणोपेते-मधःशरीरं तु मृगजातिगजलक्षणोपेतं च भवति किल, अयं गजः **मध्यम एव**॥

(13) The elephants which have Manda-gaja's qualities and appearance in upper portion of their bodies and Mṛga-gaja's in the lower, are of the middle class.

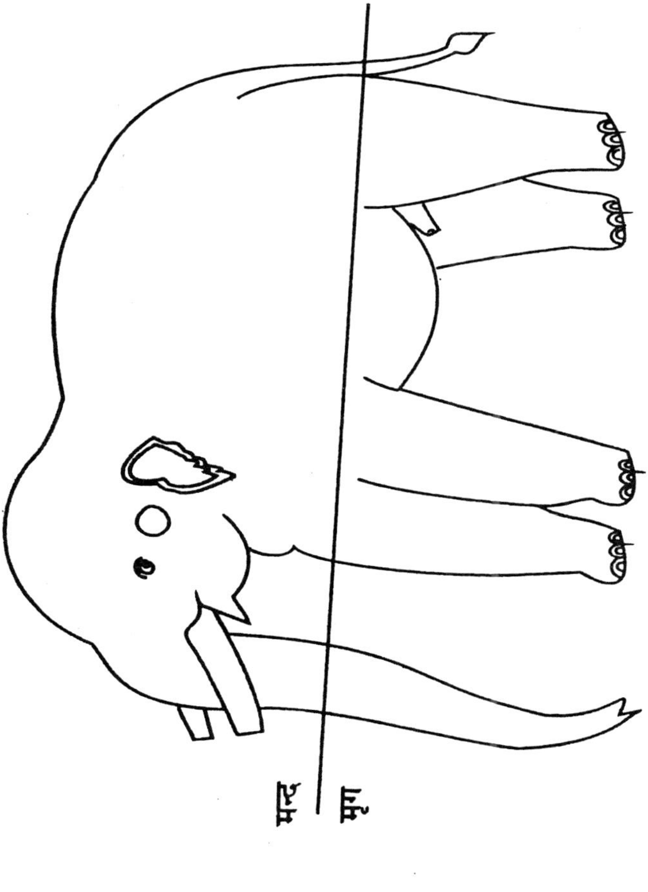

Fig. 101. : मन्दमृगगजः मध्यमः Middle class elephants

॥अथ चतुर्दशस्य ऊर्ध्वं मृगरूपाधो मन्दरूपमिश्रगजस्य लक्षणम् (14)॥

मृगरूपादिसत्त्वं च दृश्यते यस्य हस्तिनः।
अधमस्तु स विज्ञेयः सत्त्वशक्तिविवर्जितः॥

व्याख्या—अथ चतुर्दशस्य ऊर्ध्वं मृगरूपाधो मन्दरूपमिश्रगजस्य लक्षणमाह–मृगरूपादीति। यस्य गजस्य उपरिभागशरीरं तावत् मृगजातिगजलक्षणसहितमधोभागशरीरं तु मन्दजातिगजलक्षणभासुरं च विलोक्यते; अयं तु गज **अधम एव।** नास्य बलपराक्रमादिप्राप्तिरिति॥

(14) The elephants which have Mṛga-gaja's qualities and appearance in upper portion of their bodies and Manda-gaja's in the lower, are of inferior class.

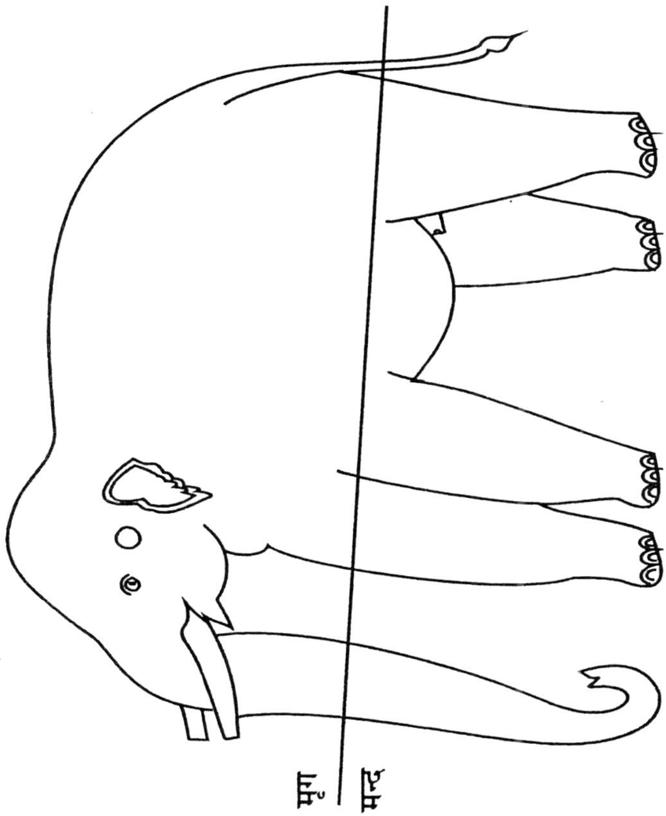

Fig. 102. : मृगमन्दगजः अधमः Inferior class elephants

॥अथ-पंचदशस्य ऊर्ध्वं मृगरूपाधो भद्ररूपमिश्रगजस्य लक्षणम् (15)॥

करदन्ताक्षिकुंभैस्तु यो मृगो ज्ञायते गजः।
शेषावयवभद्रोऽपि हीन एव भवेदसौ॥

व्याख्या—अथ पंचदशस्य ऊर्ध्वं मृगरूपाधो भद्ररूपमिश्रगजस्य लक्षण-माह-करेति। यः किल मातंगः करदन्ताक्षिमस्तकादिशरीरोर्ध्वभागेषु मृगजाति-गजलक्षणयुतः अधःशरीरे भद्रजातिगजलक्षणयुतो विलोक्यते; सोऽयं गजस्तु **अधम एव।** न **विशयः।** अतो **न क्रेतव्य इति भावः॥**

(15) The elephants which have Mṛga-gaja's qualities and appearance in upper-portion of their bodies and Bhadra-gaja's in the lower, are of inferior class.

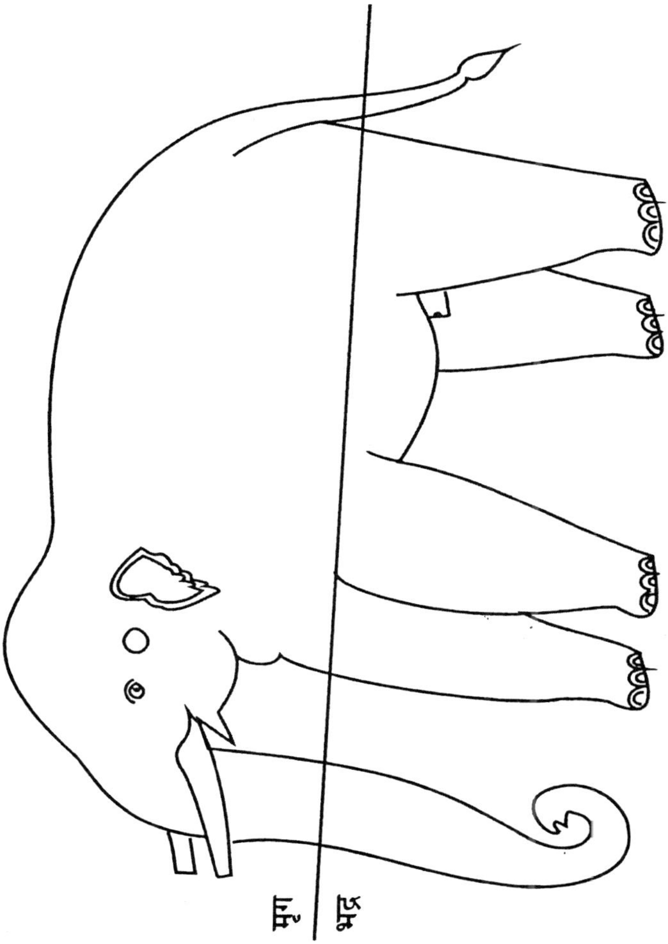

Fig. 103 : मृगभद्राजः अधमः Inferior class elephants

।।अथ-षोडशस्य ऊर्ध्वं भद्ररूपाधो मन्दमृगरूपसंकीर्णगजस्य लक्षणम् (16)।।

भद्रमन्दमृगाकारसंयुक्तो मध्यमो भवेत्।
ऊर्ध्वकायेन यो भद्रो मन्दोऽपि च मतंगजः।।
मृगगात्रमधोभागे स भवेद्वेगवान् गजः।

व्याख्या–अथ षोडशस्य ऊर्ध्वं भद्ररूपाधो मन्दमृगरूपसंकीर्णगजस्य लक्षणमाह–भद्रेति। यस्य किल गजस्य ऊर्ध्वं शरीरतलं तावत् भद्रजातिलक्षणोपेतं मध्यशरीरं तावत् मन्दजातिगजलक्षणयुतमधःशरीरं तु मृगजातिगजलक्षणयुतं च भवति; अयं तु गजः वेगवानेव। अतोऽयं **मध्यमगज इति व्यवस्था शास्त्रकाराणामिति।।**

(16) The elephants which have Bhadra-gaja's qualities and appearance in upper bodies, Manda-gaja's in the centre and Mṛga-gaja's in the lower, are of the best class.

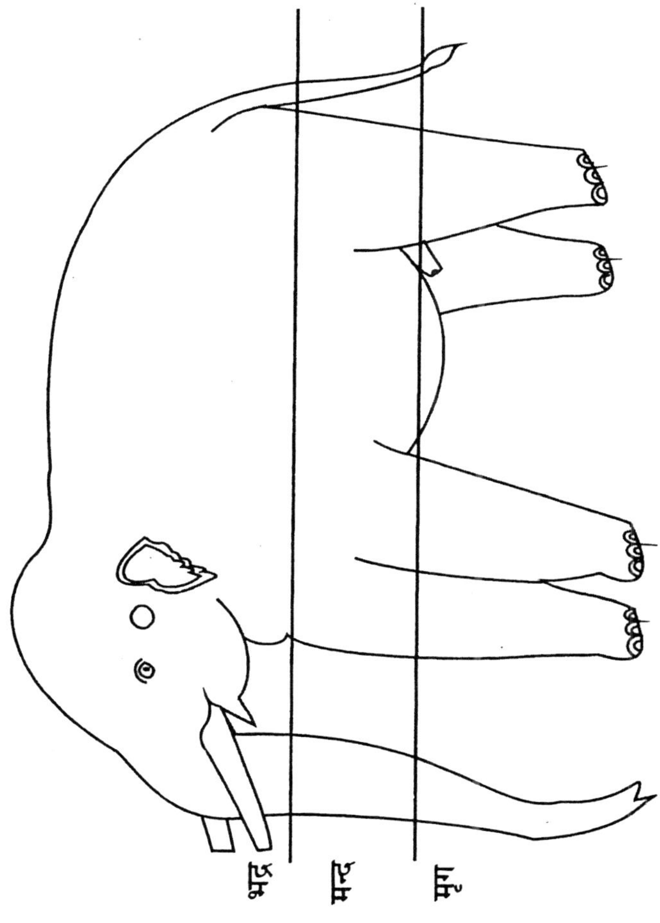

Fig. 104. : भद्रमन्दमृगगज: उत्तम: First class elephants

।।अथ सप्तदशस्य ऊर्ध्वं मन्दरूपाधो मृगभद्ररूपसंकीर्णगजस्य लक्षणम् (17)।।

मन्दावयवबाहुल्यं मृगरूपस्य चैकतः।
भद्रावयवसंयुक्तो मध्यमः स गजो भवेत्।।

व्याख्या—अथ सप्तदशस्य ऊर्ध्वं मन्दरूपाधो मृगभद्ररूपसंकीर्णगजस्य लक्षणमाह-मन्देति। यस्य गजस्य ऊर्ध्वं शरीरं मन्दजातिगजलक्षणयुक्तं मध्यशरीरं मृगजातिगजलक्षणयुक् अधःशरीरं तु भद्रजातिगजलक्षणवच्च भवति, अयमपि गजः **मध्यम एव**।।

(17) The elephants which have Manda-gaja's qualities and appearance in upper bodies, Mṛga-gaja's in the centre and Bhadra-gaja's in the lower, are of the middle class.

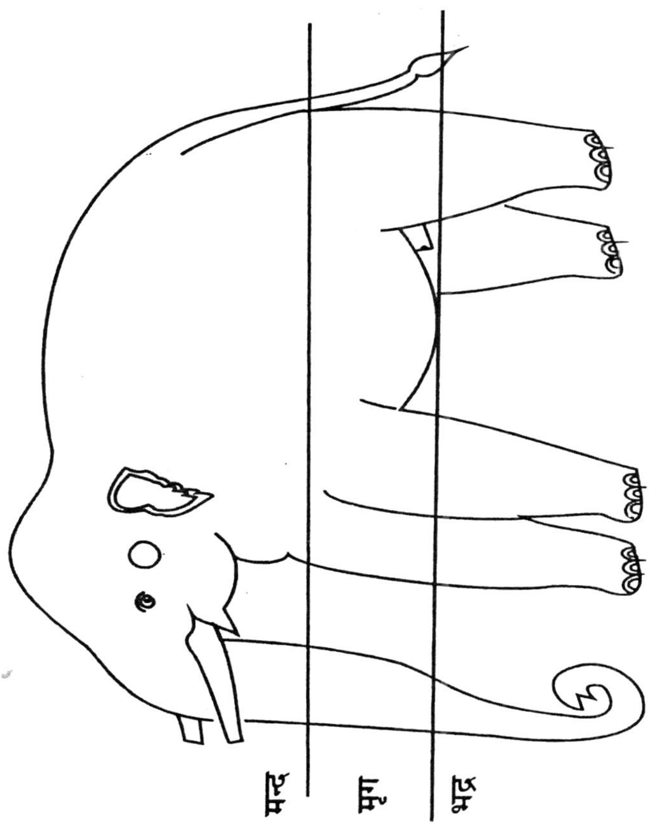

Fig. 105. : मन्दमृगाभद्रगजः मध्यमः Middle class elephants

॥अथाष्टादशस्य ऊर्ध्वं मृगरूपाधो भद्रमन्दरूपसंकीर्णगजस्य लक्षणम् (18)॥

मृगरूपादिसत्त्वं च दृश्यते यस्य हस्तिनः।
अधमस्तु स विज्ञेयः सत्त्वशक्तिविवर्जितः॥
करदन्ताक्षिकुंभैस्तु यो मृगो ज्ञायते गजः।
शेषावयवभद्रोऽपि हीन एव भवेदसौ॥

इति पालकाप्यमहर्षिप्रणीते गजशास्त्रे गजजातिलक्षणनिरूपणं नामाष्टमं प्रकरणम्॥

व्याख्या—अथाष्टादशस्य ऊर्ध्वं मृगरूपाधो भद्रमन्दरूपसंकीर्णगजस्य लक्षणमाह—मृगेति। यस्य किल गजस्य ऊर्ध्वं शरीरं तावत् मृगजातिगजलक्षणयुक् मध्यशरीरं तु भद्रजातिगजलक्षणवत् अधःशरीरं मन्दजातिगजलक्षणोपेतं च दृश्यते, स तु गजः बलहीनो भवेत्। **अतोऽधम एव।** तस्मादेवमुक्तप्रकारेणाष्टादशभेदविभक्तानां गजानां लक्षणादिकं सर्वमपि करदन्ताक्षिकुंभादिस्थानेषु निभृतं निश्चित्य ततस्तत्तज्जातिभेदं वदे**दित्युपदेशः।** एवमुक्ताष्टादशविधजातिलक्षणक्रमस्तु करिणां करिणीनां च शरीरे दृश्यमिति (द्रष्टव्य इति) **व्यवस्था** ज्ञेया।

इति श्रीमदनन्तकृष्णभट्टारकविरचितायां गजशास्त्रव्याख्यायामष्टमं प्रकरणम्॥

(18) The elephants which have Mṛga-gaja's qualities and appearance in upper portion of their bodies, Bhadra-gaja's in the centre and Manda-gaja's in the lower are of very inferior class. All these 18 classess of elephants belong to both the sexes.

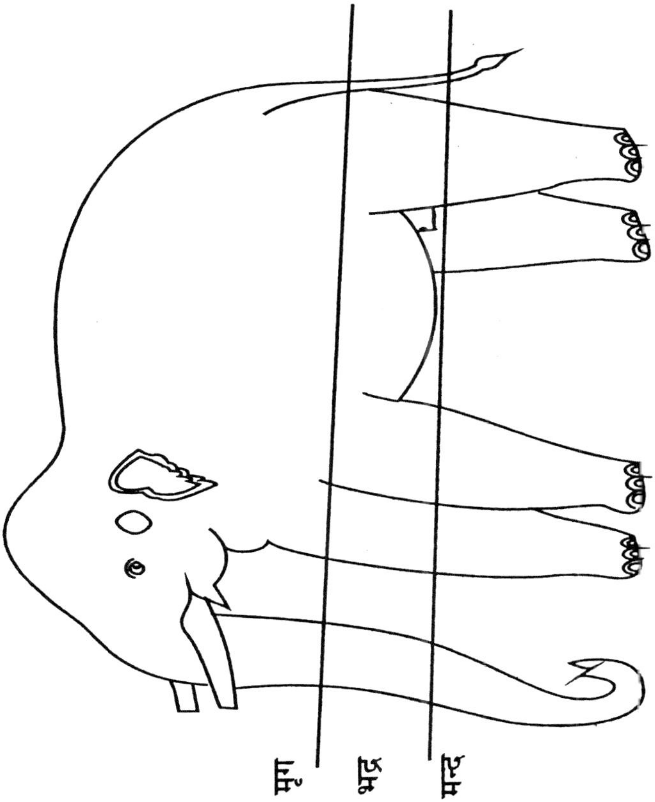

Fig. 106. : मृगभद्रमन्दगजः अधमः Inferior elephants

नवमं प्रकरणम्

अंशगजलक्षणनिरूपणम्

तत्र प्रथमस्य ब्रह्मांशगजस्य लक्षणम् (1)

संयुक्तबिन्दवो यस्य गौरवर्णो मनोहरः।
लोहिते नेत्रयोः प्रान्ते स्निग्धौ च वलिनौ रदौ॥

एवं लक्षणसंयुक्तो गजो ब्रह्मांशको मतः।
पूजार्होऽसौ नरेन्द्राणां विजयारोग्यवर्धनः॥

इत्याह भगवान् व्यासो ब्रह्मांशगजलक्षणम्।
कक्षाभागे तथा कण्ठे यः समः पृथुलांसकः॥

मुखे कोकनदच्छायो युग्मरोमविराजितः।
बहुकालमदः शूरः मेघनादेन हृष्यति॥

प्राजापत्यंशको नागः प्रजावृद्धिं करोत्यसौ।

व्याख्या—एतावता प्रबन्धे**नाष्टमे प्रकरणे** कलियुगे तत्र तत्र देशेषु जनितानां मिश्रगजसंकीर्णगजानां स्वरूपलक्षणगुणादिकं प्रतिपाद्याधुनास्मिन्**नवमे प्रकरणे** ब्रह्माद्यंशेन भासुरा ये ये गजा लसन्ति; तल्लक्षणादिकं निरूपयति-संयुक्तबिन्दव इत्यादिना। अस्मिन्नपि कलियुगे जनिताः केचिन्मतंगजाः उत्तमजातिजनिमवाप्य यतो वक्ष्यमाणसल्लक्षणविशेषभासुरा भवन्ति; अतस्ते **ब्रह्मांशगजा** इति कीर्त्यन्ते। यथा-ये ये गजाः कर्णभागे पुष्करे मुखे च रक्तवर्णबिन्दुसहिताः किंचिद्रक्तवर्णमिलितकृष्णवर्णछुरितांगाः नेत्रान्तेऽपि विशेषतः सुवर्णकांतियुताः स्निग्धमनोहरावयवोपेताः दृश्यन्ते; ते **ब्रह्मांशगजाः** भूपालचक्रवर्त्यादीनां पट्टाभिषेकादिशुभसमयसेवनयोग्याः। तेषां विजय-लक्ष्म्याद्यनेकशुभप्रदाश्च। किं चैषां ब्रह्मांशवतां गजानां मुखभागे कोकनद-

कान्तिपूरो भवति। सर्वावयवेष्वपि युग्मरोमप्राप्तिः। नितरां शौर्यादिकं चाजन्मसिद्धम्। किं चैते घनगर्जितं निशम्य मुदिता भवन्तीति।

Description of Aṁśa or creed of certain elephants

(1) Brahma-aṁśa-gajas—The elephants which have beautiful black appearance with red colour and red spots on their trunks, fore-head, and ears or with white coloured and red spots on their trunk etc. small thin hair on their whole bodies and which are fond of thunder and rain, which are naturally strong and bold and which have red colour on the corners of their eyes are called Brahmāṁśa-elaphants. These will create and develop prosperity, success, issues etc. to the kings and nobles.

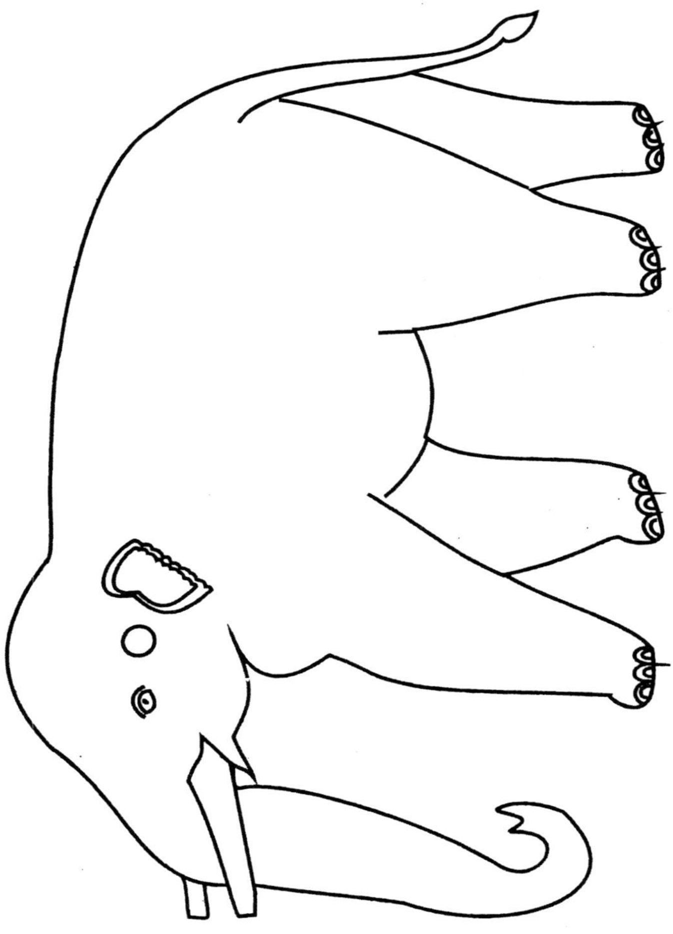

Fig. 107. : ब्रह्मांशगजः उत्तमोत्तमः Very superior elephants

॥अथ-द्वितीयस्य इन्द्रांशगजस्य लक्षणम् (2)॥

बिन्दवो बहुरेखा वा दृश्यन्ते यस्य वर्ष्मणि॥
स्वस्तिकैर्वर्धमानाब्जैर्नन्द्यावर्तैश्च सन्निभैः॥

रक्तोत्पलसमे नेत्रे यः स्यादिन्द्रांशको गजः॥
समरे विजयं दद्यात् परभूपालसंपदाम्॥

व्याख्या—अथ द्वितीयस्य इन्द्रांशगजस्य लक्षणमाह-बिन्दव इति। येषां गजानामुदरपार्श्वस्कन्धादिस्थलेषु स्वस्तिकवर्धमाननन्द्यावर्तरूपरेखा वा स्वस्तिकवर्धमाननन्द्यावर्तरूपबिन्दवो वास्पष्टं दृश्यन्ते; ते गजाः इन्द्रांशाः प्रकीर्तिताः। किं च-ये ये गजाः नितरां नीलवर्णमनोहरसर्वावयवाः कोकनद-कान्तियुतनेत्रांचलोपेताश्च दृश्यन्ते; ते सर्वेऽपि इन्द्रांशः कीर्त्यन्ते। भूपालानां युद्धादिसमयेषु विशेषतो विजयलक्ष्मीप्रदाः तद्द्वारा विविधसौख्यवर्धकाश्च भवन्तीति। अत्रैवं कापि **व्यवस्था**। यथा-पूर्वोक्तस्वस्तिकवर्धमाननन्द्यावर्तादि-चिह्नेषु एकस्यापि लक्ष्मणः स्फुरणेऽपि इन्द्रांशगजा एव। द्वयोस्त्रयाणां मेलने विशेषत इति॥

(2) Those elephants which are tall and very strong and which have Vardhamāna or lotus marks either in the form of moles or scars (strips) either on one side or both sides of their bodies are called Indrāṁśa-elephants. These will create prosperity, issues, success, long life etc. to kings and nobles.

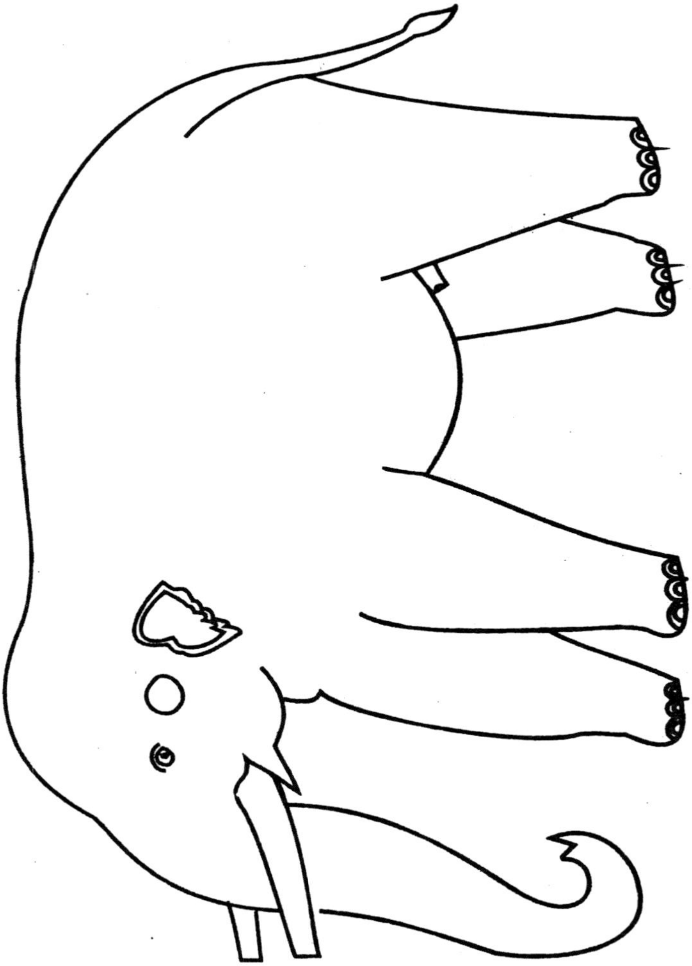

Fig. 108. : इन्द्रांशगजः उत्तमोत्तमः Very superior elephants

॥अथ तृतीयस्य धनदांशगजस्य लक्षणम् (3)॥

ताम्रावोष्ठौ तथा जिह्वा धात्रीफलसमद्युतिः।
नयने रदनौ यस्य कुंकुमोद्रेकसन्निभौ॥

धनदांश इति ख्यातो धनरत्नसमृद्धिकृत्।
नृपाणां भवने तिष्ठन् पूजितः कुंजरोत्तमः॥

व्याख्या—अथ तृतीयस्य धनदांशगजस्य लक्षणमाह-ताम्राविति। ये ये गजाः हरितवर्णच्छुरितांगाः ओष्ठभोगे जिह्वायां च विशेषतस्ताम्रवर्णभासुराः कुंकमवर्णनयनाः कुंकुमवर्णदन्तयुगलोपेतोश्च भवन्ति। ते धनदांशगजाः कीर्त्यन्ते। एते गजाः उत्तमाः यस्य वशे वर्तन्ते; तेषामधिपानां धनवृद्धिरत्न-वृद्ध्यादिकं च भवति। एते गजाः भूपालभवने वासभाजः सन्तस्तेषां नृपाणां नित्यसंपद्वृद्धिकारिणश्चेति॥

(3) Those elephants which have their lips, tongues and eyes complete red-coloured are called Kuberāṁśa-elephants. The kings and nobles, who possess these elephants, will be bestowed with emeralds, gold and wealth.

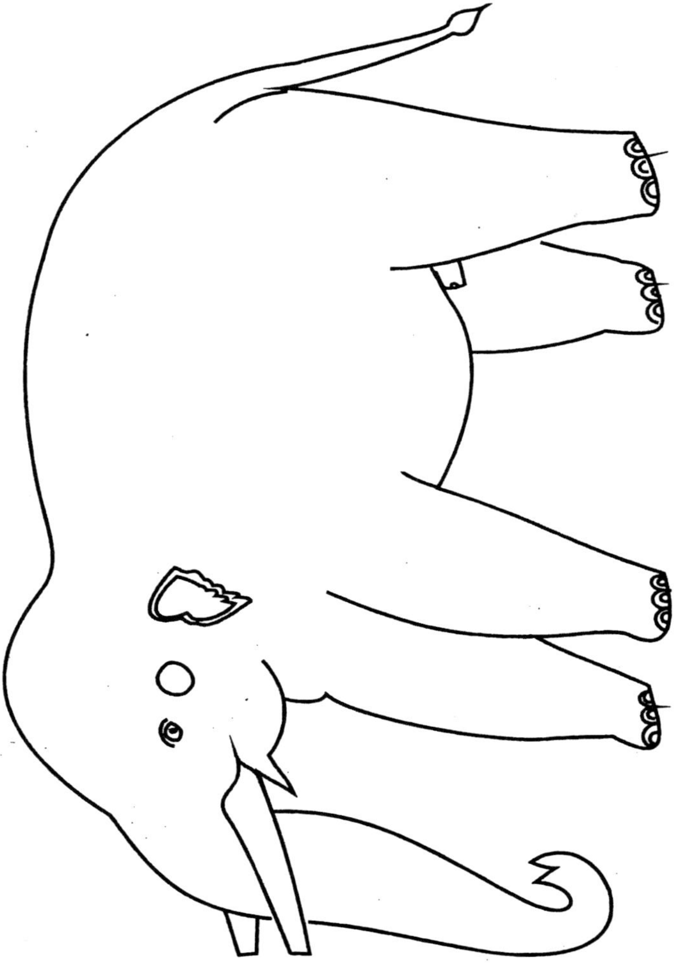

Fig. 109. : कुबेरांशगज: उत्तमोत्तम: Very superior elephants

।।अथ-चतुर्थस्य वरुणांशगजस्य लक्षणम् (4)।।

कृष्णमेघनिभो वर्णः स्त्यानसर्पिर्मदस्त्रवः।
आसने सुभगो मूर्ध्नि गंभीरो घनगर्जितः।।
स्त्रवति प्रचुरं दानं वरुणांशककुंजरः।
आहवे रिपुसंहारी निजभर्त्रे जयप्रदः।।

व्याख्या–अथ चतुर्थस्य वरुणांशगजस्य लक्षणमाह–कृष्णमेघनिभ इति। ये ये गजाः कृष्णमेघवन्मनोहरनीलवर्णछुरितांगाः विशेषतो मदजलस्त्रावयुताः घनगर्जवन्मनोहररींकारयुताः तत्र तत्रावयवेषु ह्रस्वमण्डलाकारबिन्दुयुताश्च दृश्यन्ते; ते सर्वे गजाः वरुणांशकाः उत्तमाः समरादिसमयेषु भूपालादीनां विशेषतो जयप्रदाश्च।।

(4) Those elephants which have beautiful blue colour on their bodies, awful flow of ruttish-water from temples, cry like thunder-bolts, and which are full of spots on their bodies are called Varuṇāṁśa elephants. These will not only slay their foes in war and battle, but also give success and wealth to their masters.

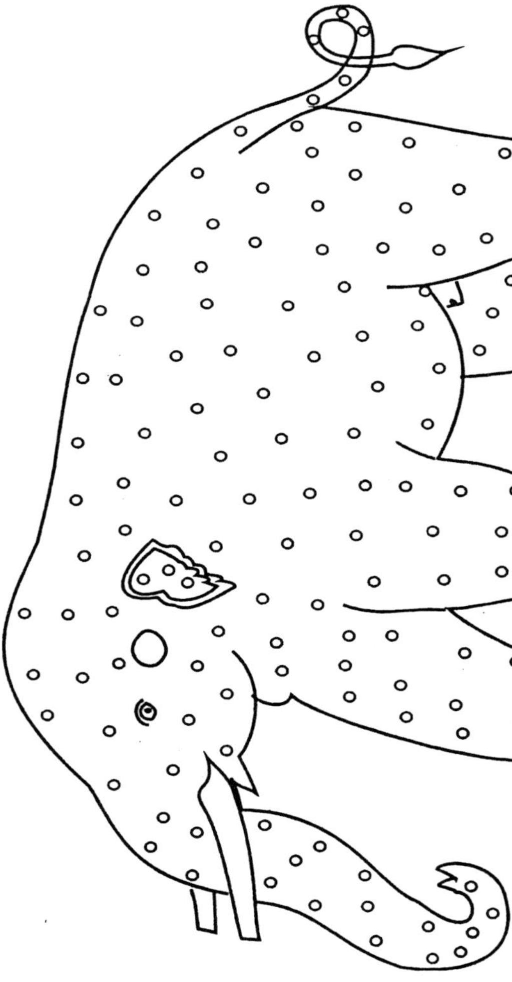

Fig. 110. : वरुणांशगजः उत्तमोत्तमः Very superior elephants

॥अथ-पंचमस्य चन्द्रांशगजस्य लक्षणम् (5)॥

त्रिवलीमण्डितः कण्ठे क्षौद्रपिंगललोचनः।
केतकछायदशनः पृथुरक्ताग्रपल्लवः॥

बिन्दुमान् पाण्डुवर्णश्च शशांकांशकभासुरः।
संगरप्रांगणे राज्ञां गजोऽयं विजयप्रदः॥

व्याख्या—अथ पंचमस्य चन्द्रांशगजस्य लक्षणमाह-त्रिवलीति। ये ये गजाः श्वेतवर्णच्छुरितसर्वावयवाः तत्र तत्रांगोपांगेषु रक्तवर्णबिन्दुभासुराः केतकछायदन्तयुगलाः किंचिद्रक्तवर्णपुष्करोपेताः कण्ठभागे त्रिवलीसहिताः क्षौद्रवत् पिंगलवर्णमनोहरनयनाश्च विलोक्यन्ते; ते सर्वे गजाः **चन्द्रांशाः** कीर्त्यन्ते। युद्धादिषु समयेषु राज्ञां विशेषतो मंगलप्रदा भवन्तीति॥

(5) The elephants which are of pure white colour with big red dots throughtout their bodies, yellowish tusks, and which have long trunks with the red colour on the end of their trunks, eyes like honey and 3 lines on their necks are called Candrāṁśa-elephants. These will not only slay their foes in wars, but also give success to their masters.

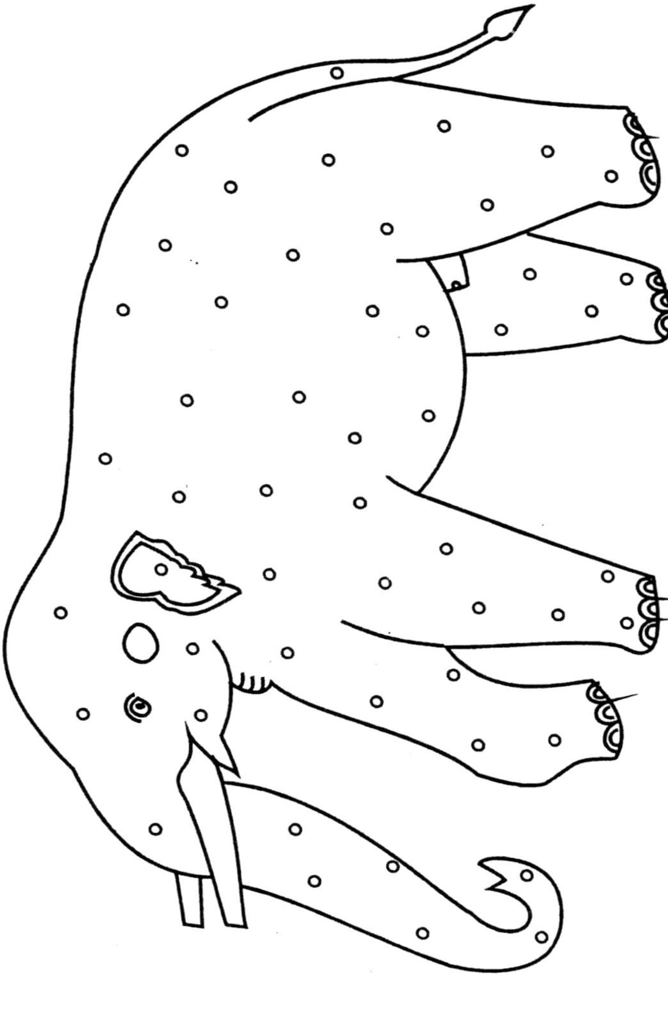

Fig. 111. : चन्द्रांशगजः उत्तमोत्तमः Very superior elephants

॥अथ-षष्ठस्य अग्न्यंशगजस्य लक्षणम् (6)॥

अग्निज्वालासदृग्रोमा केशवालेषु पिंगलः।
पिंगाक्षः पिंगतालुश्च पिंगपुष्करशोभितः॥

अग्न्यंशकसमुद्भूतः साक्षाद्वह्निरिवाहवे।
भस्मसात्कुरुते सैन्यमशेषं द्विषदां सदा॥

दोषाभावो गुणस्तस्य संजातसमरोत्सवे।
प्रचण्डत्वाद्भयं दत्ते रिपुसैन्येष्वयं गजः॥

व्याख्या—अथ षष्ठस्य अग्न्यंशगजस्य लक्षणमाह—अग्निज्वालेति। ये ये गजाः नितरां कृष्णवर्णशरीरभासुरा अपि तेषु कृष्णवर्णावयवेषु अग्निज्वालावत् रक्तवर्णरोमपुंजसहिताः मस्तकभागे पुष्करे च विशेषतः पिंगलवर्णयुताः पिंगाक्षाः पिंगतालुप्रदेशाः प्रचण्डपराक्रमाश्च दृश्यन्ते। ते सर्वे गजाः भूपालानां द्विषच्चमूं समरे भस्मीकुर्वते। स्वनायकस्य विजयलक्ष्म्याद्यनेकमंगलदायिनः॥

(6) The elephants which have red hair like flame on the whole of their bodies, red eyes, trunks and tongues are called, Agni-aṁśa-elephants. These elephants are very powerful and strong in war and burn the enemies like fire and appear to be very terrible. They will give success, long life etc. to their masters.

Fig. 112. : अन्त्यंशगाज: उत्तमोत्तम: Very superior elephants

॥अथ-सप्तमस्य विष्णवंशगजस्य लक्षणम् (7)॥

दन्तमध्यात्समारभ्य क्रमशो हीयते करः।
ताम्रपुष्करपर्यन्तः सुप्रमाणायतांगुलिः॥

सुगन्धिशीकरासारः दीर्घनिश्वाससन्ततिः।
घनवत् बृंहितध्वानो वलिहीनवपुर्दृढम्॥

मृदुसूक्ष्मांजनश्यामः सर्वांगीणतनूरुहः।
श्रीगर्भपुष्करछाया कान्तिः सर्वांगसंगिनी॥

सुवर्णवेतकोद्योतौ रदनौ वर्तुलौ दृढौ।
आयतः प्रान्ततो मध्ये निम्नः स्यात् वृत्तकुंभकः॥

आयतो रोमवानोष्ठः समदे च समे शुभे।
मुखमण्डलमत्यर्थं रम्यं दृष्टिमनोहरम्॥

पुष्पसारसमे नेत्रे पाटले प्रान्तलोहिते।
नलिनौ मृदुविस्तीर्णौ समौ छेदविवर्जितौ॥

सिराविरहितौ कर्णौ तालदुन्दुभिनिस्वनौ।
वर्तुलावुन्नतौ कुंभौ समौ लक्ष्मीकुचोपमौ॥

रम्यौ फालतलन्यासौ विपुलं चासनं समम्।
ऋजुह्रस्वो गलोद्देशः दीर्घावंसौ च मांसलौ॥

बाहू दीर्घावृजू पीनावधोऽधः क्रमशः शुभौ।
कूर्माकारतलालानस्निग्धार्न्धेन्दुनिभा नखाः॥

विंशतिर्वा दशाष्टौ वा शोभनाः परिकीर्तिताः।
उरो विशालं सद्वृत्तमुदरं प्रतनू कुचौ॥

अस्त्रस्तं मेहनं शस्तं वराहजघनं परम्।
सज्जचापनिभो वंशो वालधिश्चायतः शुभः॥

शंखचक्रगदाकारबिन्दवो वलयोऽथवा।
दृश्यन्ते यस्य नागस्य स विष्ण्वंशसमुद्भवः।।
अभिषेकोचितः पूज्यः सर्वकार्यार्थसाधकः।।

इति ब्रह्माद्यंशगजलक्षणम्।।

दीर्घांगुलिकरोदग्रसान्द्रकर्णायताननः।
जीमूतनीलः सत्त्वाढ्यो निःशंकश्चारुदर्शनः।।
यज्ञार्हः स भवेद्राज्ञो योग्यश्चैव विशांपते।

इति यज्ञार्हगजलक्षणम्।।

रक्तस्त्रोतोऽधिकजवः शतवर्षाणि जीवति।
सांग्रामिकः स राज्ञो वै कोशवर्धनकारकः।।

इति सांग्रामिकगजलक्षणम्।।

व्याख्या—अथ सप्तमस्य विष्ण्वंशगजस्य लक्षणमाह—दन्तमध्यादित्यादिना। अयमेव विष्ण्वंशगजः **नितरामुत्तमोत्तमः**। भूपालानां पट्टाभिषेकसमये समरादिसमयेषु च पुरतः कार्यः। अयं गजस्तेषां सर्वकार्यार्थसाधक इति **वाक्यार्थः**। तस्मादस्य विष्ण्वंशगजस्य लक्षणानि तु बहूनि। यथा—यस्य किल गजस्य दन्तभागादारभ्य क्रमशो हीनप्रमाणहस्तः पुष्कराग्रे ताम्रवर्णश्च भाति; एवं यस्य गजस्य सर्वेष्वप्यवयवेषु समसन्धिसमप्रमाणादिकं बलाधिक्यं शुद्धसत्त्वगुणकार्यादिकं च स्पष्टं भाति; यस्य किल गजस्य पुष्कराग्रगलनशीलशीकरः निश्वासश्च सुगन्धी; रींकारस्तावत् घनगर्जनवन्मनोहरः। सर्वेष्वप्यवयवेषु मनोहरकृष्णवर्णश्च सिराहीनकर्णतालतलं वृत्तकुंभयुगलं विंशतिसंख्या नखावलिर्वा अष्टादशसंख्याकनखावलिर्भाति; एवं गजस्य यस्य उदरपार्श्वभागे स्कन्धतले वा रेखाबिन्दुरूपशंखचक्रगदावलिः व्यक्तं दृश्यते; स एव गजः विष्ण्वंशभासुर इति। लक्षणवाक्यान्तराणि तु पुराणशैल्या स्पष्टार्थकान्येव। अतो न व्याख्यायन्ते। एवं विष्ण्वंशगजस्वरूपादिकं प्रतिपाद्याथ यज्ञार्हगजलक्षणमाह—दीर्घांगुलीति। सजलमेघवन्नीलवर्णछुरितांगानां येषां गजानां शुण्डादण्डो नितरां दीर्घः कर्णद्वयमाननतलं च विशालं; पराक्रमबल–

समृद्धिश्च दृश्यते; ते गजाः भूपालानां यज्ञार्हा निश्चिताः **पूर्वैर्महर्षिभि**रिति। एवं यज्ञार्हगजलक्षणं प्रतिपाद्याथो युद्धगजलक्षणमाह–रक्तस्रोत इति। ये ये गजाः पूर्वोक्तभद्रादितत्तत्सद्वंशजनिताः नितरां प्रचण्डबलपराक्रमोपेताः दृढगात्राः किंचिद्रक्तकरशीक**रासारा**श्च दृश्यन्ते; शतवर्षकालजीवनधारिणस्त एव **गजा विशेषतो युद्धार्हा** इति।।

इति श्रीमदनन्तकृष्णभट्टारकविरचितायां गजशास्त्रव्याख्यायां नवमं प्रकरणम्।।

7th Viṣṇu-aṁśa-gajas

The elephants which have their trunks uniform from their mouth to the end as pointed (i.e. at the beginning stout and gradually becoming thinner and thinner to the end as pointed) have their bodies uniformly and proportionately equal in size and their exhale and inhale long and big (period) with pleasant fragrance, thunder-bolt cry, small black and uniform hair throughout their bodies, red colour on their faces, beautiful and round forehead, ears, without big nerves, 20 or 18 nails on their four feet and calm appearance and temperance and which have very many best qualities, are called Viṣṇu-aṁśa-elephants. These will improve every success to their masters.

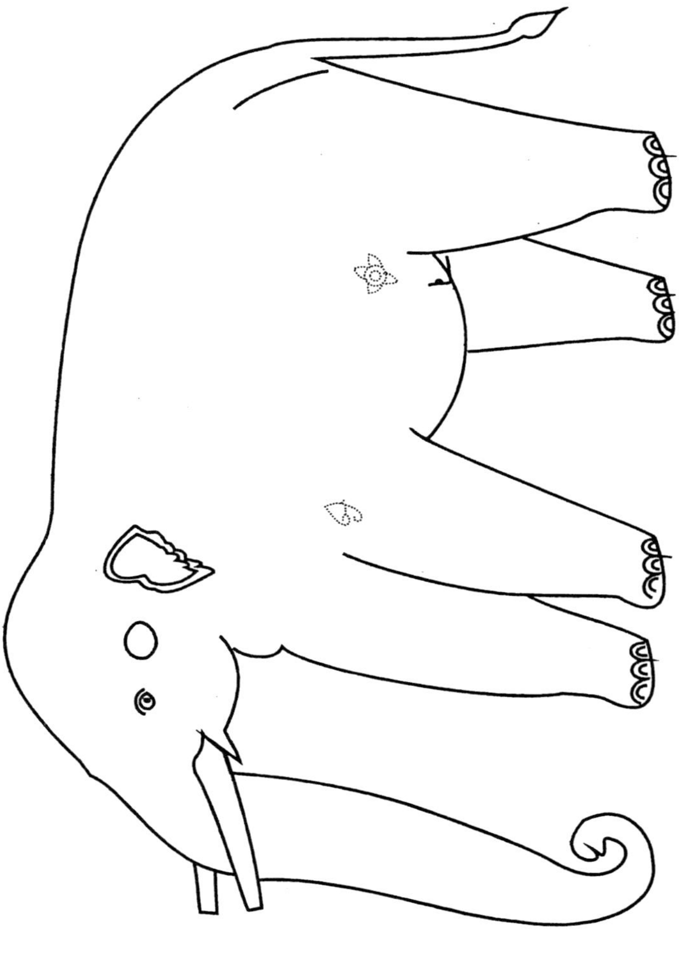

Fig. 113. : विष्णुवंशगज: उत्तमोत्तम: Very superior elephants

दशमं प्रकरणम्

वर्णगजलक्षणकथनम्

त्रयः शुद्धा महाराजा व्यामिश्रास्त्रय एव हि।
अन्तर्वर्णास्त्रयश्चापि नागानां परिकीर्तिताः॥

हरिद्रक्तश्च कृष्णश्च मातंगानाममी त्रयः।
शुद्धवर्णा इमे प्रोक्ताः गजशास्त्रविशारदैः॥

कफस्तु शुभदः श्वेतः पित्ताद्रक्तस्तथा मतः।
त्वग्रोमनखवालान्तर्वर्णः स्याद्वर्णलक्षणं॥

कृष्णो दन्ती वातजातो गजविद्भिः प्रकीर्तितः॥

व्यासप्रोक्ते गजशास्त्रे-

अन्ये चारुणपीतकालधवलैर्वर्णैश्चतुर्धाः क्रमात्।
कृष्णो वातभवः कफाच्छशिनिभः पित्ताच्च हेमप्रभः॥

इति शुद्धवर्णगजलक्षणम्॥

अथ-मिश्रवर्णगजलक्षणम्॥

हरित्कृष्णः श्वेतरक्तः कृष्णरक्तस्तथैव च।
त्रय एते महाराज वर्णाः स्युर्मिश्रसंज्ञकाः॥

व्यासप्रोक्ते गजशास्त्रे-

अन्ये ते कफवातपित्तगुणकैः व्यामिश्रवर्णा गजाः।
जायन्ते जननाय संमदकरा जात्या जगत्याममी॥

अथान्तर्वर्णगजलक्षणम्-

अन्तर्वर्णास्त्रयः प्रोक्ताः अन्तः पाण्डरलोहितः।
अन्तः पाण्डरकृष्णश्च तथान्तर्लोहितासितः॥

श्वेतपीतौ रक्तकृष्णाविति वर्णश्चतुर्विधः।
हरित्कुंकुमवर्णाभः पद्माभो रक्त एव च॥
कृष्णोंऽजननिभश्चैव व्यामिश्राख्यो गजो मतः।
भवन्ति शंखवैडूर्यविद्युज्ज्वालाघनप्रभाः॥
इति दिग्दन्तिनः सर्वे भूतले न भवन्ति ते॥

इति पालकाप्यमहर्षिप्रणीते गजशास्त्रे दशमं प्रकरणम्॥

व्याख्या–अथास्मिन् **दशमे प्रकरणे** गजानां वर्णलक्षणमाह–त्रयः शुद्धा इत्यादिना। उत्तमजातिजनितानां गजानां शरीरे वर्णपरीक्षां च कलयेदिति **प्राचां मतमवलंब्य** प्रकरणमिदमुक्तं **शास्त्रकारेण**ेति **व्यवस्था**। तत्र गजानां शरीरत्वचि रोमराजिषु नखेषु मस्तककेशेषु च तादृशवर्णस्वभावो निरीक्ष्य **इति क्रमः**। तथा चेत् गजशरीरे भासनशीलाः शुद्धवर्णास्त्रय एव। यथा–श्वेतवर्णः रक्तवर्णः कृष्णवर्णश्चेति। तत्र कफातिरेकात् गजशरीरे श्वेतवर्णो भवति। एवं पित्तातिरेकात् रक्तवर्णः वातातिरेकात् कृष्णवर्णश्च भवतीति **परिपाटी**। एवं शुद्धवर्णानां त्रयाणां स्वरूपलक्षणादिकं प्रतिपादितं ज्ञेयम्। एवं मिश्रवर्णाश्च त्रय एव केषांचित् गजानां शरीरेषु दृश्या भवन्ति। यथा–श्वेतवर्णमिश्रकृष्णवर्णः श्वेतवर्णमिश्ररक्तवर्णः कृष्णवर्णमिश्ररक्तवर्ण इति। एतादृशव्यामिश्रवर्णानां त्रयाणां स्वरूपादिकं सर्वमपि तेषु तेषु गजशरीरेषु सूक्ष्मतो ज्ञेयम्। किं चान्येषां केषांचित् गजानां शरीरेष्वन्तर्वर्णाख्यानां वर्णविशेषाणां त्रयमपि दृश्यं भवति। यथा–अन्तःपाण्डरलोहितवर्णः अन्तःपाण्डरकृष्णवर्णः अन्तर्लोहितपाण्डरवर्ण इति। अस्य **विशदार्थस्तु**–अन्तःपाण्डरलोहितवर्णो नाम तत्र तत्र गजावयवेषु ईशत्पाण्डरवर्णमिलितस्वल्पदृश्यरक्तप्रकर इत्यर्थः। एवमीषत्पाण्डरवर्णमिलितस्वल्पकृष्णवर्णप्रकरः अन्तःपाण्डरकृष्णवर्ण इत्युच्यते। अनेनैव प्रकारेण ईषल्लोहितवर्णमिलितस्वल्पश्वेतकान्तिरिति **व्यवस्था। इति पालकाप्यमहर्षिः। भगवान् व्यासस्तु**–केचित्तु गजाः अरुणवर्णदेहाः पीतवर्णदेहाः कृष्णवर्णदेहाः श्वेतवर्णदेहाश्च भवन्ति। अतो वर्णचतुष्कमपि दृश्यमिति मेने। किं च–एवमत्रोक्ताः रक्तवर्णदेहा गजाः श्वेतवर्णदेहा गजाश्चान्येऽपि भूतलेऽस्मिन् न दृश्या भवन्ति। ते तु स्वर्गादिस्थानेषु दिग्गजैः साकं संचरणशीला एव।

अतो भूतले कलौ युगे जाताः सर्वेऽपि करिणः करिण्यश्च प्रायेण संपूर्णकृष्णवर्णच्छुरितदेहा अपि तत्तन्मुखाद्यवयवेषु रक्तवर्णबिन्द्वादिलक्षण-विशेषभाजो भवन्तीति **भावः**। एतादृशविशेषवर्णलक्षणादिकं तु तत्र तत्र ज्ञेयम्।।

इत्यनन्तकृष्णभट्टारकविरचितायां
गजशास्त्रव्याख्यायां दशमं प्रकरणम्।।

Test of colours in elephants.

There are 3 main colours visible in elephant's bodies as white, red and black. Those which have more bronchite (*kapha*) will have white young ones, which have more *śleṣma* will have red young ones, and which have more *vāta* will have black young ones. There are 3 sub-colours as whitish black, whitish red, and blackish red. Again there are 3 sub-colours as red with a little white, black with a little white, and red with a little black. The elephants which have red, white, subs, and sub-sub-colours mentioned above are not available on the the face of the earth in this Kaliyuga.

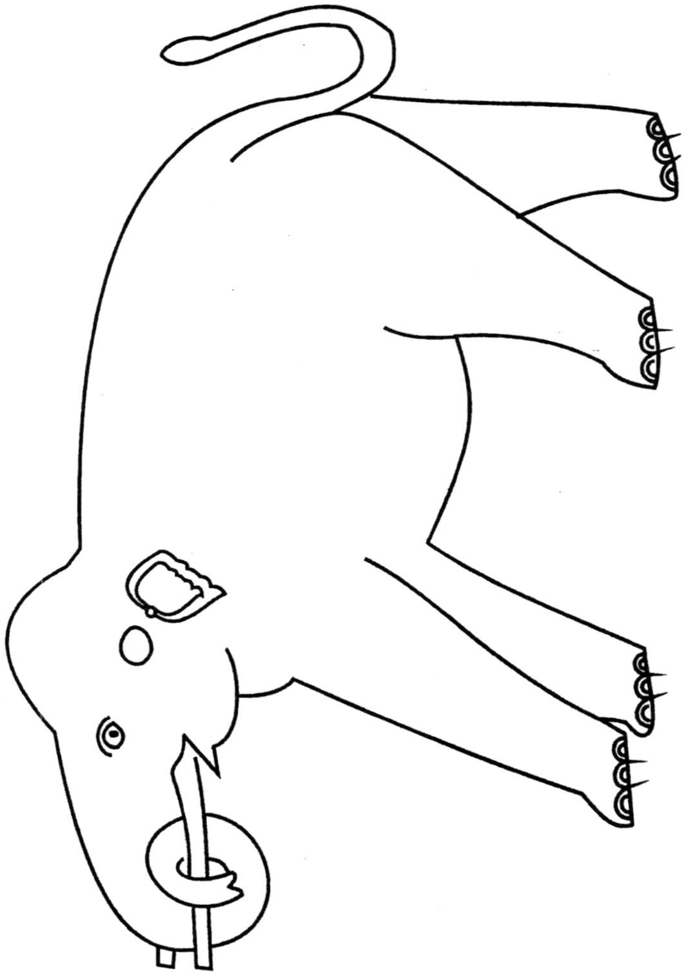

Fig. 114. : श्वेतवर्णगजः

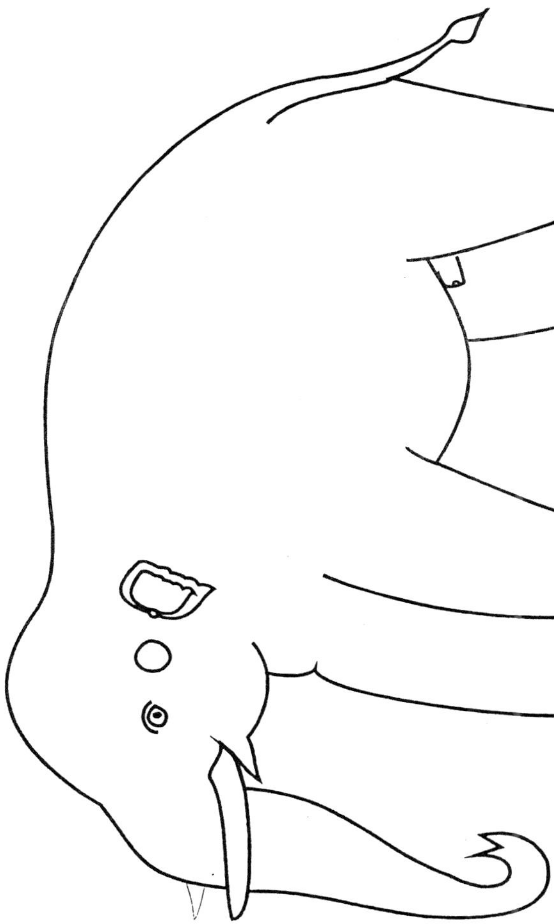

Fig. 115. : रक्तवर्णगजः

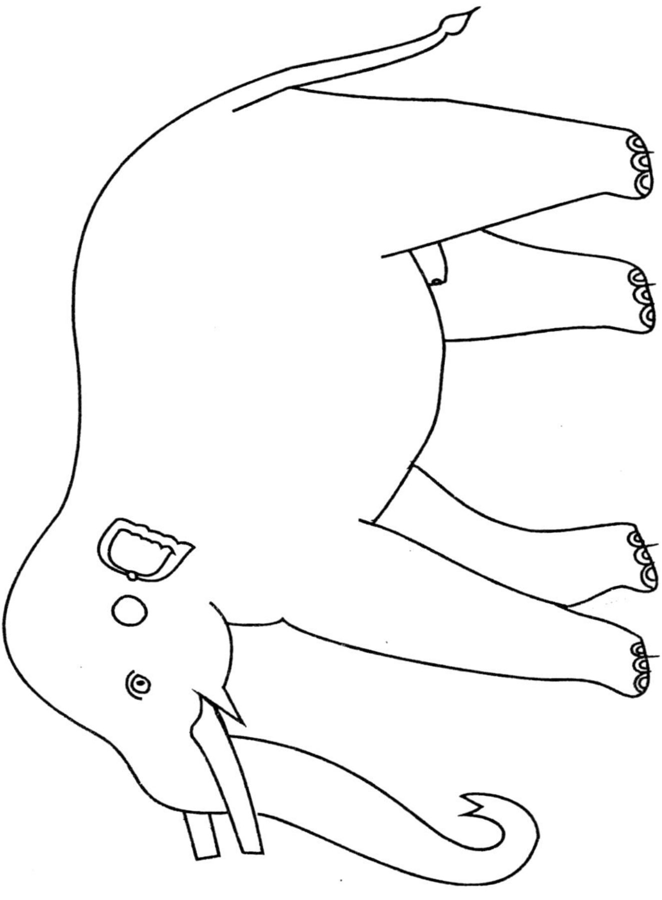

Fig. 116. : कृष्णवर्णगजः

एकादशकं प्रकरणम्

।।अथ छायानिरूपणम्।।

पार्थिवी औदकी चैव छायाग्नेयी च शोभना।
वायव्या निन्दिता छाया नाभसी तु मतंगजे।।
गंभीरा स्निग्धवर्णा च नैकवर्णा च पार्थिवी।
छायाग्नेयी घना स्निग्धा कुंजरे दृश्यते शुभा।।
स्निग्धनीलांबुदप्रख्या विज्ञेया सलिलात्मिका।
शक्रगोपकबालार्कपद्मकिंजल्कसन्निभा।।
निष्प्रभा परुषा ध्वस्ता भस्मवर्णा च वायवी।
निन्द्या चानियतछाया रूक्षा तन्वी च खात्मिका।।
इत्येवं पंचधा छाया वारणेषु प्रदृश्यते।।

इति पालकाप्यमहर्षिप्रणीते गजशास्त्रे एकादशप्रकरणम्।।

व्याख्या—अथास्मिन्नेकादशके **प्रकरणे** गजानां शरीरेषु छायापरीक्षा च कार्येत्याह—पार्थिवीति। सा तु छाया पंचविधा भवति। यथा—(१) पार्थिवी-छाया, (२) सलिलछाया, (३) अग्निछाया, (४) वायुछाया, (५) नभश्छायेति। तत्र पार्थिवी छाया सलिलछाया अग्निछाया च गजानां तन्नायकानां च क्षेमजननी। एतच्छायात्रयमपि सर्वथा **शुभप्रदम्।** अन्यत् छायाद्वयं तु **न प्रशस्तम्।** किं च—तत्र प्रथमा पार्थिवीछाया तावन्नीलकृष्णरक्तपीताद्यनेकवर्ण-स्वरूपमण्डलात्मिका भवति। सलिलछाया तु सर्वांगेष्वपि नीलवर्णप्रचुरा भवति। अग्निछाया तु शक्रगोपसमानवर्णा वा बालार्कमरीचिकांतिसमानवर्णा वा विकसितपद्मकिंजल्कसमानवर्णा वा भवति। परुषवर्णस्वरूपा भस्मवर्णस्वरूपा च वायुछाया दृश्या। द्रष्टृणां नेत्रक्लेशकारिणी अनियतस्वरूपा विकाराकारा छाया तावन्नभश्छायेति **छायालक्षणक्रमः।।**

इति श्रीमदनन्तकृष्णभट्टारकविरचितायां
गजशास्त्रव्याख्यायामेकादशकं प्रकरणम्।।

Description of the brightness of the best elephants

There are 5 kinds of brightness of the best elephants, as

1. *Pārthivīchāyā*	earth brightness
2. *Salilachāyā*	water brightness
3. *Agnichāyā*	fire brightness
4. *Vāyuchāyā*	Wind brightness.
5. *Nabhaschāyā*	Sky brightness.

The first three are the best, which will make the elephants and their masters very prosperous, and the last two are the worst, which will create worst difficulties both to the elephants and their masters.

(1) *Pārthivīchāyā*—There are many beautiful (*maṇḍala*) clear spots of blue, red, white and black on the different parts of the elephant's bodies separately.

(2) *Salilachāyā*—There will be uniform blue colour throughout elephant's bodies.

(3) *Agni-chāyā*—There will be red colour on the whole bodies of the elephants.

(4) *Vāyu-chāyā*—There will be ash-colour on the whole bodies of the elephants.

(5) *Nabhas-chāyā*—There will be ugly combination of different colours on the bodies of elephants.

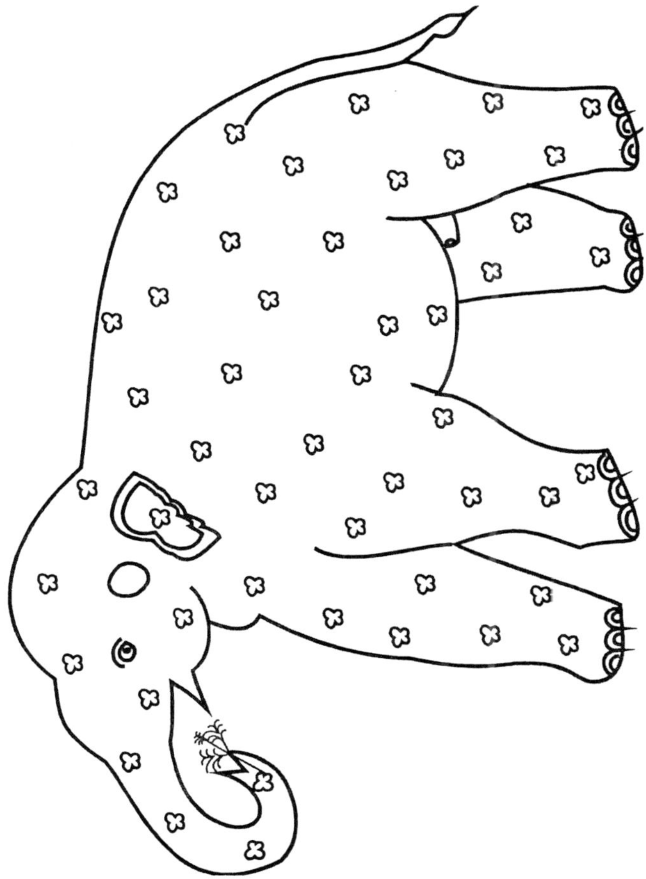

Fig. 117. पृथिवीछायायुतगजः उत्तमोत्तमः Very superior elephants having earth brightness

द्वादशकं प्रकरणम्

।।अथ-गन्धलक्षणम्।।

अथ गन्धं प्रवक्ष्यामि नागानां तु शुभाशुभम्।
स्वेदे मदे वा मूत्रे वा वमथौ वापि लक्ष्यते।।

शुभस्तु सुरभिर्गन्धः दुर्गन्धस्त्वशुभप्रदः।
उशीरघृतलाजाब्जजातिपाटलजाः शुभाः।।

गन्धाः प्रोक्ता महीपाल गजानां गजचिन्तकैः।
वस्तिगन्धो मार्गगन्धः शल्यकस्य च गंधकः।।

यश्च श्वपचगन्धः स्यात्तथा वायसगन्धकः।
निन्द्यगन्धसमायुक्तो निन्द्यः प्रोक्तो मतंगजः।।

इति वाहान् समुद्दिष्टान् गन्धज्ञानेन हस्तिनः।
पुण्यान् पूजितसर्वांगान् प्रशस्तान् शृणु तत्त्वतः।।

मत्स्यगन्धश्च यो नागः सुरागन्धश्च यो भवेत्।
गन्धर्व इति निर्दिष्टो गन्धविद्भिर्महीपते।।

जात्या यक्षो भवेन्नागोऽशोकमालतिगन्धकः।
सिन्धुवारागरुतकसगन्धी दानवः स्मृतः।।

पद्मगन्धी च यो नागः कुरंटस्योत्पलस्य च।
सप्तछदसगन्धी च देवजातिः प्रकीर्तितः।।

इति गन्धसमुद्देशः कीर्तितस्ते विशांपते।

इति पालकाप्यमहर्षिप्रणीते गजशास्त्रे द्वादशप्रकरणम्।।

व्याख्या—अथास्मिन् द्वादशके प्रकरणे गजानां शरीरे वीज्य(=क्ष्य)-

मानणा गन्धलक्षणं विशदयति-अथ गन्धं प्रवक्ष्यामीत्यादिना। तत्र गन्धपरीक्षा तावत् गजानां स्वेदजले मदजले मूत्रे वमथुप्रसारे पुष्करभागात् गलनीयशीकर-सलिले च कर्तव्येति **व्यवस्था।** तस्मादेतेषु स्वेदजलमदजलमूत्रजलादिषु शुभगन्धयुक्ता गजाः **यजमानस्य शुभवर्धका** भवेयुः। एतेषु मदजलमूत्रजलादिषु अशुभगन्धयुक्ता वारणास्तु **भर्तुरशुभदा एवेति मतिः।** तत्र शुभगन्धस्वरूपं तावत् उशीरगन्धसदृक् वा घृतगन्धसमानं वा लाजगन्धसमानं वा पद्मगन्धतुल्यं वा पाटलीपुष्पगन्धतुल्यं वा भवेत्। दुर्गन्धस्वरूपं तु वस्तिगन्धसदृक् वा अपामार्गगन्धसदृक् वा शल्यगन्धसदृक् वा श्वपचगन्धतुल्यं वा वायसगन्धतुल्यं वा विष्ठादिगन्धतुल्यं वेति **क्रमः।** तस्मादेतादृशदुर्गन्धयुक्ताः गजाः सर्वधा **न क्रेतव्या इत्युपदेशः।** किं च-पूर्वोक्तशुभगन्धवीजनशीलगजास्तावत् जातिचतुष्केन विभक्ताः। यथा-(१) मत्स्यगन्धतुल्यगन्धयुता नागाः सुरागन्ध-तुल्यगन्धयुता नागाश्च गन्धर्वगन्धगजा **इति शास्त्रज्ञा वदन्ति।** (२) एवमशोक-पुष्पगन्धतुल्यगन्धसहिता गजाः मालतीकुसुमगन्धतुल्यगन्धयुता वारणाश्च यक्षगन्धगजा इति व्यवह्रियन्ते, (३) एवं सिन्धुवारकुसुमगन्धतुल्ययुताः अगरुधूपगन्धतुल्यगन्धोपेता नागाश्च दानवगन्धगजाः, (४) अनेनैव क्रमेण कमलगन्धतुल्यगन्धोपेता वारणाः कुरंटकोत्पलसप्तछदकुसुमगन्धतुल्यगंधसहिता वारणाश्च देवगन्धगजा इति **क्रमपरिपाटी।** एवमत्रोक्ता**श्चतुर्विधगजास्तु** नितरां **प्रशस्ताः मूल्याधिक्यार्हा इति भावः॥**

इत्यनन्तकृष्णभट्टारकविरचितायां गजशास्त्रव्याख्यायां द्वादशकं प्रकरणम्॥

Description of Smell examination

The smell of ruttish water, perspiration, urine and saliva of elephants should be tested whether good or bad. The elephants having good small are the best ones and they will multiply their master's prosperity and long life whereas the others having bad smell will spoil the prosperity and increase sorrows and miseries of their masters. Good smell will be like lotus, Khus-khus, Jasmine and other best flowers and bad smell like mutton, crow and tortoise. There are 4 kinds of elephants having good smell.

(1) Those which have the scent of toddy and fish are called Gandharva-smell elephants.

(2) Those which have the scent of Aśoka and Mālatī-flowers are called Yakṣa-smell-elephants.

(3) Those which have the scent of Sindhuvāra flowers and Agaru-smoke are called Dānava-smell elephants.

(4) Those which have the scent of lotus, night lotus, Kuraṇṭaka-flowers and Seven-leave's trees are called Deva-smell elephants.

त्रयोदशकं प्रकरणम्

।।अथ-गजबलसत्त्वपरीक्षानिरूपणम्।।

गुरुत्वं रूपतः श्रेष्ठं गुरुत्वादधिकं बलम्।
बलादप्यधिकं सत्त्वं तस्मात्सत्त्वं परीक्षयेत्।।

शुद्धस्फटिकसंकाशं सत्त्वं हृदि शरीरिणाम्।
दुर्लभं तत्परिज्ञेयमुपायेन परीक्षयेत्।।

जांबूनदस्य ताम्रस्य पलानां रजतस्य वा।
अष्टादशसहस्त्राणां भारं संगृह्य वेगवान्।।

यो गजो गजमध्येन गच्छति श्रमवर्जितः।
दशयोजनमध्वानं स तूत्तमबलः स्मृतः।।

यश्चतुर्दशसाहस्त्रं भारमादाय गच्छति।
सप्तयोजनमध्वानं स तु मध्यबलः स्मृतः।।

दशसाहस्त्रिकं भारं गृहीत्वा पंचयोजनम्।
अध्वानं यो गजो यायात्स हीनबल उच्यते।।

व्याख्या–अथास्मिन् **त्रयोदशके प्रकरणे** सर्वेषामप्युत्तमगजानां बलपरीक्षाक्रमं सत्त्वपरीक्षाक्रमं च क्रमेण विशदयते-गुरुत्वमित्यादिना। ये ये गजाः गजान्तरापेक्षया किंचिदौन्नत्याधिक्यवन्तः ते गजाः विशेषसौन्दर्य-हीना अपि **श्रेष्ठा इति क्रमः**। तादृशगुरुत्वापेक्षया बलमेव श्रेष्ठम्। तादृशबलापेक्षया सत्त्वमेव श्रेष्ठतमं भवति। तस्मात् बलवतो गजान् सत्त्ववतो गजांश्च स्वीकुर्या**दित्युपदेशः**। तत्र बलपरीक्षा कथं कर्तव्येत्याकांक्षाया-माह-जांबूनदस्येत्यादिना। यो गजस्तावत् अष्टादशसहस्त्रपलतुलितं जांबूनद-खण्डराशिं वा ताम्रखण्डराशिं वा रजतखण्डराशिं वा स्वोपरि धृत्वा श्रमवर्जितः

सन् दशयोजनदूरमध्वानं गच्छति, स तु **उत्तमबलवान् गज** इति व्यवह्रियते। एवं यो वारणस्तावत् चतुर्दशसहस्रपलतुलितं जांबूनदखण्डराशिं वा ताम्रखंडराशिं वा स्वोपरि धृत्वा अनायासः सन् सप्तयोजनदूरमध्वानं गच्छति; स तु **मध्यमबलवानिति** कीर्त्यते। अपि च-एवं प्रकारेण यो गजः दशसहस्र-पलतुलितं जांबूनदखण्डराशिं वा रजतखण्डराशिं वा स्वोपरि धृत्वा पंचयो-जनदूरमध्वानं श्रमहीनो गच्छति; स तु हीनबल **इति क्रमः।** एवं दशसहस्र-पलतुलितभारवहनेऽप्यसमर्थाः सर्वेऽपि **गजाः अधमाः अधमाधमाश्**चेति **भावः।** तथा च-महीपालादयः एवं रीत्या उत्तमबलगजं मध्यमबलगजं हीनबलगजं च क्रमात् परीक्ष्य तत्राद्यौ स्वीकुर्यादि(=स्वीकुर्युरि)**त्युपदेशः॥**

Test of Elephants' strength and patience.

The elephants being taller in nature are better than the more beautiful, having more strength are better than the taller and having more patience are much better than the stronger. Therefore the strongest and the most patient ones should be purchased.

Test of strength

1. The elephants which can carry very easily 18000 *palas* of gold, silver or copper to a distance of 10 *yojanas* are the strongest of all the elephants.
2. The elephants which can carry very easily 14000 *palas* of gold, silver or copper to a distance of 7 *yojanas* are stronger than the others as middle class.
3. Those which can carry very easily 10000 *palas* of gold, silver or copper to a distance of 5 *yojanas* are 3rd class ones (stronger).
4. Those which can not carry even 10000 *palas* of weight to 5 *yojanas* even once are considered to be inferior class ones.

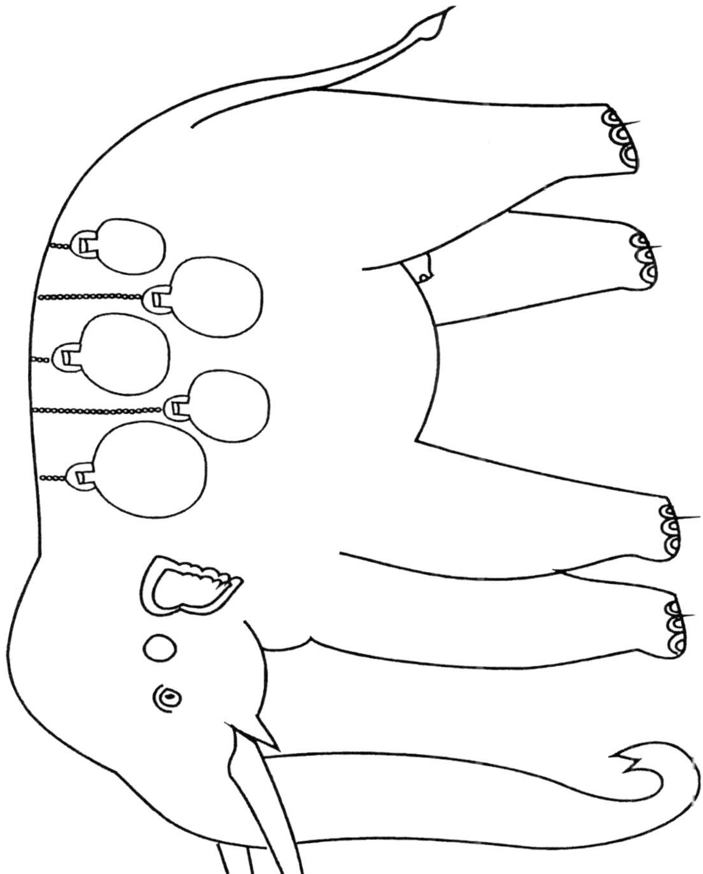

Fig. 118. : उत्तमबलगजः उत्तमः Very superior elephants

॥अथ-सत्त्वपरीक्षाक्रमः॥

पाषाणैरिष्टकाभिर्वा दारुकैः फलकैर्घनैः।
सुसंकल्पितमूलैस्तु कारयेच्च समं स्थलम्॥

उच्छ्रायेण त्रिहस्तं स्यादायामेन चतुर्दश।
हस्ताष्टकं पृथुत्वेन परितो धृतकर्णिकम्॥

बाणपातद्वयायामपार्श्वसारितभूतलम्।
मातंगं मंत्रपूतेन प्रोक्षयेत्सलिलेन तु॥

मंत्रेशनाथ भूतेश विघ्ननाथ गणाधिप।
गजानां सत्त्वसन्देहे कुरु सत्त्वविनिर्णयम्॥

सुप्रशस्तदिने तत्र गजौ गैरिकमण्डितौ।
अन्योन्यस्पर्धया युक्तौ पार्श्वे विवृतकंबलौ॥

वेणुदारुकृतास्फोटैः दन्तसंवृतिभेदकैः।
कृते करेणुघाते तु वेदनां यो न मन्यते॥

हस्तदन्तकृतास्फालः संहतं हन्तुमिच्छति।
नापसर्पति घातेषु प्रतिघातं करोति च॥

घण्टागर्जितनादेषु प्रतिपूरितदिङ्मुखे।
निवर्तते न दुःखेन स भवेत्सत्त्ववान् गजः॥

इति पालकाप्यमहर्षिप्रणीते गजशास्त्रे त्रयोदशकं प्रकरणम्॥

व्याख्या—एवं बलपरीक्षाक्रममुपदिश्यानन्तरं सत्त्वरीक्षाक्रममाह पाषाणैरित्यादिना। पाषाणखण्डैर्वा दृढदारुफलकादिभिर्वा त्रिहस्तप्रमाणाधारकल्पनयुतं चतुर्दशकरौन्नत्ययुतमष्टकरप्रथुलं कमपि स्तंभं ग्रामनगरबहिः प्रदेशे कालक्रमेण दृढं निर्मापयित्वा मंत्रनाथं प्रार्थ्य गणेशमंत्राभिमंत्रणेन परिभूतसलिलेन गजशरीरं प्रोक्ष्य तादृशगजद्वयमन्योन्यजिगीषास्पर्धायुक्तं समवयस्कं पार्श्वभागे विवृतकंबलं घण्टाकिंकिणिकाद्यलंकारमण्डितं च कारयित्वा शुभदिने शुभसमये तादृशगजद्वयं परस्परं मुखेन मुखं दन्तेन दन्तं घट्टितं हस्तिपकादिभिः चोदनं कार्यम्। तदनु

तस्मिन् स्तंभे घट्टितुं प्रेरणा कार्या। एवं कृते सति तस्मिन् समये यो यो मातंगः प्रतिगजघट्टनादिना जातां स्ववेदनां किंचिदप्यजानन् भीतिरहितः सन् स्थिरो भूत्वा रुषान्वितस्तमेव प्रतिगजं वा तादृशस्तंभं वा पुनर्घट्टयितुं प्रतिघातं वा कलयितुं यतते; तथा करोति; स एव गजः उत्तमसात्त्विक सत्त्व वानिति **सात्त्विकपरीक्षाक्रमः॥**

इत्यनन्तकृष्णभट्टारकविरचितायां गजशास्त्रव्याख्यायां त्रयोदशकं प्रकरणम्॥

Test of patience

(1) The two elephants on either side with two *mahouts* on their backs should be induced to dash each other, when one dashes the other with full force running from half a furlong, the other one should patiently endure the pain and defend it (re-attack). These elephants are the best ones.

(2) The two elephants with two *mahouts* on their backs should be induced to dash one by one separately, a big and strong brick or stone pillar 2½ feat long, 2½ feet wide and 15 feet high with strong foundation on the outside of the town or village. It should dash the pillar down and then the other elephant standing on the other side of the pillar *vice versa*. The elephants which are able to do this are the most patient and best ones. They can withstand all the difficulties and blows of the enemies in the battle and war. The elephants of the two varieties carrying the heaviest weight and the most patient are more valuable in price.

इष्टिकास्तम्भ-Brick-pillar

Fig. 119. : उत्तमसत्त्वगजः उत्तमः Very superior elephants

चतुर्दशकं प्रकरणम्

।।अथ सात्त्विकनिरूपणम्।।

तत्र सात्त्विकगुणगजलक्षणम् (१)

सुमनाः सुप्रभश्चण्डः तेजस्वी दृढविक्रमः।
कुतूहली प्रतापी च क्रीडने हर्षणे च यः।।
कृतज्ञश्च भवेन्नागः सात्त्विको गजसत्तमः।।

अथ-राजसगुणगजलक्षणम् (२)

दुर्मना दुर्गतिर्नागः सततं धेनुकामनाः।
आशावान् दुर्बरः क्रूरः विस्मार्युत्तानवेदिता।।

अथ-तामसगुणगजलक्षणम् (३)

कृच्छ्रेण किंचिज्जानीते नर्म चास्य प्रणश्यति।
निद्रालुर्मूढसंज्ञश्च तामसो गज उच्यते।।

व्याख्या—अथास्मिन् **चतुर्दशके प्रकरणे** सर्वेषामप्युत्तमगजानां सत्त्वगुणादिपरीक्षां कलयेदित्याशयेन तत्क्रमं व्यक्तीकरोति-सुमना इति। तत्र मानुषाणामिव गजानामपि गुणत्रयं दृश्यं भवति। यथा-सत्त्वगुणः रजोगुणः तमोगुण इति भेदात्। तथा च-केचित् गजाः सत्त्वगुणयुताः भवन्ति। अन्ये तु राजसगुणयुताः। परे तु तामसगुणसहिताः दृश्यन्त इत्युक्तं भवति। तत्र सात्त्विकगुणयुता गजाः कीदृशा इत्याकांक्षायामाह-सुमना इति। ये ये गजाः सन्ततं सन्तुष्टमानसाः मनोहरसौन्दर्ययुताः कार्यकाले स्वबलपराक्रनप्रदर्शनशीलाः हस्तिपकभूपालादिनिर्दिष्टभारवहनमृगयासमरादिकार्यकरणे लोलुपाः क्रीडनादिषु हर्षयुक्ताः कृतज्ञाश्च विलोक्यन्ते; ते सर्वेऽपि सत्त्वगुणगजा इति कीर्त्यन्ते। एवं ये ये गजाः बलपराक्रमहीनाः हस्तिपकादिनिर्दिष्टकार्याणि

कर्तुं मनःखेदयुक्ताः सन्ततं करिणीसंभोगनिरताः दुष्टगतिचर्याद्युपेताः क्रूरहृदयाः हस्तिपकादिभिः शिक्षितकार्याणि विस्मृतवन्तश्च विलोक्यन्ते; ते सर्वेऽपि राजसगुणगजा निर्दिष्टाः। एवं ये ये गजाः सन्ततभक्षणसन्ततनिद्रादिषु बद्धाशयाः यजमानादिप्रदर्शितकार्याणि कृच्छ्रेण जानतः शृंगारक्रीडादिहीनाः मूढचेतसो मूढकार्याश्च दृश्यन्ते; एते सर्वेऽपि तामसगुणगजा ज्ञेया इति **क्रमार्थः। अत्रोक्तेषु गजेषु सत्त्वगुणयुता एव मातंगाः स्वीकार्याः। न राजसतामसगुणगजा इत्युपदेशः॥**

Description of main character of Elephants

The elephants too have 3 main characters as *Sattva-guṇa*, *Rajoguṇa* and *Tamo-guṇa*, like human beings.

(1) *Sattva-guṇa*-elephants will have always good characters, temper, more beauty and glittering-good-strength in wars, more zeal and interest in work and patience, smartness, energy etc.

(2) *Rajoguṇa*-elephants are lazy and shirking-natured in work, very bad-natured, very passionate, avaricious in eating, not much strong, forgetful of work, training and instructions. They will not work unless they receive instruction and punishment.

(3) *Tamo-guṇa* elephants are very dull natured, very difficult in grasping the instructions and very sleepy. They do not know the enjoyment and pleasure.

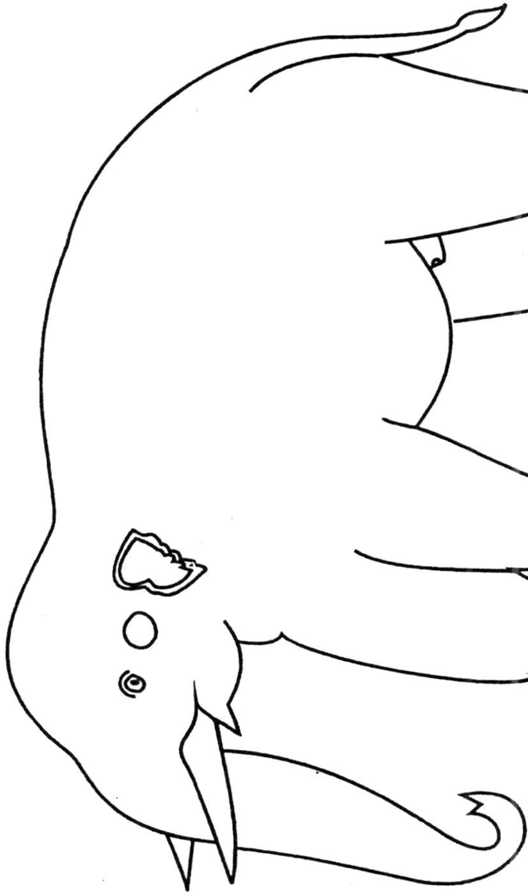

Fig. 120. : सत्त्वगुणगज: उत्तम: Superior elephants

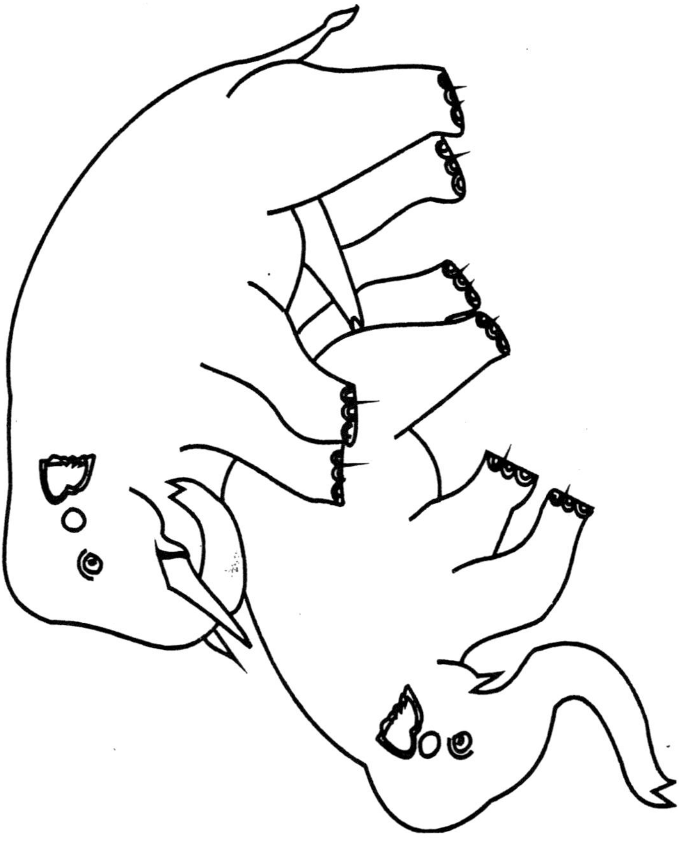

Fig. 121. : रजोगुणगजः अधमः Inferior elephants

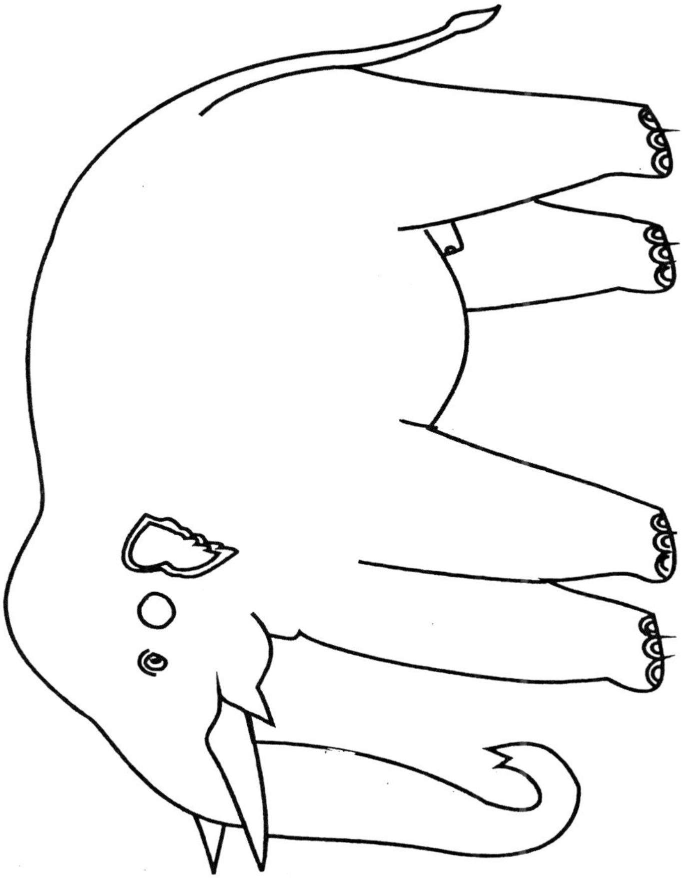

Fig. 122. : तमोगुणगजः अधमः Inferior elephants

देवांगना दर्शनीयास्तथा राक्षसकन्यकाः।
पिशाचानां च याः कन्याः नागकन्यास्तथैव च॥

गन्धर्वयक्षकन्याश्च कामयाना गजोत्तमान्।
वशारूपमुपस्थाय संगता दिग्गजैः पुरा॥

सर्वतः पतितं शुक्लं गर्भं गृह्णन्ति ताः क्वचित्।
प्रसूतिस्तत्क्षणादेव दिग्गजानां महीपते॥

तासां ये गर्भसंभूताः नागा दिव्यांगनोद्भवाः।
देवमानुषगन्धर्वपिशाचोरगराक्षसाः॥

तत्र प्रथमस्य देवसत्त्वगजस्य लक्षणम् (१)

यः कान्तिमान् कुमुदचन्दनसप्तपर्ण-
सारंगपद्मचतुरंगुलतुल्यगन्धः।
फुल्लाननः कलभकौतुकवानजस्त्रं
मानोन्नतः प्रियकरः स तु देवसत्त्वः॥

व्यासप्रोक्ते गजशास्त्रे-

अभिषेकोचितः पूज्यः सर्वकार्यार्थसाधकः।
अव्याहाररतो नित्यं वल्लीरेखाविवर्जितः॥
अनामयः स्थिरः शूरः देवसत्त्वो भवेद्गजः।

व्याख्या–एवंप्रकारेण गजानां गुणत्रयकार्यादिकं प्रतिपाद्याधुना देवमानुषगन्धर्वादिसत्त्वयुतानां गजानां लक्षणं विशदयितुं तत्पूर्ववृत्तं कथयति-देवांगना इत्यादिना। पूर्वं त्रेतायुगे द्वापरयुगे च तत्र तत्र संचरणशीलानां मनोहरांगानां दिग्गजानां स्वरूपलक्षणादिकं निरीक्ष्य तरलितमानसाः तत्संभोगाभिलाषयुक्ताः सत्यः काश्चित् देवांगनाः काश्चित् राक्षसकन्याः काश्चित् पिशाचकन्याः काश्चित् नागकन्याः काश्चित् गन्धर्वकन्याः काश्चित् यक्षकन्याश्च करिणीरूपमवाप्य तत्र तत्र रमणीयप्रदेशेषु तैर्दिग्गजैः साकं संभोगमकुर्वन्। तस्मात्तादृशदिग्गजेन्द्रियप्रभावात् तासां देवकन्यादीनामुदरे जनिताः केचित्

गजाः तत्तदंशसंयुक्ता एवाविर्बभूवुः। ततःप्रभृति तादृशगजवंशजनिताः केचित् गजाः अद्याप्यस्मिन् कलियुगे तत्र तत्र दृश्यन्ते। तस्मात् तेषां देवसत्त्वमानुषसत्त्व-गन्धर्वसत्त्वादिसत्त्वयुतानां गजानां लक्षणादिकमपि निरीक्ष्य तेषु उत्तमसत्त्वयुतानेव वारणान् स्वीकुर्यादित्युपदेशः। तत्राद्यस्य देवसत्त्वगजस्य लक्षणमाह **शास्त्रकारः** कान्तिमानिति। यो यो गजः सर्वेष्वप्यवयवेषु मनोहरस्निग्धकृष्णकान्तिपूरयुक्तः कुमुदस्येव वा चन्दनवृक्षस्येव वा सप्तपर्णवृक्षस्येव वा सारंगमृगस्येव वा पद्मस्येव वा चतुरंगुलपत्रवृक्षस्येव वा गन्धवीजनशीलः प्रसन्नवदनः सन्तुष्टदृष्टिः मानोन्नतः शौर्ययुतश्च दृश्यते; स देवसत्त्वगज इति कीर्त्यते **शास्त्रज्ञैः**। एतादृशगज **उत्तमः**। मूल्याधिक्येनापि क्रेतव्य **इति भावः। व्यासस्तु**-एवं लक्षणोपेतः रोगहीनः पुष्टांगः बलाढ्यश्च यो देवसत्त्वगजो दृश्यते स एव राज्ञामभिषेककाले **सेवनार्हः**। तेषां नित्यसंपन्नित्यमंगलवृद्धिकारीति।।

In ancient times the daughters of Devas, Rākṣasas, Piśācas, Nāgas, Gandharvas and Yakṣas seeing the beautiful divine elephant free roaming, enjoyments independence etc. desired to take their forms and have intercourse with them. Accordingly they took their sex forms and enjoyed happily with them. No sooner had they sexual intercourse with them than the childern elephants according to their mothers were born to them.

(1) Description of Deva-sattva-elephants

The elephants which are very beautiful and shining, very pleasant and happy, very healthy even in their old ages and have always good fragrance like lotus or sandal ever pleasing sight and which work always with zeal and energy are called *Deva-sattva* elephants. They should be ridden over at the time of coronation. They will give all sorts of prosperity, success, long life etc. to their masters.

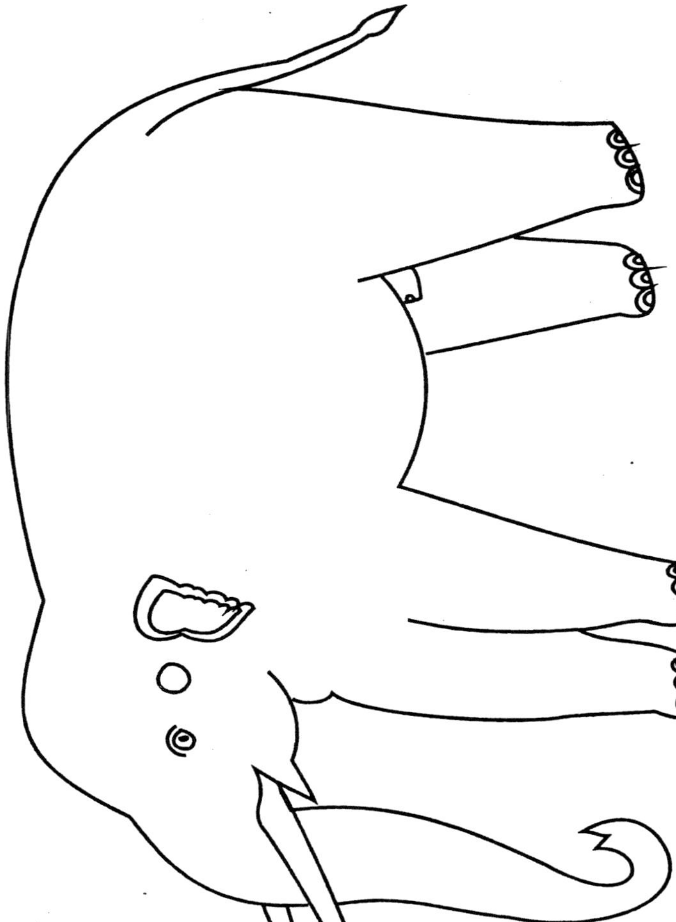

Fig. 123. : देवसत्त्वगजः उत्तमः First class elephants superior

।।अथ-मानुषसत्त्वे ब्राह्मणसत्त्वगजस्य लक्षणम् (२)

विप्रः शुचिर्मधुपयः परमान्नसर्पि-
श्चूतप्रसूनसमगंधसुगंधितांगः।।
सामप्रियः सकलनागहितः सुशान्तः
स्नानप्रियः शुभगतिर्गदितो मुनीन्द्रैः।।

व्यासप्रोक्ते गजशास्त्रे-

जलावगाहनासक्तः कोपनः कातरो भृशम्।
भोजने लंपटो नित्यं कुंजरो विप्रसत्त्वजः।।

व्याख्या–एवं देवसत्त्वगजस्वरूपगुणादिकं संग्रहेण प्रतिपाद्याधुना क्रमप्राप्तमानुषसत्त्वगजलक्षणं विशदयति–विप्र इति। **अत्रैवमान्तरालिक-व्यवस्था ज्ञेया।** यथा–मानुषसत्त्वगजवर्गे केचित् गजाः विप्रसत्त्वाः अन्ये तु वारणाः क्षत्रियसत्त्वा परे तु वैश्यसत्त्वा। इतरे तु शूद्रसत्त्वा इति। तस्मात् तत्राद्यस्य ब्राह्मणसत्त्वगजस्य लक्षणं तावदेवं ज्ञेयम्। यथा–यो यो गजः मधुरक्षीरपरमान्नधृतरसालकुसुमतुल्यगन्धयुक्तः सामवाक्येन लालनशीलः सकलगजहितः सन्ततं शान्तस्वभावः जलावगाहनलोलुपः शुभगतिशुभ-चर्यादियुक्तश्च विलोक्यते; स ब्राह्मणसत्त्वगज इति निर्दिष्टः **पूर्वमुनीन्द्रैरिति पालकाप्यः। व्यासस्तु**-यो यो गजो जलावगाहननिरतः स्वल्पकोपयुतः युद्धादिविषये भीरुः सन्ततभक्षणे बद्धाशयो विलोक्यते; स एव विप्रसत्त्वगज इति।।

(2) *Mānuṣa-sattva* elephants are divided into 4 classes as Brāhmaṇas, Kṣatriyas, Vaiśyas and Śūdras. Brāhmaṇa-sattva-elephants are always very pure and clean and have a good odour like honey, milk, ghee, good-mangoes etc. They easily grasp the good and sweet words. They are not in any way hindrance to other elephants. But very friendly, amusing, very calm in temper, anxious of ever bathing in water and have good nature. Vyāsa says that they will suddenly lose temper (hot tempered). But very cowardice in works and wars and very avaricious always in eating as Brāhmaṇas.

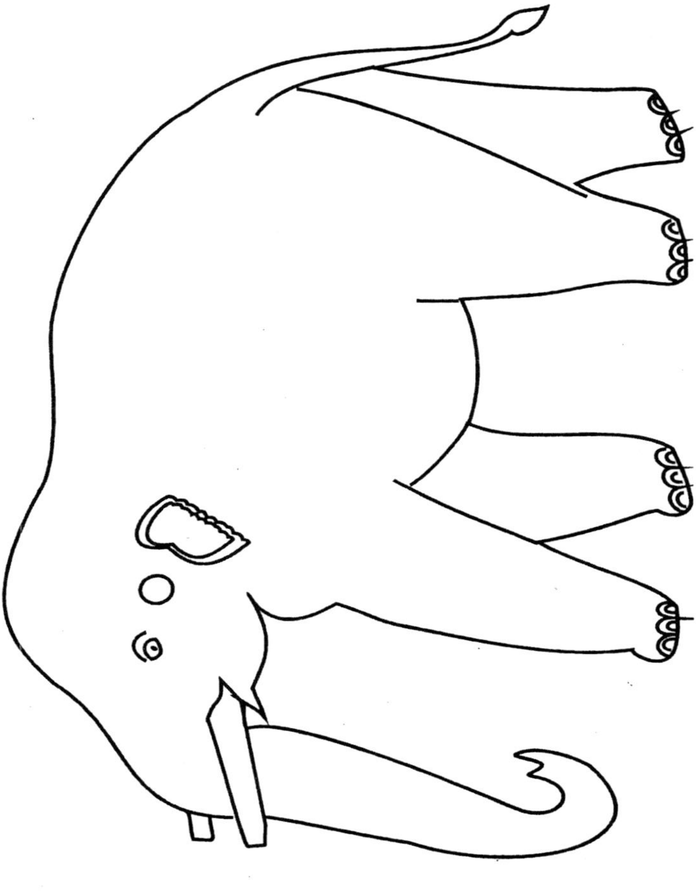

Fig. 124. : : ब्राह्मणसत्त्वगजः उत्तमः Superior elephants

॥अथ-मानुषसत्त्वे क्षत्रियसत्त्वगजस्य लक्षणम् (३)॥

यश्चन्दनाब्जहरितालमनःशिलानां
गन्धैः समो विमलगुग्गुलुकस्य वापि।
सन्नाहकर्मकुशलो युधि निर्भयश्च
स क्षत्रियो विविधशस्त्रनिपातधीरः॥

व्यासप्रोक्ते गजशास्त्रे-

शान्तः शूरः सदोत्साही बली युद्धविशारदः।
अभीरुराहवे धीरः कुंजरः क्षत्रसत्त्वजः॥

व्याख्या–अथ क्रमप्राप्तस्य तृतीयस्य, (द्वितीयस्य) क्षत्रियसत्त्वगजस्य लक्षणमाह–य इति। यो यो गजः चन्दनस्येव वा कमलस्येव वा हरितालस्येव वा मनःशिलाया इव वा गुग्गुलुधूपस्येव वा मनोहरगन्धयुतः मुखपट-कंबलाद्यलंकारः भयरहितो युद्धोत्सुकः शस्त्रपातादिजनितव्रणवेदनां तुच्छी-कुर्वंश्च दृश्यते; स क्षत्रियसत्त्वगज इति **पालकाप्यः**। **व्यासस्तु**-यो यो गजः शौर्यवानपि शान्तस्वभावः मृगयादिकार्यं प्रत्युत्साहवान् युद्धे धीरो भयहीनश्च दृश्यते; स क्षत्रियसत्त्वगज इति॥

(3) *Kṣatriya-sattva*-elephants will have good odour like sandal, luxurious, very bold, very willing for works and war, very reckless of wounds etc. Vyāsa says that though they are very bold and strong, they will be calm, very anxious and courageous in war and hunting.

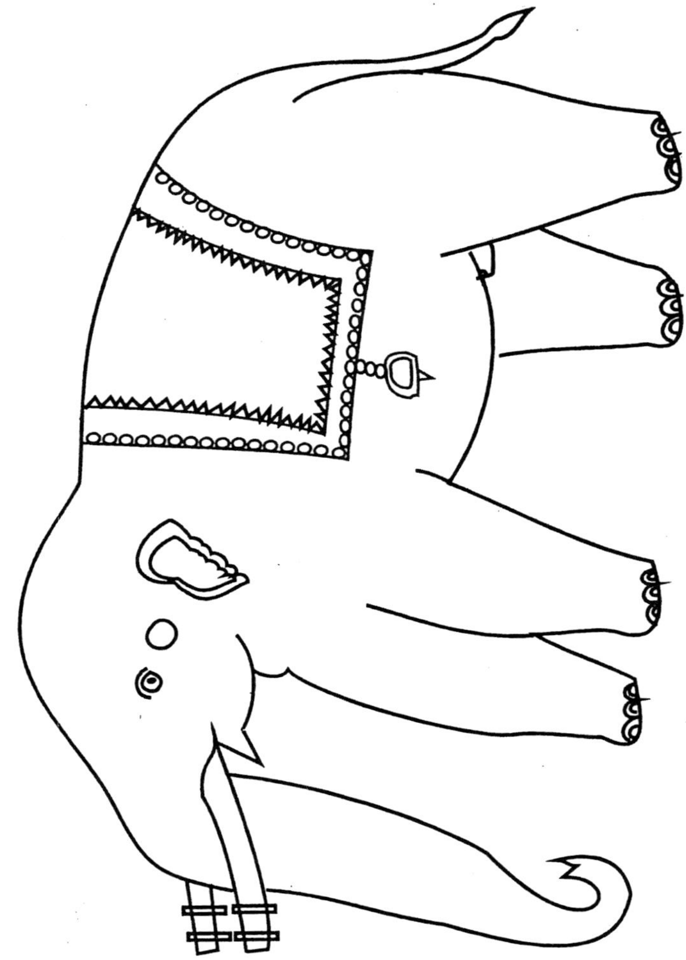

Fig. 125. : क्षत्रियसत्त्वगजः उत्तमः Best elephants

॥अथ-मानुषसत्त्वे वैश्यसत्त्वगजस्य लक्षणम् (४)॥

बन्धूकशालितिलकेतकमालतीनां
गन्धेन यस्तु समलंकृततालुजिह्वः।
क्लेशक्षमः पिशितभुक् प्रियसान्त्वनश्च
क्रुद्धोऽपि तूर्णमुपशाम्यति वैश्यसत्त्वः॥

व्यासप्रोक्ते गजशास्त्रे-

कपटो दुष्टचेष्टश्च कुशलो विकलस्वरः।
भीरुराहवकाले च कुंजरो वैश्यसत्त्वजः॥

व्याख्या-अथ चतुर्थस्य, तृतीयस्य वैश्यसत्त्वगजस्य लक्षणमाह-बन्धूकेति। यो यो गजः बन्धूककुसुमस्येव वा शालिमंजर्या इव केतककुसुमस्येव वा शुभगन्धवीजनशीलः मनोहरावयवः गमनागमनादिविविधक्लेशसहनशीलः मांसभोजनलोलुपः प्रियवाक्यश्रवणरतः क्रुद्धोऽपि तत्क्षणादेव तच्छान्तियुतश्च दृश्यते; स वैश्यसत्त्वगज इति **पालकाप्यः। व्यासस्तु**-यो यो गजः कपटस्वभावः दुष्टकार्यनिरतोऽपि समर्थो विकलस्वरः समरादिषु भीरुश्च विलोक्यते; स वैश्यसत्त्वगज इति॥

Vaiśya-sattva elephants will have good smell like paddy, *ginglly* crops and Mālatī flowers. They are very patient and they can endure any amount of sun's heat and cold. They are eager to eat mutton and flesh, drunkards and very willing to hear good instructions though in anger. Vyāsa says that they are always very selfish, cunning, always inclined to do mischievous and wicked deeds, very capable in work and have a peculiar cry. They are cowards in war and hunting.

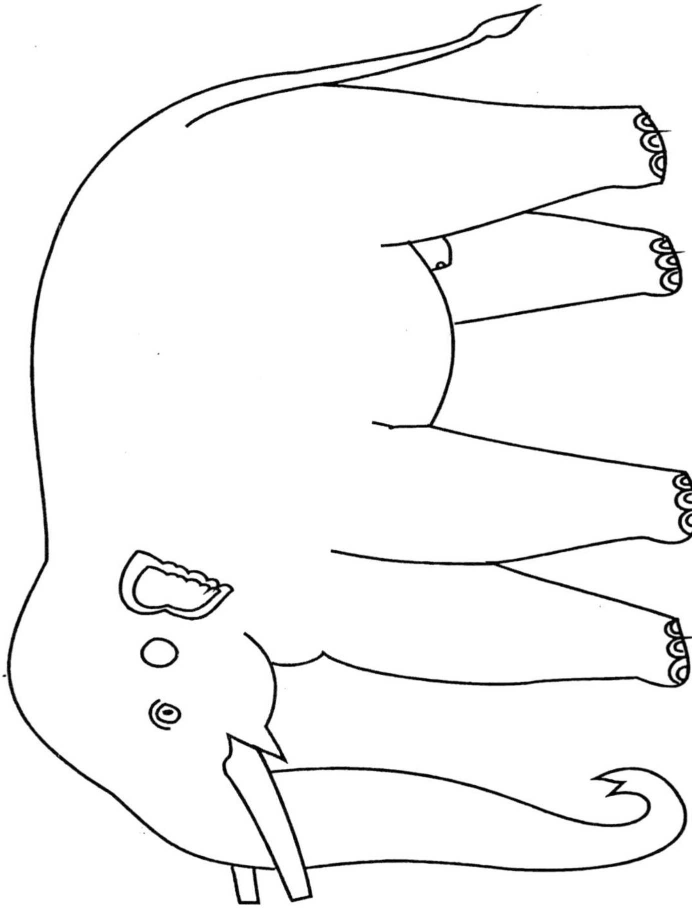

Fig. 126. : वैश्यसत्त्वगजः उत्तमः Superior elephants

॥अथ मानुषसत्त्वे शूद्रसत्त्वगजस्य लक्षणम् (५)॥

उच्छिष्टहृष्टः सहसैव भीरुः शुष्कान्नभोजी सकुलीरगन्धः।
क्रुद्धो भवेद्यः कृपणः कृतघ्नः सत्त्वेन शूद्रः स गजाधमश्च॥

व्यासप्रोक्ते गजशास्त्रे-

दण्डसाध्यस्तथा नीचो मूर्खश्च मलिनाशनः।
आहवानिरतोऽशूरः शूद्रसत्त्वो भवेद्गजः॥

व्याख्या–अथ पंचमस्य (चतुर्थस्य) शूद्रसत्त्वगजस्य लक्षणमाह–उच्छिष्टहृष्ट इति। यो यो गजो मानवभुक्तोच्छिष्टद्रव्यभक्षणनिरतः सततं भीरुः निःसारतृणकाष्ठादिभोजी कर्कटतुल्यगन्धः कृपणः कोपशीलः कृतघ्नश्च विलोक्यते, स शूद्रसत्त्वगज इति **पालकाप्यः। व्यासस्तु**-यो यो गजः दण्डसाध्यः सान्त्ववाक्यपराङ्मुखः नीचस्वभावः नीचकार्यनिरतः मूर्खः कुत्सितद्रव्यभोजी आहवादिभीरुश्च दृश्यते; स शूद्रसत्त्वगज इति॥

(5) They will eat the remnant and useless things of human-beings. They are very cowards. They will eat the dry-branches, twigs etc. They have a bad smell like big black scorpions, and ungrateful. Vyāsa says that all kinds of works should be extracted from them by giving them punishment. They are very mean. They are quite unfit for war and hunting as they are foolish and dull. *These elephants are bad ones and should not be purchased*. They are unfit for hard work. But fit for carrying heavy loads.

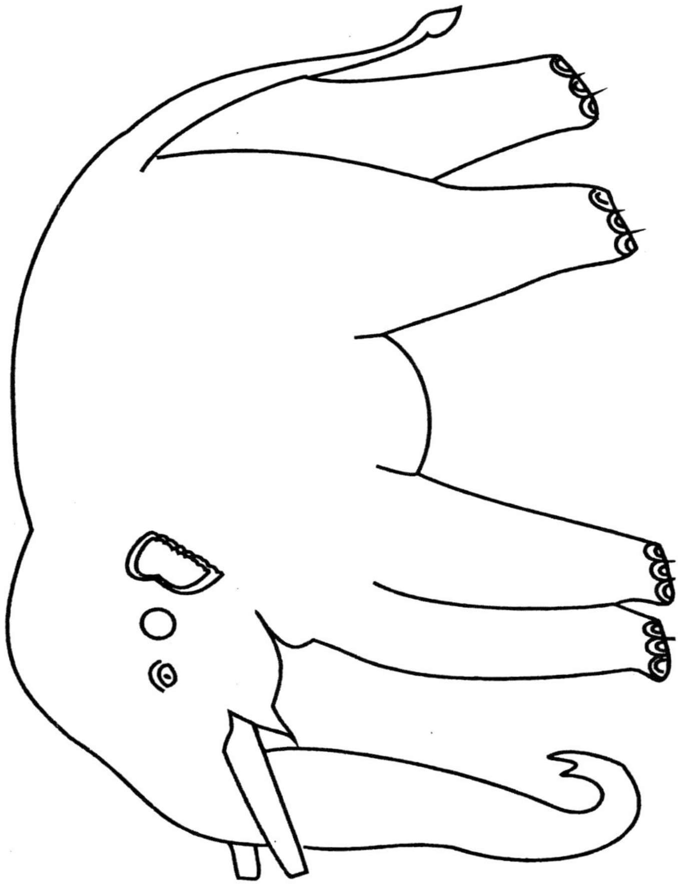

Fig. 127. : शूद्रसत्त्वगजः अधमः Inferior elephants

॥अथ गन्धर्वसत्त्वगजस्य लक्षणम् (६)॥

गन्धर्वमाहुरतिमुक्तकयूथिकाब्जपुन्नागनागदलचन्दनतुल्यगन्धः।
नादप्रियः शुभगतिः शुभदन्तनेत्रकुंभोत्तमांगकरपुष्करबाहुसन्धिः॥

व्यासप्रोक्ते गजशास्त्रे-

मेधावी च क्रियादक्षः कामुकश्चपलः पटुः।
स्तंभप्रेक्षणकः शस्तो गजो गन्धर्वसत्त्वजः॥

व्याख्या—एवमत्रोक्ताः देवसत्त्वगजाः ब्राह्मणसत्त्वगजाः क्षत्रियसत्त्वगजाश्च **उत्तमाः**। वैश्यसत्त्वगजास्तु **मध्यमाः**। शूद्रसत्त्वगजास्त्व**धमाः न स्वीकार्या** इत्युपदिश्याधुना क्रमप्राप्तस्य षष्ठस्य गंधर्वसत्त्वगजस्य लक्षणमाह–गन्धर्वमिति। ये ये गजाः अतिमुक्तकुसुमस्येव वा वनमल्लीकुसुमस्येव वा कमलस्येव वा पुन्नागकुसुमस्येव वा नागकुसुमस्येव आर्द्रचन्दनस्येव वा मनोहरगन्धवीजनयुताः संगीतभेर्यादिशुभवाद्यश्रवणलालसाः शुभगतयः शुभनेत्रशुभदन्तादिनोपेताश्च भवन्ति; ते सर्वेऽपि गन्धर्वसत्त्वगजा इति **पालकाप्यः**। **व्यासस्तु**–ये ये वारणाः नितरां मेधाविनः विविधकार्येषु दक्षाः कामाधिक्यवन्तश्चपलस्वभावाः समरकाले स्वस्थान एव स्थातुमभिलाषयुक्ता भवन्ति; ते सर्वे गन्धर्वसत्त्वगजा निर्दिष्टाः। इमेऽपि गजाः **श्रेष्ठाः**। **क्रेतव्या इत्युपदेशः॥**

(6) They are very fond of music. They have the smell of Punnāga-trees, lotus, sandal etc. Their mode of walk is very nice and beautiful. They are very intelligent and will never fail in any work. But a little lazy. They are passionate. They are fit for any good work.

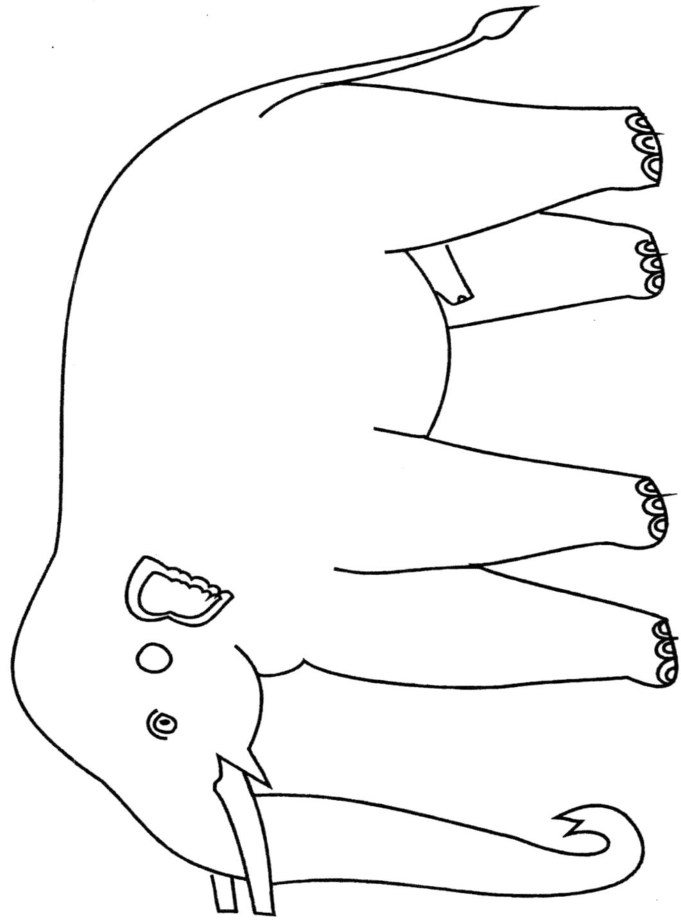

Fig. 128. : गन्धर्वसत्त्वगजः उत्तमः Superior class elephants

॥अथ-पिशाचसत्त्वगजस्य लक्षणम् (७)॥

शून्यप्रियः कुणपदेहसमानगन्धी
भ्रान्तो निशासु विचरन् घननिस्वनश्च।
यः सर्वदैव परिकुप्यति यश्च मूढः
तं सूरयो गजमुशन्ति पिशाचसत्त्वम्॥

व्यासप्रोक्ते गजशास्त्रे-

राजसः पित्तभूयिष्ठः पित्तलः स्तब्धविग्रहः।
उन्मार्गेण सदा भाति विवेकरहितो भृशम्॥
उन्मत्त इव चेष्टायां द्विपः पैशाचसत्त्वजः।

व्याख्या—एवं शुभसत्त्वगजलक्षणं प्रतिपाद्याधुना दुष्टसत्त्वगजलक्षणमाह-शून्यप्रिय इति। तत्र पिशाचभुजंगराक्षससत्त्वयुक्ताः **गजाः** सर्वधा **दूरतस्त्याज्या** इति व्यवस्थां मनसि कृत्वा तत्र प्रथमतः पिशाचसत्त्वगजस्य लक्षणं विशदयति-शून्यप्रिय इति। ये ये गजाः पिशाचा इव शून्यस्थले निवासपराः विकृतशरीराः कुणपशरीरगन्धवत् दुर्गन्धिवीजनयुताः भ्रान्तस्वभावाः निशायामेव संचारलालसाः भयंकररींकारयुताः सन्ततं कोपयुक्ताः मूढात्मानश्च विलोक्यन्ते, ते सर्वेऽपि पिशाचसत्त्वगजा इति **पालकाप्यः। व्यासस्तु**-ये ये गजाः राजसगुणयुताः पित्तशरीराः पित्तस्तंभितदेहाः उन्मार्गगामिनः विवेकहीनाः उन्मत्ता इव चेष्टां कुर्वन्ति; ते पिशाचसत्त्वगजा इति॥

(7) They resemble Piśācas in above characters etc. They like to remain in secluded places. They have the smell of crops. They roam about always in night and they will have terrible cry. They are very foolish, very bad and hot tempered, very wicked and mischievous. They are useless for any good work. *They should not at all be purchased.*

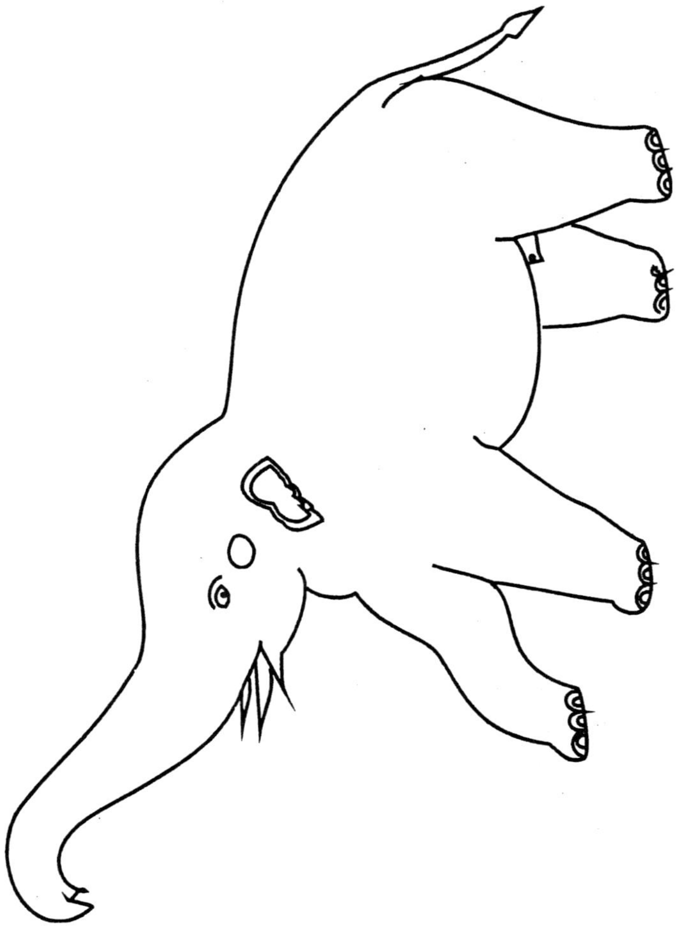

Fig. 129. : पिशाचसत्त्वगजः अधमः Inferior elephants

॥अथ-सर्पसत्त्वगजस्य लक्षणम् (८)॥

यो भूतिशैवलफणिर्ज्जककर्दमानां
गन्धैः सुरापिशितयोरपि तुल्यगन्धः।
त्रस्तो भवेज्जलदशब्दमपि ब्रुवाणः
क्रुद्धोऽनिशं सजलपांसुरतो भुजंगः॥

व्यासप्रोक्ते गजशास्त्रे-

विश्वासघातकः क्रूरः गमने कुटिलक्रमः।
न भुंक्ते च मदेऽत्यर्थं सर्पसत्त्वः करी मतः॥

व्याख्या–अथाष्टमस्य भुजंगसत्त्वगजस्य लक्षणमाह–य इति। ये ये गजाः भस्मशैवलनागवल्लीसुरामांसकर्दमानामिव गन्धयुताः सततं भीरवः मेघगर्जनश्रवणभयसहिताः क्रूराः क्रुद्धाश्च विलोक्यन्ते, ते ते गजाः भुजगसत्त्वाः कीर्त्यन्त इति **पालकाप्यः। व्यासस्तु**–यजमानहस्तिपपोषकादिषु विश्वासहीनाः क्रूरचेष्टाः कुटिलगमनाः मदप्रादुर्भावसमये भुक्तिविमुखाश्च ये ये गजा विलोक्यन्ते, ते नागसत्त्वा इति॥

(8) They have the bad smell of sponze, toddy, mud and flesh. They will be always producing sounds like serpents and they are hot tempered. They will very suddenly cut down friendship. They will always walk in streets in curved way like serpents. They will never eat food at the time of rut. They are unfit for any work. *They should not be purchased.*

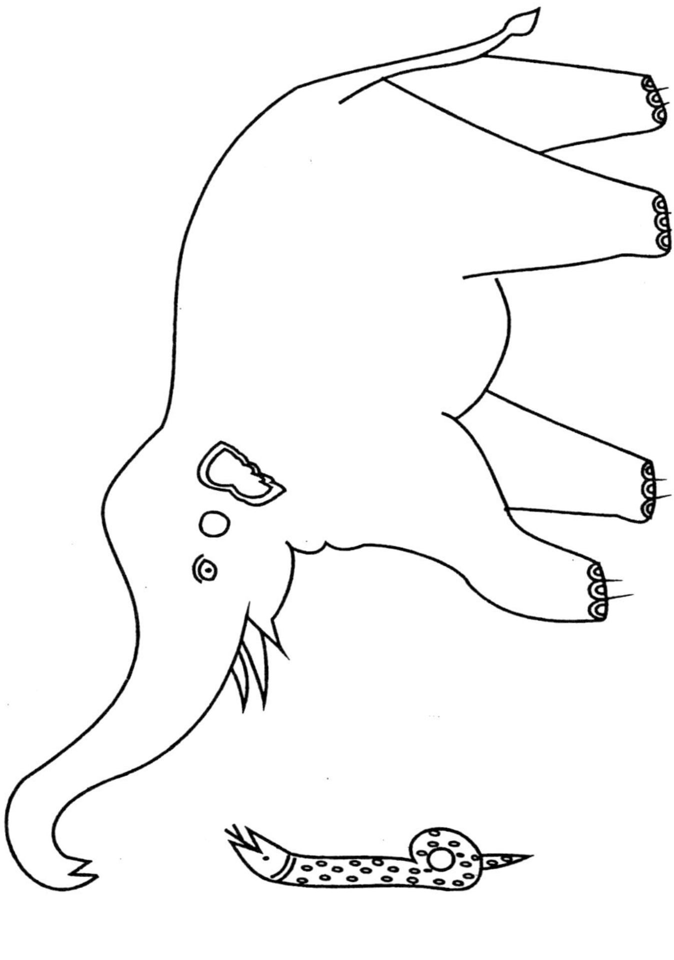

Fig. 130. : सर्पसत्त्वगजः अधमः Inferior elephants

॥अथ-राक्षससत्त्वगजस्य लक्षणम् (९)॥

यः काकवानरखरोष्ट्रबिडालमूत्र-
विट्पूतिग[न्धम]निशं भृशदारुणश्च।
इष्टान्नमांसरुधिरोऽविनयी कृतघ्नः
सत्त्वेन राक्षस इति प्रतिकूलकारी॥

व्यासप्रोक्ते गजशास्त्रे-

निशायां चरति स्वैरं मनुष्याणां वधे रतः।
वेगवान् बलवान् हस्ती रक्षःसत्त्वसमुद्भवः॥
एतौ द्वौ तामसौ सत्त्वौ तामसौ वातुलौ भृशम्।
सवातो दृश्यते रक्षः निद्रालुश्चपलो गजः॥
देवगन्धर्वसत्त्वः स्यात् शुभो राजाधिरोहणे।
सान्नाह्यः क्षत्रियो नागः वैश्यस्त्वारोग्यकर्मसु॥
परिक्लेशसहः प्रोक्तः शूद्रो भाण्डादिवाहने।
पिशाचराक्षसाः स्कन्धघातार्थं सन्धिकर्मसु॥

व्याख्या—अथ क्रमप्राप्तस्य नवमस्य राक्षससत्त्वगजस्य लक्षणमाह-य इति। काकवानरखरोष्ट्रबिडालानां मूत्रगन्धसदृशगन्धयुताः नितरां दारुणस्वभावाः रक्तमांसादिभक्षणलोलुपाः विनयादिसद्गुणदूरगाः कृतघ्नाश्च ये ये गजा दृश्यन्ते; ते राक्षससत्त्वगजा इति **पालकाप्यः। व्यासस्तु**—ये ये गजाः निशासंचारशीलाः मानुषवधे निरताः अत्यन्तं वेगगत्यः राक्षसा इव विकृतशरीराश्च दृश्यन्ते; ते राक्षससत्त्वगजा इति। किं च पूर्वोक्तभुजगसत्त्व-गजः अयं च राक्षससत्त्वगजः तामसगुणपूर्णौ चपलस्वभावौ निद्राप्रियौ च। **तस्मादेतौ न क्रेतव्यावित्युपदेशः।** अपि च-एवंरीत्या अत्रोक्तानां नवविधसत्त्वभाजां गजानां कार्यमाह देवगन्धर्वेति। देवसत्त्वगजा गन्धर्वसत्त्व-गजाश्च राज्ञां पट्टाभिषेकादिशुभसमयेषु आरोहणार्हौ। तेषां मंगलदायिनः **इति भावः।** क्षत्रियसत्त्वगजास्तु प्रासादद्वारशालाद्यलंकरणार्थं नियोक्तव्याः। वैश्यसत्त्वगजास्तु केवलवाहनयोग्या एव। शूद्रसत्त्वगजाश्च भारवहनाय नियो-क्तव्याः। पिशाचसत्त्वगजाः राक्षससत्त्वगजाश्च शत्रुसेनाभंजनाय प्रेष्या **इति व्यवस्था।**

(9) They have the bad smell of cat, crow, monkey and donkey and the smell of their dungs. They are very fond of eating flesh and drinking blood like Rākṣasas. They are very indifferent and ungrateful. They roam about always in nights. They are fond of killing human beings. They are very swift and strong. They are unfit for any work. *They should not at all be purchased.*

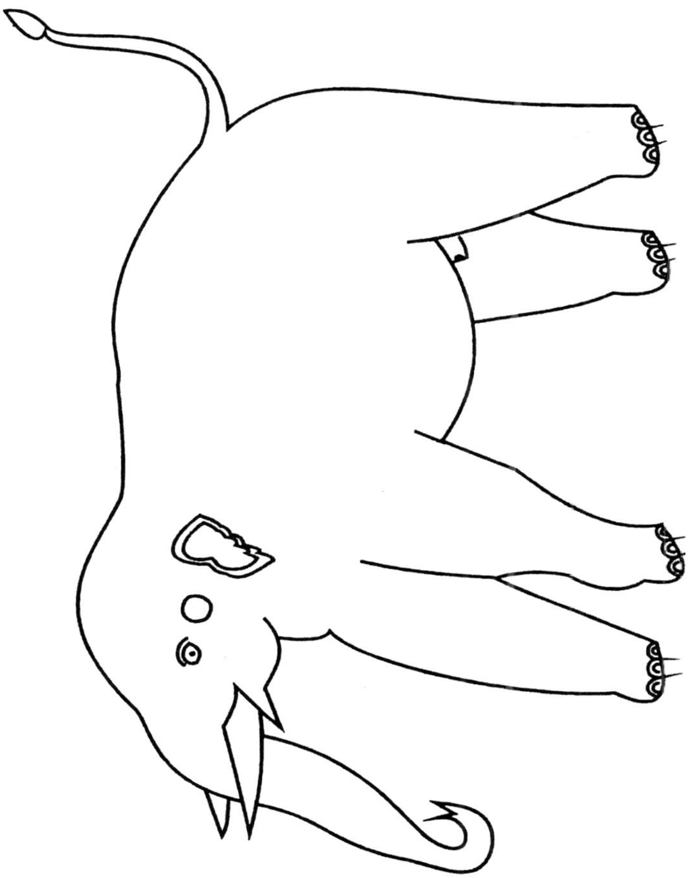

Fig. 131. : राक्षससत्त्वगजः अधमः Inferior elephants

॥अथ गजनेत्रवर्णलक्षणम्॥

मधुनो घृतपिण्डस्य गोमेदकमणेस्तथा।
आदित्यस्यानलस्यापि सवर्णे यस्य चक्षुषी॥
स एव वारणो राजन् समरेषु जयावहः।

॥अथ-गजस्वरलक्षणम्॥

शंखमेघकलहंसदुन्दुभिव्याघ्रसिंहवृक्षसन्निभस्वराः।
पूजिताः करिवरस्य.........
....॥

इतःप्रभृति मातृकायां मूलमात्रमेव दृश्यते। न तु व्याख्या।

गण्डतालुशिरः कण्ठजिह्वाहस्तोदरश्रुतेः।
जनितो ब्रह्मिताख्यः स्यात् तालुजश्च विशेषतः॥

गर्जितं गलजं विद्यात् शंखस्वरसमं तथा।
मेघनादसमं प्राहुः रवं च हृदि संस्थितम्॥

हंसदुन्दुभितुल्यः स्यात् जिह्वाकर्णसमुत्थितः।
उत्क्रोशं गण्डजं विद्यात् व्याघ्रस्वरसमं तथा॥

निनदं हस्तिशिरसो मृगेन्द्रवृषसंमितम्।
एतत्स्थानसमुत्थाः शब्दा ये चात्र वारणेन्द्राणाम्॥

एवं ब्रह्मितसंज्ञाः शुभावहा मानवेन्द्राणाम्।
ब्रह्मितगर्जितफेनायितमिति शब्दस्त्रिधैव नागानाम्॥
ब्रह्मितमिह तालूत्थं कण्ठप्रभवं तु गर्जितं विद्यात्॥

जिह्वामूलसमुत्थं फेनायितमित्यभिख्यातम्।
शुककाकवन्यजंबुकक्रोडवानररवाः न शोभनाः॥

॥अथ शुभस्वरविशिष्टगजलक्षणम्॥

हस्तेन मृदंगरवं कर्णाभ्यां दुन्दुभिस्वनं चैव।
दर्दुरनिनदं मुखतः करोति यः पूजितः स गजः॥

इति पालकाप्यमहर्षिप्रणीते गजशास्त्रे चतुर्दशकं प्रकरणम्॥

पंचदशकं प्रकरणम्

॥अथ गजगतिलक्षणनिरूपणम्॥

तत्र शुभगतिलक्षणं यथा-

मल्लसिंहशुकव्याघ्रशार्दूलवृषसन्निभा।
समासना समपदा समदेहा गतिः शुभा॥

समा च लघुपादा च वेगेऽप्यम्लानकारिणी।
शुभलक्षणयुक्तस्य हयस्य करिणोऽपि वा॥

मत्तस्य मुदितस्यापि गतिस्तुल्या शुभा मता।

॥अथ-अशुभगतिलक्षणम्॥

वृकस्य कृकलासस्य खरस्य नकुलस्य च।
समा गतिर्दन्तिनो या सा दुष्टेति मता बुधैः॥

पृष्ठवालादिगात्रेषु विषमा विकटासना।
वेगेऽपि मन्दसंचारा विशेषान्दोलितासना।
गतिर्विगर्हिता प्रोक्ता करिणां शास्त्रचिन्तकैः।

व्यासप्रोक्ते गजशास्त्रे-

वल्मीकस्थाणुगुल्मक्षपतरुमनस्येच्छया दत्तदृष्टिः
यायाद्गात्रानुलोमत्वरितगतिपरो वक्त्रमुन्नम्य चोच्चैः।

कक्ष्यासन्नाहकाले जनयति च मुहुः कंपनं बृंहितं वा
तत्काले वामदन्तं जयकृदथ रदं वेष्टयन् दक्षिणं वा॥

इति पालकाप्यमहर्षिप्रणीते गजशास्त्रे पंचदशप्रकरणम्॥

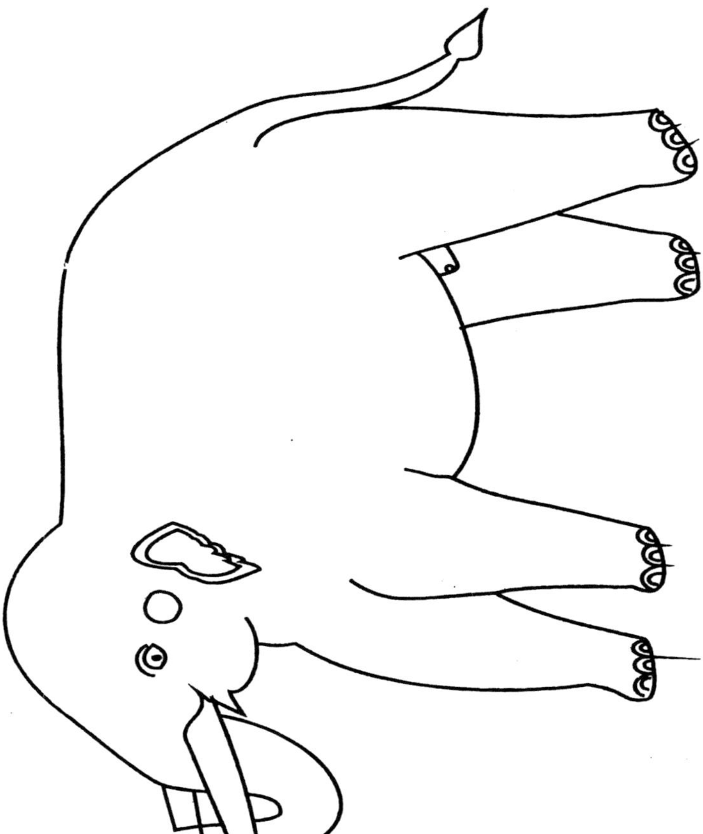

Fig.132. : कक्ष्यासन्नाहसमये दक्षिणदन्तवेष्टनकृद् गजः उत्तमः, Best elephants

।।अथ षोडशमावर्तलक्षणप्रकरणम्।।

अथावर्तान् प्रवक्ष्यामि यथावदनुपूर्वशः।
सर्वकालफलाः सर्वे प्रशस्तांश्च निबोध मे।।

तत्र शुभावर्तस्थानानि-

पिंगूषे पुष्करे चैव वक्षस्युभयपक्षयोः।
तथांसफलके चैव तथा रन्ध्रोपरन्ध्रयोः।।

भुजयोः कक्षयोश्चापि वालवृन्ते तथैव च।
फाले लांगूलवंशे च मण्डूक्ये वक्त्रसंस्थिते।।

आवर्ताः सुप्रशस्ता वै क्षेमारोग्यजयावहाः।
सर्वकामफला ह्येते तेषामाकृतयस्त्विमाः।।

अथ-शुभावर्तस्वरूपाणि-

शंखाब्जकुंभमत्स्याभैः वर्धमाननिभैस्तथा।
प्राकारादर्शवृषभदीपप्रासादतोरणैः।।

वेदीयूपनिभैश्चैव शक्तिपट्टशसन्निभैः।
शरासचामराकारैः अंकुशछत्रसन्निभैः।।

तनुभिर्बिन्दुभिर्भव्यवलिभिः सद्विवर्तनैः।
वलीनां संगमाद्वापि लक्षयेदाकृतीर्बुधः।।

दक्षिणे दक्षिणावर्तो हस्तिनो यस्य दृश्यते।
विशेषाच्छुभदः प्रोक्तः इतरेऽशुभदायिनः।।

हस्तिनो यस्य दृश्येत वामावर्तस्तु वामके।

विशेषाच्छुभदः प्रोक्तः इतरेऽशुभदायिनः।।

अथ-अशुभावर्तस्थानानि-

गात्रापरे कटे गण्डे गले हृदि हनौ तथा।
तथा मेढ्रे तथा कुक्षे प्रोथभागे नखेषु च।।

अण्डपाते च वृषणे जंघातत्परपेचके।
कुष्ठीवतोश्च विज्ञेयो द्व्यंगुलौ मस्तके तथा।।

वाहित्थे प्रतिमाने च कृष्णान्ते च निगालके।
आवर्तास्त्वप्रशस्ताः स्युः कुलकोशक्षयावहाः।।

।।अथ-अंगदोषाशुभावर्तापवादः।।

यस्यांगुलिः प्रशस्ता वै हस्तदोषनिवारणे।
दन्तस्थान् हस्तिनो हस्तः दन्तौ च मुखजान् पुनः।।

मुखं च नेत्रयोर्दोषान् नेत्रं तु मुखजांस्तथा।
नखाः स्फिग्गतदोषांश्च स्फिजावूर्वोपरि स्थितान्।।

अपरो वालजांश्चैव वालधिः केशसंस्थितान्।
कोशो निहन्ति निर्दोषः सर्वांगोपांगसंस्थितान्।।

यस्यांगुलिः प्रशस्ता वै हस्त्यलक्षणवानपि।
स बाह्यस्थैस्तथान्तःस्थैः दोषैर्न प्रतिहन्यते।।

दन्तदोषस्तु यस्यैष मुखजं हन्ति लक्षणम्।

इति पालकाप्यमहर्षिप्रणीते गजशास्त्रे षोडशकं प्रकरणम्।

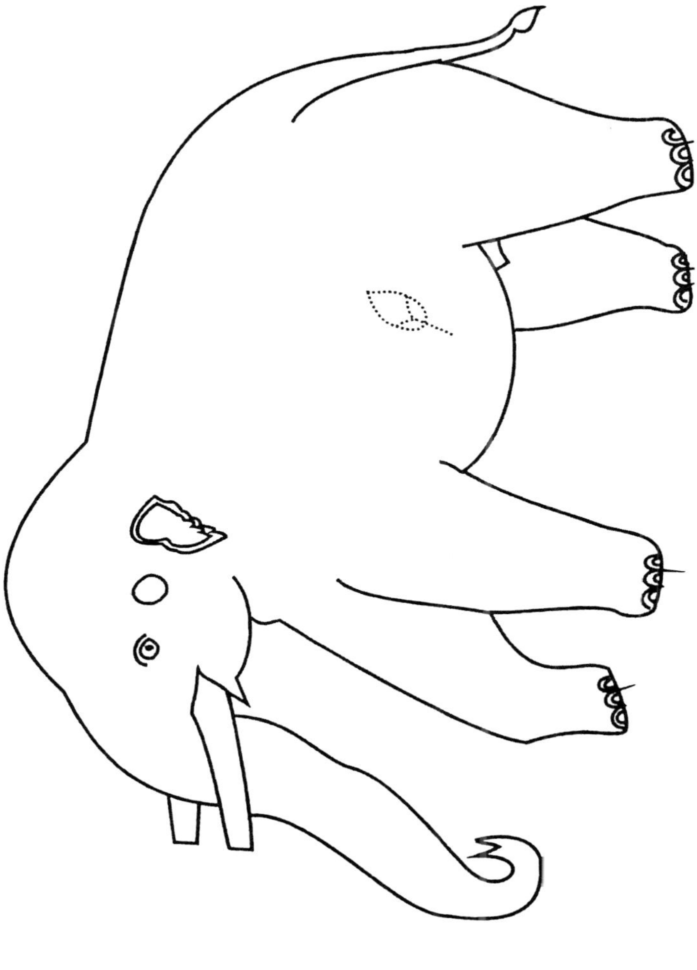

Fig.133. : उदरभागे पद्माकारावर्तयुत गजः, उत्तमः Best elephants

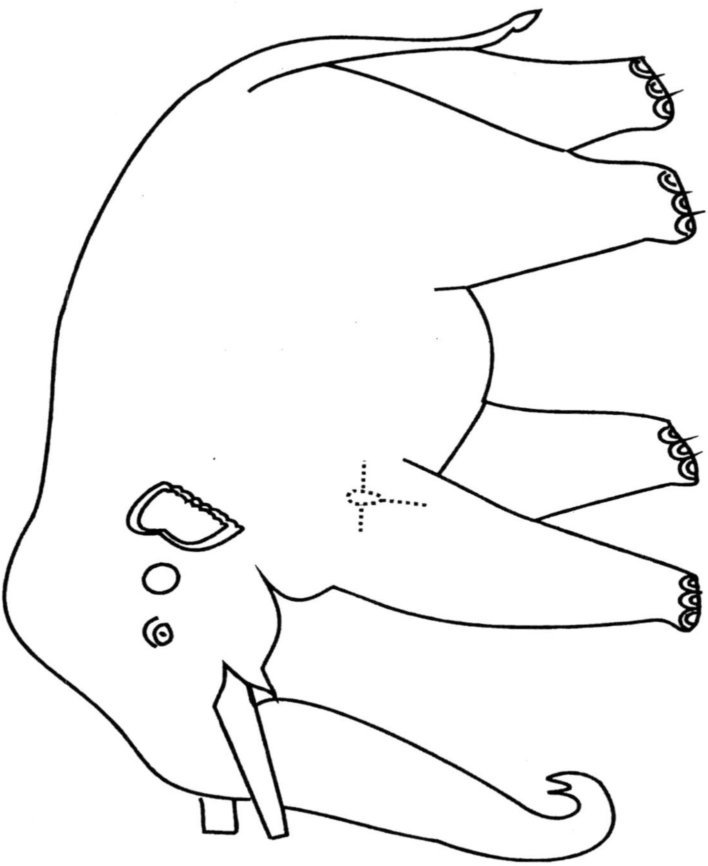

Fig.134. : अंगदस्थाने छत्राकारावर्तयुतः गजः, उत्तमः Best elephants

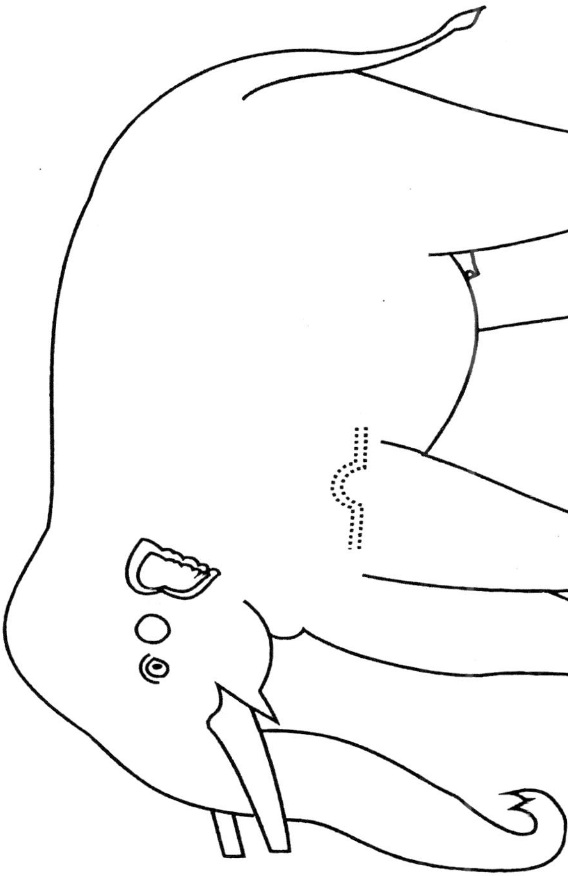

Fig.135. : अंगदस्थाने डोलाकारावर्तयुतः गजः, उत्तमः Best elephants

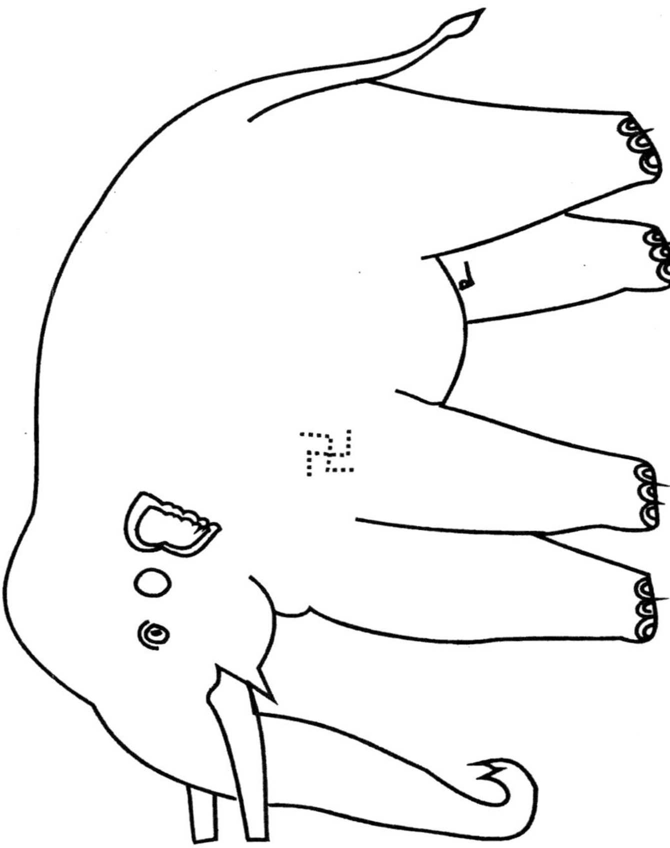

Fig.136. : अंगदस्थाने स्वस्तिकाकारावर्तयुतः गजः, उत्तमः Best elephants

सप्तदशकं प्रकरणम्

।।अथ गजमहादोषनिरूपणम्।।

त्रिदन्ता अधिकांगाश्च समुष्का ये च निस्पृहाः।
अधिपादाश्च ये नागाः गर्भिणीव सदोदकाः।।

पूतनामातृकश्चैव मायिको मत्कुणस्तथा।
गात्राभ्यामपराभ्यां च कटाभ्यामपि वारणः।।

तयोरेकेन वा हीनः व्यालहस्ती तथैव च।
वालदण्डेन कोशेन हस्तेनांगुलिना तथा।।

श्रोत्रान्तरेण नाभ्या च नासया च मतंगजः।
अधिकोऽप्यथवा हीनः मूकश्च बधिरस्तथा।।

छायाहीनश्च कुब्जश्च पैशाचश्च मतंगजः।
भुजाप्रविष्टरोमा च कचव्याप्तशरीरकः।।
विषमैर्लोमभिर्युक्तः राजानं हन्ति वारणः।।

यस्यास्ति ये निर्विकृताः केशाश्चासनशोभनाः।
अन्ये च दारुणफलाः महादोषाः प्रकीर्तिताः।।

इति पालकाप्यमहर्षिप्रणीते गजशास्त्रे सप्तदशप्रकरणम्-

१. त्रिदन्ता गजाः — दन्तत्रययुता गजाः **अधमाधमाः**। महादोषवन्तः कीर्त्याः। एतादृशमहादोषयुक्ता गजाः **न क्रेतव्याः वर्ज्या इत्युपदेशः**। एवमुत्तरत्रापि योज्यम्।।

२. अधिकांगा गजाः — प्रमाणाधिक्ययुतावयवोपेता गजाश्च **अधमाधमा** इत्यर्थः।

३. समुष्का गजाः — स्पष्टं बहिर्दृश्यमुष्कयुता गजाश्च **अधमाधमाः**।

४. निस्पृहा गजा:	करिणीं निरीक्ष्यापि कामेच्छारहिता गजाश्च अधमाधमा:।
५. अधिपादा गजा:	पंचमपादसहिता गजाश्च अधमाधमा:।
६. सदोदका गजा:	पुष्कराग्रभागात् मेहनाच्च सततं जलस्रावयुता गजाश्चा अधमाधमा:।
७. पूतनामातृकगजा:	यजमानं गजान्तरं प्रति वा सततं दुर्बुद्धियुता गजाश्च अधमाधमा:।
८. मायिकगजा:	कपटस्वरूपयुता गजाश्च अधमाधमा:।
९. मत्कुणगजा:	यजमानकृतपूर्वशिक्षावैरादिस्मरणभाज: अत एवाकाले तद्वधाय कृतोद्यमा गजाश्च अधमाधमा:।
१०. पूर्वगात्रहीना गजा:	पूर्वभागशरीरे किंचित्प्रमाणन्यूनावयवोपेता गजाश्च अधमाधमा:।
११. अपरगात्रहीना गजा:	पश्चाद्भागशरीरे किंचित्प्रमाणन्यूनावयवोपेता गजाश्च अधमाधमा:।
१२. कटहीना गजा:	क्षुद्रगण्डस्थलयुता गजाश्च अधमाधमा:।
१३. कटाधिकगजा:	अत्यन्तं विशालगण्डस्थलोपेता गजाश्च अधमा-धमा:।
१४. व्यालगजा:	क्रूरमुखयुता गजाश्च अधमाधमा:।
१५. वालदण्डाधिकगजा:	धेनोरिवात्यन्तं दीर्घेण वालदण्डेनोपेता गजाश्च अधमाधमा:।
१६. वालदण्डहीनगजा:	नितरां ह्रस्वेन वालदण्डेनोपेता गजाश्च अधमा-धमा:।
१७. कोशाधिकगजा:	नितरां बृहन्मेहनयुता गजाश्च अधमाधमा:।
१८. कोशहीनगजा:	नितरां ह्रस्वमेहनयुता गजाश्च अधमाधमा:।
१९. हस्ताधिकगजा:	नितरां दीर्घशुण्डादण्डयुता गजाश्च अधमाधमा:।
२०. हस्तहीनगजा:	नितरां ह्रस्वशुण्डायुता गजाश्च अधमाधमा:।
२१. अंगुल्यधिकगजा:	पुष्कराग्रभागे नितरां दैर्घ्ययुता गजाश्च अधमाधमा:।
२२. अंगुलिहीनगजा:	पुष्कराग्रभागे नितरां ह्रस्वप्रमाणयुता गजाश्च अधमाधमा:।

२३. श्रोत्राधिकगजा:	नितरां बृहता कर्णविवरेण चोपेता गजाश्च अधमाधमा:।
२४. श्रोत्रहीनगजा:	नितरां ह्रस्वेन कर्णविवरेण चोपेता गजाश्च अधमाधमा:।
२५. नाभ्यधिकगजा:	नितरां बृहता नाभिभागेन युता गजाश्च अधमाधमा:।
२६. नाभिहीनगजा:	नितरां ह्रस्वेन नाभिभागेन युता गजाश्च अधमा-धमा:।
२७. नासाधिकगजा:	पुष्कराग्रे नितरां बृहद्विवरयुता गजाश्च अधमा-धमा:।
२८. नासाहीनगजा:	पुष्कराग्रे नितरां ह्रस्वविवरयुता गजाश्च अधमा-धमा:।
२९. मूकगजा:	प्रसिद्धा:। एतेऽपि गजा अधमाधमा:।
३०. बधिरगजा:	प्रसिद्धा:। एतेऽपि गजा अधमाधमा:।
३१. छायाहीनगजा:	मनोहरशरीरकान्तिहीना: (Ash-coloured) गजाश्च अधमाधमा:।
३२. कुब्जगजा:	नितरां वामना गजाश्च अधमाधमा:।
३३. पिशाचगजा:	पिशाचा इव रात्रिसंचारशीला: दुष्कार्यकरणलोलुपा: गजाश्च अधमाधमा:।
३४. भुजाप्रविष्टरोमकूप-युता गजा:	भुजमध्यभागे निबिडरोमयुता गजाश्च अधमाधमा:।
३५. सर्वांगकेशगजा:	सर्वांगेष्वपि भल्लूकादिवत् रोमावल्याधिक्ययुता गजाश्च अधमाधमा:।
३६. विषमकेशा गजा:	शरीरावयवेष्वेकत्र रोमप्रसार: परत्र तद्व्याप्तिहीन इत्यादिदोषयुता: गजाश्च अधमाधमा:।
३७. विकृतलिंगगजा:	कुण्डाकारमेहनाग्रभागयुता गजाश्च अधमाधमा:।

एवमत्र निर्दिष्टशैल्या सप्तत्रिंशद्विधमहादोषयुता: गजा: न क्रेतव्या इति व्यवस्था।।

अष्टादशकं प्रकणम्

।।अथ-परिमाणकथनम्।।

नवाष्टौ सप्त चायामाः सप्त षट् पंच चोच्छ्रयाः।
नाहे दश नवाष्टौ च भद्रमन्दमृगाः क्रमात्।।

अरालगजप्रमाणम्-

अष्टारत्निदशायामे चैकादश च नाहतः।
अरालः स तु विज्ञेयः सर्वकर्मसु गर्हितः।।

व्यासप्रोक्ते गजशास्त्रे-

अष्टहस्तोच्छ्रितो नागः दशहस्तायतस्तथा।
एकादशपरीणाहो ह्यराल इति तं विदुः।।

इति सामान्यारालगजलक्षणम्।।

पंचोन्नतः सप्तकरैश्च दीर्घः
ह्यष्टौ च हस्ताः परिणाहयुक्ताः।
एतद्विवृद्ध्या मृगमन्दभद्राः
संकीर्णनागोऽनियतप्रमाणः।।

अरत्निमात्रेणाधिक्यान्निन्द्यौ मानाधिकाविमौ।
अरत्निमात्रेणाधिक्यादरालस्तु निगद्यते।
अत्यरालो व्ययाधिक्यान्निन्द्यौ मानाधिकाविमौ।।

नवारत्न्युन्नतो नागः तथैवैकादशायतः।
नाहतो द्वादशारत्निः अत्यराल इति स्मृतः।।
अत्यरालमरालं च न गृह्णीयात्कदाचन।

उत्तमगजप्रमाणम्-

सप्तारत्निसमुत्सेधो नवारत्न्यायतस्तथा।।
दशारत्निपरीणाहः स गजो मानतः शुभः।
अरत्निमात्रहीनो यः स मध्यो मानतो गजः।।

अरत्निद्वयहीनश्चेत् कनिष्ठः परिकीर्तितः।
कनिष्ठादपि हीनो यः वामनः स निगद्यते।।

वामनादपि हीनो यः कुब्जो निन्द्यौ गजाविमौ।

मानप्रकरणतः योजनप्रमाणं यथा-

परमाणुः सुसूक्ष्मत्वात् भूमौ ग्राह्यो न चक्षुषा।
ते चाष्टौ त्रसरेणुः स्यात् त्रसरेणोस्तथाष्टकम्।
रथरेणुस्तदष्टाभिः वालाग्रं समुदाहृतम्।।

वालाग्राणि तथा चाष्टौ लीक्षेति समुदाहृतौ।
अष्टौ लीक्षा भवेद्यूकास्ताश्चाष्टौ यव उच्यते।।
अङ्गुलं स्याद्यवाश्चाष्टौ पादो रत्नेः षडंगुलः।
द्विवितस्तिररत्निः स्याद्वितस्तिर्द्वादशांगुला।।

चतुर्वितस्तिः किष्कुः स्यात् द्वौ किष्कू धनुरुच्यते।
धनुःसहस्त्रं गोलः स्यात् क्रोशः स्याद् गोलयुग्मतः।।

क्रोशद्वयं तु गव्यूतिः तदद्वयं योजनं स्मृतम्।
अष्टौ धनुःसहस्त्राणि योजनं परिकीर्तितम्।।

इति पालकाप्यमहर्षिप्रणीते गजशास्त्रे।
अष्टादशकं प्रकरणम्।।

एकोनविंशतिकं प्रकरणम्

।।अथ-आसनलक्षणकथनम्।।

उत्कृष्टं मध्यमं चैव ह्यवकृष्टमिति त्रिधा।
गजानामासनं प्रोक्तं गजशास्त्रविशारदैः।।

मन्दादिजातौ युद्धे च प्रोक्तमुत्कृष्टमासनम्।
समं दृढं च संलग्नं जानुसन्धिसमाहितम्।।

आसनत्रितयेऽप्येवं सौष्ठवं परिकल्पयेत्।
गजस्य प्रेरणार्थाय पुरस्तादासनं जगुः।।

इति पालकाप्यमहर्षिप्रणीते गजशास्त्रे
एकोनविंशतिकं प्रकरणं समाप्तम्।।

गजशास्त्रं च समाप्तम्।।

APPENDIX - I

अथ षष्ठश्रेणी।

गजगुणादिवर्णनम्।

त्रयोदशविधा लोके जायंतेऽरण्यवासिनः॥232॥
मतंगजाः कृष्णकायाः नयनानंददायिनः॥
मृगयारसिका मंजुसंचारा दृढविक्रमाः॥233॥
क्षुद्रनेत्रा बृहत्कर्णाः स्थूलोदरसमन्विताः॥
शुंडादंडसमोपेता दंतद्वयविराजिताः॥234॥
शत्रुविध्वंसनकाः संपत्संप्राप्तिहेतवः॥
स्ववाहिनीबलकराः राष्ट्रक्षेमविवर्धकाः॥235॥
महाबलवतामेषां मतंगानां मनोहरः॥
प्रावृट्कालो वसंतश्च कामोद्दीपनदायकः॥236॥
नवमे दशमे वर्षे कलभा दृढविक्रमाः॥
संपूर्णयौवनारूढा मत्ता मदजलस्रवाः॥237॥
महाबलास्ते मातंगा भृशं कामजवान्वितः॥
विस्मृताहारपानाश्च वशानामंतिकाश्रयाः॥238॥
ताभिर्विहारभाजाः स्युस्तत्संभोगाभिलाषिणः॥
वशाश्च कामसंपन्नास्तुल्यकाममदान्विताः॥239॥
संभोगभाजस्तैः साकं विहारमुदिताशयाः॥
महीरुहाणां छायासु कुजेषु च विशेषतः॥240॥
जलेषु च नदीकूलेष्वपि कामान्विता गजाः॥

चिरं विहृत्य संतोषात् शुंडादंडादिकेलिभिः।।241।।
निःशब्दे निर्भये शांते तमासाच्छादितस्थले।।
परस्पराभिलाषेण ते चिरं भोगकांक्षिणः।।242।।
गजा बलवशादेकं दिनं दिवसद्वयम्।।
दृढमेढ्रप्रहारैस्ताः स्त्रासयेयुर्वशा मुहुः।।243।।
तदानीमेव तासां तु गर्भप्राप्तिश्च निश्चिता।।
कामं कामकलातृप्ता गजा मलिनरेतसः।।244।।
पुनः संभोगविमुखा इति शास्त्रविनिश्चयः।।
केचिद्बलयुता नागा यौवने वर्षपंचकम्।।245।।
सततं मैथुनासक्ता गण्यंते हीनवीर्यकाः।।
अन्येषामेकभोगेन मनस्तृप्तिश्च निश्चिता।।246।।
गजांतराभिसरणविमुखास्ता वशाः परम्।।
हीनानां त्वन्यथा वृत्तिः सर्वत्र परिकीर्तिता।।247।।
अतः सहनिवासेन करिणा प्राप्तमैथुना।।
सद्य एव वशा प्राप्तसत्त्वा निद्रान्विता मता।।248।।
प्राप्तसत्त्वां वशां नागो लालयन्नन्वहं मुहुः।।
मुंजातृणेक्षुकदलीनलिनीकंददो मुदा।।249।।
रक्षको भवति प्रायस्तद्दर्शनकुतूहली।।
वृषाणां तुरगाणां च हरिणानां शुनामपि।।250।।
शुकानां च पिकानां च चक्राणां केकिनामपि।।
कारंडवानां हंसानां गजानां च विशेषतः।।251।।
पारावतानामन्येषां सत्त्वानां यौवनोदये।।
।वेविधाः कामलीलास्तु लोचनोल्लासहेतवः।।252।।
तस्मान्मयात्र तास्वेका निर्दिष्टा क्रमपंक्तिका।।
प्रमोदात्करिणा साकं खेलन्ती करिणी तदा।।253।।
प्राप्तसत्त्वोदया क्लांता चान्वहं निद्रयान्विता।।
हस्तिहस्तसमानीतकंदतोयादिभक्षिणी।।254।।

तरोश्छायासु कुंजेषु शयाना गर्भविव्हला॥
एकविंशति मासं वा द्वाविंशतिकमासकम्॥255॥
चतुर्विंशतिमासं वा नीत्वा सा करिणी तदा॥
सूते कलरवं शावं कुंजगेहांतराशया॥256॥
प्रसूय करिणी प्रायः एकद्वित्रिदिनावधि॥
तृणाहारमनिच्छंती डिंभस्य स्तन्यदायिनी॥257॥
मुहुः क्लमभरात्सुप्ता पोतालोकनहर्षिता॥
पोतसंरक्षणपरा तद्वात्सल्यवती वशा॥258॥
स तु डिंभः स्तन्यपायी पंककेल्यादितत्परः॥
जनन्या सहितो वर्षवयस्को वृद्धिभाङ्मतः॥259॥
द्वितीये वत्सरेऽतीते भयहीनः स्वयं गजः॥
वनांतरप्रचारी च गजसंघसमन्वितः॥260॥
जलेषु खेलनं कुर्वन् कलयन् बृंहितं मुहुः॥
तृणेक्षुकदलीकांडसल्लकीभक्षणः क्रमात्॥261॥
सप्तमं वर्षमासाद्य यौवनं प्राप्य सत्वरम्॥
धेनुकासहितः क्रीडन् तदा दानजलो बली॥262॥
स्वेच्छाविहारशीलश्च नानागुणसमन्वितः॥
भूपालैःसंगरे योज्यः सर्वप्राणिहिते रतः॥263॥
एवं गजशिशूत्पत्तिवृद्धिसत्त्वादिकः क्रमः॥
एतेषां जातिभेदस्तु क्रमादत्र निरूप्यते॥264॥

दंतिनः। (1)

दंतिनो नीलवर्णाश्च पृथुदंतलसन्मुखाः॥
पट्करोन्नतिमानाश्च दीर्घशुंडाविराजिताः॥265॥
शूराश्च कार्यदक्षाश्च नित्यं दृढपराक्रमाः॥
मृगयारसिका मंजुनादा मंजुलनेत्रकाः॥266॥
दीर्घपादाः स्थूलमेढ्रा मंदगंभीरगामिनः॥

स्थूलदेहा दीर्घपुच्छाः सांत्ववाक्यरताश्च ते॥267॥
स्वनाथवात्सल्ययुता गंभीरा दृढमेधसः॥
कोपहीना भारसहाः स्वल्पकामाश्च ते मताः॥268॥

दंतावलाः। (2)

दंतावलास्तुंगकायाः कृष्णवर्णशरीरिणः॥
पृथुकुंभद्वयोपेताः नितरां वेगगामिनः॥269॥
पृथुमस्तकसंयुक्ताः नितरां स्थूलदेहकाः॥
पद्भ्यां चंचलकायाश्च मेधायुक्तिविभूषिताः॥270॥
प्रचंडयुद्धलोलाश्च जलक्रीडारसान्विताः॥
पंकधूलीकेलिभाजः पूर्णकामाश्च ते मताः॥271॥
दृढस्मरणायुक्ताश्च शिक्षणे मृदुतां गताः॥
शुद्धाः सुगंधिदेहाश्च गंभीराकृतयश्च ते॥272॥
गंभीरझींकारयुता बहुभोजनतत्पराः॥
दर्गुणैः संवियुक्ताश्च कार्यकालपराक्रमाः॥273॥
स्वकुलेषु पुरोगाश्च ताडने कोपसंयुताः॥

हस्तिनः। (3)

हस्तिनो मंदसंचाराः किंचित् हीनपराक्रमाः॥274॥
पूर्वद्वेषस्मृतियुताः सुंदरांगाश्च ते मताः॥
स्वनाथवात्सल्ययुताः कार्यनिर्वहणोत्सुकाः॥295॥
पूर्णकामाः स्थूलमेढ्रा नित्यं कार्याभिलाषिणः॥
पंकपांसुजलक्रीडालोलुपा लोलनेत्रकाः॥276॥
संगीतावाद्यलोलाश्च यौवने मदमंथराः॥
शिक्षां प्राप्यैव कार्याणि चाशु कुर्वंति तत्क्षणात्॥277॥

द्विरदाः। (4)

द्विरदास्ते समाख्याताः स्वच्छदंतद्वयान्विताः॥
ह्रस्वकाया बलयुताः दृढस्थूलशरीरिणः॥278॥

स्थूलशुंडा बृहत्कुंभा मंदसंचारका मताः॥
जलावगाहनासक्ताः संततं भक्षणे रताः॥279॥
गंभीरझींकारवंतः स्वल्पकार्यश्रमान्विताः॥
स्वभावात् भीरवश्चैव सुंदरांगाश्च ते मताः॥280॥
नीतोपद्रवकार्यास्ते नागवद्भृशकोपनाः॥
अलंकृतिप्रिया नित्यं यंतृचित्तानुवर्तिनः॥281॥
नितरां कृष्णदेहाश्च दीर्घश्वासाश्च ते मताः॥

गजाः। (5)

गजा बृहत्काययुता नीलवर्णमनोहराः॥282॥
गर्वकोपादिहीनाश्च बलवंतश्च ते मताः॥
श्रमकार्यक्षमा नित्यं असाध्या यौवनोदये॥283॥
गंडस्रवन्मदजला स्थूलोदरसमन्विताः॥
पूर्णकामयुताः काले यंतृचित्तानुवर्तिनः॥284॥
किंचित्कृष्णरदोपेता मुहुः शुंडाप्रचालिनः॥
रक्तबिंदुलसद्वक्त्रा यौवने तु विशेषतः॥285॥
महापराक्रमयुताः दीर्घस्थूलकरा मताः॥
शरवद्वेगगतयो मृदुस्पर्शाश्च ते भृशम्॥286॥
मनोज्ञनेत्रसंयुक्ता मंजुझींकारमानिताः॥
वंचनादिविमुक्ताश्च ते चिरंजीविनो मताः॥287॥

भद्रगजाः। (6)

भद्रास्ते कथिता नागाः ये भृशं तुंगकायकाः॥
स्थूलमात्रा दीर्घशुंडा नितरां बलशालिनः॥288॥
मृदुस्पर्शा मंजुनेत्रा रक्तपुष्करभासुराः॥
सितबिंदुमुखाश्चापि रक्तबिंद्वाननाः परे॥289॥
भृशं मदजलस्रावाः स्थूलोदरसमन्विताः॥
यंतृचित्तानुकूलास्ते सुखसाध्याश्च ते मताः॥290॥
शुभावर्तयुताः प्रायो मधुरध्वनिकंठकाः॥

कार्यक्षमाः क्षमायुक्ताः संपद्वृद्धिकराश्च ते।।291।।
दृढमेधासमायुक्ताः शुभगंधशरीरिणः।।
आखेटरसिका युद्धनिपुणाः पूर्णपौरुषाः।।292।।
जितशात्रवसेनास्ते स्वामिनां विजयप्रदाः।।
गंभीरगमनाः प्रायः कोपे तु द्रुतगामिनः।।293।।
पट्टाभिषेकसेव्यास्ते नृपाणां मंगलप्रदाः।।

मंदगजाः। (7)

मंदा गजा नातितुंगा नितरां स्थूलकायकाः।।294।।
स्थूलोदराः स्थूलशुंडा नयनानंददायकाः।।
सिंहनेत्रा भृशं मंदगमना रक्तपुष्कराः।।295।।
स्वल्पकोपसमायुक्ता बुद्धिमंतश्च ते मताः।।
शिक्षणे स्मरणोपेता गंभीराकृतयश्च ते।।296।।
नीलवर्णलसत्कायाः कार्ये दुःखितचेतसः।।
कदलीघासपुंड्रेक्षुभक्षणे लोलुपा भृशम्।।297।।
संपूर्णबलसंयुक्ता असाध्या यौवनोदये।।
भृशं कामसमोपेता दृढदीर्घशेफान्विताः।।298।।
युद्धकाले प्रवीणाश्च दृढघट्टनलालसाः।।
दृढभारवहाः शांताः कोपे ह्रींकृतिभीरवः।।299।।
मृगयारसिका वीरा वशासंभोगलालसाः।।

मृगगजाः। (8)

प्रायो मृगगजा लोके कृशदेहाः प्रकीर्तिताः।।300।।
कृशशुंडा दीर्घपादा बलहीनाश्च ते मताः।।
स्थूलनेत्रा ह्रस्वपुच्छाः सौंदर्येण विराजिताः।। 301।।
चलचित्ताः कोपशीलाः धूम्रवर्णांगकाश्च ते।।
बुद्धिभ्रंशयुता जातु नितरां कार्यभीरवः।।302।।
दंड्या दुर्गंधसंयुक्ताः कामकामान्विता मताः।।

विकृतावयवोपेताः कृशदंतद्वयान्विताः॥303॥
अकाले विवशाः प्रायः कार्यभ्रष्टाश्च निश्चिताः॥

संकीर्णगजाः। (9)

भद्रमंदमृगाणां च ये गुणाः परिकीर्तिताः॥304॥
संकीर्णा इति गण्यंते तैर्गुणैः सहिता गजाः॥
संकीर्णद्विपपोतास्तु बहवः संभवंति हि॥305॥
संकीर्णद्विरदाः प्रायः शुभदा एव कीर्तिताः॥
सुखसाध्याः सुलभ्याश्च यंतृचित्तानुवर्तिनः॥306॥
कार्ये पराक्रमोपेता नयनानंददायिनः॥
शिक्षाभिर्मृदुतां नीता मनुष्याणां हिते रताः॥307॥
सर्वकर्मसु दक्षाश्च घासदानादितर्पिताः॥
संकीर्णा अपि नागाश्च संरक्ष्या भूमिपालकैः॥308॥

मतंगजाः। (10)

मतंगजा महावेगा महाकायसमुज्ज्वलाः॥
नीलाश्च कृष्णवर्णाश्च श्वेतरक्तस्फुटान्विताः॥309॥
शुंडाचलनशीलाश्च संततं वेगगामिनः॥
तरुभंजनलीलासु संततं वेगगामिनः॥310॥
बुद्धिमंतः क्षमायुक्ताः शांताः पूर्णपराक्रमाः॥
वशासंभोगलोलाश्च तत्पार्श्वाश्रयणे रताः॥311॥
सांत्ववाक्यरता नित्यं नाथप्रीतिविवृद्धिदाः॥
यौवने गर्वसंयुक्ताः शरवद्वेगगामिनः॥312॥
शीतवातातपादिभ्यो न भीताश्च भवंति ते॥
वारिलीला लोलचित्ताः कथितास्ते सुखासनाः॥313॥

पद्मिनः। (11)

ये पद्मसरसीस्नानलोलाः पुष्पसुगंधिनः॥
लतावलोकनासक्ताः संगीतश्रवणे रताः॥314॥
घंटादुकूलपट्टादिधारणे दत्तचेतसः॥

छायासेवनलोलाश्च ये दृश्यंते मतंगजाः॥315॥
ते पद्मिनः समाख्याताः स्वामिनां शुभदायकाः॥
नितरां सुंदरांगाश्च शांतचित्ताश्च ते मताः॥316॥
कार्येषु दक्षाः सततं स्वल्पशिक्षापरायणाः॥
यंतृचित्तानुकूलाश्च बुद्धिमंतश्च निश्चिताः॥317॥
क्षुत्तृट्सहा नाथवश्या दुर्गुणैस्तु विवर्जिताः॥
मंत्रिसेनेशयोग्याश्च युवराजार्हकाश्च ते॥318॥
संततं शुभदाः प्रोक्ताः स्वीकार्या मृगयास्वपि॥

इभाः। (12)

पर्जन्यनिनदा ये तु संततं कोपसंयुताः॥319॥
नातितुंगा नातिनीचाः कृष्णवर्णा मतंगजाः॥
इभास्ते कथिता नाम्ना कृच्छ्रसाध्याश्च ते मताः॥320॥
मुहुर्धावनशीलाश्च गर्वेण च समन्विताः॥
शीतवाताध्वखेदादिसहास्ते वेगगामिनः॥321॥
यौवने मदसंपन्नाः कर्कशस्पर्शदेहकाः॥
सेनानां पुरतः कार्याः संगरे भूमिपालकैः॥322॥
कुपिता दुर्निवाराश्च रिपुसेनाविनाशिनः॥
चोदिता भीषणाः कामं जवने न च मानिताः॥323॥
पटगेहादिरक्षायै नियोक्तव्याश्च ते मताः॥
आखेटादिषु कालेषु ज्वलन्नेत्राश्च निश्चिताः॥324॥

स्तंबेरमाः। (13)

स्तंबेरमास्ते कथिता ये ह्रस्वतनवो गजाः॥
मृदुस्पर्शा नीलवर्णा मिताहाराश्च ये गजाः॥325॥
संपूर्णबलसंपन्ना दक्षा मेधान्विताश्च ये॥
सुखशिक्षाः क्लेशसहाः सद्गुणैर्ये समुज्ज्वलाः॥326॥
वयःक्रमेण ते भिन्नगुणवंतश्च कीर्तिताः॥
सांत्ववाक्यरता नित्यं नाथवात्सल्यमानिताः॥327॥

कोपहीना भृशं मत्ताः-सिंहनेत्राश्च ते मताः॥
नातिस्थूला नातिकृशाः समावयवसंयुताः॥328॥
शुभगंधाः शुभच्छायाः सर्वप्राणिहिते रताः॥
एवं बहुविधा नागा जायंतेऽरण्यभूमिषु॥329॥
गुणक्रियासत्त्वभेदात् निश्चितव्याश्च ते परम्॥

हस्तिनी (14)

करिण्यश्च गजैस्तुल्यरूपचेष्टादिसंयुताः॥330॥
दंतहीनाः शांतचित्ता लज्जावत्यश्च कीर्तिताः॥
किंचिध्रस्वशरीराश्च बलमेधादिपुष्कलाः॥331॥
क्रौर्यहीनाः सुंदराङ्ग्यो मृदुस्पर्शा मिताशनाः॥
मनोज्ञगमनापेतास्त्रिचतुस्तनया मताः॥332॥
डिंभेष्वत्यंतवात्सल्याः सर्वप्राणिहिते रताः॥
करिणां करिणीनां च चत्वारिंशद्वयोऽवधि॥333॥
बलसंपत्पूर्णशोभा तदूर्ध्वं जरयान्विताः॥
जरादूषितसर्वांगाः परुषाकृतयश्च ते॥334॥
अयोग्याः कार्यकालेषु रक्षितव्याः प्रयत्नतः॥
तस्मादेकसमाः पोताः द्विवर्षाश्च त्रिवर्षकाः॥335॥
जलबंधादियोगेन सुखलभ्या वनेचरैः॥
क्षुधितास्तर्जि(र्पि)ताः काले करिणीभिश्च यत्नतः॥336॥
नीत्वा सुचित्ततां शांत्या मृदूक्तिभिरनुक्षणम्॥
शालायां रक्षितव्याश्च घासादानादिभिर्नृपैः॥337॥
अनर्घं रत्नमित्येव गजमाह सुनंदकः॥
तस्मान्नृपतिभिर्नागाः शिक्षितव्याश्च यत्नतः॥338॥
शतं वर्षाणि करिणां परमायुरितीरितम्॥
जातिक्रियास्वरूपेण ते गजा राजसोत्तमाः॥339॥

APPENDIX - II

GIVING INFORMATION ABOUT THE NATIONAL PARKS, WILD LIFE SANCTUARIES AND TIGER RESERVES WHERE ELEPHANTS ARE FOUND AND THE STATE-WISE AREA IN SQ.KMS.

	NAME OF THE NATIONAL PARK	STATE	AREA IN SQ.KMS.
1.	Rajaji N.P.	Uttaranchal	820.00
2.	Corbett N.T.R.	do	1378.54
3.	Dudhwa T.R.	Uttar Pradesh	884.00
4.	Dandeli W.L.S.	Karnatak	843.16
5.	Palamu T.R.	Jharkhand	1026.00
6.	Kaziranga N.P.	Assam	471.71
7.	Manas T.R.	do	2840.00
8.	Buxa T.R. and Jaldapara W.L.S.	West Bengal	760.92
9.	Simlipal T.R.	Orissa	2750.00
10.	Nagarhole N.P.	Karnatak	643.39
11.	Bandipur T.R.	do	847.00
12.	Madhumalai W.L.S.	Tamilnadu	217.70
13.	Silent Valley N.P.	Kerala	89.52
14.	Indira Gandhi N.P. (Annamalai and Parambikulam W.L.S.)	Tamilnadu	117.10
15.	Eravikulan N.P.	Kerala	97.00
16.	Periyar T.R.	do	777.00

This information is reproduced from the Book: *Wildlife Reserves of India'* by Sanjay Monga, Published by the India Book House Pvt. Ltd. in 2002 A.D. Mumbai.

APPENDIX - III

A GLOSSARY giving the Meanings of some parts of an Elephant's body, Elephant-food, some terms regarding measurement-units etc.

(1) अपर	Apara : Hind portion of the body of an elephanrt.
(2) अरत्नि	Aratni : A cubit of the middle length, from the elbow to the tip of the middle finger.
(3) अरुष्कर	Aruṣkara : Marking nut.
(4) अराल	Arāla : A large-sized elephant.
(5) अत्यराल	Atyarāla : A very huge elephant.
(6) अङ्गुली	Aṅgulī : The tip of an elephant's trunk; A unit of measure; A toe; A finger.
(7) अंसफलक	Aṁsaphalaka : Scapula (shoulder-blade).
(8) अण्डपात	Aṇḍapāta : The desent (descending) of the testicles of an elephant,usually, during rut or must-period.
(9) आयाम	Āyāma : Length.
(10) आनाह	Ānāha : Circumference of an elephant's body.
(11) आलानबन्ध	Ālānabandha : A Pillar for tying an elephant.
(12) उच्छ्राय	Ucchrāya : Height.
(13) उन्नत	Unnata : Raised high.
(14) कट	Kaṭa : The temples of an elephant.

(15) कटप्रभेद Kaṭaprabheda : Appearance of rut from an elephant's temple.

(16) कटोदक Kaṭodaka : The fluid flowing from the temples of an elephant.

(17) कुक्षि Kukṣi : Flank or side of the belly.

(18) कोष्ठ Koṣṭha : Flank side of the belly.

(19) कोश Kośa : Scrotal sack.

(20) कोशहीन Kośahīna : Without a scrotal sack.

(21) कोशाधिक Kośādhika : With an extra scrotal sack; With a large scrotum.

(22) कुम्भ Kumbha : The frontal globe on the head of an elphant.

(23) क्रोश Krośa : A measuring unit (of length) about 2000 yards, about 1¼ miles.

(24) कक्षा Kakṣā : Armpit (Fore-leg related skin-fold).

(25) कर Kara : The trunk of an elephant.

(26) कट Kaṭa : The temple of an elephant.

(27) कलविङ्कनेत्र Kalaviṅkanetra : Having eyes like a sparrow.

(28) कडङ्गर Kaḍaṅgara : Straw, hard dry grass.

(29) कण्ठ Kaṇṭha : Neck

(30) गण्डगण्डस्थल Gaṇḍa/ Gaṇḍashthala : An elephant's temple, cheek.

(31) गल Gala : Throat, outer portion of the neck.

(32) गण्डफलक Gaṇḍaphalaka : A broad cheek.

(33) गण्डभित्ति	Gaṇḍabhitti : The opening in the temple of an elephant, from which rut flow exudes or oozes.
(34) गजमार्ग	Gajamārga : The elephant track.
(25) चि(चु)बुक	Ci (cu) buka : The chin portion.
(36) छवि	Cchavi : Colour of the skin.
(37) छुरि	Cchuri : An elephant's colour or complexion.
(38) जङ्घा	Jaṅghā : The lower portion of the legs.
(39) नाह	Nāha : Circumference of an elephant's body.
(40) परिणाह	Pariṇāha : Circumference.
(41) पादपाश	Pādapāśa : Foot-trap or a leg-trap.
(42) पादप्रचारलिङ्ग	Pādapracāraliṅga : Elephant's footsteps or track.
(43) पादजाल	Pādajāla : Foot-net or trap.
(44) परिखा	Parikhā : Moat or trench full of water around a field chosen for catching of the elephants.
(45) पिङ्गूष	Piṅgūṣa : Front of the ear.
(46) पुष्कर	Puṣkara : The tip of the elephant's tongue.
(47) पेचक	Pecaka : The root of the elephant's tail.
(48) पक्ष	Pakṣa : Side of an elephant.
(49) पिङ्गाक्ष	Piṅgākṣa : Having reddish-brown eyes.
(50) फाल (भाल)	Phāla : The forehead (for Bhāla ?).
(51) बन्ध	Bandha : The catching of elephant, also known as Khedda.

(52) मुष्क	Muṣka : the scrotum.
(53) मेहनकोश	Mehanakośa : The extended skin of the penis.
(54) योजन	Yojana : A measurement of length, about 4 to 5 miles.
(55) यवस	Yavasa : Grass, fodder, meadow-grass-an elephant's food.
(56) रन्ध्र	Randhra : Opening of the skin for the flow of rut-fluid.
(57) उपरन्ध्र	Uparandhra : The sub-opening of the skin for the flow of rut.
(58) रिङ्कार	Riṅkāra : An elephant's shrill cry.
(59) लाङ्गूलवंश	Lāṅgūlavaṁśa : The length of the tail of an elephant.
(60) वाल/वालधी	Vāla/ Vāladhī : Backbone of an elephant.
(61) वालकेश	Vālakeśa : Hair on the back-bone portion.
(62) वक्त्र	Vaktra : Mouth.
(63) वक्ष	Vakṣa : Chest.
(64) वंश	Vaṁśa : Back, back-bone.
(65) वंशलाङ्गूल	Vaṁśalāṅgūla : the bony portion of the elephant's tail.
(66) वर्ष्म	Varṣma : A measure;height.
(67) सृक्क(क्व)णि	Sṛkkaṇi/ Sṛkkvaṇi : The corner or angle of the mouth.
(68) हस्त	Hasta : The trunk of an elephant.
(69) हस्तिप(क)	Hastipa/ Hastipaka : A mahout or a person who rides and controls the elephant.

BIBLIOGRAPHY

(1) Gajaśāstram of Pālakāpya Muni, with Extracts from other Works and Coloured Illustrations-Edited with Translation in Tamil by Shri Mantramurti K.S. Subrahmanya Sastri, Sanskrit Pandit, Saraswati Mahal Library, Tanjore and Summary in English by Shri S. Gopalan, Hon. Secretary, Saraswati Mahal Library, Tanjore. Saraswati Mahal Series No. 76, Published by Shri S. Gopalan, Hon. Secretary for the Administrative Commitee, T.M.S.S.M. Library, Tanjore, 1958. Price: Rs. 10/-

(2) Gajaśāstra-Marathi Version by Raja Serfoji II of Tanjore (1798-1832 A.D.). Supplement to Gajaśāstram in Sanskrit-the above book- Tanjore Saraswati Mahal Series No. 76-A, Edited by Shri G. Nagaraja Rao, Marathi Pandit, SML, Tanjore; Publisher—the same as above. 1958; Rs. 1-50/-

(3) Gajashastrasara Pakshilakshana ani Chikitsa (Bajanama) va Chitta Vahagas Chikitsa (Yujanama) (in Marathi)—Science of Elephants and Training and Treatment of Falcons, Hunting Cheetas, Rams and Smaller Birds. Sampadaka-Rajeshri E. Krishnaswami Mehadick Rao-saheb; Publisher the same as above. 1952. Rs. 3.00/- Tanjore S.M. Granthamala Book. 40-41.

(4) Gajagrahaṇaprakāra-A Metrical work dealing with Catching and Training of Elephants by Nārāyaṇa Dīkṣita; Edition with an Introduction by E.R. Sreekrishna Sarma. S.V.U.O. Journal-Texts and Studies-off-print No. 1. Pub: Sri Venkateswara University Oriental Research Institute, Tirupati; 1968.

(5) Gajaśikṣā by Nāradamuni, with the Commentry Vyakti of

Umāpatyācārya-Edited with Introduction by Prof. E. R. Sreekrishna Sarma. S.V.U.O. Journal Vol. XVIII—Texts and Studies-off-print No. 5. Pub: As above. 1975.

(6) The Elephant-Lore of the Hindus: The Elephant-Sport (Mātaṅgalīlā) of Nīlakaṇṭha-Translated from the Original Sanskrit, with Introduction, Notes and Glossary by Franklin Edgerton, New Haven, Yale University Press, 1931. Rs.8/-

(7) Pālakāpyamuniviracito Hastyāyurvedaḥ (Sanskrit) Śivadattaśarmaṇā Saṁśodhitaḥ. Anandashram Sanskrit Series No. 26. 1894. Pune. Rs. 7-6-0.

(8) Hastivijñāna (Marathi) by Mahadev Mukund Joshi, Maji Hattikamdara, Baroda Hathikhana. Vidyavilas Press, Baroda. 1910. Rs.1- 4- 0.

(9) Haṁsadevakṛta Mṛgapakṣiśāstra- Ṣaṣṭhaśreṇī (Sanskrit) Oriental Institute, Baroda, Manuscript No. 13516. Folios: 163; Grs. 1760.

(10) Carakasaṁhitā of Caraka, with the Āyurvedadīpikāvyākhyā by Cakrapāṇidatta. Nirtnay Sagar Press, Bombay.

(11) Suśrutasaṁhitā of Suśruta, with the Nibandhasaṅgrahākhyavyākhyā by Dalhaṇācārya, Nirnay Sagar Press, Bombay.